WATCH OFFICER'S

16th EDITION

GUIDE

Titles in the Series

THE U.S. NAVAL INSTITUTE
Blue & Gold Professional Library

For more than one hundred years, U.S. Navy professionals have counted on specialized books published by the Naval Institute Press to prepare them for their responsibilities as they advance in their careers and to serve as ready references and refreshers when needed. From the days of coal-fired battleships to the era of unmanned aerial vehicles and laser weaponry, such perennials as *The Bluejacket's Manual* and the *Watch Officer's Guide* have guided generations of sailors through the complex challenges of naval service. As these books are updated and new ones are added to the list, they will carry the distinctive mark of the Blue & Gold Professional Library series to remind and reassure their users that they have been prepared by naval professionals and meet the exacting standards that sailors have long expected from the U.S. Naval Institute.

BLUE & GOLD
PROFESSIONAL LIBRARY

WATCH OFFICER'S GUIDE

16th EDITION

ADM James Stavridis, USN (Ret.), RADM Robert P. Girrier, USN (Ret.), CAPT Tom Ogden, USN, and CAPT Jeff Heames, USN

NAVAL INSTITUTE PRESS
Annapolis, Maryland

Naval Institute Press
291 Wood Road
Annapolis, MD 21402

Library of Congress Cataloging-in-Publication Data
Names: Stavridis, James, author.
Title: Watch officer's guide, 16th edition / ADM James Stavridis, USN (Ret.); RADM Robert
    Girrier, USN (Ret.); CAPT Jeffrey Heames, USN; CAPT Thomas Ogden, USN.
Description: 16th edition. | Annapolis : Naval Institute Press, 2020. | Series: Blue & gold
    professional library | Includes bibliographical references and index.
Identifiers: LCCN 2020016807 | ISBN 9781682475164 (hardback)
Subjects: LCSH: United States. Navy—Watch duty—Handbooks, manuals, etc. |
    United States. Navy—Officers' handbooks.
Classification: LCC V133 .S725 2020 | DDC 359—dc22
LC record available at https://lccn.loc.gov/2020016807

Unless otherwise noted, all photos are from official U.S. government sources.

Contents

Preface

The sea is eternally demanding, presenting myriad challenges to the watch-stander: shiphandling, weather, the rules of the nautical road, engineering, formation and convoy steaming, communications, navigation, and underway safety, to name just a few. In port, the watch officer faces other challenges, including safety, force protection, the management of boats and vehicles, the rendering of honors, and the execution of ceremonies. Both at sea and in port, the watch officer must stand a taut watch, exhibit forehandedness, remain ever vigilant and alert, and maintain a scrupulously accurate deck log. These are challenging duties, not learned in a day or exclusively from reading books like the *Watch Officer's Guide.* In fact, honing the classic skills of a seasoned watch officer requires a combination of study, education, training, review, and—above all—experience. In addition, it involves the skills to effectively leverage all available information and decision-making aids and systems—which are ever-increasing and advancing. This edition is meant to provide a consolidated guide with a great deal of useful information in a single volume.

This classic of the profession has now been through sixteen editions since its initial publication in 1911. It is the result of the contributions of hundreds of naval officers and mariners who have worked to modernize and improve over a century since it first appeared on the bridge and quarterdeck of many ships. In addition to updated appendices, this edition offers important new material, including the introduction of fundamental shipboard operating principles (chapter 1); a description of crew endurance and human factors (chapters 5 and 7); the five broad themes identified from analysis of the U.S. Navy's comprehensive review of surface incidents between 2007 and 2017 (chapter 7); and specifics for the littoral combat ship, the future frigate, and ZUMWALT destroyer. The other material in the volume has been reviewed, brought into line with current practice, and improved. The assistance of CAPT Andrew Carlson of USS ZUMWALT, CAPT J. P. Cordle, USN (Ret.), CDR Kevin Meehan, LT Tyson Eberhardt, and LTJG Jack Hanley of USS CHUNG-HOON is appreciated.

This edition is the product of officers who have served at sea in U.S. Navy ships. In particular, we would like to thank several great Navy captains who taught us much of what we know of ships, the sea, and shiphandling: CAPT R. F. Gaylord, USN (Ret.); RADM T. C. Lockhart, USN (Ret.); CAPT L. E. Eddingfield, USN (Ret.); ADM W. F. Doran, USN (Ret.); CAPT W. G. Wheeler, USN (Ret.); CAPT F. W. Pfirrmann, USN (Ret.); and CAPT R. D. Collins. We would also like to thank the many other naval officers who took the time to teach us about the sea and the standing of watches. Above all, we owe a great debt to our wives: Laura (herself a Navy junior), June, Stephanie, and Nancy; and our children: Christina, Julia, Noah, Taylor, Truman, and Griffin; they are the inspiration for all that we have been fortunate enough to accomplish in our careers.

Standing a proper watch involves receiving data and information from numerous sources, sorting their relevance and accuracy, and taking action appropriately. It is dynamic—the pace will vary—but the importance of the duty is never diminished. The successful watch officer is one who is always willing to learn, to accept critical feedback, to grow, and to adapt. Failure to adapt is a sure precursor to danger, even disaster, at sea. Be flexible, forehanded, and take proper action as a watch officer, and you will do a great job and stand a safe and effective watch, carrying out your ship's missions.

Acronyms and Abbreviations

1MC	battle and general announcement system
ACCO	auxiliaries control console operator
ACP	allied communications publication
AIS	automatic identification system
ALCON	all concerned
AMCROSS	American Red Cross
APU	auxiliary power unit
ARPA	automatic radar piloting aid
ASTAC	antisubmarine tactical air controller
ASW	antisubmarine warfare
ATFP	antiterrorism / force protection
ATP	allied tactical publication
ATTWO	antiterrorism tactical watch officer
AUXO	auxiliaries officer
BMOW	boatswain's mate of the watch
BRM	bridge resource management
BTB	bridge-to-bridge
BWPT	bilge water processing tank
C&D	command and decision
CCS	central control station
CDC	command and decision center
CDO	command duty officer

CE	communications electronics division
CG	guided-missile cruiser
CHENG	chief engineer
CHT	collection, holding, and transfer
CIC	combat information center
CICWO	combat information center watch officer
CICWS	combat information center watch supervisor
CLF	Combat Logistics Force
CMAA	command master at arms
CMC	command master chief
CNMOC	Commander, Naval Meteorology and Oceanography Command
CNO	chief of naval operations
CNSP	Commander, Naval Surface Forces Pacific
CO	commanding officer
COLREGS	Convention on the International Regulations for Preventing Collisions at Sea
COMMO	communications officer
COMMS	communications
CONN	conning officer
CONOPS	concepts of operation
CONREPS	connected replenishments
COTS	commercial off the shelf
CPA	closest point of approach
CSE	course
CSOOW	combat systems officer of the watch
CSOSS	Combat Systems Operational Sequencing System
CTG	commander, task group
CUES	Code for Unplanned Encounters at Sea
CVN	aircraft carrier (nuclear-powered)
DDG	guided-missile destroyer
DESRON	destroyer squadron
DH	department head

DIET	duty in-port emergency team
DLQ	deck landing qualifications
DOD	Department of Defense
DR	dead reckoning
ECDIS-N	Electronic Chart Display and Information System–Navy
EDO	engineering duty officer
EDORM	Engineering Department Organization and Regulations Manual
EHF	extremely high frequency
ELO	electrical officer
EMC	electrician's mate chief
EMCON	emissions control
ENG	engineer officer
ENL	emergency navigation laptop
EOCC	engineering operational casualty control
EOOW	engineering officer of the watch
EOP	engineering operational procedures
EOSS	Engineering Operational Sequencing System
EOT	engine-order telegraph
EPCC	electrical plant control console
EPT	engineering plant technicians
ERO	engine room operator
ETA	estimated time of arrival
FF	fast frigate
FNMOC	Fleet Numerical Meteorology and Oceanography Center
FOD	foreign object debris
FOM	figure of merit
FPCON	force protection condition
FWC-N	Fleet Weather Center Norfolk
FWC-SD	Fleet Weather Center San Diego
FXP	fleet exercise publication
GPS	global positioning system
GTM	gas turbine motor

GUNNO	gunnery officer
HCC	hazard characteristic code
HCO	helicopter control officer
HF	high frequency
HIFR	helicopter in-flight refueling
HM	hazardous material
HM	hospital corpsman
HSO	helm safety officer
HW	hazardous waste
IAD	international air distress
IAW	in accordance with
IC	interior communications
IDLH	immediately dangerous to life or health
INS	inertial navigation system
IVCS	Interior Voice Communications System
JOOD	junior officer of the deck
JOOW	junior officer of the watch
JTWC	Joint Typhoon Warning Center
kHz	kilohertz
LCS	littoral combat ship
LHA	landing helicopter assault (AMERICA-class general-purpose amphibious assault ship)
LHD	landing helicopter dock (WASP-class amphibious assault ship)
LOGREQ	logistic requirement
LOI	letter of instruction
LPD	amphibious ship dock
LSD	dock landing ship
LSE	landing signalman enlisted
MAA	master-at-arms
MAD	military air distress
MC	intercommunications voice unit
MEDEVAC	medical evacuation
MHz	megahertz

MIL	man in the loop
mo board	maneuvering board
MOVREP	movement report
MPA	main propulsion assistant
MRC	maintenance requirement card
MSC	Military Sealift Command
MTP	Maritime Tactical Signal and Maneuvering Publication
MUC	Meritorious Unit Commendation
NATO	North Atlantic Treaty Organization
NATOPS	Naval Air Training and Operating Standardization
NAV	navigator
NAVDORM	Navigational Department Organization and Regulations Manual
NAVOCEANO	Naval Oceanographic Office
NAVSSI	Navigation Sensor System Interface
NBC	nuclear/biological/chemical
NDP	naval doctrine publication
NM	nautical mile
NMOC	Naval Meteorology and Oceanography Command
NOAC-Y	Naval Oceanography Antisubmarine Warfare Center Yokosuka
NOOC	Naval Oceanography Operations Command
NSTM	naval ships technical manual
NTP	Navy Tactical Publication
NTRP	Navy Tactical Reference Publication
NUC	Navy Unit Commendation
NVD	night vision device
NWP	naval warfare publication
OCE	officer conducting the exercise
OCM	oil content monitor
OJT	on-the-job training
OOD	officer of the deck
OPAREA	operations area

OPCON	operational control
OpNavInst	Office of the Chief of Naval Operations Instruction
OPORD	operation order
OPTASK	operational task
ORM	operational risk management
OS	operations specialist
OTC	officer in tactical command
OTSR	optimum track ship routing
OWS	oil–water separator
PACC	propulsion and auxiliary control console
PAX	personnel transfer
PBED	plan, brief, execute, debrief
PIM	position of intended movement
PMAP	Protective Measures Assessment Protocol
PMS	planned maintenance system
POD	plan of the day
POOW	petty officer of the watch
POW	prisoner of war
PPM	parts per million
PQS	personnel qualification standard
PRE-EX	pre-exercise message
PUC	Presidential Unit Citation
PWT	plumbing waste tank
QM	quartermaster
QMOW	quartermaster of the watch
RAS	replenishment at sea
RAST	recovery, assist, secure, and traverse
RCO	readiness control officer
RHIB	rigid-hull inflatable boat
RMD	restricted maneuvering doctrine
ROE	rules of engagement
ROR	rules of the road
rpm	revolutions per minute

RSD	rapid securing device
R/T	radiotelephone
SAR	search and rescue
SCC	ship control console
SHF	super-high frequency
SOFA	status of forces agreement
SOP	standard operating procedure
SOPA	senior officer present afloat
SORM	Standard Organization and Regulations Manual
STBD	starboard
SUPPO	supply officer
SUWC	surface warfare coordinator
SWO	senior watch officer
TACON	tactical control
TAO	tactical action officer
TSS	traffic separation scheme
TUM	Tag-Out User's Manual
UA	unauthorized absence
UAS	unmanned aircraft system
UCMJ	Uniform Code of Military Justice
UHF	ultra-high frequency
UNREP	underway replenishment
USNS	U.S. Naval Ship
VERTREP	vertical replenishment
VHF	very high frequency
VMS	Voyage Management System
WEAX	route weather forecasts
WIG	wing-in-ground-effect
WOCT	waste oil collecting tank
XO	executive officer

1

INTRODUCTION

The OOD reports directly to the Commanding Officer for the safe navigation and general operation of the ship; to the Executive Officer (and CDO if appointed) for carrying out the ship's routine; and to the Navigator on sighting navigational landmarks, and on making course/speed changes.

OPNAVINST 3120.32D

THE OFFICER OF THE DECK

The officer of the deck (OOD) occupies a unique position in a naval ship. Nowhere in military or civilian life is there a parallel to the range and degree of responsibility that is placed in the hands of the OOD. As direct representative of the captain, the OOD acts with all the authority of command and, next to the captain and the executive officer (XO), is the most important person in the ship. Modern technology has given the OOD sophisticated tools but also has added to the scope of traditional duties and responsibilities. Qualification as OOD is the cornerstone of professional growth for a surface line officer and the most critical milestone of the surface-warfare qualification.

The pathway to OOD qualification generally includes a combination of formal classroom instruction and training, navigation and seamanship simulators, and live training at sea. Qualification usually occurs after many months of careful study and direct observation. Newer ship classes such as the littoral combat ship (LCS) variants and the ZUMWALT-class destroyers (DDG 1000) are equipped with technological advances that offer minimal manning config-urations and require unique qualification paths. For the LCS, multiple crews assigned to a single hull require specialized training to develop and maintain crew proficiency using high-fidelity simulation environments to deliver OODs that are highly trained prior to stepping aboard their ships.

Regardless of the pathway to qualification, a junior officer must devote every possible moment to learning the skills to qualify as an OOD and, while doing so, must expect to be closely and critically observed in both live and virtual training environments. Simulators offer navigation and seamanship training in a benign environment as well as ample opportunity to debrief individual and team performance after each event. At sea, mistakes will be corrected on the spot because, in the fast-paced atmosphere of modern fleet operations, there often is no time for lengthy critiques and explanations. As demanding as this learning process may be, its rewards are superbly satisfying. There is no feeling quite like that of standing watch for the first time as a fully qualified OOD, knowing that you are in control of the ship at sea. Whether that ship is a fleet tug or an aircraft carrier, the trust given to the OOD carries with it a time-honored and unique distinction.

RESPONSIBILITY AND AUTHORITY

The duties, responsibilities, and authority of the OOD are delineated in OpNavInst 3120.32D Standard Organization and Regulations of the U.S. Navy. These regulations have legal status under Title 10 of the U.S. Code of Federal Regulations. They prescribe *minimum* duties and responsibilities. Factors such as the special mission of a ship, command policy, and guidance for a particular situation may add to these duties and responsibilities but not reduce them. Even more important than the letter of the regulations is the unwritten but traditional requirement that an OOD apply good judgment, intelligence, and initiative to his or her duties and exercise authority fully. This can be difficult. Given the diverse and often complex activities that take place aboard a ship at sea, it is easy for a watch officer to unwittingly allow authority to be delegated to a subordi-nate, particularly where specialized operations are concerned. There is nothing wrong with delegating authority, but the OOD must clearly understand that, regardless of who carries out duties, the responsibility for their being carried out is always his or hers. It is good practice, for example, to allow the quartermaster or the junior officer of the deck (JOOD) to take and plot navigational fixes. This does not, however, relieve the OOD of responsibility for the safe navigation of the ship. "Experts" who perform some of the many tasks required on a watch are assistants, never surrogates.

ACCOUNTABILITY

> On the sea there is a tradition older even than the traditions of the country itself and wiser in its age. . . . It is the tradition that with responsibility goes authority and with them both goes accountability.
>
> "HOBSON'S CHOICE," *WALL STREET JOURNAL*, 14 MAY 1952

Accountability is a subtle responsibility that is often misunderstood. A naval officer is accountable for the outcome of his or her duties, good or bad. Just as the commanding officer (CO) is inescapably accountable to a superior for everything that happens aboard the ship, so the OOD is accountable to the CO for everything that happens during his or her watch. The only exceptions are those laid down by law or regulation. As the captain's direct representative, the OOD is the only person on board who can make decisions that affect the safety of the ship and the lives of her crew. The captain cannot be on the bridge at all times, and as history has repeatedly demonstrated, the OOD sometimes has to take actions that determine whether shipmates live or die. Accountability is one of the reasons why the OOD holds a unique position. No OOD should ever forget that.

PRIORITIES

There is nothing that indicates which of the watch officer's duties are most important, for the simple reason that they are all important. Judgment is required, however, to balance priorities, as these will continually shift depending on the specific operations the ship is engaged in. The OOD can expect to be constantly confronted with the need to decide without delay where to focus his or her attention. Training a watch, for example, is always important, yet there will be times when training must be skipped to carry out other duties. The safety of the ship and the fulfillment of her mission always come first and must never be neglected. On the other hand, there will be times when the ship's activities allow the OOD to delegate many responsibilities and to become, for a while, a teacher and observer. At such times, the JOOD should run the watch. Not only does this give the junior officer self-confidence, it also gives the OOD a chance to step back and observe just how well he or she has performed.

Although theoretically responsible for all the things that go on during a watch, the OOD obviously cannot exercise personal control over everything. Total control would hopelessly enmesh the OOD in too much detail, drawing attention away from those aspects of the ship's operation over which he or she *must* have direct control.

Making a distinction between what is of direct concern and what is not requires a well-developed sense of judgment, and acquiring that sense is a vital part of a watch officer's training. The OOD should not become involved, for example, in how a petty officer on the forecastle assigns a paint-chipping job. However, if the OOD sees one of the crew using a power tool without regard for safety, the situation must be corrected immediately. This sort of action can cause conflict. A department head or a senior officer may want to take an action that is in itself proper but will interfere with more important tactical operations being controlled by the watch. Here again, the duty of the OOD is to keep priorities straight, even if it means referring the matter to the XO or the captain for resolution.

COMMAND RELATIONSHIPS

Regardless of ship class, the OOD's command relationship with the CO of the ship is clear and fixed. His or her other command relationships are equally important but much less clearly defined. Although regulations imply that the XO has authority over the OOD only on matters pertaining to the ship's routine, in most ships the XO is empowered to correct or modify any action taken by the watch officer. Because the extent of the XO's authority is a matter of individual command policy, the OOD must be familiar with the ship's regulations and with the CO's standing orders and directives that deal with this subject.

The XO is second only to the captain as the most senior and experienced warfare-qualified officer on board. Therefore, that person's advice and authority should be carefully weighed by the OOD. In addition, the OOD has a responsibility to the XO for the complete and accurate execution of the ship's routine. The OOD must keep the XO informed of changes that may affect the ship's routine, just as he or she must keep the CO informed of changes that may affect the operational picture.

The relationship between the OOD and the engineering officer of the watch (EOOW) must be clearly understood by both. All regulations are very specific in stating that the EOOW reports to the OOD. However, each captain must outline—in writing—the policy regarding any automatic actions by the EOOW. This policy is established in the commanding officer's standing orders, which are standardized according to ship class with minor variation allowed to accommodate a captain's preference. For example, it may be a captain's policy that, in the event of an engineering casualty, the EOOW is to automatically take whatever action is required and to keep the OOD informed of the status of the propulsion plant. Another captain may require that the EOOW get the permission of the OOD before altering any propulsion plant condition, regardless of the casualty.

Another possibility is a policy directing automatic actions by the EOOW except under certain conditions when the permission of the OOD is required. The OOD and the EOOW must each have a clear understanding of the captain's policy and standing orders. It is a good idea for the OOD, upon relieving the watch, to review with the EOOW ship's policy regarding automatic actions by the latter.

In the rapidly changing world of modern warfare, a ship must be capable of the quickest possible reaction to a threat. Often there is not sufficient time to move from a routine underway condition to general quarters with weapons systems ready. To enhance weapons system readiness and reduce response time, the tactical action officer (TAO) concept has evolved. The TAO is a qualified OOD charged with the immense responsibility of employing the ship's weapons and sensors to achieve the ship's mission. The TAO must have a deep knowledge of tactics and the ship's weapons systems capabilities as well as potential enemy threat and capabilities. Knowledge and oversight of the ship's specific weapons status and posture are critical to performing this task. The TAO normally stands watch in the combat information center (CIC) and is empowered with the authority to employ the ship's weapons systems.

The relationship between the OOD and the TAO is especially important because it involves a significant exception to the concept that the OOD is the final decision maker during a watch. Tactical control of the ship, particularly in the areas of threat analysis and reaction, belongs to the TAO in the CIC. This officer is normally a department head and is often senior in rank and experience to the OOD. In the CIC, the TAO has direct access to sensor information and weapons control as well as the means to evaluate enemy threats quickly and to take immediate action against them. OpNavInst 3120.32D and the ship's tactical doctrine may authorize him or her to direct the OOD to the tactical handling of the ship and, depending on circumstances and readiness levels, to fire weapons without permission from the OOD. Even when a TAO watch is set, however, the OOD remains responsible for the safety of the ship. If, in his or her judgment, a course of action directed by the TAO would put the ship in immediate danger, he or she may decline to follow it but must immediately inform the CO of the situation. Assignment of the decision-making responsibilities must be clearly understood by both watch officers at all times. In the fast-paced environment of modern warfare, there is not likely to be time to discuss a decision or to debate who should make it. Specifically, control of the ship may be shifted, by positive command, to the TAO in the CIC or, in some cases, to other watch station officers, but the safety of the ship remains the responsibility of the OOD.

A TAO is stationed when the threat or the tactical situation requires that the ship be capable of assessing and reacting to a rapidly changing environment. The OOD must know the source of the TAO's authority and understand his or her relationship to the TAO.

The OOD has a unique relationship with the navigator. While on watch, the OOD is responsible for the safe navigation of the ship. This is a dual responsibility, shared with the navigator, who is at all times responsible for the safe navigation of the ship. It is quite clear, therefore, that the OOD must understand the navigation plan, the intended track, the potential dangers to navigation, and the quality of fixes available. The navigator may be authorized by the captain to relieve the OOD if in his or her judgment the OOD is endangering the ship from a navigation standpoint. Such a policy, established in writing, would only be executed in rare situations.

Normally the quartermaster of the watch (QMOW) maintains the navigation picture for the OOD and is the navigator's representative while the navigator is away from the bridge.

Many large ships are organized to provide for the assignment of a command duty officer (CDO) at sea. He or she is required to keep informed of the tactical situation and the status of equipment and must be prepared to assume operational direction of the ship. The CDO's position relative to the OOD is similar to that of XO to the OOD. The CDO may be, and usually is, authorized by the CO to relieve the OOD if necessary. When a ship under way has a CDO assigned, the OOD should make all the reports to that person that he or she normally would make to the XO and the CO.

These brief comments show that, although the OOD's relationships with other key watchstanders are regulated, there is latitude for each command to supplement and to some extent modify the various regulations. This is a prerogative of the CO, whose duty it is to see that his or her watch organization is the best one possible to meet the needs of the ship. This might mean that in wartime the captain would order the TAO to direct combat. When a TAO watch does not seem necessary, the captain might decide not to set one in order to use the crew to better advantage. These are command decisions that will, in all cases, be communicated either orally or in writing to the watch officers concerned. It then becomes the duty of the watch officer to understand clearly and without any doubt his or her position in the organization.

SHIPBOARD OPERATING PRINCIPLES

While there are a wide variety of roles, responsibilities, and policy guidance that shape watch officer relationships within a ship, the six shipboard operating principles apply to all hands at all times and offer a foundation for safe and effective operations. These principles include integrity, formality, level of knowledge, a questioning attitude, procedural compliance, and forceful backup.

Integrity is the expectation of honesty and ownership of individual tasks. A warship is a complex system requiring the coordinated effort of numerous specialized personnel and teams. Integrity provides the foundation of trust upon which each shipmate operates within a team or unit.

Formality describes the climate of standards and rules that govern behavior. Maintaining a high degree of formality in how we perform watchstanding duties, communicate, conduct maintenance, and complete other actions is key to successful operations.

Level of knowledge is the foundation of sound decision making. Establishing and maintaining a high level of knowledge enables intelligent and responsive decision making when issues emerge. You should strive to continually improve your level of knowledge and professional competencies.

A questioning attitude is a critical thinking skill. It is an individual trait that is learned and must be continually exercised to remain sharp. Approach your watch station or environment with the knowledge that you will find something worth fixing. An individual with a questioning attitude frequently asks:

- What is wrong with this situation?
- Is this action the correct one?
- Am I sure?
- What do I expect to happen?
- Is he or she about to make a mistake?

Having a questioning attitude contributes to a safe environment, leads to process improvement, and increases knowledge through learning about the "why" in our actions and procedures.

Procedural compliance is strict adherence to processes or procedures as written or ordered. With few exceptions, there exists a procedure for everything that must be done on a ship. Strict compliance with procedure improves safety and keeps equipment operating correctly. You should always know and refer to the reference material governing your and your shipmates' actions. History is replete with examples where failure to comply with existing procedure resulted in disaster, loss of life, or damage to equipment.

Forceful backup (on your own part) means willingness to step in when an evolution or event is not being conducted properly. It means having the courage to step forward and say something when you feel something is wrong, even if that means confronting your seniors.

CHARACTERISTICS OF THE OOD

The shipboard operating principles offer a foundation for safe and effective operations in general. Several additional characteristics are necessary for an OOD to fulfill his or her mission effectively.

Forehandedness

The watch officer should be ready for any situation. For that reason, the most important faculty for the watch officer to cultivate is forehandedness. If there is a reason to think that there will be fog during a watch, he or she should check over the fog procedure before taking the deck. If the ship is to take part in fleet exercises, the watch officer should arrange to study the orders, pre-exercise messages (PRE-EXs), and applicable instructions before going on watch. If the ship is to enter New York Harbor, for example, the watch officer should review the inland rules of the road. If there are to be ceremonies during the watch, the watch officer should be letter perfect in the honors required and put a little extra snap in his or her own appearance. The watch officer must always look ahead—a minute, an hour, and a day—and make it a matter of pride never to be caught unprepared.

The wise watch officer will mentally rehearse the action to take in the event of a fire, a man overboard, a steering failure, or any other serious casualty. This habit is not difficult to acquire and is certain to pay large dividends.

Developing forehandedness requires experience as well as a deliberate focus on learning. One proven method for learning is through the plan, brief, execute, and debrief (PBED) process. Specific evolutions of a technical or complex nature should be planned and briefed in advance with all the major participants attending. The OOD is usually a central figure in these briefings. Proper preparation for complex evolutions not only results in smooth running operations but also keeps them safe. All participants should carefully observe the activity in order to provide feedback during a post-event debrief. Debriefing events are vital to ensuring execution issues are effectively captured and learned from. A constant focus on learning is vital to developing forehandedness and is the mark of the successful watch officer.

Vigilance

Next to forehandedness, the most important quality for the OOD is vigilance. Vigilance is essential to safety. The OOD must, of course, observe intelligently all that comes within his or her vision, both outside and inside the ship, but vigilance extends beyond the visible. The OOD should also encourage vigilance on the part of all others on watch.

Judgment

A third important quality for the OOD is judgment, which means a sense of proportion and of the fitness of things. Watches vary all the way from extreme tenseness, when the OOD must be alert every instant, as in high-speed work at night in a darkened ship, down to the calm of a Sunday afternoon at anchor, when the OOD is just keeping ship. On a darkened ship, only essentials count, and the OOD must key his or her mind to its keenest pitch. On a quiet Sunday afternoon, it may be that the most immediate responsibility is to be affable to visitors.

Intuition and Experience

Most officers who have spent some time at sea have a special sense for what is going on around them. An experienced chief engineer will awaken immediately if the sound of a blower or a pump is not right, just as a good navigator will go to the bridge to check the weather at even the smallest change in the ship's motion. There is nothing magical about this ability, and it requires no special talent. It is the product of experience and of the carefully cultivated habit of close and continuous observation. To a new officer, so many things seem to be happening at once that concentration on one detail is almost impossible. With experience, however, things begin to sort themselves out, and before long what seemed like a confusing and impossibly complex environment becomes understandable. At this point the learning process that makes a good watch officer begins. Once the basics of the watch become second nature, he or she can turn attention to developing an ability to observe and evaluate everything that is going on during the watch. Subtle errors that are detected early can be corrected before they incur serious consequences.

Leadership

The fifth important quality is leadership, which the Navy officially defines as "the sum of those qualities of intellect, of human understanding, and of moral character that enable a person to inspire and to manage a group of people successfully." Every watch officer should cultivate dignity, forcefulness, confidence, and precision in his or her manner and should exact similar qualities from assistants. Striving to avoid any indication of confusion or peevishness and to perform quietly, the watch officer should always act the part of what he or she really is—next to the captain and the XO, the most important person in the ship, and the leader of the watch team.

Energy

A sixth quality that marks a superb watch officer is a high energy level. It can become tedious standing watch on the bridge. Many watches seem to go on forever, and even the best watch officers can feel fatigue and a certain sense of complacency. On exciting watches, the level of effort required to keep track of everything that's going on can likewise begin to wear down the watch officer.

There are several things a watch officer can do to enhance his or her level of energy while on watch. Getting the proper amount of rest is critical, as is eating a balanced diet. Watching a movie until 2230 and gulping down a soda and hot dog for dinner is bound to reduce the energy of an officer on the midwatch. Additionally, attitude is important. Maintain an upbeat approach to watchstanding. To pass the time on long, slower watches, train the watch section. Just as conducting prebriefs for complex evolutions are an essential element of forehandedness, conducting watch station debriefs immediately following an event or exercise is equally important. The process of learning and self-improvement is a never-ending pursuit. Stay enthusiastic and your energy level will remain high.

CONCLUSION

We have talked about some of the bedrock qualities that lead to the standing of a good and competent watch. But there are some intangibles as well. What are some of these intangible but important qualities a captain looks for in a good OOD?

Confidence comes first—a serene inner sense of assurance that will quickly radiate to the entire bridge team. Enjoyment of responsibility is certainly an important component as well. Another key attribute is a sense of humor. Don't take *yourself* too seriously, but always take your responsibility as OOD very seriously. There is a big difference.

Finally, you should always, always stay calm. You will not be able to control many things on the bridge of a ship—the wind, the seas, the equipment casualties, the requirements and missions—but there is one thing you can always control: your own temperament. Stay calm and focused, work hard to learn what you must, and admit your mistakes.

2

THE WATCH IN GENERAL

DUTIES, RESPONSIBILITIES, AND AUTHORITY. The OOD under way shall:

(1) Be aware of the tactical situation and geographic factors which may affect safe navigation and take action to avoid the danger of grounding or collision following tactical doctrine, the U.S. Coast Guard Navigation Rules of the Road, and the orders of the Commanding Officer or other proper authority.

(2) Be informed of current operation plans and orders, intentions of the OTC and the Commanding Officer, and other matters of ship or force operations.

(3) Issue necessary orders to the helm and main engine control to avoid danger to take or keep an assigned station, and to change course and speed following orders of proper authority.

(4) Make all required reports to the Commanding Officer. When a CDO is specified for the watch, make the same reports to the CDO.

(5) Ensure that required reports to the OOD concerning tests and inspections and the routine reports of patrols, watches, and lifeboat crews are made promptly and that the bridge watch and lookouts are posted and alert.

(6) Supervise the personnel on watch on the bridge, ensure that all required deck log entries are made, and sign the log at the end of the watch.

(7) Issue orders for rendering honors to passing ships as required by regulations and custom.

(8) Ensure that the Executive Officer, CDO (In-Port) (when assigned), and department heads concerned remain informed of changes in the tactical situation, operations schedule, approach of heavy weather, and other circumstances which may require a change in the ship's routine or other actions.

(9)   Be aware of the status of the engineering plant, and keep the EOOW advised of power requirements and the operational situation so they may operate the engineering plant effectively.

(10) Carry out the routine of the ship as published in the POD and other ship directives. Keep the Executive Officer advised of any changes in routine.

(11) Supervise usage of the general announcing system; the general chemical, collision, sonar, and steering casualty alarms; and the ship's whistle.

(12) Permit no person to go aloft on the masts or stacks or to work over the side except when wind and sea conditions permit and then only when all applicable safety precautions are observed.

(13) Supervise transmissions and acknowledgments on the primary and secondary tactical voice radio circuits, and ensure that proper phraseology and procedures are used in all transmissions.

(14) Supervise and conduct on-the-job training (OJT) for the junior officer of the watch (JOOW), the JOOD, and enlisted personnel of the bridge watch.

(15) Assume other responsibilities as assigned by the Commanding Officer.

(16) Supervise the striking of the ship's bell to denote the hours and the half-hours from reveille to taps. Request permission of the Commanding Officer to strike eight bells at the hours of 0800, 1200, and 2000.

(17) Permit no person on weather decks during heavy weather conditions without permission of the OOD and then only when all applicable safety precautions are observed.

OPNAVINST 3120.32D

PREPARATION

The more thorough the preparation before going on watch, the more likely the OOD is to perform duties effectively.

A newly commissioned officer reporting to his or her first ship, or an experienced officer ordered to one that is unfamiliar, will be required to quickly learn about the ship, her organization, and the people who run her. To get this information, there are some helpful references available. OpNavInst 3120.32D Change 1, supplemented by instructions for the particular type and class of ship concerned, constitutes the Standard Organization and Regulations Manual, familiarly known by its acronym, SORM. At first the sheer bulk of all this material may be dismaying, but most of the chapters of SORM contain material that can be absorbed gradually, as the newly reported officer becomes acquainted with the ship's operation. A watch officer should immediately begin familiarizing himself or herself with the ship's watch organization. The SORM chapter, usually chapter 4, on this subject contains the most important regulations of the watch and details precisely the duties and responsibilities of, and relationships among, watchstanders. There are a number of ship's instructions that detail the specific duties of the various watchstanders, such as sounding-and-security patrol and roving patrol. Because the first duties of a JOOD are likely to involve checking in some way on the performance of these watchstanders, it is important to know what their duties are, especially if the ship has special watch requirements, which may be described in a ship-specific instruction.

Although a warship's organization for damage control is quite complex, the basics of that organization—including the location of repair lockers, the number and composition of repair parties, and the essential components of installed firefighting and drainage systems—should be learned as soon as possible.

Today's fleet operations require a watch officer to be familiar with a wide range of tactical and operational situations on any given watch. It is therefore foolish for an oncoming OOD or TAO to assume the watch after only a ten- or fifteen-minute rundown of what is happening. Preparation must be longer than that. Many professionals in other fields, such as professional sports, spend considerable amount of time (sometimes as much as five to seven times more for preparation than for execution) preparing for each play and evolution. Pre-exercise messages (PRE-EXs), standard operating procedures (SOPs), letters of instruction (LOI), operation orders (OPORDs), concepts of operations (CONOPs), operational tasks (OPTASKs), and supplements should all be studied carefully, well before the information is needed, and not in the corner of a darkened bridge or CIC on a rough night. Essentially, preparation for the underway watch begins before the ship gets under way. The OOD must participate in pre-exercise briefings and be familiar with the strike group commander's standing orders. However, the immediate situation must be absorbed and reviewed just prior to the watch. The best place to do this sort of preparation is usually the CIC, where formation disposition, tactical data, and communications plans are all displayed. However, the CIC is not the only place the OOD should stop before relieving the watch. It is a good idea to visit the EOOW and CSOOW and find out the details of engineering plant and combat system status as well as any possible extra drills, maintenance, or repairs that are being planned. A tour of topside spaces will give firsthand knowledge of readiness for heavy weather and send a signal to the lookouts that the officer will be in charge for the next watch.

The OOD should be physically prepared, fresh, and well rested before assuming the watch. He or she should be dressed for the weather and take along his or her own equipment—flashlight with red filter, notebook, and so on; the OOD should not expect to borrow them from the officer being relieved. On a night watch, the OOD should allow at least twenty minutes to become night-adapted before even considering taking over. If a special evolution is ongoing or planned for early in the watch, it may require the watchstander to arrive earlier to ensure a more complete understanding of the situation. It is most important to be psychologically prepared. For the entirety of a watch, the OOD's mind should be on nothing else—not divisional duties, administrative concerns or paperwork, or any other non-watch-related task. In a fast-moving tactical situation, only a few seconds of inattention can cause an OOD to become confused, sometimes with disastrous results.

RELIEVING THE WATCH

The process of relieving the watch should not be undertaken until the relief is absolutely familiar with the general situation. It used to be that the oncoming OOD would appear on deck fifteen minutes before the hour, but modern operations at sea usually demand more discussion between the offgoing and the oncoming watch than is possible in the traditional fifteen-minute turnover. Additionally, the various watch turnovers throughout the ship can be synchronized to ensure continuity of awareness. Unless the oncoming officer is prepared, the information the offgoing officer passes on during the turnover will make little sense. The new OOD will then be in the unpleasant position of either having to ask for information or, worse, taking over without really understanding what is going on and then spending the rest of the watch trying to catch up.

No matter how thoroughly the relieving officer has prepared before reporting ready to relieve, the oral turnover is still important. This is the last chance to clear up anything that may seem vague or confusing, and it is the on-watch officer's opportunity to pass on to the relief any necessary miscellaneous information. For example, there might have been some last-minute changes to the watch team. Perhaps the officer in tactical command (OTC) has a weak transmitter on a tactical circuit and can barely be heard. This is the sort of information the relieving OOD needs to run a smooth watch.

The oral turnover should be formal. The officer coming on duty should step up to the officer being relieved, salute, and say, "I am ready to relieve you, sir (or ma'am)." The officer being relieved returns the salute and says, "I am ready to be relieved." Aside from setting an example of formality and military courtesy and observing a time-honored custom of the service, there are very sound reasons for this procedure. The key word is "ready." By declaring himself or herself ready to relieve the watch, the officer is stating that he or she has made all reasonable preparations, gathered all available information, and needs but an oral turnover to assume duties. A mumbled, "What's going on?" is not an acceptable substitute. The officer being relieved describes the operational situation, being sure to cover everything about other ships in the formation and other contacts. He or she should outline all known events scheduled to take place during the upcoming watch, then give a rundown on the propulsion plant status, highlighting any limitations.

While receiving information about the watch, the oncoming OOD has an opportunity to observe what is going on, both on board and outside the ship. When the OOD thoroughly understands the situation, has heard all the off-going OOD has to say, and has asked any necessary questions, it is his or her duty to salute again and say, "I relieve you, sir (or ma'am)." It must be stressed that this is an obligation, not to be dispensed with a sloppy, "Okay, I've got it." The officer being relieved returns the salute and replies, "I stand relieved." Both officers then inform the bridge watch and report to the captain that the watch has been relieved.

DECLINING TO RELIEVE THE WATCH

Some junior officers feel they may be considered timid if they exercise their option and decline to relieve the watch. However, it is an officer's duty to do so if, for example, the ship is out of position in the formation or a busy watch in port has become confused, with boats astray or out of fuel. Of course, a ship may be out of position for good reason and be headed back to her station, in which case it would be proper to relieve the watch. In the case of declining to relieve the watch, the oncoming watch officer should attempt to assist the watch by providing forceful backup as able. The oncoming officer should also call the senior watch officer and executive officer, or the commanding officer if necessary, to the control station to assist in resolving the situation.

A reputation for being detailed in taking over a watch is not a bad thing to acquire. It will keep the preceding watch officer on his or her toes, ready to turn over the watch without leaving embarrassing loose ends. The oncoming watch officer must remember that once he or she has said, "I relieve you, sir (or ma'am)," the full responsibility and authority of the watch is his or hers. If difficulties arise, he or she cannot then try to pass the blame back to the officer just relieved.

It is usually best not to relieve in the middle of a complex operation. Rather, it is better to stand back and observe the situation and, when feasible, step forward to relieve.

LEADERSHIP RESPONSIBILITIES

In addition to responsibilities for the operation of the ship, the watch officer has an important role as leader of a watch team. No matter how competent or well prepared the OOD may be, he or she cannot hope to perform well without positive control of the watchstanders. In all likelihood, some of the people on the watch will be experienced, others inexperienced. Some will be fully qualified, some will be in the process of qualifying, and some may be standing watch for the first time. As the leader of the team, you should know the strengths and weaknesses of your watchstanders and provide forceful backup while training to shore up whatever weak areas you find. Your watch team's performance will be no better than the leadership and training given them by the watch officer.

Consciously or unconsciously, they will take their lead from what they see the watch officer doing. The OOD is the center of action and the most visible person on the watch team. His or her manner must therefore convey an attitude of seriousness, concentration, and self-discipline. The OOD should insist that officers on his or her watch continually check, inspect, and train their subordinates. He or she should not hesitate to relieve a person on watch who is clearly incompetent or not trained to perform a job.

A mindset of continuous training is an integral part of every watch. The high rate of turnover that most ships experience means that a watch officer can expect the training of new people to be a major and continuing duty. In addition, depending on command policy, he or she may be authorized to sign off on certain portions of a junior officer's surface-warfare personnel qualification standards (PQS). Not only does the training of watchstanders bring about obvious improvements in the readiness of the ship, it also does a great deal for the morale and enthusiasm of the watchstander. A watch officer who shows a sincere interest in improving the skills of subordinates almost always gets a good response and builds a team he or she can be proud of. The quality of a watch helps significantly to determine a watch officer's professional reputation. He or she must exercise leadership by insisting on high standards of performance and appearance. He or she should take care that in the relieving process not all key watchstanders are relieved at once. One other point should be noted: All of the ship's resources are available to the OOD. He or she must never hesitate to use these resources when necessary.

A proven method for effective team learning is to follow the plan, brief, execute, debrief (PBED) process. High-performing watch teams plan their watches together, conduct prewatch briefs as a team, continually provide forceful backup to each other during execution, and then conduct event debriefs that critically examine their performance. Teams that implement PBED learn more effectively by ensuring that debrief points are addressed in the planning process for upcoming events. PBED allows a watch team leader to create an environment where the watchstanding and operating principles of integrity, formality, questioning attitude, level of knowledge, and procedural compliance can flourish.

ROUTINE

An intelligently conceived and punctiliously executed routine is essential to good shipboard organization. It is the OOD's job to supervise and closely control the manner in which this routine is carried out. If the plan of the day calls for "Sweepers" at 0800, he or she must be sure that, as far as can be determined, the crew does execute at that time. If reveille is scheduled for 0600, he or she must see that all hands are turned out at that time. If something about the plan of the day does not seem right, the OOD should consult the XO, but until the routine is changed, he or she must see that it is carried out. The plan of the day is a directive. All hands must follow it, whether or not the word is passed over the general announcing system.

The boatswain's mate of the watch (BMOW) is a critical leader of the bridge watch team and handles much of the detail of carrying out the daily routine. That person should be made to feel accountable for the watch routine and for the instruction, behavior, and appearance of the deck watch. It is his or her duty to see that all stations are manned and that the previous watch has been relieved.

Like the OOD, the BMOW exercises all the attributes of leadership required of a naval officer. One of the boatswain's mate's major duties is to carry out the plan of the day. He or she must know what is happening on board ship and must pass the word in accordance with the prescribed routine. The OOD should supervise the boatswain's mate in carrying out the watch routine rather than deal directly with the people on watch. The standard routine is usually written into the ship's organization and regulations manual and is varied only by specific instructions in the plan of the day. When it seems advisable to change the routine because of unusual and unforeseen circumstances, the OOD must obtain permission for such change from the XO or the CDO.

PASSING THE WORD

For the ship's routine to be carried out as planned, the word must be passed. Few daily evolutions are more basic, or more abused, than the passing of the word. The amount of control the watch has over the general announcing system, designated the 1MC, is one of the best indicators of how well the ship is being run and how much attention the watch officer is paying to what is happening in the ship. Except in unusual or urgent situations, the 1MC should not be used as a paging system. The habit of passing the word for individuals (in most cases, simply because it is the easiest way to contact people) is one that is easy to get into and hard to break. Unless watch officers monitor what goes out over the 1MC, its abuse will quickly become part of accepted shipboard procedure. People will become so accustomed to hearing the 1MC every five minutes that when something really important is passed, no one will listen. By controlling the system, the OOD can prevent this from happening but also can avert problems in carrying out the ship's routine. If, for example, a ten-hand working party has been called away and fifteen minutes later the quarterdeck is asked to pass the word to "bear a hand in mustering the ten-hand working party," the proper reaction should be to turn down the request and instead find out why the party was not properly mustered.

General announcements are disruptive to the ship's routine if they are lengthy or made too frequently. When the word is passed, standard phraseology should always be used. This is not only the mark of a smart, seamanlike ship, but it is also the best way to ensure that the message gets out with maximum clarity, brevity, and formality. Standard phraseology (see chapter 4) is found in the SORM. A copy of the word to be passed for ship's routine and other standard announcements should be available on the bridge and at the quarterdeck station.

Things to Avoid in Passing the Word

1. Use of clumsy or redundant language such as, "All personnel not actually on watch," "For the information of all hands," "Now bear a hand," or "That is all."

2. Improper use of circuits. SOPA (senior officer present afloat) regulations and regulations in many foreign ports prohibit the use of topside speakers except in emergencies.

3. Use of the 1MC during religious services or ceremonies, except in emergencies.

4. Addressing a long list of people.

5. Asking officers or chief petty officers to "muster" or "lay to." Courtesy demands the phrase "please assemble."
6. Pauses, hesitations, and breaks in the course of a message. If the watch is not sure what to say, the message should be written down and read.
7. Speaking too quickly or in an unclear manner.

APPEARANCE OF THE WATCH

The OOD, circumstances permitting, must see that the men and women on watch are in clean regulation uniform. The OOD sets an example, at all times, for the whole ship. At sea, particularly in bad weather, he or she should be dressed to keep warm and dry and should see that the watchstanders are similarly protected. In port, when visitors are coming aboard, the maximum spit and polish is expected; uniforms should be in excellent condition, shoes polished, and personal appearance neat.

The BMOW is responsible for the appearance of the watch, and the OOD should not hesitate to have him or her order any person who does not come up to standard to change. Wrinkled, ill-fitting, or dirty uniforms and work shoes may be worn about the deck when a clean uniform might get soiled, but they are not good enough for a messenger of the watch on the quarterdeck. Similarly, the appearance of the bridge or quarterdeck should be a matter of interest to the OOD. He or she should have the BMOW keep the area clean and tidy. Sweeping the deck, emptying trash buckets, and keeping empty coffee cups out of sight are all details to which an alert BMOW attends.

CONDUCT ON WATCH

There is need for formality on watch. This does not require pomposity; on the contrary, often a touch of humor is appropriate. But watchstanders must never be permitted to forget that they are on duty and that what they are doing is important. This formality adds to the professionalism of the watch and to the reputation of the OOD. It is usually the small things that count most. For example, it is inappropriate for officers on watch to address each other by first names, even if they are roommates. Officers should address crew members by formal title, and crew members on watch should similarly address each other.

A ship is always subject to emergency or disaster; fire, man overboard, and dozens of other events can disrupt the dullest watch. The OOD should make it a practice to run a taut watch and to prevent noisy and idle chatter; he or she should use common sense and not be arbitrary or harsh in dealing with subordinates.

RELATIONS WITH THE STAFF

The OOD of a flagship has the additional responsibilities of keeping the embarked staff informed as to what is going on, handling additional boats and vehicles, and rendering honors.

The staff duty officer is usually the person who receives special reports. In general, the events and sightings normally reported to the CO should also be reported to the staff duty officer. He or she bears approximately the same relation to the admiral and squadron or division commander as an OOD does to the CO.

The flag lieutenant is generally responsible to the admiral for the scheduling of honors and advises the OOD what honors are to take place. In return, the OOD advises the flag lieutenant as well as the staff duty officer of unscheduled visits that may require honors.

Staff officers take care to preserve the flagship's unity of command and do not give orders directly to the OOD. Routine requests may be made to the ship's officers, but in matters of any importance the chief of staff usually deals with the CO of the flagship. An OOD will not be inconvenienced by an embarked staff as long as he or she remembers to consider their needs and to keep them informed.

At a minimum, the OOD should review the Staff Standing Orders on a monthly basis and keep a copy available at the watch station to ensure procedural compliance with the orders from the embarked commander and staff.

TURNING OVER THE WATCH

As a watch draws to a close, the OOD gives the relief all available information for maximum continuity. Both the relieved and the relieving officer must see that this is done. It may be necessary to make notes or to keep a checklist; in any event, the relieved officer should remember, even while turning over the watch, to be alert and on the job. The task of turning over the watch must not divert attention from maintaining a proper watch. If the OOD feels that the pace of operations makes the scheduled turnover inappropriate or even unsafe, he or she should so inform the relief, and a delay or change should be arranged. The oncoming relief must be flexible in this regard.

When the CO is on the bridge, the oncoming watch officer should say, "Request permission to relieve the officer of the deck," and the offgoing OOD should report, "I have been properly relieved as officer of the deck by_____."

KNOWING THE SHIP

Listed below are some of the basic facts that an officer should begin learning about a ship as soon as he or she reports on board. The "OOD under way" part of the surface-warfare officer's PQS contains other things that he or she will be required to know as part of the qualification process. The surface-warfare officer's qualification process is designed to lead to various watch officer qualifications, and following that process is the best way to qualify as OOD. However, by going through the following list a few items at a time during a quiet watch or in-port duty day, an officer will soon improve his or her feel for the ship and how she operates.

1. Principal dimensions (beam, draft, length, displacement, etc.).
2. Fuel and water capacity, fuel consumption at various speeds, most economical speed.
3. Maximum speed available under different engineering plant configurations.
4. Capabilities and limitations of weapon systems.
5. Capabilities and limitations of sensors.
6. Angles for standard, full, and hard rudder.
7. Steering-engine controls and steering-engine combinations; emergency steering procedures.
8. Location, sound, appearance, and meaning of all alarm systems on the bridge.
9. Location of and normal use for all radio and communications stations.
10. Procedures and safety precautions for raising and lowering boats.

11. Preparations for underway replenishment.
12. Preparations for entering and leaving port.
13. Operation and tuning of radar repeaters.
14. Operation of electronic navigation systems.
15. Operation of bearing circles, alidades, and stadimeters.
16. Publications kept on the bridge, where they are to be found, and how they are accounted for.
17. Procedure for manning watch and battle stations.
18. Make-up and check-in requirements for various security watches.
19. Regulations concerning disposal of trash and garbage.
20. Regulations concerning pumping bilges, oil spills, and environmental protection.
21. Characteristics and limitations of onboard aircraft or helicopters.
22. Operational, administrative, and task organizations that affect the OOD and where his or her ship is in the organization.
23. Required reports to the OOD.
24. Location and use of emergency signals.
25. Precautions to be taken in heavy weather.
26. Basic ship's tactical information, such as turning-circle diameters under various conditions and limitations on acceleration and deceleration.
27. Thumb rules and quick procedures for assessing the situation.

A SEQUENCE FOR RELIEVING

A reasonable and formal procedure should be established for the process of relieving. While this is generally a matter of personal preference, a reasonable guideline is for the outgoing OOD to inform the oncoming OOD about:

1. The quartermaster and navigation plot.
2. The bridge combat system terminal if installed.
3. Bridge status boards.

The following is the minimum amount of information the watch officer should know before relieving the watch:

1. Course, speed, position, and intended track of the ship.
2. Water depth, predicted set and drift, and navigational aids.
3. Rocks, shoals, shipping, and other dangers to navigation in the vicinity or on the proposed track.
4. Gyro error, magnetic variation, and magnetic heading on the present course.
5. Weather conditions, the force and direction of the wind, temperature, barometer reading, and the rate of change.
6. Status of lifeboats and ability of lifeboat crew to respond instantly.
7. Status of fathometer, global positioning system (GPS), ship's gyros (WSN-5/7), electronic navigation system, and radar navigation information as applicable.
8. General tactical situation, including assigned position in the formation, location of the guide, and the ship's actual position in the formation.
9. Major equipment in use and out of commission and the readiness of the armament, engineering plant, and ordered/set damage-control material condition.
10. Any recent course and speed changes required by the previous watch to maintain station.
11. All unexecuted orders (the OOD reads and signs the captain's night orders and staff night orders if a commander is embarked).
12. Location and voice call of the OTC, the tactical voice nets in use, and the location and disposition information of other ships.
13. Identification of all ships in the formation visually and on the radarscope.
14. Status of shipping and current closest points of approach (CPAs).
15. Turbines, engines, or boilers in use and maximum speed possible; status of off-line equipment and respective power train.
16. Watch status in the CIC; aircraft under control.
17. Emission-control condition and specific restrictions placed on electronic emissions.
18. Radar guard assignments, air defense sector assignments, and nets utilized for reporting.

19. Authentication and challenging information.
20. Status of all electronic equipment.
21. Status of the towed array: scope of the cable, depth of the array, and minimum depth associated with that scope (if applicable).
22. Status of embarked helicopters (if applicable), time of flight quarters, ceiling, visibility, dew-point spread, and the best course to place the ship in the envelope for acceptable winds, pitch and roll, status of flight-deck nets (raised or lowered), and any maneuvering restrictions.
23. Lighting measures in effect.
24. Generators in use and status of off-line generators.
25. Steering cables and units in use.
26. Contents of the plan of the day, including any special events that may occur during the watch and preparations.
27. The location of the captain.

RELIEVING ANY WATCH

This excerpt, taken from OpNavInst 3120.32D, is an excellent summary of the protocol for taking *any* watch on board a U.S. Navy warship. You should be very familiar with the procedure and use it in all your relieving processes.

ROLES FOR RELIEVING THE WATCH. Relieving the watch shall be controlled and precise. The ability to handle casualties and tactical decisions is significantly reduced during the transition period between watches. Accordingly, the following rules will apply:

(1) The relieving watch is to be on station in sufficient time to become familiar with equipment conditions and the overall situation and still relieve on time.

(2) The relieving watch inspects all spaces and equipment as required by the Commanding Officer before relieving the watch.

(3) If practical, the relieving watch examines all applicable equipment log readings on the station since they last had the watch, noting any unusual variations such as voltages, pressures, and temperatures.

Such variations shall be discussed and resolved prior to watch relief. (Check that the preceding watch has completed the log sheets as required.)

(4) The relieving watch reads the remarks sections of applicable logs from the last time that they were on watch (or from the time of getting under way, plant start-up, equipment light-off; or for the preceding three watches if continuity of watches has been interrupted), carefully noting and discussing unusual conditions, deviations, or other matters of importance.

(5) Both the relieved watch and the relieving watch are responsible for ensuring that the relieving watch is completely aware of all unusual conditions. These include tactical situations, equipment out of commission or in repair, personnel working aloft, outstanding orders, deviations from normal plant or equipment line-up, forthcoming evolutions (if known), and any other matters pertinent to the watch.

(6) The relief is executed smartly under the following guidelines:

(a) Permission is obtained from the appropriate watch supervisor to relieve the watch.

(b) Relief reports, "Ready to relieve."

(c) Person being relieved gives a status report of the watch section.

(d) Relief tours the watch station.

(e) Person being relieved completes briefing of relief (including unexecuted orders and anticipated evolutions) and answers any questions.

(f) When the relief is fully satisfied that they are completely informed regarding the watch, they relieve the watch by saying, "I relieve you."

(g) Responsibility for the watch station then shifts to the oncoming watchstander, and the person being relieved states, "I stand relieved."

(h) The person assuming the watch reports their relief to the same person from whom permission was requested to relieve.

(i) On stations where a log is maintained, the log is completed and signed by the offgoing watchstander before leaving the watch station.

(7) On nuclear-powered ships, the relief of the EOOW shall be conducted following the procedures listed in the OpNavInst 9210.2 (series).

TRAINING THE WATCH

A good watch officer is always ready to train the watch team. Particularly when a watch is long and dull, it is important to keep the watch team occupied and interested in being at their stations—whether on the bridge, in CIC, or in engineering spaces. The best way to do this is to conduct training at every opportunity. A few ideas:

1. Set up a competition between the bridge and CIC in solving various problems, maneuvering boards, looking up answers to questions in publications, communications procedures, tactical signals, and the like.

2. Have a question-and-answer competition among bridge watchstanders— who can locate the flight-deck crash alarm, the fog signal switch, the various radio circuits on the bridge, and so forth.

3. Show the lookouts profiles of various air and surface contacts operating in the theater.

4. Have an engineer come to the bridge to cover damage control or engineering training on station. This is particularly important to ensure the bridge team thoroughly understands and complies with the Engineering Operational Sequencing System (EOSS) and Engineering Operational Casualty Control (EOCC) procedures. Interactions between the engineering control stations and the bridge must always be crisp and clear—whether during routine procedures or emergencies.

5. Have a corpsman come up to conduct first-aid training.

6. Cross-train the boatswain's mate to navigate or the quartermaster in tactical communications.

7. Discuss your watch team's preplanned responses to various emergencies. Who will do what (how and when)? Rehearse the actions.

3

THE SHIP'S DECK LOG

All U.S. Navy ships in commission shall maintain a ship's deck log.

OPNAVINST 3100.7C

The deck log shall be a complete daily record, by watches, which shall describe every occurrence of importance concerning the crew and the operation and safety of the ship or items of historical value.

OPNAVINST 3120.32D

GENERAL

The deck log is the official record of a ship's history during her commission. It presents a complete narrative of noteworthy incidents in the life of the ship and her officers and crew. Everything of significance pertaining to the ship's complement, material, operations, or state of readiness is entered in the deck log. It is a detailed source of factual data. Watch officers responsible for the maintenance of the log must appreciate the importance of their undertaking. They must ensure that all entries are complete, accurate, clear, concise, and expressed in standard naval phraseology. Taken together, the entries should constitute a true and understandable historical and legal record of the ship.

The ship's deck log must be kept with care. It must be clear enough to stand alone as the official legal record of the ship's activity and significant occurrences of any one day, under way or in port. The entries in the deck log for each day must give so complete an account of the events of that day, from 0000 until 2400, that reference to the previous day's log is not necessary. This is why the entry made by the midwatch must recapitulate the situation existing at midnight. This entry includes the conditions of readiness in force, the status of the engineering plant, the command organization, course and speed, other units present, and required tactical information.

The deck log is one of several logs that must be diligently maintained at all times with appropriate classification markings in place. The deck log is a legal record and can be used as evidence before legal bodies. The magnetic compass record book, the engineering log, and the engineer's bell book are vital operational documents that are maintained on board between three and five years. Consequently, it is important that the remarks be complete and accurate. Erasures in any of these records would bring their validity as evidence into question. The OOD must initial corrections of errors in these logs.

Logs are often consulted in the settlement of claims for pensions by persons who claim to have been injured while serving in the armed forces. A complete entry, therefore, must be made in the log concerning every injury, accident, and casualty, including accidents that could later lead to the discovery of injuries to the officers, crew, or passengers on board. This is necessary both to protect the government from false claims and to furnish a record for honest claimants. Deck logs represent an enduring element of a ship's history: they are maintained by the Navy History and Heritage Command for thirty years and then transferred to the National Archives and Records Administration for permanent retention.

The navigator has charge of the preparation of the deck log. Regulations require that he or she examine the logbook daily to see that it is prepared in accordance with instructions and call to the attention of watch officers any inaccuracies or omissions in their entries. The navigator is responsible for log entries being in proper form, but the OOD is responsible for the entries made during his or her watch.

Increasingly, entries' signatures are in digital form as archives are pushed to digital records. Handwritten entries are still made in some cases but must be signed with a ballpoint pen in black ink. The remarks must be legible, and while the JOOD or QMOW may write the log, it must be signed by the OOD responsible for the watch. A sample computerized deck log instruction follows.

COMPUTERIZED DECK LOG: POLICY AND INSTRUCTION

Start a New Deck Log. Select the icon folder "Deck Logs" and then open the template file "In-port Deck Logs."

Fill Out the Uniform Entries. Double click on the uniform entries. The only thing that needs to be changed is the month and day. The information is automatic for each page.

Fill Out the Midwatch Entries. Double click on the log entry lines and then type all the following information:

				0000–0400
2345				ASSUMED THE WATCH MOORED IN (CITY, COUNTRY) AT
				(PIER NAME) STBD/PORT SIDE TO, BOW IN/OUT WITH 6
				STANDARD MOORING LINES DOUBLED/ TRIPLED. OTHER
				LINES BEING USED: (LIST ANY).
				CENTERLINE ANCHOR IS UNDERFOOT/ HAWSED.
				STBD ANCHOR IS UNDERFOOT/HAWSED.
				ENGINEERING PLANT STATUS AS FOLLOWS: (LIST ALL).
				SHORE SERVICES BEING USED: (LIST ALL).
				MATERIAL CONDITION YOKE IS SET THROUGHOUT THE SHIP.
				AREA SOPA IS (NAME OF SOPA).
				PIER SOPA IS (NAME OF SHIP & HULL #).
				OTHER SHIPS PRESENT ARE: (LIST ALL).
				CO IS ABOARD or ASHORE.
				XO IS ABOARD or ASHORE.
				CDO IS (RANK & NAME).
				OOD IS (RANK & NAME).

Save the New Day. Once finished with the midwatch entry, go to "save" or "save as," if starting a new month, select the folder "Deck Logs," and name the new file using the year, month, unit name, and hull number for file name; for example: 2018–04 USS BUNKER HILL (CG 52).

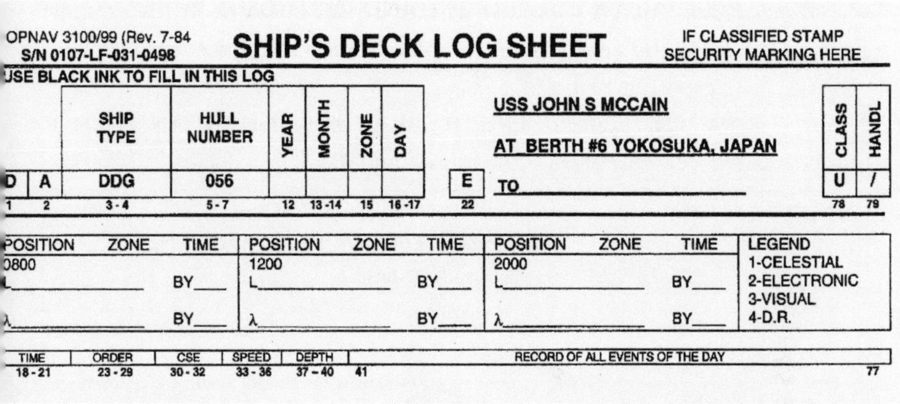
OPNAV 3100/99 (Rev. 7-84
S/N 0107-LF-031-0498

SHIP'S DECK LOG SHEET

IF CLASSIFIED STAMP
SECURITY MARKING HERE

USE BLACK INK TO FILL IN THIS LOG

		SHIP TYPE	HULL NUMBER	YEAR	MONTH	ZONE	DAY		USS JOHN S MCCAIN AT BERTH #6 YOKOSUKA, JAPAN	CLASS	HANDL
D	A	DDG	056					E	TO	U	/
1	2	3-4	5-7	12	13-14	15	16-17	22		78	79

POSITION ZONE TIME	POSITION ZONE TIME	POSITION ZONE TIME	LEGEND
0800	1200	2000	1-CELESTIAL
L____ BY___	L____ BY___	L____ BY___	2-ELECTRONIC 3-VISUAL
λ____ BY___	λ____ BY___	λ____ BY___	4-D.R.

TIME	ORDER	CSE	SPEED	DEPTH	RECORD OF ALL EVENTS OF THE DAY
18-21	23-29	30-32	33-36	37-40	41 77

FIGURE 3-1 Ship's Deck Log Sheet

The First Entry. Every page will start with watch time (0000–0400, 0400–0700 CONTINUED, etc.).

TIME	ORDER	CSE	SPEED	DEPTH	RECORD OF ALL EVENTS OF THE DAY
18–21	23–29	30–32	33–36	37–40	41 77

				0000–0400 CONTINUED

Log Entries. Every entry is in past tense and CAPITAL letters. Enter the time for entries in the "Time" column (18–21). Each log entry will start in the "Depth" column (37) and stop at column 77. Press the "tab" key to move to the next line.

TIME	ORDER	CSE	SPEED	DEPTH	RECORD OF ALL EVENTS OF THE DAY
18–21	23–29	30–32	33–36	37–40	41 77

				0300–0700
0430				RECEIVED MUSTER REPORT
0500				XO ARRIVED
0600				ROVING PATROL REPORTED ALL CONDITIONS NORMAL
0630				OBSERVED SUNRISE

Watch Relief. The OOD watch relief is typed as shown in the example below. After the OOD's name, skip one space before starting the next watch.

TIME	ORDER	CSE	SPEED	DEPTH	RECORD OF ALL EVENTS OF THE DAY
18–21	23–29	30–32	33–36	37–40	41 77
				0800–1200 CONTINUED	
1145				WATCH PROPERLY RELIEVED BY PSC KANNONBALL	
				Signature	
				PRINT NAME	
				1200–1600	
1145				ASSUMED THE WATCH MOORED AS BEFORE	

Last Entry of the Day. The last watch will end the log as shown in the example below.

TIME	ORDER	CSE	SPEED	DEPTH	RECORD OF ALL EVENTS OF THE DAY
18–21	23–29	30–32	33–36	37–40	41 77
				2000–2400	
2345				WATCH PROPERLY RELIEVED BY PSC KANNONBALL	
				SIGN NAME	
				PRINT NAME	

Save the Deck Logs. To keep from losing the information you have entered in the deck logs, save them to the hard drive by pressing "Ctrl-S" every fifteen minutes.

OOD Signs Out. OODs are mustered the following day to sign deck logs.

Routine Log Entries. Anything that affects the ship and its crew in any way must be logged in accordance with the Deck Log Instruction (OpNavInst 3100.7B) and the Commanding Officer's Policy.

CO and XO Arriving and Departing the Ship. The first arrival of the day is recorded as "arrived." Then all subsequent arrivals are described as "returned."

TIME	ORDER	CSE	SPEED	DEPTH	RECORD OF ALL EVENTS OF THE DAY
18–21	23–29	30–32	33–36	37–40	41 77
					1200–1600 CONTINUED
1230					CO ARRIVED
1235					CO DEPARTED
1315					CO RETURNED
1330					XO ARRIVED
1345					XO DEPARTED
1400					XO RETURNED

Official Visitors. Any official person will be logged arriving and departing the ship. If an official is above the rank O-5 without a title, log his or her rank and name. This includes U.S. and foreign officers.

TIME	ORDER	CSE	SPEED	DEPTH	RECORD OF ALL EVENTS OF THE DAY
18–21	23–29	30–32	33–36	37–40	41 77
					1200–1600 CONTINUED
1300					USS PREBLE ARRIVED
1315					7TH FLT ARRIVED
1430					USS MUSTIN DEPARTED
1515					CAPT. JOHN WILLIAMS DEPARTED
1530					CDR. Always at Sea, USN
1600					JS UMIGIRI ARRIVED

Observing Sunrise, Sunset, and Colors. Log sunrise, morning colors, evening colors, and sunset.

TIME	ORDER	CSE	SPEED	DEPTH	RECORD OF ALL EVENTS OF THE DAY
18–21	23–29	30–32	33–36	37–40	41 77
					0800–1600 CONTINUED
0530					OBSERVED SUNRISE
0800					OBSERVED MORNING COLORS
1630					OBSERVED SUNSET AND EVENING COLORS

Twelve o'clock Reports. The 0700–1200 watch will log all twelve o'clock reports received.

TIME	ORDER	CSE	SPEED	DEPTH	RECORD OF ALL EVENTS OF THE DAY	
18–21	23–29	30–32	33–36	37–40	41	77
					0700–1200	
0700					RECEIVED CHRONOMETER REPORT	
0800					RECEIVED BOAT REPORT	
0900					RECEIVED COMBAT SYSTEMS REPORT	
1000					RECEIVED FUEL AND WATER REPORT	
1100					RECEIVED DRAFT REPORT	
1130					RECEIVED MUSTER REPORT	
1200					RECEIVED VEHICLE REPORT	

Roving Patrol. Be sure to include the periodic reports from the roving patrol or other security personnel providing routine reports.

TIME	ORDER	CSE	SPEED	DEPTH	RECORD OF ALL EVENTS OF THE DAY	
18–21	23–29	30–32	33–36	37–40	41	77
					1200–1600 CONTINUED	
1300					ROVING PATROL REPORTED ALL CONDITIONS	
					NORMAL	

Shifting Watch to the Pilothouse. The watch is stood either on the quarterdeck or in the pilothouse.

TIME	ORDER	CSE	SPEED	DEPTH	RECORD OF ALL EVENTS OF THE DAY	
18–21	23–29	30–32	33–36	37–40	41	77
					0800–1200 CONTINUED	
11145					OOD SHIFTED WATCH FROM AMIDSHIPS QUARTERDECK	
					TO THE PILOTHOUSE	
					WATCH PROPERLY RELIEVED BY PSC KANNONBALL	

				Signature
				PRINT NAME
				1200–1600
11145				ASSUMED THE WATCH MOORED AS BEFORE

Other Things to Be Logged. Anything significant happening during the watch should be logged. Appropriate entries would include any special evolutions or activities the ship is engaged in.

TIME	ORDER	CSE	SPEED	DEPTH	RECORD OF ALL EVENTS OF THE DAY
18–21	23–29	30–32	33–36	37–40	41 77
					0700–1200
0700					COMMENCED/SECURED PERSONNEL WORKING ALOFT
0800					COMMENCED/SECURED DIVING OPERATIONS
0900					(NAME OF) BARGE ALONGSIDE / CAST OFF
1000					COMMENCED/SECURED SECURITY ALERT (LIST REASON)
1100					COMMENCED/SECURED (NAME OF) DRILL
1130					PERSONNEL/EQUIPMENT CASUALTY
					FIRES, FLOODING, SECURITY ALERTS

When there are personnel or equipment casualties, it is very important to include as much information as possible in the deck log. The entry should include (but is not limited to):

- Rank and name of casualty.
- Where the accident occurred.
- Injuries sustained.
- Who reported the accident.
- What is being done for medical attention.
- Who was notified (CO, XO, CDO, duty hospital corpsman [HM], duty master-at-arms [MAA], etc.).

- What happened.
- Status of casualty.
- Relevant amplifying information.

Emergencies such as fires, flooding, security alerts, and so on should also be logged. The entry should include the following information:

- Where and what type of emergency.
- What team was called away (duty in-port emergency team [DIET], security force).
- Who reported it.
- What's happening in relation to the emergency.
- Who was notified (CO, XO, CDO, etc.).
- Did the casualty result in damage, was it repaired, or was the leak or flooding stopped, and so on.

While the deck log should be thorough, it need not be exhaustive: entries that do not add to the historical, legal, or operational value of the log are not required (e.g., reveille, meal times).

DECK-LOG ENTRIES

Because the deck log is an official record, particular care must be taken in the recording of numbers. Where a signature is required, the name is to be printed under the individual's signature. Deck logs that are illegible for any reason, including poor penmanship, will be returned for remedial action. No lines may be skipped, except between the beginning and end of successive watch entries. Only abbreviations that are accepted throughout the Navy by reason of long and continued usage may be entered in the log. The following are some of the most commonly used abbreviations, drawn from OpNavInst 3100.7C:

145 rpm	145 revolutions per minute
AE STOP	All engines stop
AEA ⅓	All engines ahead ⅓
AEA FLK	All engines ahead flank

AEA FUL	All engines ahead full
AEA STD	All engines ahead standard
CPA	Closest point of approach
H(R/L)R	Hard (right/left) rudder
MEET HR	Meet her
OCE	Officer conducting the exercise
OOD	Officer of the deck
OTC	Officer in tactical command
P(S) EA ⅓	Port (starboard) engine ahead ⅓
P(S) EB ⅓	Port (starboard) engine back ⅓
R(L) 050	Right (left) to course 050°T
R(L) 15R	Right (left) 15° rudder
R(L) FR	Right (left) full rudder
R/A	Rudder amidships
UA	Unauthorized absence

The following sample entries are to be used as guides for recording the remarks of a watch. They are not all-inclusive, nor are they to be construed as the only acceptable ones. Any entry that is complete, accurate, and in standard naval phraseology is acceptable. A comprehensive list of required entries is provided in OpNavInst 3100.7.

MIDWATCH
Under Way

00–04

0000   Steaming in company with Task Group 30.5, composed of COMCARSTRKGRU 11 and COMDESRON 23, plus USS JOHN PAUL JONES (DDG 53) and USS HIGGINS (DDG 76), en route from Pearl Harbor, Hawaii, to San Diego, California, in accordance with CTG 30.5, 161514Z AUG 18. PRINCETON (CG 59) is in station 2 in a formation 1. Formation course 220°T, SPEED 15 knots. SOPA and OTC is CTG 30.5, COMCARSTRKGRU 11 in USS NIMITZ (CVN 68), HIGGINS is guide, bearing 220°T, distance

5,000 yds. Condition of readiness 3 and material condition YOKE set. Ship darkened except for running lights.

Note: On succeeding watches the first entry is "Under way as before."

In Port

00–04

0000   Moored starboard side to USS BAINBRIDGE (DDG 96) with standard mooring lines in a nest of three ships. USS FORREST SHERMAN (DDG 98) moored inboard of BAINBRIDGE to starboard. FORREST SHERMAN moored starboard side to pier _____, berth _____, Norfolk, VA. Ships present: _____, SOPA _____.

00–04

0000   Anchored in berth B-4, Trinidad, West Indies, in 12 fathoms of water, mud bottom, with 60 fathoms of chain to the starboard anchor on the following anchorage bearings: South Point Light 060, etc. Ship in condition of readiness 3, material condition YOKE set and darkened except for anchor lights. Engineering Department on 30-minute notice before getting under way. Heavy weather plan in effect. Anchor detail standing by. Wind 45 knots from 070. Weather reports indicate possibility of winds up to 60 knots before 0400. Ships present: _____, SOPA _____.

00–04

0000   Moored starboard side to pier 3, berth 35, U.S. Naval Station, Norfolk, VA, with standard mooring lines doubled. Receiving miscellaneous services from the pier. Ships present include _____, SOPA _____.

00–04

0000   Resting on keel blocks in dry dock no. 3, U.S. Naval Shipyard, Bremerton, Wash., receiving miscellaneous services from the dock. Ships present include _____, SOPA _____.

Note: On succeeding watches the first entry is "Moored as before," "Anchored as before," or "Dry-docked as before."

AIR OPERATIONS
Entries Applicable to Carriers

1000   Flight quarters.

1005   Commenced launching aircraft for (carrier qualification) (refresher operations) (group tactics), etc.

1025   Completed launching aircraft, having launched 40 aircraft.

1030   Commenced recovering aircraft.

1035   Commenced maneuvering while recovering (launching) aircraft (while conducting task group [force] flight operations).

1055   Completed recovering aircraft, having recovered 40 aircraft.

1143   F-18 bureau no. 12345 of VFA-87, pilot LCDR Ben B. BOOMS, USN, crashed into the sea off the port bow at latitude 30°50′N, longitude 150°20′W, and sank in 500 fathoms of water. Pilot ejected clear of aircraft.

1144   USS MAHAN (DDG 72) and helicopter commenced recovery of pilot.

1145   Pilot recovered by helicopter and delivered on board USS GEORGE WASHINGTON (CVN 73). Injuries to pilot: (description).

1215   Secured from flight quarters.

1300   F/A18, bureau no. 67890 of VFA-87, pilot ENS John P. JONES, USNR, crashed into barrier no. 2. Pilot sustained mild abrasion to left forearm and contusions to both legs. Damage to aircraft: (major) (minor) (strike).

1315   CDR A. B. SEA, USN, Commanding Officer, VFA-87, departed with 15 aircraft for Oceana, VA, TAD completed.

1330   CDR X. Y. ZEE, USN, Commanding Officer, VAW-124, landed aboard with 4 aircraft from NAS, Norfolk, VA, for TAD.

Entries Applicable to All Ships

2100   Maneuvering to take plane guard station no. 1R on USS THEODORE ROOSEVELT (CVN 71).

2110   On station.

2115   Commenced flight operations.

2210   F/A 18 aircraft crashed into the sea off starboard bow. Maneuvering to recover pilot.

2214   Recovered pilot LTJG Harvey H. GOTZ, USN VFA-87. Injuries to pilot: (description).

Entries Applicable to Ships Carrying Helicopters

1435   Flight quarters.

1455   Launched helicopter. Pilot LTJG Ray WINGS, USN; passenger BMC A. CLEAT, USN.

1505   Recovered helicopter on main deck aft.

1510   Secured from flight quarters.

LOADING AND TRANSFERRING OPERATIONS

Ammunition

1400   Commenced loading (transferring) ammunition.

1600   Completed loading (transferring) ammunition, having received from (transferred to) USS BRIDGE (T-AOE 10) 300 rounds 5″/54 cal. Illum. Projectiles, 300 5″/54 cal. full charges, and 30 5″/54 cal. reduced charges.

> *Note:* For entries regarding expenditures of ammunition, see "Gunnery" under "Drills and Exercises."

DAMAGE

Collisions

1155   USS OAK HILL (LSD 51), in coming alongside to port, carried away 39 feet of the ship's port life line forward, with stanchions, and indented the ship's side to a depth of 4 inches over an area of 10 feet long and 4 feet high in the vicinity of frames 46–51. No personnel casualties.

1401   Starboard lifeboat carried away by heavy sea. Boat and all equipment lost. No personnel casualties.

Engineering Casualties

1018   Lost fires in no. 1A boiler due to high water level. Maximum speed available, 18 knots.

1019   Lit fires in no. 1B boiler.

1130   No. 1B boiler on the line. All conditions normal. Maximum speed available, 27 knots.

DRILLS AND EXERCISES

General

1000   Exercised at general drills.

Abandon Ship

1005   Commenced abandon-ship drill.

1045   Secured from abandon-ship drill.

Alarms

0800   Tested general, chemical, collision alarms. All conditions normal.

NBC Attack

1440   Set material condition ZEBRA and NBC condition WILLIAM.

1450   Set NBC condition CIRCLE WILLIAM.

1500   (SIMULATED) nuclear (underwater) (air) burst, bearing 045°T, distance 15,000 yards. Maneuvering to avoid base surge and fallout.

1530   Rejoined formation and took station L6 in formation.

Collision

1350   Held collision drill.

1354   Material condition ZEBRA set.

1410   Secured from collision drill. Set material condition YOKE.

Rescue and Assistance

1100   Held fire drill.

1110   Secured from fire drill.

1300   Called away the rescue and assistance party.

1305   Rescue and assistance party embarked in starboard boat and clear of ship.

1330   Rescue and assistance party returned aboard. Further assistance not required.

Gunnery

1245   Went to general quarters. Set material condition ZEBRA.

1300   Commenced missile exercise.

1304   Commenced firing. Fired one _____ missile to starboard (port).

1308   Ceased firing.

1320   Set material condition YOKE.

1325   Secured from general quarters. Ammunition expended: 89 rounds 5"54/cal. High-explosive projectiles with 89 rounds full-service smokeless (flashless) powder cartridges with no casualties.

> *Note:* For several exercises fired in close succession, the ammunition expended for all may be grouped in one entry. Normally, material condition will be set and batteries secured before securing from general quarters.

FORMATIONS

General

0700   Maneuvering to take station in SCREEN Kilo formation. Guide is USS JOHN S. MCCAIN (DDG 56).

0800   Rotated both screen sector boundaries 30° clockwise.

0900   New formation guide is USS ANTIETAM (CG 54).

Officer in Tactical Command (OTC)

0900   COMCARSTRKGRU 7 embarked in USS RONALD REAGAN (CVN 76) assumed OTC.

1000   Commanding Officer, USS MCCAMPBELL (DDG 85), was designated OTC.

> *Note:* All shifts of tactical command should be logged. When the OTC is the CO of the log writer's ship, the following terminology should be used: "OTC is Commanding Officer, USS ANTIETAM (CG 54)." In every case, the command title of the OTC (for example, COMCARSTRKGRU 7) should be used, and not his or her name and grade. Entry should state in which ship OTC is embarked.

Rendezvous

0800   USS MOMSEN (DDG 92) made rendezvous with this ship (the formation) and took designated station (took station in the screen) (took plane guard station).

2200   Joined rendezvous with TG 70.2 and took designated station in SCREEN K, with guide in USS LASSEN (DDG 82), distance 2,400 yards. OTC is COMCARSTRKGRU 5 in USS RONALD REAGAN (CVN 76).

Tactical Exercises

1000   Commenced division tactical exercises. Steering various courses at various speeds (in area HOTEL) (conforming to maneuvers signaled by COMDESRON 21) (on signals from COMDESRON 21).

Zigzagging

1300   Commenced zigzagging in accordance with plan no. 1A, base course 090°T.

1500   Ceased zigzagging and set course 010°T.

FUELING

In Port

1000   Commenced fueling at Naval Fuel Depot, San Diego, draft forward 22', aft 23'.

1130   Ceased pumping. Received 254,031 gals. of JP-5.

At Sea

1345   Set the special sea and replenishment detail. Commenced preparations for refueling from USNS RICHARD E BYRD (T-AKE 4).

1426   Maneuvering to take station astern USNS RICHARD E BYRD.

1438   On station.

1442   Commenced approach. Captain (at the conn) (conning).

1453   On station alongside port side of RICHARD E BYRD.

1456   First line over.

1510   Received first fuel hose.

1515   Commenced receiving fuel.

1559   Fueling completed. Received 233,198 gals. of DFM/F-76.

1606   All lines and hoses clear. Maneuvering to clear port side of RICHARD E BYRD.

1610   Clear of RICHARD E BYRD.

1612   Secured the replenishment detail.

HONORS, CEREMONIES, AND OFFICIAL VISITS
Personal Flags

1200   RADM D. D. WAVE, USN, COMCARSTRKGRU 5, broke his flag in this ship.

1300   The Honorable _____, Secretary of the Navy, came aboard; broke the flag of the Secretary of the Navy.

1500   The Secretary of the Navy departed; hauled down the flag of SECNAV.

1530   COMPHIBGRU 3 shifted flag from USS MAKIN ISLAND (LHD 8) to USS AMERICA (LHA 6).

Manning the Rail

1000   Manned the rail as the President of the United States came aboard for an official visit. Fired 21-gun salute, broke the President's flag at the main truck.

Visits

1430   Their Majesties, the King and Queen of _____, made an official call on VADM D. G. FARRAGUT, USN, COMSIXTHFLT, with their official party. Rendered honors and fired a salute of 21 guns.

1530   The royal party departed. Rendered honors and fired a salute of 21 guns.

Calls

1000   The Commanding Officer left the ship to make an official call on COMCARSTRKGRU 2.

1605   RADM V. A. MOSS, USN, COMCARSTRKGRU 2, came aboard to return the official call of the Commanding Officer.

INSPECTIONS
Administrative and Material

0930   RADM S. DECATUR, USN, COMCARSTRKGRU 3, accompanied by members of staff and inspecting party, came on board and commenced administrative inspection. Broke flag of COMCARSTRKGRU 3.

1100   COMCARSTRKGRU 3, members of staff, and inspecting party left the ship. Hauled down flag of COMCARSTRKGRU 3.

Lower Deck
1315   Commenced captain's inspection of lower decks, holds, and storerooms.
1400   Secured from inspection.

Personnel
0900   Mustered the crew at quarters for captain's inspection (of personnel and upper decks).

NAVIGATION
Anchoring
1600   Anchored in Area South HOTEL, berth 44, Hampton Roads, VA, in 6 fathoms of water, mud bottom, with 30 fathoms of chain to the port anchor on the following bearings: Fort Wook 040°T, Middle Ground Light 217°T, Sewall's Point 072°T. Ships present: _____, SOPA _____.

Contacts
1405   Sighted merchant ship bearing 280°T, distance about 6 miles on approximately parallel course.
1430   Identified merchant ship as SS SEAKAY, U.S. registry, routed independently from Aruba, NWI, to New York, NY.
1441   Passed SS SEAKAY abeam to port, distance about 2 miles.
1620   Obtained unidentified radar contact bearing 090°T, distance 28,800 yards.
1629   Unidentified contact tracked and determined to be on course 180°T, speed 15 knots. CPA 042°T, distance 4.2 miles.
1636   Contact identified as USS BARRY (DDG 52) by USS ARLEIGH BURKE (DDG 51).
1715   Obtained sonar contact bearing 172°T, range 2,500 yards.
1717   Contact evaluated as possible submarine. Commenced attacking (tracking) (investigating).
1720   Lost contact.

1721   Contact regained bearing 020°T, range 2,000 yards. Oil slick sighted on that bearing and range. Commenced reattack.

1724   Sonar reported hearing breaking-up noises.

1725   Lost contact.

> *Note:* Contacts at sea are logged when they will pass in the vicinity of logging ship. Although the exact distance is not specified, normally contacts that pass within three nautical miles are logged.

Dry-Docking

1420   Commercial tug SEAGOOSE came alongside to port. Pilot C. U. FINE came aboard.

1426   USN tug YTB-68 came alongside port bow, USN tug YTB-63 came alongside port quarter.

1431   First line to dock starboard bow.

1435   First line to dock port bow.

1440   Bow passed over sill of dock.

1442   Cast off all tugs.

1450   Caisson in place.

1455   Commenced pumping water out of dry dock.

1540   Resting on keel blocks.

1545   Pilot left the ship.

1550   Commenced receiving electrical power and fresh water from the dock.

1630   Inspection of all hull openings completed.

Overhaul, Conversion, and Inactivation

1635   Commenced undergoing (overhaul) (conversion) (inactivation). Commenced limited log entries for duration of (overhaul) (conversion) (inactivation).

0850   Inspection of all hull openings completed.

0900   Flooding commenced in dry dock.

0918   All services disconnected from ship.

0920   Inspection of all spaces for watertight integrity completed.

0925   Ship clear of keel blocks.

0930   Handling lines secure on ship.

0935   Pilot U. C. FINE came aboard.

0950	Commenced moving ship clear of dock.
0958	Stern passed over sill.
1005	USN tug YTB 63 came alongside port bow, USN tug YTB 68 came alongside port quarter.
1009	Bow passed over sill.

Note: Upon termination of overhaul or conversion, deck-log entries must be recorded daily by watches.

Getting Under Way

0600	Commenced preparations for getting under way. Set material condition YOKE.
0730	Stationed the special sea detail.
0800	Under way for Norfolk, VA (for sea), as a unit of Task Group 20.2 in compliance with COMCARSTRKGRU 2 serial 063 (CTG 20.2 Op Order 7-06). Maneuvering to clear the anchorage. Captain conning (at the conn), navigator on the bridge.
0810	Standing out of Boston Harbor.
0830	OOD was given the conn. Set readiness condition 3, anchor detail on deck. (Secured the special sea detail, set the regular steaming watch.)
0845	Entered international waters.

Entering Harbor

0551	Passed sea buoy (number/name) abeam to port, distance 1,000 yards.
0554	Stationed special sea detail. OOD (conning) (at the conn), captain and navigator on the bridge.
0600	Commenced maneuvering while conforming to Gedney Channel.
0650	Passed lighted buoy no. 12 abeam to starboard.
0705	USN tug no. 216 came alongside port quarter. Pilot B. A. WATCHER came aboard and took the conn.
0706	Maneuvering to go alongside the pier.
0715	Moored port side to berth 3A, U.S. Naval Ammunition Depot, Earle, NJ, with standard mooring lines. Ships present _____, SOPA is COMDESRON 22 in USS MITSCHER (DDG 57).
0720	Pilot left the ship.

Mooring

1006   Moored port side to Standard Oil Dock, berth 76, Los Angeles Inner Harbor, CA, with standard mooring lines.

1015   Commenced receiving miscellaneous services from the pier.

Sighting Aids to Navigation

0102   Sighted Cape Henry Light bearing 225°T, distance about 20 miles.

0157   Passed Cape Henry Light abeam to starboard, distance 7.3 miles.

0300   Cape Henry Light passed from view bearing 315°T, distance about 20 miles.

Tide

0733   Commenced swinging to flood tide, stern to port.

1046   Completed swinging to flood tide, bearing 347°T.

Time-Zone Changes

0001   Set clocks ahead 1 hour to conform with +3-zone time.

Sea and Weather

1130   Visibility decreased to 1 mile due to fog (heavy rain). Commenced sounding fog signals and stationed (extra lookouts) (lookouts in the eyes of the ship). Winds southeast 25 knots. Sea southeast 8 feet and increasing.

1212   Visibility increased to 5 miles. Ceased sounding fog signals.

Note: Commencement and cessation of sounding fog signals must always be entered.

PERSONNEL

Absentees

0800   Mustered the crew (at quarters) (at foul-weather parade) (on stations) (at quarters for captain's inspection). Absentees: (none) (no new absentees) (SA ROSCOE BADEGG, USN, absent without authority from muster) (FN M. A. WOHL, USN, UA since 0700 this date).

Note: There is no legal distinction between absence beyond leave and absence without leave. Both are logged as unauthorized absence, or UA. The initial entry indicating a person's absence suffices until he or she returns, is declared a deserter, or is otherwise detached from the ship.

0900   A systematic search of the entire ship for SA ROSCOE BADEGG, USN, who missed 0800 muster, disclosed that (he was not on board) (he was found to be sleeping in BOSN's locker comp. A-301-A).

1000   NAVSTA msg 0311600Z reports that BTFN Arch CULPRET, USN, UA since 0800, 15 Apr 2018, returned to naval custody and was being held at that station pending disposition of charges.

Note: An entry such as the above shows that an absentee has returned to naval jurisdiction.

Return of Absentees

2200   PN3 Guy ROAMER, USNR, (returned aboard) (was delivered on board by base security), having been UA since 0800 this date.

2300   SH3 C. A. HAZE, USN, UA since 0700 this date, was delivered on board under guard from NAVSTA, accused of drunk and disorderly conduct at that station. By order of the Commanding Officer, he was restricted to the limits of the ship pending disposition of the charges.

Reports

0800   Sounding-and-security watch reported. All conditions normal.

0830   Roving patrol reported all conditions normal.

Court of Inquiry

1000   The court of inquiry, CAPT A. B. SEA, USN, senior member, appointed by COMNAVSURFOR ltr [letter] serial 2634 of 2 Apr 2006 met in the case of the late BM3 Andrew J. SPIRIT, USN.

1030   The court of inquiry in the case of the late BM3 Andrew J. SPIRIT, USN, adjourned to meet ashore at the scene of his death.

Courts-Martial

1000   The special court-martial, CDR Jonathan Q. DOE, USN, senior member, appointed by CO, USS NIMITZ (CVN 63), ltr serial 102 of 1 Mar 2006, met in the case of SA Ralph O. WEARY, USN.

1200   The special court-martial that met in the case of SA Ralph O. WEARY, USN, recessed to meet again at 1300 this date.

Note: A court adjourns if it will not meet again that date, but if it is to meet again on the same date, it recesses. If known, the date and time of the next meeting are logged.

Deaths

0416   GM1 William P. SEA, USN, died on board as a result of _____.

Deserters

0800   PN3 Guy ROAMER, USNR, was this date declared a deserter from this ship, having been UA since 0800 1 May 2018, a period of 30 days.

Injuries

1035   During drill on the 5″ loading machine, GMSN Ira M. JONAH, USN, suffered a compound fracture of the right foot when a drill shell fell on his foot. Injury not due to his own misconduct. Treatment administered by the medical officer. Disposition: placed on the sick list.

Note: To protect the government from false claims and to establish a record of facts for honest claimants, it is important that there be an accurate and complete entry, including all pertinent details, of *every* injury, accident, or casualty, however slight, among the officers, crew, visitors, passengers, longshoremen, harbor workers, or repairmen.

Temporary Additional Duty

1400   Pursuant to COMNAVAIRPAC ltr serial 104 of 2 Feb 2006, ENS Willy A. BRITE, USN, left the ship for TAD with NAS, Barber's Point, Hawaii.

1700   ENS Willy A. BRITE, USN, having completed TAD with NAS, Barber's Point, Hawaii, returned aboard and resumed his regular duties.

Passengers

1000   Mr. Delbert Z. Brown, civilian technician, embarked for transportation to Guam, M.I. Authority: CNO 141120Z May.

Note: All passengers should be logged in and out with social security number.

Patients

1306   Transferred LT Lawrence A. LEVY, USN, to U.S. Naval Hospital, Yokosuka, Japan, for treatment. Diagnosis _____.

Note: A ship sailing in U.S. continental waters should log a patient's transfer if his or her absence is expected to exceed thirty days; outside those waters, such a transfer should be logged regardless of how long the absence is expected to last. Diagnosis, if known, should be included.

Shore Patrol

1305   Pursuant to orders of the Commanding Officer, BM1 Marvin A. FORCE, USN, in charge of 17 men, left the ship to report to senior shore patrol officer, Norfolk, VA, for TAD.

0200   The shore patrol detail with BM1 Marvin A. Force, USN, in charge, returned to ship, having completed TAD.

Leave

1100   COMDESRON 21 hauled down his pennant and departed on 5 days' leave.

1110   The Commanding Officer departed on 5 days' leave.

0700   The Commanding Officer returned from 5 days' leave.

       Note: Flag officers and unit commanders embarked and COs are the only personnel who must be logged in and out on leave.

SAFETY

Divers

0900   Secured injection pumps in preparation for divers going over side.

0915   Divers in the water for inspection of STBD shaft.

0945   Divers out of the water.

0950   Restored all equipment to normal operation.

Men Aloft

0915   Secured all transmitters and rotating antennas in preparation for personnel going aloft.

0920   Men working aloft.

0945   Personnel secured from working aloft.

0950   Restored all conditions to normal operation.

SHIP MOVEMENTS

1100   USS MITSCHER (DDG 57) got under way and stood out of the harbor.

1130   USS MILIUS (DDG 69) stood into the harbor and anchored (in berth D-3) (moored alongside pier 4).

1300   USS MONTEREY (CG 61) got under way from alongside this ship and anchored in berth D-8.

1600   USS JOHN PAUL JONES (DDG 53) stood in and moored alongside (to port) (outboard) of USS MONTEREY (CG 61).

SHIP'S OPERATIONAL CONTROL

0705   Changed operational control to COMUSNAVEUR, deactivated TG 85.3, and activated TG 65.4, composed of DESRON 26 and DESRON 14, en route to Mediterranean area from Norfolk, VA.

1045   Detached by COMDESRON 26 from TG 65.4 to proceed independently to San Remo, Italy.

1435   Detached from CTU 58.3.2; changed operational control to CTU 57.4.3.

> *Note:* For sample entries regarding commencement of operational control and changes thereto, see "Under Way," under "Midwatch," and "Rendezvous," under "Formations."

SHIPS PRESENT

Ships present: USS EISENHOWER (CVN 69) (COMCARSTRKGRU 12 embarked), USS CAPE ST. GEORGE (CG 71), USNS RICHARD E BYRD (T-AKE 4), and various units of the U.S. Atlantic Fleet, and service craft. SOPA is COMCARSTRKGRU 12 in EISENHOWER (CVN 69).

Ships present: Task Group 63.1 less DESRON 23 plus USS THEODORE ROOSEVELT (CVN 71) and various units of the British and French navies. SOPA is COMCARSTRKGRU 9 (CTG 63.1) in THEODORE ROOSEVELT (CVN 71).

SPECIAL OPERATIONS

0904   Under way for special operations in accordance with COMTHIRDFLT execution order 110518, 17 January 2018. Maneuvering on various courses at various speeds conforming to SOCAL OPAREA. Captain (at the conn) (conning).

1125   Secured the maneuvering watch. Commenced special operations. Commenced limiting log entries to nonoperational data as directed by the chief of naval operations.

1840   Ceased special operations in accordance with COMTHIRDFLT patrol order 110518, 17 January 2018. Commenced operating in accordance with COMSUBRON 1 transit order 2-18.

> *Note:* OpNavInst 3100.7 provides specific guidance on special log-keeping and classification requirements for special operations.

ENVIRONMENTAL CONDITIONS

In describing significant changes in wind, weather, and atmosphere, terminology similar to the following should be used:

State of the Sea	*Motion of the Ship*
Cross sea	Pitching deeply and heavily
Discolored water	Pitching moderately
Heavy following sea	Rolling heavily
Heavy ground swell	Rolling easily
Heavy rolling sea	Rolling deeply
Heavy sea	Pitching badly
Heavy swell from the _____	Pitching easily
Light following sea	Laboring greatly
Light ground swell	Rolling quickly
Light swell from the _____	
Riptides	
Rough sea	
Short chopping sea	
Smooth sea	

4

COMMUNICATIONS

Transmissions shall be as short and concise as practicable, consistent with clarity. The use of standard phraseology enhances brevity.

ALLIED COMMUNICATIONS PUBLICATION (ACP) 125G

Communications have been called "the voice of command." The way a ship uses communications circuits indicates professionalism in command. Indeed, without good communications, every ship and every station within a ship would be isolated. As a basic function of command and control, shipboard communications are centralized in key control spaces, including the bridge, CIC, and damage-control center. Communications systems range from the most basic, such as voice tube and buzzer, to the most modern and sophisticated satellite and laser paths—including extensive use of internet protocols. They also include wireless mobile communication systems for internal shipboard applications, useful in damage control, engineering, combat systems, and force protection watchstanders. Each system has specific functions and characteristics, but all are meant to enable clear, concise communications. To properly exercise command-and-control authority, the watch officer must be familiar with the systems and how best to use them to accomplish the mission.

INTERNAL COMMUNICATIONS

Internal communications provide the means for informing and directing the ship's company. The various systems can be complicated, mastered by the specialists responsible for their maintenance. A relatively small number of circuits and types of equipment relate to the duties of the watch officer, but he or she should have detailed knowledge of those installed in the area of the watch station—the bridge, the central control station, the pilothouse, and in CIC.

Sound-powered telephone circuits are proven, reliable, and have stood the test of many casualties. They are installed in most ships and include the following:

JA	Captain's battle circuit
JC	Weapons control circuit
JF	Flag officer's circuit
1JG	Aircraft control circuit
JL	Lookout circuit
1JS	Combat information center information circuit
1JV	Maneuvering and docking circuit
JW	Ship-control bearing and navigation circuit
JX	Radio and signals circuit
JZ	Damage control circuit

Although mostly used as backup circuits, the JA, JL, and 1JV are the most commonly used. The watch officer should learn where they go, who monitors them, and which station controls which circuit. The proper voice procedure to use on these circuits differs somewhat from voice-radio procedure, and the OOD should know procedures and enforce compliance and formality at all times. It may appear unimportant that informal conversation is occasionally passed over the sound-powered telephones, but when an emergency arises it will be evident that only trained watchstanders, using standard phraseology, can get the correct word from station to station. A ship in which a lack of formality is permitted over the telephones is not only incapable of first-rate performance in an emergency but also liable to be the scene of confusion and mistakes during routine operations.

Intercommunications voice (MC) units are installed in important stations of most ships and normally used to pass urgent information between officers and petty officers at the station or to amplify sound-powered telephone communications. Here again, circuit formality and procedural compliance must be enforced by the OOD. To avoid confusion and speed up transmissions, the standard procedure for the sound-powered phone talker is used on MC circuits.

A representative list of some of the more traditional MC circuits follows:

One-Way Systems	Purpose
1MC	Battle and general announcements
2MC	Engineers
3MC	Hangar deck
4MC	Damage control
5MC	Flight deck
6MC	Boat control
7MC	Submarine control
10MC	Docking control
18MC	Bridge

Two-Way Systems	Purpose
19MC	Ready room
20MC	Combat information
21MC	Captain's command
22MC	Radio room
23MC	Distribution control
24MC	Flag officer's command
25MC	Wardroom
26MC	Machinery control
27MC	Sonar control
28MC	Aircraft squadron
29MC	Sonar information
30MC	Bomb shop
31MC	Escape trunk

Many ships employ a digital system called the Integrated Voice Communication System (IVCS), which provides tremendous flexibility for accessing and organizing internal communications. The IVCS features dial telephone operation, functionally organized "nets," command and decision (C&D) intercom access, sound-powered phone interfaces, announcing system, and radio call access. Certain types of ships have a general announcing system instead of the 1MC and special station-to-station systems. Regardless of the system, the principles are the same and formality should be maintained. The OOD must know what communications systems are available and who is on the other end. During an emergency, there is no time to figure it out.

Another important responsibility of the OOD is the *management* of 1MC circuits. It is a good practice to keep topside 1MC speakers off while in port, except in emergencies or for safety announcements, to minimize noise and to get the attention of the crew when something of vital importance is passed. The 1MC should not be used to call every member of the crew to the quarterdeck for a phone call or a visitor. Other internal circuits or the messenger should be used for this sort of task. Proper and concise use of the 1MC is the mark of a thinking, professional watch officer.

The 1MC System

The 1MC system is the most important internal communications circuit in the ship and should be the one most closely controlled by the OOD. As mentioned earlier, the control that the watch has over its use is an indicator of how well a ship is being run. More important, however, is ensuring that messages passed over the system, particularly in critical situations, are phrased as clearly as possible. The following list of basic 1MC messages gives the standard phraseology in which they are passed. Your ship or unit may have specific instruction for passing the word, so you should make yourself familiar with that guidance.

EVENT	PIPE	WORD TO BE PASSED
Abandon ship (prepare)	All hands	"All hands prepare to abandon ship. Execute emergency destruction. Nearest land bears _____ degrees magnetic relative position (port bow). _____ miles designated enemy (friendly)." Repeat word.
Abandon ship	All hands	"All hands abandon ship. Nearest land bears _____ degrees magnetic relative position (port bow). _____ miles designated enemy (friendly)." Repeat word.

EVENT	PIPE	WORD TO BE PASSED
Anchored	All hands	"Anchored, shift colors."
Away the RHIB	Long boat call	"Away the RHIB, away." If the captain is not in the boat, omit the second "away."
Belay the word	Attention	"Belay my last."
Boarding	All hands	"Away the boarding party." Pass the word twice.
Boat call	Attention	"Away the RHIB."
Casting off	Attention	"Stand by to cast off (ship) to port (starboard)."
CO arriving or departing	Number of boat gongs depends on rank.	"(Title of officer.)"
Church call	None	"Divine services are now being held in _____ (space). Maintain silence about the decks."
Collision (standby)	Collision alarm	"Stand by for collision, starboard (port) side, frame _____ (number). All hands close all watertight doors Aft (forward) of frame _____ (number)."
Collision	Collision alarm	"Collision, collision, starboard (port) side, frame _____ (number)."
Colors (first call)	None	"First call, first call to colors." No word is passed for the execution or for the carry-on whistle.
	1 whistle	To execute.
	3 whistles	To carry on.
Condition III	Attention	"On deck condition III, watch (number)."
Crew members working aloft	None	"There are personnel working aloft. Do not rotate, radiate, or energize any electronic equipment while personnel are working aloft." Pass the word every thirty minutes.
Divers	None	"There are divers working over the side. Do not operate any equipment, rotate screws, cycle rudder (planes or torpedo-tube shutters), take suction from or discharge to the sea, blow or vent any tanks, activate sonar or underwater electrical equipment, open or close any valves, or cycle trash-disposal unit before checking with the diving supervisor (name and rate) or the officer of the deck."

EVENT	PIPE	WORD TO BE PASSED
Divers (completed)	None	"Diving operations are completed."
Eight o'clock reports (in port)	Attention	"On deck all eight o'clock reports."
Eight o'clock reports (under way)	Attention	"Lay before the mast all eight o'clock reports."
Fire (in port)	Rapid ringing of ship's bell	"Fire, fire, fire, class _____. Fire, fire in compartment _____ (number), (compartment name), away the in-port emergency team. Provide from repair _____ (number)." Pass the word twice.
Flight quarters	All hands	"Flight quarters, flight quarters. All hands man your flight quarters stations for (HIFR) (VERTREP) (land/launch). All hands not involved in flight quarters stand clear."
Securing from flight quarters	All hands	"Secure from flight quarters."
General quarters	General quarters alarm	"General quarters, general quarters. All hands man your battle stations." Pass the word twice.
Holiday routine	All hands	"Commence holiday routine."
Inspection (personnel)	All hands	"Quarters for captain's personnel inspection."
Inspection (material)	All hands	"Stand by all lower (upper) deck spaces for inspection."
Inspection (berthing and messing)	All hands	"Captain's (XO's) inspection of messing and berthing."
Knock off	Pipe down	"Knock off ship's work."
Liberty	All hands	"Liberty call, liberty call. Liberty commences for sections _____ to expire on board at _____."
Mail call	Attention	"Mail call."
Man overboard	None	"Man overboard port (starboard) side. (Type of recovery)." Pass the word twice.
Mast	Attention	"All mast cases, witnesses, and division officers concerned assemble _____ (place)."

EVENT	PIPE	WORD TO BE PASSED
Material condition	Attention	"Set material condition (Yoke) (Zebra) (X-ray). Duty damage-control petty officer make reports to _____ (place)."
Meals	Pipe down	None.
Movie call	Attention	"Movie call."
Muster of restricted crew members	Attention	"Muster all restricted men (personnel)."
Officers (unidentified)	Number of boat gongs depends on rank.	"(Rank of officer, service). Arriving/ Departing."
Preparation for entering port	All hands	"Make all preparations for entering port. The ship expects to moor (anchor) at _____."
Preparation for getting under way	All hands	"Make all preparation for getting under way. The ship expects to be under way at _____."
Quarters	All hands	"All hands to quarters for muster, instruction, and inspection."
Quarters (foul weather)	All hands	"All hands to quarters for muster, instruction, and inspection, foul-weather parade."
Rain squall	Attention	"Haul over all hatch hoods and gun covers."
Readiness reports	Attention	"All department heads make ready for sea reports to the officer of the deck on the bridge."
Receiving alongside	Attention	"Stand by to receive (ship) (barge) alongside to port (starboard)."
Relieving the watch	Attention	"Relieve the watch, relieve the watch, relieve the wheel and lookouts, on deck section ___."
Repel boarders	All hands	"All hands repel boarders." Pass the word twice.
Replenishment (refueling)	Attention	"Station the replenishment (refueling) detail."
Rescue and assistance	Attention	"Away the rescue-and-assistance detail. Muster at _____ (area). Section _____ provide."
Reveille	All hands	"Reveille, reveille. All hands heave out."
Secure the sea and anchor detail	Pipe down	"Secure the sea and anchor detail."

EVENT	PIPE	WORD TO BE PASSED
Secure	Pipe down	"Secure from (event)."
Shifting the watch	Attention	"The officer of the deck is shifting the watch to the quarterdeck (bridge)."
Security alert	None	"Security alert, security alert. Away the security alert force. All hands stand fast."
Side boys	Attention	"Lay to the quarterdeck the side boys."
Smoking lamp (lighted)	Attention	"The smoking lamp is lighted in all authorized spaces."
Smoking lamp (out)	Attention	"The smoking lamp is out throughout the ship while . . ." or "The smoking lamp is out in (space or area) while . . ."
Sea and Anchor detail	All hands	"Station the sea and anchor detail."
Sweepers (at sea)	Sweepers	"Sweepers, sweepers, man your brooms, give the ship a clean sweep down fore and aft, sweep down all lower decks, ladder wells, and passageways. Now, sweepers."
Sweepers (in port)	Sweepers	"Sweepers, sweepers, man your brooms, give the ship a clean sweep down fore and aft, sweep down all lower decks, ladder wells, and passageways, take all trash to the receptacles provided on the pier."
Taps	None	"Taps, taps, lights out, all hands turn into your bunks. Maintain silence about the decks. Taps."
Test alarms	None	"The following is a test of the general, chemical, and collision alarms from the _____ (space)."
Turn to	Turn to	"Turn to, continue ship's work" or "Turn to, commence ship's work."
Visit and search	All hands	"Away the visit-and-search crew." Pass the word twice.
Working party	All hands	"Now muster a _____ (number)-hand working party (place) with (person in charge)."

Sound-Powered Telephone Procedures

Standard phraseology and discipline must be maintained over sound-powered telephone circuits. When unofficial conversation is the norm and discipline breaks down, information is lost or, even worse, the wrong information is passed. The formality of sound-powered phone circuits is a reflection of the professionalism of the OOD.

When headphones are worn by phone talkers at both stations, a message can be stated with the call-up. For example, if the CIC talker has data to pass to the bridge talker, the following is passed:

CIC talker: "Bridge combat. Combat reports a contact bearing 040°T, 10,000 yards, on course 330°T, speed 10 knots. CPA is 270°T, 5,000 yards, at time 1045."

The receiving talker repeats the message and answers as follows:

Bridge talker: "Bridge, aye. Contact bearing 040°T, 10,000 yards, on course 330°T, speed 10 knots. CPA is 270°T, 5,000 yards, at time 1045."

The repeat-back procedures ensure that the proper word is received.

Standard Phraseology for Internal Communications

Circuit Test. To find out if telephone stations are manned and ready, the talker at control says, "All stations, control, comm check." Each talker then acknowledges in the order previously assigned. Each station responds in order but does not wait more than a few seconds for the station immediately preceding to acknowledge.

Sending. When sending a message, first call the station, identify your own station, and then state the message. "Forecastle, bridge, prepare to anchor in five minutes."

Receiving. When receiving a message, first identify yourself and then repeat the message. "Bridge, forecastle, prepare to anchor in five minutes, aye."

Repeats. When a message is not clear to the listener at the receiving end, he or she should say, "Say again." Never use the word "repeat."

Spelling. Difficult words are spelled by using the phonetic alphabet preceded by the proword (procedure word), "I spell." Pronounce the word before and after spelling it. "Forecastle—I spell—Foxtrot, Oscar, Romeo, Echo, Charlie, Alfa, Sierra, Tango, Lima, Echo—forecastle."

Leaving Circuit. When a phone talker is relieved by another talker, the former informs the control station that he or she is shifting phones. "Bridge, after steering, shifting phone-talkers." And upon returning: "Bridge, after steering, back on the line."

Securing. Before securing phones, always get permission. "Bridge, fantail, request permission to secure."

Ship's Alarms

All ships are equipped with a general alarm, a chemical alarm, and some form of collision alarm. Each of these alarms has a distinctive sound that should be immediately recognizable to all hands. In addition to these universal alarms, some ships have special-purpose signals to provide safety or security for critical spaces and situations. Most ships have some sort of alarm system designed to provide a signal on the bridge and at the quarterdeck station as well as at local stations when the temperature in the magazines reaches a certain degree. Non-aviation ships that carry helicopters have an alarm that signals a helicopter crash. Ship's routine usually calls for testing the various alarms on the morning watch and before getting under way. Specialized alarms are normally tested as part of a planned maintenance system.

Boat Gongs and Side Boys

Most ships sound gongs to indicate the prospective departure of boats and the arrival or departure of visiting officers, embarked unit commanders, and the CO. As boat signals, gongs are sounded *three* times ten minutes before the departure of the boat, *twice* when there are five minutes to go, and *once* with one minute to go.

When used to indicate the arrival or departure of an officer, gongs are sounded in pairs, the same number as the number of side boys the officer rates, followed by the name of the officer's command or by the word "staff." Gongs, when used this way, are not honors but merely inform those aboard of the arrival and departure of senior officers and the departure of crew's boats. In a nest, the ships may agree, or the senior CO direct, that such gongs will not be sounded for captains of outboard ships making routine crossings of inboard ships. Officers rate side boys and gongs as follows:

Rank	*Side Boys and Gongs*
Admiral and vice admiral	Eight
Rear admiral	Six
Captain and commander	Four
Lieutenant commander through ensign	Two

EXTERNAL COMMUNICATIONS

As a rule, categories of external communications relate to the watch officer: voice, visual, and record. Each of these modes meets a specific type of communications requirement, and a ship at sea is likely to be using all of them simultaneously to transmit and receive information. Technical control of all voice and record communications equipment is the responsibility of the radio watch supervisor or, on larger ships, the communications watch officer. In this regard, the term "technical control" should be clearly understood. The watch supervisor in radio does not control what messages are transmitted or received. What he or she does is maintain the communications path by monitoring the performance of equipment and placing traffic on a circuit.

Voice Communications

Voice communication is a primary command-and-control tool for the watch officer on the bridge and in the CIC. Voice radiotelephone (R/T) is used to pass tactical signals, to report sensor information, and to coordinate operations between units. The use of each R/T circuit is established in the operational commander's OPTASK communications or communications plan (COMMS Plan), as is the use of the net control station, if any, and special instructions and procedures for the use of the circuit. Depending on their function, R/T circuits may be controlled by operators on the bridge, in the CIC, or at other locations. It is extremely important that there be no confusion between the CIC and the bridge over who controls, answers, or logs a given circuit, and each watch officer should confirm, as he or she begins a watch, what the circuit-guarding arrangement is.

Most ships are now equipped with digital voice circuit recorders or some other means to digitally capture the communications circuits on the ship. Recording devices are typically located in the pilothouse, in the CIC, and some cases the communications center. In the pilothouse, the recorder might be as simple as a manually operated handheld digital recording device for recording very high frequency (VHF) communication exchanges. Recording devices in the CIC and communications center are typically installed hardware with a range of selectable functions. Regardless of format or medium, the watch officer should be aware of the recording equipment in use and occasionally check to ensure the ship's communications are being properly captured in accordance with ship's policy. These recordings have use when debriefing watch teams after events as they may be used to develop a reliable chronology of events as they occurred, not as remembered by the watch team.

Voice-radio circuits can be established on almost any frequency but are most commonly in the high-frequency (HF) band, between 2 and 30 megahertz (MHz); the ultra-high-frequency (UHF) band, between 225 and 400 MHz (either line of sight or satellite); and the super-high frequency (SHF) and extremely high frequency (EHF) bands for satellite communications. Both HF and satellite communications are usually allocated to long-range circuits for dispersed formations, while the UHF band circuits are used mainly for short-range, line-of-sight communications. Because of its relative short range, transmissions over UHF have the advantage of being more difficult for an enemy to detect at long range. HF transmissions, on the other hand, can be detected for thousands of miles. The following is a list of voice-radio bands (V = very, L = low, M = medium, S = super, E = extremely):

VLF	3–30 kHz (kilohertz)
LF	30–300 kHz
MF	300 kHz–3 MHz
HF	3–30 MHz (Navy HF 2–30 MHz)
VHF	30–300 MHz

UHF	300–3000 MHz (Navy UHF 225–400 MHz)
SHF	3–30 GHz (S, C, X, Ku, K bands)
EHF	30+ GHz (Ka, Q, V, W bands)

For HF, it is better to use higher frequencies by day and lower frequencies by night due to their electromagnetic propagation characteristics and the daily cyclical changes in the atmosphere.

Correct use of the R/T should be one of the first things that a junior watch officer learns. Use of proper procedures and terminology and the ability to authenticate and quickly encode and decode information are basic skills. The competence with which a watch officer handles R/T communications is one of the most visible measures of professionalism as well as one of the best indicators of a ship's operational smartness. From time to time every ship experiences some difficulty with voice communications. The extent to which such difficulties affect operations and the speed with which they are resolved are usually in direct proportion to the watch officer's knowledge of communications. When it appears that R/T signals are not being heard by other ships, the most common error is for the watch officer or CIC to assume that the equipment is bad and to order that it be shifted or that new gear be put on the line. As often as not, after new equipment is patched in, the problem still exists or new problems have arisen. At this point both the OOD and the CIC watch officer are ordering new circuit patches, antennas, and equipment, and the radio watch has lost all control of the equipment setup. The problem eventually gets solved, but not without considerable frustration, misunderstanding, and loss of tempers.

To avoid this sort of confusion, watch officers in CIC and on the bridge must allow communicators to do their job. When a circuit suddenly stops working, a systematic investigation of all equipment, remote units, and patching systems will be the most effective means to discover the cause. If the watch in radio is allowed to carry out its responsibility for technical control of the circuit, in all likelihood the problem will be found and corrected. If, on the other hand, the watch is constantly setting up new equipment or changing patches at the insistence of the bridge and the CIC, chances are that before long no one will have control of the situation. The watch officer who understands this and has the patience to allow communicators to do their job minimizes such trouble.

Two general categories of signals are transmitted over unsecure R/T circuits: executive and nonexecutive. Nonexecutive signals are administrative or contain information. Executive signals contain the word "execute" and require an action by the ship. They are subdivided into "delayed executive" and "immediate executive." Delayed executive signals give the OOD time to calculate the action to be carried out when the signal is executed. Immediate executive messages require an immediate response. The OOD must understand the different categories and what is required of him or her and the ship.

Allied Communications Publication 125

One of the most important publications that the watch officer should constantly review is Allied Communications Publication 125, Communication Instructions Radiotelephone Procedure. ACP-125 is a short, unclassified, and easily readable publication that you should pick up and read cover to cover about once a quarter. If your unit does not have a copy, it is easily found with a simple internet search. Some of the key sections include a general discussion of communications security, the keeping of circuit logs, the pronunciation of alphabet and numerals, and—most importantly—a list of "prowords." This list is usually in chapter 3 and contains the key phrases and words that are universally recognized as appropriate for use on R/T circuits. Memorize all of them. There are four pages' worth in ACP-125, and if you talk on an R/T circuit, you will use them daily.

The publication also includes details on messages, operating rules, and various miscellaneous procedures for everything from reporting enemy contacts to letting everyone know that an intruder is on the circuit. ACP-125 has an absolute wealth of information, and your copy should be dog-eared from frequent review and use.

Bridge-to-Bridge and VHF Communications

VHF circuits are usually reserved for direct conversations between the watch officers of ships to clarify intentions, weather reports, Coast Guard safety information, or routine coordination during unplanned encounters at sea with international maritime units. The general channel assignments, as specified by the Vessel Bridge-to-Bridge Radiotelephone Act, are these:

Channel 16   Coast Guard emergency use

Channel 13   General bridge-to-bridge traffic

If a conversation of any length is required, the OOD should recommend switching to a channel other than 16 or 13. The Vessel Bridge-to-Bridge Radio-telephone Act is applicable on waters subject to the U.S. inland rules. See U.S. Coast Guard navigation rules for complete details of this act. It is vital that the OOD carefully monitor the VHF circuits for safety information, especially when entering or leaving port. In addition, a log of applicable transmissions is required.

Visual Communications

Visual communications are the most secure of all but are limited by both distance and visibility. Maximum use should be made of visual communications, especially when a force wants to remain undetected. All officers standing watch on deck should be able to read their own ship's flashing-light call sign and, regardless of what kind of visual watch is being kept, be constantly alert for the signals of other ships. Signal flags should be committed to memory. Learning to recognize all the flags is not difficult and is well worth the effort. Flash cards are useful in this regard and may be ordered through the Navy stock system. Most flag signals are taken from the Allied Maritime Tactical Signal and Maneuvering Book (ATP-1, vol. 2) or, when a merchant ship is being signaled, from Pub 102, International Code of Signals. The instructions for use at the beginning of these publications must be thoroughly understood in order for the officer to encode and decode signals correctly. Specific signals, even those often used, should *not* be memorized because ATP-1 is subject to change at any time. The practice of breaking or encoding signals from memory can lead to potentially dangerous mistakes.

It is most important for the OOD to know the ships for which he or she has visual responsibility. Of particular importance is the difference between flag hoists at the dip and closed up. When in port, the OOD must be alert for the signal flags flying on units moored nearby that may indicate a special evolution such as man aloft, divers in the water, or another ship coming alongside.

Record Communications

Most of the Navy's and ships' formal nontactical communications are handled as record communications. These messages are handled via a variety of secure paths including internet protocol–compatible routing. The watch officer on the bridge or in CIC is usually authorized to release various types of messages such as weather reports, bathythermograph reports, or, in the case of the CIC, certain contact reports. His or her responsibility as releasing officer is to make sure that these messages are in the correct format and addressed properly. In addition, it is a good idea occasionally to check the breakdown of coded and formatted information in standardized weather and bathythermograph messages to ensure outgoing information is correct.

E-Mail and Chat

E-mail and chat via internet protocol (in both secure and nonsecure forms) are used to coordinate both tactical and nontactical operations, though tactical operations are most often directed using voice circuits. E-mail and chat can enable an order-of-magnitude increase in information exchange and are typically monitored in the CIC. It is incumbent upon the watchstanders to know which "chat rooms" are required to be monitored and the type of information being exchanged on each. Although e-mail and chat yield an additional layer of redundancy to communications at sea, voice circuits will likely remain the fundamental path to exchange information.

CONCLUSION

The mark of a good watchstander is his or her ability to communicate on and off the ship and to lead the watch team. You will instantly impress your chain of command if you master the requirements of ACP-125, tactical-level communications guidance, and the other important information contained in this chapter. Your communication skills are central to standing an effective and safe watch.

5

THE WATCH UNDER WAY

The stern and impartial sea . . . offers no opportunities but to those
who know how to grasp them with a ready hand and undaunted heart.

JOSEPH CONRAD, POLISH-BORN ENGLISH AUTHOR AND MASTER MARINER

The position of watch officer under way carries with it unmatched responsibility and authority. When the CO certifies an officer as qualified to be in charge of the underway watch, he or she is displaying a significant degree of trust in that person's judgment, ability, and intelligence. It is a trust that cannot be taken lightly, and one that must be repeatedly justified by performance. Watchstanding at sea is the most important of a junior officer's duties and is the yardstick by which his or her potential will be judged. It also offers the finest kind of reward in terms of professional achievement and personal satisfaction. Qualification as a watch officer marks the completion of the first major step toward command at sea and should be the primary initial goal of every seagoing officer.

PREPARING FOR THE WATCH

Preparation for standing a watch under way does not begin when an officer climbs the ladder to the bridge or CIC. Physical and psychological preparation must begin long before that. The performance of an officer who goes on watch tired, cold, or hungry will be impaired, no matter how capable he or she may be, and preoccupation with other matters will prevent the high level of concentration that makes the true professional. The specific way to prepare for a watch is a matter of personal preference, but there are certain things that should become habitual: being dressed properly for the situation, donning foul-weather gear if necessary; on a cold night, drinking some soup or eating hot food before taking over; and bringing one's personal equipment. This last is, again, a matter of personal preference, but a watch officer should always bring a flashlight fitted with a red lens, something to write with, a pad or notebook, and polarized sunglasses on bright days.

CREW ENDURANCE

The concept of crew endurance applies to all watchstanders. Crew endurance may be understood as the ability to sustain operational performance while enduring job-related physical, physiological, and environmental challenges. Mission and operational effectiveness depend on crew endurance. There are numerous human factors that affect an individual's ability to perform their duties on watch. Inadequate rest, hunger, sickness, and personal or work-related issues each have potential to affect performance on watch. If your watch team members are overly fatigued or distracted, mission accomplishment, performance, and safety are in jeopardy. Chronic sleep debt has long-term physical and mental health consequences and degrades human performance.

Fatigue is a critical consideration for any watchstander. Decades of scientific research and maritime safety studies have shown that fatigue has a negative impact on decision making and the way the human body and mind perform, especially under stress. The human need for sleep is a physiologically driven event that dominates our daily activities and is central to our ability to perform both physical and cognitive tasks. The quantity and quality of sleep is a significant factor in determining how well humans function within a system. Most adult humans require an average of eight hours of sleep per day; when this sleep requirement is not met, performance can suffer dramatically. The human circadian rhythm is a human's natural daily cycle—roughly twenty-four hours in duration—and governs things such as hormone release and alertness; performance degradations frequently result from disruption of circadian rhythms from jet lag or shift work. Any traveler transiting time zones, particularly traveling east, will testify to the cognitive challenges posed by jet lag. Watchstanders are likely to experience the same type of challenges, especially in a rotation that disrupts the body's normal circadian cycle, shortens sleep periods, or degrades the quality of sleep.

The literature on shiftwork is rife with examples of diminished performance and health risks associated with working night-shift and swing-shift schedules. Some aspects of performance are more susceptible to sleep deprivation than others; given that sleepiness causes increased eye blinks, longer eye closure durations, and even brief bursts of sleep called "microsleep," it is understandable that tasks depending on visual input are particularly sensitive to sleep disruption. Studies have demonstrated that individuals whose jobs require them to perform vigilance tasks (e.g., monitoring visual displays with little or no external visual stimulation) tend to miss subtle pattern changes. This vigilance decrement has major implications for the Department of Defense (DOD), given that individuals standing watch in combat information, fire control, and sonar stations may be required to monitor visual or auditory displays for extended periods of time. It can also affect other watch standers such as on the bridge of a ship or monitoring and engineering display. Figure 5-1 shows the results of one study that was designed to measure the impact on performance of various levels of sleep deprivation for an individual; the various graphs show degradation in performance based on the hours of sleep obtained during the study period.

The bottom line is that sleep is a biological imperative and a vital requirement for life, often defined as "the rest and recovery from the wear and tear of wakefulness." In addition to its impact on real-time performance, lack of sleep can have detrimental health effects long after an individual has left the service. Just as shipboard equipment requires periodic maintenance to operate in peak condition and meet its expected service life, the human body must have sufficient sleep to function properly, especially in an arduous shipboard environment.[1]

Fatigue is often listed as a causal or contributing factor by the National Transportation Safety Board in maritime accidents. Recently the U.S. Navy has implemented measures to reduce fatigue that center around three "guiding principles":

1. Use a Circadian Watch Rotation. The first guiding principle is the use of the circadian-based watch rotation that leverages the human body's natural circadian rhythm, based on a twenty-four-hour day, to build a

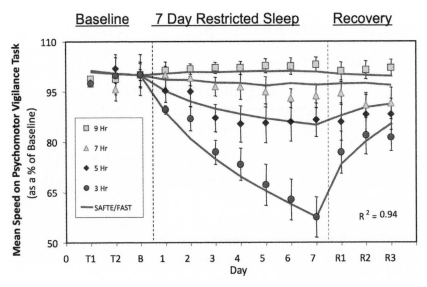

FIGURE 5-1. Graph of how lack of sleep affects performance (Source: Belenky et al. 2003)

watch schedule. In general, any combination of watch durations that adds up to twenty-four hours will support this process. Some examples are: four on / eight off, three on /nine off, or six on / eighteen off. A hierarchy of preferable watch bills based on the type of watch in the number of sections available follows in figure 5-2.

Numerous studies have shown that watchstanders are more alert when using fixed circadian watch rotations and that reaction times and decision making are improved compared to rotating watch bills. Ships mays choose a static watch bill where everyone stands the same watch all the time, or rotate on a periodic basis. In general, three weeks is the ideal duration of a shift, and the preferred rotation direction is forward (add one hour to the evening and night watches to shift the rotation). This process requires detailed planning, a qualification path to the desired number of watch sections, and frequent review to develop the required watch rotation. Designating fixed watch teams early and setting qualification goals well prior to deployment is one way to ensure even distribution of experience and talent, and to foster team cohesion and ownership of the process.

NUMBER OF AVAILABLE SECTIONS

Use These Watchbills

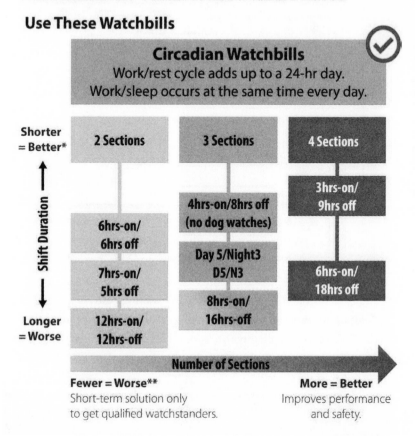

FIGURE 5-2. Circadian Watchbill
(Source: Naval Postgraduate School Crew Endurance Handbook)

2. Build a stable ship's routine around the watch rotation. The second guiding principle of a good watch rotation is a supporting schedule. Department heads and executive officers should strive to build a daily routine that supports protected sleep at specified times for those individuals expected to stand watch at night. This can include such measures as restricting announcements during morning and evening hours, adjusting meal hours to accommodate the chosen watch rotation, and

focusing the bulk of training, meetings, and drills during the heart of the day—for example between 0900 and 1500. Most ships conduct a daily operations/intelligence brief; doing this in the late afternoon instead of after dinner can allow the watch team to attend the brief and maintain situational awareness while still executing their assigned watch and sleep rotations. Figure 5.3, below, shows one of many notional schedules that leverage a circadian rotation; each ship will need to tailor their schedule to fit the unique operational requirements of their command.

3. Focus on alert watchstanders. The final guiding principle is to focus on alert watchstanders; review the schedule periodically and watch for violations of protected sleep; conduct individual risk assessments based on rest prior to an event, and plan ahead for upcoming evolutions to either ensure that watchstanders and participants are rested or, if that is not possible, allow time after the event to catch up. Certainly operational commitments and unforeseen emergencies will arise; maintaining a "sleep reservoir" by using a circadian watch rotation and supporting schedule will result in more resilient crew members who are more likely to perform better under stressful conditions.

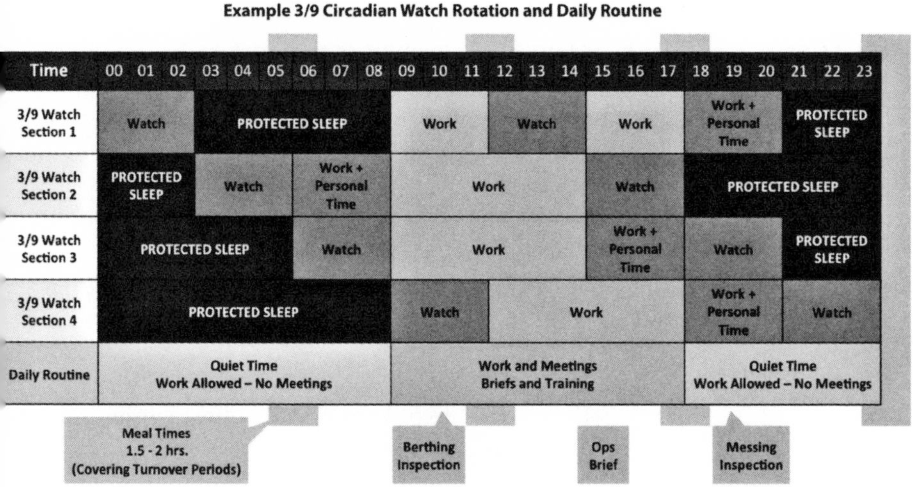

Example 3/9 Circadian Watch Rotation and Daily Routine

FIGURE 5-3. Notional four-section circadian watch rotation with supporting schedule (Source: Naval Postgraduate School Crew Endurance Handbook).

These guiding principles work together to produce well-rested watchstanders, giving them better situational awareness during routine operations and increased resilience in case of an emergency. This process can improve watch team performance, reduce fatigue, improve morale and productivity, and decrease the risk of a mishap. Best practices and lessons can be found and shared and a Crew Endurance Handbook downloaded at the following website under the "Knowledge Center" tab: http://my.nps.edu/web/crewendurance.

CONCENTRATION

The ability to concentrate is vital to an exacting task. This is as true for watch officers as it is for surgeons and professional athletes. A watch officer cannot under any circumstances be distracted from his or her duties. No departmental project or personal problem can be allowed to supersede concentration on the watch. If a watch officer has a personal problem that is serious enough to interfere with performance, he or she should discuss the situation with the captain or senior watch officer and, if necessary, ask to be temporarily taken off the watch bill. The CO will respect the judgment of the officer concerned.

GETTING THE PICTURE

Standing a deck watch on a modern warship is far too demanding a task to be undertaken without advance briefing. The value of this briefing depends upon whether the officer knows what questions to ask and what to look for.

Information from the CIC

An officer should always check in with the CIC before appearing on the bridge. It may be worthwhile for your watch team to do this together, but turnover requirements and timing may prevent it. The following is a partial list of the kinds of information a watch officer should expect to get from the CIC:

1. Formation disposition and the location of the OTC and guide(s).
2. Ship's condition of readiness; which weapons are manned; and the status of weapon systems.
3. What emissions-control (EMCON) plan is in effect.

4. Changes in the schedule of events, operations order, or task group commander's letter of instruction since the watch officer's last watch.

5. Which tactical voice circuits are guarded by the CIC and which by the bridge; net-control authority, if assigned; and type of call signs to be used.

6. What recognition and authentication systems are in effect.

7. What intelligence is available on enemy, allied, and other forces.

8. What intelligence-reporting requirements are assigned to the ship.

9. The assignment of surface, air, subsurface, and electronic-warfare reporting within the task group, with particular emphasis on the ship's responsibilities.

10. The status of combat air patrol, electronic-warfare aircraft, and other air assets; the ship's control, duties, if any.

11. The ship's scheduled flight operations, helicopter or fixed wing.

12. The status of embarked aircraft and status of the flight deck (clear, fouled, or designated as a "ready deck").

13. The status of active or passive sonars including towed array systems (tail wet or dry) as applicable.

14. Any shipboard evolutions that could restrict the safe maneuvering of the ship (e.g., small-arms shoots, PMS, ordnance handling).

Information from the TAO and the CIC Watch Officer

No attempt will be made here to discuss in detail the duties of the tactical action officer (TAO), but the OOD should have a precise understanding of the command relationship between himself or herself and the TAO. The ten or fifteen minutes that the OOD takes in planning with the TAO for the upcoming watch will do a great deal toward ensuring a smooth, well-coordinated watch. When a CIC watch officer rather than a TAO is assigned, the same procedure should be followed even though the command relationship differs. See chapter 17 for further details. A good reference to use and to have on hand at each controlling watch station is the turnover checklist from the class tactical manual.

Information from Other Control Centers

Depending on the mission of the ship, other watch stations of importance to the OOD may be manned. In a destroyer engaged in antisubmarine warfare

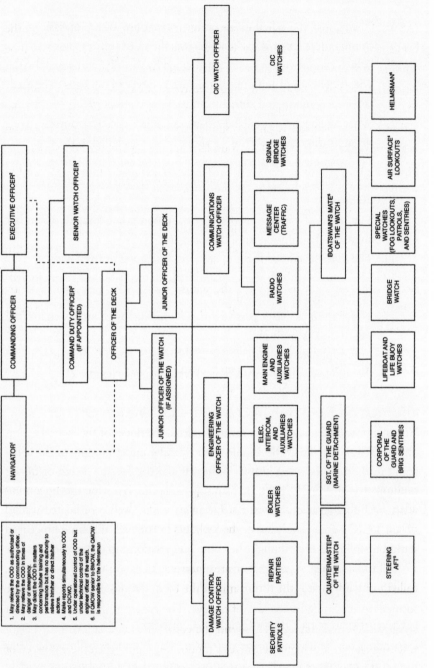

FIGURE 5-4. Watch Organization Under Way, Condition Watch IV

(ASW), for example, the watch in sonar control is as important as those on the bridge and in the CIC. Therefore, before going on watch, the OOD should be familiar with the status and duties of other watch stations. In the case of a ship with an ASW mission, he or she should be aware of environmental conditions, the active and passive equipment in use and its mode of operation, and the action to take if contact is gained. Similarly, in a ship whose primary mission is flight operations, the OOD must understand the capabilities and limitations of operating aircraft and be aware of the carrier's maneuvering restrictions and the type of missions to be expected on the watch. In the case of a guided-missile cruiser or destroyer with a primary antiair warfare focus, the OOD should have a general idea of mission battery status, air search and fire-control radars, defensive counter-air aircraft under the ship's control, and the air threat. As noted in an earlier chapter, the watch officer should stop by the engineering-control station and discuss with the EOOW the status of the propulsion plant and any training, preventive maintenance, or corrective maintenance that the engineers would like to conduct, operations permitting. A tour of topside spaces will quickly prepare the oncoming OOD for heavy weather. A walk-through of other watch stations will demonstrate to the watchstanders the interest of the OOD and remind them that he or she is in charge.

ON THE BRIDGE

When the watch officer has all the necessary information from the CIC and other watch stations, it is time to begin the turnover process on the bridge. If it is a night watch, the OOD should take the time, before and during this process, to adapt his or her eyes to the darkness. The safety of the ship at night may depend on the OOD's ability and that of the lookouts to see in the dark. This is called dark adaptation.

All vision depends on light-sensitive nerve endings in the retina of the eye, called rods and cones, which transmit to the brain an impression of the image formed on the retina by the lens of the eye. The cones, in the center, are color sensitive. The rods, in a circle around the cones, detect variations in the light intensity and are also highly sensitive to motion. At night, when there is no color to see, the cones tend to make spots in front of the eyes if a fixed point is stared at too long; looking out of the corners of the eyes forces the motion-sensitive rods to take over. They will not tell the color of a ship ahead, but they may enable an observer to see that the ship is moving.

Daylight, in which the cones furnish color perception, is composed of all the colors in the spectrum. The rods are active only in the lower, red range of the spectrum; thus, dim red lights have little adverse effect on night vision. It is possible to work on a bridge or in a pilothouse so lighted, then move out to the bridge wing and be able to see perfectly.

Exposure to white light at night greatly reduces vision. A carelessly used flashlight, an open hatch, even the flare of a match may so reduce the conning officer's perception that he or she fails to see a small craft or other object in the water.

Good night vision depends on a slow, roving gaze that systematically covers the field of vision in a simple geometric pattern. Dim objects, almost invisible if looked at directly, will be picked up. If something is sighted and then lost, the way to relocate it is to move the eyes in a circle around the spot. If the object is moving, the rods in the eyes will find it again. In addition to an effective visual scan, the use of night vision devices (NVDs) is also recommended and on some vessels is required. These portable, battery-powered instruments amplify existing ambient light to greatly improve the detection of small contacts at sea. NVDs are especially useful in detecting and avoiding objects unseen by radar such as small vessels, buoys, and fishing-related obstructions.

The effect of bright sunlight on the eyes lasts long after the sun goes down. People exposed to strong sunlight during the day can see only half as well as others at night; they should wear dark sunglasses topside on bright days.

During those first few minutes on the bridge, it is a good idea for the OOD to begin getting the feel of the watch. If it is nighttime, the OOD should stand clear of all personnel on watch while his or her eyes become adapted. Only then should the OOD start the watch by reading the captain's night orders.

THE NIGHT ORDER BOOK

Night orders are a statement in writing of how the captain wants the ship to be run when he or she is not on the bridge. They are divided into two parts: standing orders, which express the CO's policy and directions under *all* circumstances, and orders for dealing with the situation for each day (see appendix A). The OOD should study and thoroughly understand the standing orders before assuming a first watch on the bridge of a ship and should review them at least monthly and after any long period in port (a signature page is usually attached to document these reviews). The second part of the night orders contains a summary of tactical, navigational, and readiness information. Additional information and guidance are added by the captain and the navigator in the narrative sections of the orders. The night orders are signed each night by the navigator, XO, and captain, and the information they contain may not be changed without the permission of the captain. They are also signed by the OOD and JOOD on a watch-to-watch basis. When ships are steaming in company, night intentions can be signaled by the OTC, the screen commander, or some other unit commander. They can also be transmitted as a part of a "daily intentions message." Night intentions should be studied with the same care as the night orders because they are in a broader sense the "night orders" of the CO.

THE ORAL TURNOVER

The final and most important phase of relieving the watch is the oral turnover. At this time the officer taking over must obtain or verify all the information needed to stand the watch, making sure that he or she understands exactly what is expected. The following is a list of the minimum amount of information to be obtained during a turnover.

Navigational Information

1. Position of the ship, how and when determined, and fix accuracy.
2. Course and speed; engine revolutions per minute (rpm) required to keep station or maintain required speed of advance.
3. Method of plotting the ship's position (visual, radar, GPS, dead reckoning, etc.) and frequency with which fixes are to be taken.
4. Time and position of expected radar or visual landfall, if any.
5. Aids to navigation in sight or expected; times and positions of expected sightings.
6. Depth of water.

7. Planned changes of course and speed.
8. Possible hazards to navigation.
9. Weather and hydrographic conditions, including winds, currents, barometer trends, and any unusual weather that may be expected.

Tactical Information

1. The ship's station, location of the guide, and visual identification of the guide.
2. If the ship is in a line or multiple-line formation, the prescribed order, distance interval, and sequence numbers.
3. Zigzag or evasive steering plan in effect.
4. Base course, signaled speed, base speed, stationing speed, and maximum speed expected during the watch.
5. Amount and frequency of course and speed changes required to remain in station or in sector, and effects of weather on station-keeping.
6. Expected changes in formation or dispositions, attachments and detachments, and rendezvous information.
7. Maneuvering peculiarities and limitations of other ships in the formation, and approach limits for ships unable to maneuver freely.
8. Lighting and deceptive measures in force.
9. The OTC's emergency instructions.
10. Status of all contacts.
11. Status and depth of towed array (if ship is equipped).
12. Mode of operation of ship's sonar systems (active or passive) as applicable.

Readiness Information

1. Status of engineering plant. Speed limitation, equipment on the line, generator and boiler lineup, casualties to equipment or machinery that affect the speed or maneuverability of the ship.
2. Expected times of light-off or securing of main propulsion (boilers, gas turbines, etc.).
3. Readiness and material conditions set, expected changes to existing conditions.

4. Status of lookouts, watches, and special details, if set.
5. Status of the watch relief.
6. Unexecuted orders, signals, or evolutions.
7. Changes to scheduled evolution, watch assignments, and watchstanding personnel.
8. Officer with the conn.
9. Location of the captain and flag or unit commanders embarked.
10. Staff duty officer and staff watches assigned, if applicable.
11. Specific flight-deck status to include flight-deck nets (stowed or lowered) as applicable.

RELIEVING THE WATCH

Once satisfied that he or she has all the information needed to stand the watch and a grasp of the current situation, the oncoming duty officer is ready to relieve the watch. Although the relieving should certainly not be done hastily, it is discourteous to drag it out with questions about minutiae. The relief should be ready to take over about fifteen minutes before the hour. No matter how well prepared the new watch may be, it is never wise to take over during an evolution or maneuver, unless it is absolutely necessary.

Relieving a watch is, as stated in an earlier chapter, a formal process. By saying, "I relieve you, sir (or ma'am)," the new OOD is announcing to the watch that he or she has formally accepted responsibility for the watch. Use of any other terminology can leave the matter in doubt. As soon as the OOD has taken over, he or she should inform the watch by announcing clearly, "This is _____. I have the deck (and, if so, the conn)." The helmsman and lee helmsman will acknowledge this by calling out, "Helm aye, aye, sir (or ma'am)," and repeating the course steered, magnetic heading, engine order, and rpm rung up. This procedure should always be followed when a new watch comes on duty.

ORGANIZING THE WATCH

When the entire watch has been relieved, the OOD should check its organization to make sure that it is set up properly. There will probably be a number of people on watch undergoing watch qualification and instruction. Supervising the training of these people is an important duty for the OOD and watch leaders. The BMOW has specific duties in regard to training the watch, as do other senior petty officers in the section, and they should be made to take an active part in the training of the new watchstanders. It is part of the OOD's duty to see that the personnel under instruction are indeed being instructed by competent, qualified personnel and in accordance with the level of knowledge and proficiency requirements of the relevant PQS.

Training applies to all watchstanders. Some watchstanders are more experienced than others and are usually very capable at training junior watchstanders. In some ships, however, senior boatswain's mates and quartermasters may not be assigned on the watch bill; they assign junior-rated people or promising strikers as BMOWs and QMOWs under way. Although there is nothing inherently wrong with this, it often means that a junior sailor is in charge of a watch composed of peers. Unless that person is a very strong leader, he or she may have difficulty setting and enforcing standards on the watch, and the watch officer will be deprived of the most important watch leader, trainer, and supervisor.

A watch officer in this situation will have to either train the BMOW to acceptable standards or, if that fails, find a qualified person or call the senior petty officer to assist. If the situation cannot be resolved, the best long-term solution is to take the matter up with the senior watch officer. The BMOW is the most important enlisted member of a watch team and should be able to perform to the required standards. If he or she cannot, it will be almost impossible to train the rest of the watch.

A similar situation often occurs with the QMOW. The duties assigned to that person are wide-ranging and require considerable knowledge as well as completion of an extensive PQS program. The QMOW's responsibilities in the areas of log keeping, weather observation, and navigational assistance to the OOD affect not only the operation of the watch but also such things as the accuracy of weather forecasts sent to the ship, the credibility of the deck log, and, in some circumstances, the safe navigation of the ship.

A QMOW's ability to do the job properly is something that the OOD must verify by reading weather data recorded, checking the accuracy of the navigational plot, and closely examining log entries. The OOD may find, for example, that a wind whose velocity and direction have been constant for some time suddenly shifts and shows a radical change in speed when the watch is relieved. Some watchstanders are so oblivious to conditions that they will walk onto the lee wing of the bridge in a gale, record a low wind speed or similar inaccurate observation, and think nothing of it. When sent to a weather facility for analysis, inaccurate data can result in a ship's receiving an inaccurate forecast and, consequently, being in considerable danger. Quartermasters should be trained to observe, to use common sense, and, if in doubt, to call the navigator.

Once a general idea of the qualifications of his or her watchstanders is established, the OOD can decide how and in what areas to train them during the watch. If the ship is steaming independently and there are no other ships or hazards in the area, emergency steering drills and procedures should always be carried out. The process of shifting steering units and steering control from station to station and making reports is not very difficult, but it must be understood thoroughly by all watchstanders, and the best way to understand it is to do it. Knowing the location and use of alarms, backup systems, and special lights is also an important training requirement, particularly on night watches. This kind of training should be pushed as hard as the tactical situation permits. It will pay big dividends, not only in terms of watch proficiency but also in the satisfaction and pride of the watchstanders. Most people enjoy knowing that they are doing something well and will appreciate the OOD's efforts to help them qualify.

Every watch station qualification is governed by a formal PQS. Checking the PQS status of each of the watchstanders and taking the opportunity to validate their level of knowledge and competency through demonstration prior to signing off PQS items is a superb way of conducting on-watch training.

The watchstanders will feel a sense of accomplishment in seeing actual progress toward a goal, and the OOD will be qualifying his or her watchstanders, not just "breaking them in." Innovative ideas on training that meet with the captain's permission will prevent the development of slothful habits and help keep the team alert.

JOODs should play an important role in training the watch. Their active participation in all training will strengthen the watch team and advance their understanding of equipment and processes.

THE CONN

"To conn" means to control, or direct by rudder angles and engine-order tele-graph (EOT), the movements of a ship. "The conn" means the station of the conning officer. The OOD may have both the deck and the conn, but some-times the CO may take the conn when an intricate or dangerous maneuver is to be performed. It is also customary for the OOD to assist in such maneuvers by checking on how the members of the bridge watch are performing and by keeping a watchful eye on the entire maneuver so as to inform the CO of any danger that might escape his or her notice. Likewise, when the OOD has the conn during a delicate maneuver or in restricted waters, it is customary for the CO to be watching on the bridge. In effect, then, there is a two-person system in which one person has the conn, giving orders to the wheel and the engines, while another assists and advises.

Directing the movements of a modern warship at high speed and in prox-imity to other ships is a job that requires intense concentration and foresight. At night or when a number of ships are maneuvering simultaneously, it takes only a minute or two of distraction for a conning officer to become so disoriented that the ship is placed in danger. For this reason, the officer who has the conn must be able to concentrate attention on the job at hand. During maneuvers, the officer at the conn should not be concerned with getting the word passed, signing sounding-and-security logs, or any of the other duties of running the watch. When at the conn, the OOD should delegate these duties to the JOOD, and similarly, when the JOOD has the conn, the OOD should assume respon-sibility for carrying out the routine of the watch. Firm enforcement of the pol-icy of not allowing the conning officer to be distracted goes a long way toward reducing the possibility of confusion in tight situations.

Although there is no official set of rules about the conn other than those set out in each captain's standing orders, the following principles have been accepted by experienced seagoing naval officers:

1. One and only one person can give steering and engine orders at any given time.
2. The identity of the person giving these orders must be known to the people on the bridge.

3. The OOD may delegate the conn to another officer, but he or she retains responsibility for the ship's safety.

4. The CO may take over the deck or the conn. When the CO takes over the deck, the OOD has no technical responsibility for the direction of the ship's movements, except as specifically detailed by the CO. But when the latter takes over the conn, the OOD carries out all the duties assigned to him or her by regulations and assists and advises the CO.

5. In taking the conn from the OOD, the CO should see that all personnel on the bridge watch are notified of the fact. If the CO takes over during an emergency, however, the issuing of a direct steering or engine order constitutes legal assumption of responsibility for directing the ship's movements. When taking the conn in this manner, the CO retains that responsibility until the conn is turned over to another person.

6. Every CO establishes a procedure for letting it be known beyond doubt that he or she has assumed direct control of the ship and thereby relieved the conning officer of all responsibility for such control. The procedure for delegating control to a conning officer must be equally clear. Transfer of control is usually announced like this: "This is _____. I have the conn." All bridge personnel, but especially the helmsman and lee helmsman, must acknowledge the information with the words, "Aye, aye, sir (or ma'am)." It is also customary for the helmsman and lee helmsman to respond by sounding off the course being steered, the magnetic-compass course, and the speed and rpm.

The OOD has no problem if the above principles are observed at all times. But even the best of COs are fallible and may, while concentrating on the vital matters at hand, neglect to follow recommended procedures in taking over or relinquishing the conn. Under these circumstances, it is up to the OOD to clarify the situation with a polite, "Do you have the conn, sir (or ma'am)?" or "I have the conn, sir (or ma'am)." Then he or she must see that critical persons on the bridge know who has the conn.

The OOD who does not have the conn should assist the officer who does. One of the best ways of doing this is by making sure that the conning officer's orders are understood and acted upon correctly by the helmsman and other bridge personnel, and that the conning officer knows that his or her orders are being executed. The OOD may take whatever station is most conducive to maintaining a lookout.

COMBAT INFORMATION CENTER

In modern naval operations, the CIC and the bridge function as components of a tactical team. Their roles vary according to the type of operations the ship is carrying out but are never separate. Since the position of the TAO came into being, the CIC and the bridge have become even more interdependent, and no officer who stands a watch in either of these control stations should attempt to "go it alone."

It used to be the function of the CIC to collect, evaluate, display, and disseminate information pertaining to the control of the ship. In today's warships, however, the function of evaluating has been expanded to include, in many situations, actual control of the ship, its sensors, and its weapons systems. Formerly, the CO's general quarters station was the bridge. Nowadays, he or she exercises control from the CIC because the information available to help in decision making cannot be presented on the bridge. This arrangement in no way lessens the importance of the OOD as the officer responsible for the safety and proper operation of the ship. It does, however, require that person to possess a broad and intimate knowledge of how the CIC operates and what its capabilities and limitations are. The OOD must also know at all times what his or her command relationship with the TAO is. Confusion on this point leads, at best, to poor coordination between the bridge and the CIC, and, at worst, to disaster. It is for this reason that the prewatch briefing mentioned earlier in this chapter is so important.

Although it is equipped with a variety of sensors, evaluating devices, and data-processing equipment, the CIC does have certain limitations. The array of equipment in the modern CIC is so impressive, sometimes so overwhelming, that it is easy to forget this fact. Next to a multi-million-dollar radar, the eyes of a lookout may seem unreliable indeed. Yet there are times when the only reliable source of information is that lookout, and the usefulness of the entire complex of systems and sensors depends on the accuracy of the information that he or she can provide. Regardless of how sophisticated a CIC may be or how well trained its watch team, it sometimes happens, especially when maneuvering at close quarters, that the information furnished to the bridge by the CIC is incomplete or inaccurate. This is where the OOD's judgment and confidence become critical. The OOD must always be aware that he or she is not only a user of the information provided by the CIC but also a major contributor, evaluator, and verifier of the tactical picture. When the CIC proposes the wrong course of action, it is probably because coordination with the bridge has somehow broken down. It is the responsibility of the OOD to set the situation straight and, when there is time, to go over the event with the CIC watch officer or the TAO to find out what went wrong. What the OOD should *not* do in this kind of situation is engage in argument with the CIC watch while the situation is deteriorating.

In many evolutions, key channels of routine communication between the bridge and the CIC include communications "nets" accessible through Internal Voice Communications Systems (IVCS) and sound-powered telephone circuits. In most ships the principal communications net for coordinating between the bridge, CIC, and engineering-control stations is the ship's Battle Net. It is common procedure to have the Battle Net amplified on the bridge and accessible on the bridge wings for maximum awareness among the watch team. In times of high activity, an operator may be assigned the responsibility of monitoring all communications and informing the JOOD and OOD of pertinent information.

In addition to the ship's Battle Net, phone talkers are designated for communications between the bridge and CIC. On an ARLEIGH BURKE–class destroyer, the position of "Bright Bridge" operates a radar console on the bridge and maintains constant communications with the CIC. "Bright" refers to the illumination from the display that must be masked with curtains at night to preserve night vision for the bridge team.

No matter what the quality and quantity of information between the two stations, its usefulness depends on the ability of the few individuals, usually very junior, who man the circuits. The performance of communications net phone talkers, particularly those on the bridge, can be a major source of conflict and misunderstanding. The bridge talker is often a junior officer or enlisted sailor who may have very little idea of what goes on in the CIC and less understanding of the terms, acronyms, and figures being passed. If the bridge talker makes a mistake and is reprimanded by the OOD or, even worse, ridiculed by the CIC talker at the other end of the line, he or she may become frustrated or freeze up completely. Thus, at the very time help is most needed, the bridge talker is unable to give it. To prevent this from happening the OOD should make the bridge phone talker aware of the importance of the job and encourage familiarization with the CIC to clear up the meaning of information entrusted to him or her.

On a quiet watch, when no demanding evolutions are expected, watchstanders can be rotated into the CIC for indoctrination on radarscopes, combat system consoles, contact reporting, and basic procedures. At the same time, it is a good idea to man the bridge telephones and, if possible, one of the lookout stations with CIC watchstanders. It will be an education for both parties and probably a welcome change from routine duties.

For special evolutions, the OOD should not hesitate to put a more senior talker on the phones, calling that person to the bridge if necessary. The same applies to bridge and engineering-control stations. The OOD should always remember that all the resources of the ship are at his or her disposal and should not hesitate to use any of them.

The most important thing to remember about bridge-CIC relations is that both watch centers are part of the ship-control team and that they share responsibility for providing the CO, the OOD, and the TAO with the best possible support of the ship's mission. Standing watch in the CIC is discussed in chapter 17.

AIRCRAFT CARRIER FLIGHT OPERATIONS

In an aircraft carrier, the OOD meets situations not encountered in other types of ships. Flight operations themselves greatly complicate the routine of a ship. Her very size makes the efficient administration of a carrier difficult. In carriers, the OOD is supported by a JOOD as well as a junior officer of the watch. The latter frequently handles routine matters under way, such as passing the word and enforcing the ship's routine. The JOOD handles tactical circuits and relays information between the CO and the OOD, who is, of course, in overall charge of the watch team.

When an aircraft carrier is operating with lifeguard destroyers, the OOD has a special responsibility to keep those destroyers informed of the progress of flight operations, unexpected changes in course and speed, and modifications to lighting measures. The lighting and shape of an aircraft carrier make it extremely difficult for another ship to visually determine her aspect, her direction of turn, and her distance. Therefore, watch officers on the lifeguard destroyers rely heavily on the carrier's OOD to tell them *immediately* of any course and speed changes. The importance of coordination between carriers and destroyers has been underscored by tragic accidents and the loss of life at sea. Most carriers have a "plane guard" or "horizon reference unit" SOP detailing specific procedures for maneuvering in their vicinity.

It is essential for officers who stand deck watches on carriers to become familiar with those of their duties that concern aircraft. These include the following:

1. Aircraft turnups and jet blasts and related safety precautions.
2. Operation of aircraft elevators and hangar-bay doors.
3. Operation of helicopters.
4. Cooperation between the weapons department and the air department in the matter of respotting aircraft and boats.
5. No smoking during the fueling and defueling of airplanes, helicopters, and so forth.
6. The use of rescue destroyers and helicopters in plane crashes and the need to keep them informed.
7. Restrictions on blowing tubes (never during launching and recovery or when soot may blow over the flight deck).
8. Wind and weather conditions for flight operations.
9. Required relative winds (direction and speed) for each aircraft type.
10. Restrictions on ship's angle of roll when making turns.
11. Informing the air department when high winds are expected so that aircraft may be secured.

HELICOPTER OPERATIONS

The use of helicopters in ASW, amphibious operations, vertical replenishment, and other logistic and tactical roles continues to increase. Similarly, the use of unmanned aircraft systems (UAS) are playing a growing role in naval operations. Most warships now either carry a helicopter or are configured so that they can operate the helicopters of other ships. An OOD should be familiar with helicopter operations in general and should have a thorough knowledge of the helicopter-operating capabilities (levels and classes of certification) of his or her own ship. If the ship carries a helicopter, the OOD should also have a basic knowledge of its limitations, special operating requirements, and operational parameters.

Wind is always a critical factor when helicopters are being operated. Each type of ship and each type of helicopter must operate within certain wind "envelopes" to spread rotors, start engines, engage rotors, and launch and recover. Relative wind directions and velocities that constitute given envelopes for both day and night operating conditions are graphically displayed in Naval Air Training and Operating Standardization (NATOPS) series manuals. These tables must always be available on the bridge and, no matter how often helicopters are operated, should always be consulted before a rotor engagement, launch, or recovery is approved. Only in an extreme emergency and with the CO's permission should helicopters be operated outside the envelope.

Destroyers use "polar plots" to graphically display the risk of water intrusion on the flight deck based on sea conditions, ship's heading, and ship's speed. The OOD shall use the polar plots prior to any flight-deck operations including traversing helicopters, rotor engagement, launch, and recovery.

Ship's roll and pitch also affect helicopter operations. Each helicopter has a specified envelope for wind and roll and pitch in both day and night operations. It is the responsibility of the OOD to adjust course and speed not only to provide acceptable wind across the deck but also to minimize roll and pitch. As with all special evolutions, it is essential to keep a checklist handy to ensure that these critical conditions are provided.

Shipboard Procedures

All OODs should be conversant with their own ship's bills and procedures for operating, fueling, and receiving helicopters. One of the best ways to begin acquiring this information on ships that have a helicopter detachment is to talk to the pilots and deck crew. They will be glad to give the OOD information because their lives might well depend on how thoroughly he or she understands their problems and requirements.

Before any helicopter operations can be undertaken, a number of preparations must be made. The OOD is responsible for seeing that they are carried out and that the ship is ready to perform the evolution safely, smartly, and on time. The sequence of events in preparing for and conducting helicopter operations is usually as follows (appendix G includes a sample checklist):

1. Pilots and crew are briefed on the mission, weather, expected ship's movement, fields to which they might be diverted, communications, and emergency procedures. It is not necessary for the OOD to know all of these things, only to have access to them through the CIC.

2. Before flight quarters is called, helicopters should be brought on deck and preflighted. The OOD and the helicopter flight crew must maintain close liaison, especially when a helicopter is being rolled out of the hangar. During this phase, the ship's motion should be minimized, and hard turns that may cause the ship to heel should be avoided.

3. When the preliminary checks have been completed, flight quarters should be called and a foreign object damage (or foreign object debris, FOD) walkdown conducted on the flight deck. The flight operations area should be secured and all hands periodically warned to stand clear of it. The smoking lamp should be extinguished in the area of flight operations.

4. After the detail has been manned and communications have been checked, the helicopter is given permission to start engines. At this point, the OOD should have a good idea of the flight course and should ensure that the ship will be able to maneuver for launch.

5. When the pilot is ready to engage rotors, the ship is maneuvered to within the engagement envelope and the OOD gives permission to engage. Final radio communications checks are made.

6. When the helicopter is completely ready, the pilot requests a "green deck" for launch. At this time, the ship should come to flight course, and the pilot should be informed of relative wind direction and velocity, altimeter setting, and ship's pitch and roll. The deck crew then removes tie-down chains and wheel chocks and launches the helicopter. When the helicopter is well clear of the ship and the pilot has reported operations normal, flight quarters are usually secured and the ship returns to base course until it is time to recover. Cruisers, destroyers, and frigates equipped to embark helicopters also employ a recovery, assist, secure, and traverse (RAST) system featuring a rapid securing device (RSD). This system is used to move the aircraft from the hangar to its "spot" on deck and includes a single-point attachment to "anchor" the aircraft to the deck via a probe and trap arrangement. The system was designed to safely and rapidly secure helicopters to smaller flight decks—especially in higher sea states.

Conditions of Readiness

Depending on the tactical situation, the OTC usually assigns ready or "alert" helicopters to such missions as search and rescue (SAR), lifeguard, and ASW and specifies a given readiness status, which can be any one of the following:

- *Ready 5.* Ready for launch five minutes from signal. All preflight checks complete, pilots in aircraft, and engines warmed and ready to launch. Crew at flight quarters.
- *Ready 15.* Aircraft spotted, rotors spread, and most preflight checks complete. Pilots in flight gear, briefed, and on call. Flight quarters not set.
- *Ready 30.* Aircraft ready to launch within thirty minutes. All daily preflight checks complete. Depending on limitations of ship, aircraft may or may not be spotted. Crew not at flight quarters.

Each readiness condition has advantages and disadvantages. Ready 5 provides the fastest reaction time but, because of crew fatigue resulting from the need for constant readiness to launch, cannot be maintained for long. Ready 15 does not provide as rapid a reaction time and is contingent upon the crew's ability to get to flight quarters on short notice. However, it has the advantage of requiring fewer people to be on station for a long period of time and can be maintained longer.

A final note: One of the many actions taken when flight quarters is called away on cruiser- or destroyer-type units is to lower the safety nets located along the periphery of the flight deck. When the nets are lowered on some units, they introduce additional maneuvering considerations with which the OOD must be familiar.

Emergencies

The OOD on a ship that operates with helicopters should be familiar with basic procedures for both in-flight and on-deck emergencies because one of the first things an aircraft in trouble will attempt to do is land on deck. He or she should be prepared to recover aircraft on very short notice and, if the situation dictates, without flight quarters being fully manned. The time the pilot has in which to land safely may be so short that the risk of recovering that person without a full flight-deck crew is justified. This is essentially the pilot's decision, and if such action is considered necessary it is probably because his or her life depends on it.

In the case of on-deck emergencies such as crashes or fires, the OOD may have to decide, after the crew is safe, whether to save the helicopter or to jettison it and thereby avoid danger to the ship. The OOD should plan in advance how to handle such a situation and know what equipment is available to assist in each kind of emergency. For example, fin stabilizers, with which some ships are equipped, contain a device that induces a large roll of the ship, a capability that could be extremely useful in getting a burning aircraft over the side. An OOD should also be very familiar with procedures for lost communications and aircraft-in-the-water accidents.

SUBMARINE OPERATIONS

The duties of the OOD of a surfaced submarine differ from those of the OOD of a surface ship in several ways. First of all, a submarine is extremely vulnerable if she is involved in a collision. The OOD must keep this fact in mind and never allow the submarine to get into a situation where there is appreciable risk of collision. He or she must always be alert for the presence of other vessels because the silhouette a submarine presents to another ship is deceptive. This is true both night and day but particularly at night because the lights of a submarine, which may not conform to the rules of the road, are grouped so closely that she gives the appearance of a fishing boat or a small ship. There is a tendency, then, for vessels approaching a surfaced submarine at night to be unconcerned. Similarly, a submarine tends to present a small "pip" on radar, which also leads to her classification by approaching ships as a small vessel.

The OOD of a submarine must be cognizant of the status of "rig for dive" at all times. An underway submarine should be ready to dive at any time. Once she has been reported "rigged for dive," permission to alter the status of that rig or to do anything that might interfere with diving must be obtained from the CO.

Because a submarine is extremely low in the water, certain safety precautions must be followed at all times at sea. Some of these are as follows:

1. No one should be allowed on the main deck without the CO's permission. Save in exceptional circumstances, all personnel going to the main deck must use life jackets and safety lines.
2. In rough seas, the OOD and lookouts should wear safety belts and have lifelines secured to a part of the ship that would not be carried away by a boarding sea.
3. In rough seas, the OOD should shut the conning tower or upper-bridge hatch to prevent flooding.
4. In a following sea, the OOD should be alert to the danger of water being taken into the ship through the air-induction system. In submarines equipped with dual-induction systems, the main air-induction system should be shut and the snorkel system used to get air into the ship.

When a submarine submerges, the OOD becomes the diving officer and the conning officer takes over the functions of the OOD. The duties and responsibilities are not a great deal different from those on a conventional submarine. Nuclear submarines spend so little time on the surface, however, that bridge personnel may forget what those duties and responsibilities are. Following a prolonged period of submergence, the OOD should review the standing instructions and orders covering surface watchstanding and should brief the watch section as necessary.

SEARCH AND RESCUE

The armed services and the Coast Guard jointly maintain an almost worldwide SAR organization that uses existing commands, bases, and facilities to search for and rescue people involved in air, surface, and subsurface accidents. There are three SAR areas: the Inland Region, whose designated commander is the chief of staff of the U.S. Air Force; the Maritime Region, whose commander is the commandant of the U.S. Coast Guard; and the Overseas Region, whose commander is a designated unified commander. The commander of the unit that arrives first at the scene of a disaster is known as the on-scene commander. When an accident occurs, certain radio frequencies are specified for the use of those involved in SAR operations and a carefully planned procedure is followed.

Detailed information concerning the SAR organization and its procedures can be found in most fleet instructions and OPORDs. The SAR folder on the bridge and in the CIC contains the Navy Search and Rescue Manual (NWP 3-50.1) and pertinent SAR directives from current OPORDs.

The OOD should be familiar with these directives and know the radio frequencies to be used, the rescue procedures, and the special signals made by ships and aircraft in distress. At a minimum, the international air distress (IAD) frequency of 121.5 MHz and military air distress (MAD) frequency of 243.0 MHz should be known by both bridge and CIC watchstanders. Bridge-to-bridge (BTB) VHF channel 16, which must be continuously guarded for vessel safety, is also a potential source of SAR-related information, to include actual distress calls.

REPLENISHMENT AT SEA

Replenishment at sea (RAS) refers to the transfer of fuel, stores, mail, ammunition, and sometimes people from one ship to another while both are under way. Most replenishments are scheduled, but a "RAS of opportunity" can be ordered whenever circumstances warrant it. RAS requires special skills and maneuvering with which all officers must be familiar because they are likely to be involved in the evolution either as OOD or as conning officer. This is especially true on destroyers and other small ships, not only because of the large number of people involved in the evolution but also because it is likely to occur often. When RAS is scheduled, the OOD should put in motion the following things (a comprehensive underway replenishment checklist should be a part of the OOD's on-hand references—a sample is provided in appendix H):

1. Review Underway Replenishment (NWP 4-01.4) for details of the entire procedure. Check *Knight's Modern Seamanship* for a description of the equipment used, a brief discussion of shiphandling involved, and for safety precautions to be observed. The *Naval Shiphandler's Guide* also contains an excellent discussion of underway replenishment in chapter 9.

2. Notify the heads of the departments concerned as soon as practicable in order to make preparations and conduct required prebriefs.

3. Order that information about the time of the operation and the stations to be manned be passed over the 1MC circuit.

4. Supervise the use of prescribed signals while the ship is approaching and alongside the replenishing ship.

5. Assist the conning officer in relaying orders to the helmsman, operator of the EOT, and rpm indicator.

6. Notify the EOOW as far in advance as possible so that he or she can make appropriate changes in the status of the plant—for example, lighting off extra boilers, placing generators on standby, and, if refueling is scheduled, shifting the fuel load. Engineering preparations will usually include the conduct of steering checks, and placing the plant in a "maximum reliability" configuration (which entails both an increase

in watch station manning and placing additional equipment on line for improved redundancy). Most ships also employ some type of "restricted maneuvering doctrine" (RMD), temporarily modifying normal engineering casualty control procedures in the interests of maximizing ship control safety during close quarters maneuvering.

7. Study the characteristics and replenishment arrangements of the ship alongside of which his or her own ship will be. Set stadimeters to the correct masthead height for the units he or she will be working with. If equipped, ensure battery-powered laser range finders are operable and available.

8. Check to see that communications equipment includes a radio, a flashing light, electric megaphones, sound-powered telephones, flags, paddles, and wands. During the actual operation, the use of radio between delivery and receiving ships is normally confined to emergencies. Electric megaphones are used during the approach and until telephone lines are connected. Thereafter, they are the main standby method of communicating.

HEAVY WEATHER

One of the attributes of a good naval officer and seaman is knowledge of the weather. He or she should know what weather is expected and be prepared to meet its effects on shipboard operations. Kotsch's *Weather for the Mariner* and Kotsch and Henderson's *Heavy Weather Guide* are excellent references providing a rich background.

When heavy seas and winds of high intensity are anticipated, the OOD must take the following precautions (specific actions should be included in a heavy-weather checklist as an OOD reference):

1. Have the word passed over all circuits: "Prepare ship for heavy weather."
2. Designate divisions to rig inboard lifelines on weather decks.
3. Pass, as appropriate, the word: "Close all hatches on main deck forward." "Close all topside hatches forward (or aft) of frame____." "Close all topside hatches, doors, and ports on starboard (port) side."

Pass the word for personnel to remain clear of the weather decks as necessary for safety.

4. Require personnel assigned topside in heavy weather to wear life jackets and safety lines. Crew thus exposed should also wear warm jackets.

DAMAGE-CONTROL SETTINGS

The OOD's responsibility for effective damage control and watertight integrity procedures is an important one. An OOD should have completed the PQS for general damage control and should know the exact location and capabilities of all major and secondary damage-control systems in the ship (an all-hands requirement). The OOD must see that the proper damage-control condition is set and that exceptions to that condition are reported and entered in the damage-control closure logbook. When the sounding-and-security watch reports to the bridge "All secure" and presents readings, the OOD should examine them carefully before initialing them. Unexplained changes to soundings in tanks or a requirement to pump spaces frequently ought to be given close scrutiny, particularly in heavy weather when the ship may be making water because hatches or other deck openings have not been properly secured.

While opening and closing doors and hatches may seem dull, they are matters of great importance to the safety of the ship and the lives of the crew. A sudden grounding or collision can result in rapid and cascading disaster. History has shown time and again the importance of watertight integrity as well as swift response in maintaining ship stability after damage. Even half a ship will stay afloat and permit the rescue of many crew members if her watertight integrity has been maintained. The OOD must always strive to combat carelessness and to see that the proper closure setting is maintained.

MATERIAL CASUALTIES

The OOD must ensure, to the extent possible, that all machinery and electronic gear is operable. This means exercising foresight and testing equipment such as winches, radar, and voice circuits that may be used in the immediate future. In addition, the OOD should make certain that the right officer is notified of any material casualties that occur. He or she must know what effect a given casualty will have and take action to cause the necessary reports to the OTC, as well as intraship reports. For example, the OOD should report an important electronics system failure to the electronics officer as well as to the combat systems officer of the watch (CSOOW) and obtain an estimate of repair time. The captain (and embarked commander, if applicable) will then usually be notified via the TAO or OOD depending on the current watch condition in effect.

The OOD is interested in how a casualty affects the performance, maneuverability, or safety of the ship, *not* in how repairs are to be made, who is to do them, or how long they will take. An OOD who badgers people on the scene of a casualty not only makes no contribution but also often adds to the problem and impedes its correction.

BINOCULARS

The OOD should know how to adjust, clean, and use binoculars; know his or her own focus and interpupillary setting; and instruct lookouts and other personnel in the care and use of glasses. Careless handling, especially dropping, can soon make a pair of glasses unfit for use. The watch should be taught to use the neck strap and to keep the glasses in their case when they are not in use. Nothing is more unseaman-like and just plain wasteful of public funds than letting binoculars lie around. The top of a chart table may seem like safe stowage, but when the ship takes a roll, the user has to lean over and pick up a pair of glasses that are no longer of help. Binocular lenses should be cleaned only with lens paper.

REFUSE DISPOSAL AND POLLUTION CONTROL

The Navy's ability to accomplish its mission requires both the conduct of daily operations in the land, sea, and air environments and good stewardship of our world's resources. The bottom line is very simply that the Navy is committed to operating in a manner compatible with the environment. National defense and environmental protection are and must continue to be compatible goals. Therefore, a very important part of the Navy's mission is to prevent pollution, protect the environment, and preserve natural, historic, and cultural resources. In order to accomplish this mission element, personnel must be aware of the environmental and natural resources laws and regulations that have been established by federal, state, and local governments. The Navy chain of command must provide leadership and a personal commitment to ensure that all Navy personnel develop and exhibit an environmental protection ethic.

You will find that the number of environmental regulations has increased significantly in recent years, and these regulations are in a continuous state of change. You must be generally familiar with an overview of federal regulations, DOD requirements, and Navy requirements that apply to Navy ships. In addition, while your ship is tied up along a pier, you as an OOD must ensure you are aware of, understand, and comply with the additional requirements imposed upon your ship by state and local governments. All the information you will need can be found in the detailed instructions, OpNavInst 5090.1D (10 January 2014), the Environmental Readiness Program, and in Opnav M-5090.1, the Environmental Readiness Program Manual.

One of the key items you must have complete familiarity with as an underway OOD are the regulations for overboard discharge of any matter from the ship. The basic guidelines are noted below (and in greater detail in appendix J):

- *Sewage Disposal.* As of 1 April 1981, all ships are required to be equipped with tanks capable of holding waste, transferring it ashore, or dumping it at sea beyond three nautical miles of the shore's low-water baseline.
- *Garbage.* Garbage may not be thrown overboard within the navigable waters of the United States and the contiguous zone, roughly twenty-five nautical miles to sea. In foreign waters it is a matter of courtesy to use the same standards that are used in the United States.
- *Oil and Oily Water.* Oil may not be deliberately pumped into the ocean. Bilge pumping is not permitted within fifty miles of the coastline. Caution should be exercised to prevent the spillage of oil.
- *Solid Waste.* Solid waste, trash, and refuse may not be discharged at sea within twenty-five miles of any shore.
- *Hazardous Material.* Never discharge hazardous materials at sea.
- *Medical Waste.* Medical waste is not to be disposed of at sea except in extreme circumstances, and then in weighted containers more than fifty miles at sea with records maintained.

- *Plastics.* Plastics are not to be disposed of at sea. Most ships are equipped with plastic waste processors that facilitate long-term storage and disposal of all plastic waste ashore.

Besides the environmental dangers associated with the discharge of oil and refuse at sea, there are operational considerations. Even in mid-ocean, trash should never be dumped over the side unless it is rigged to sink, and under no circumstances should trash be dumped during flight operations because of the danger of creating FOD. Dumping should not be permitted during ASW operations because solid material can return false echoes. It should also be obvious that any potential slick left by a ship at sea would assist enemy forces in finding her.

REPORTS TO THE CO

Policy on reports to the CO requires exact compliance. As unimportant as some reports may appear, they all contain information that, for one reason or another, the CO needs. Exceptions or changes to what is to be reported can be made only by the CO, not the OOD or any other officer onboard ship. The CO is the most experienced mariner onboard. His or her standing orders define the required reports with the specific purpose of bringing that considerable experience to bear in a timely way. A seemingly small omission can mean the difference between early and effective action and disaster. As unkind as it may seem to awaken a tired CO, it is much worse to have to call that person to the bridge unprepared when the ship is already in danger. Failure to make required reports to the CO is a lesson all too often painfully and tragically relearned.

Reports to the CO should be concise and specific and should include the OOD's proposed course of action. They should systematically "build a clear picture" for the CO. For example, the OOD may report a contact in this manner: "Captain, this is the OOD. I am presently on a course of 276 degrees at a speed of twelve knots. I have a contact broad on my starboard bow at nine thousand yards. She has a target angle of 330 degrees relative. Her present CPA is off the port bow at one thousand yards. My intention is to alter course 30 degrees to starboard in order to open the CPA to four thousand yards off my port beam." If a certain format or sequence is prescribed by the captain for reporting information such as surface contacts, it must be adhered to exactly. COs will address the desired report format in their standing orders. No CO enjoys being awakened at night to hear a rambling discourse or a collection of disjointed information.

In case of doubt, it is always the wisest course to call the captain. The CO is accustomed to interrupted sleep when under way and will gain peace of mind from an OOD who pays conscientious attention to duty. Some people can acknowledge a message without being fully awake. Therefore, the OOD should make certain that important messages are understood. If possible, such messages should be communicated by the OOD in person rather than by messenger.

Notes

1.   Nita Lewis Miller and Michael Firehammer, "Avoiding a Second Hollow Force: The Case for Including Crew Endurance Factors in the Afloat Staffing Policies of the US Navy," *Naval Engineers Journal* 119, no. 1 (October 2007): 83–96, https://doi.org/10.1111/j.0028-1425.2007.00007.x.

2.   Department of the Navy, Comprehensive Fatigue and Endurance Management Policy, COMNAVSURFORINST 3120.2, 30 November 2017, https://federalnews network.com/wp-content/uploads/2017/12/113017_navyrestpolicy.pdf.

6

SHIPHANDLING

The mark of a great shiphandler is never getting into a situation that requires great shiphandling.

FLEET ADMIRAL ERNEST J. KING, USN, COMMANDER IN CHIEF,
U.S. FLEET AND CHIEF OF NAVAL OPERATIONS DURING WORLD WAR II

Shiphandling is an exciting and challenging aspect of a watch officer's job. The key to becoming a competent shiphandler is an understanding of the basic forces affecting the ship, knowledge of shiphandling procedures, and confidence. This chapter provides the basics, but a career of continuous study and practice is required of anyone who wants to become and remain a fully capable conning officer.

DEFINITIONS

Pivot Point. The pivot point is the point of rotation within a ship as she makes a turn. For a destroyer-type ship, it is generally about one-third the length of the ship from the bow and fairly close to the bridge (when the ship is going ahead).

Turning Circle. The turning circle is the path described by a ship when she turns. It varies according to the amount of rudder and speed. See figure 6.1.

Advance. For any turn, the advance is the distance gained in the direction of the original course from the time the rudder is put over until the ship is on the new course.

Transfer. For any turn, the transfer is the distance gained in a direction perpendicular to that of the original course from the time the rudder is put over until the ship is on the new course.

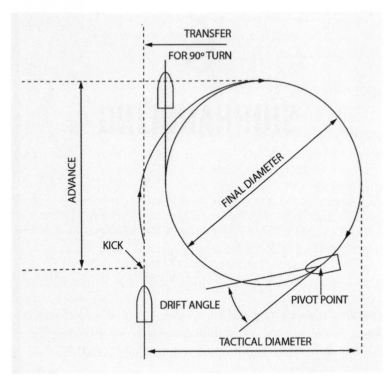

FIGURE 6-1. Turning Circle

Tactical Diameter. For any amount of constant rudder angle, the tactical diameter is the distance made good in a direction perpendicular to that of the original course from the time the rudder is put over until the ship is on a reverse heading. It is the transfer for a turn of 180 degrees.

Standard Rudder. Standard rudder (usually 15 degrees) is the angle of rudder that, under normal conditions, gives the ship standard tactical diameter.

Full Rudder. Full rudder (usually 30 degrees) is a prescribed angle of rudder, usually a safe distance—5 degrees—short of the stops, that gives the ship reduced tactical diameter.

Hard Rudder. This means putting the rudder over to the indicated side as far as the wheel allows (the more modern steering systems, such as those on guided-missile destroyers [DDGs], have safeties built in to prevent driving the rudder into the stops). Usually 35 degrees.

Acceleration and Deceleration Rates. Acceleration and deceleration rates are those at which a ship picks up or loses headway after a change of speed. This rate is usually measured in yards per knot.

GENERAL PRINCIPLES

An officer who wants to become an efficient shiphandler should be aware of certain general principles and their specific application to his or her ship. Examples of these principles follow.

Effect of the Wind upon Turning

Most ships, particularly those with high bows, turn slowly into the wind when going ahead and rapidly when turning away from it. Conversely, they turn rapidly into the wind when backing. The effect on a particular ship can be estimated by comparing the "sail area" forward of the pivot point with that abaft the pivot point. A ship whose sail area is greater forward has the above tendencies. One with greater sail area aft has the opposite tendencies; this is particularly true of aircraft carriers. The term "sail area" refers to those surfaces of the hull and superstructure above the waterline against which the wind can exert force.

Effect of Speed upon Turning

With constant rudder angle, at speeds appreciably above steerageway, any increase in speed makes the turning circle larger. This is because the inertia of the ship tends to keep her going in the original direction of motion. The amount by which the turning circle increases varies from ship to ship and is most noticeable when ships of different types are operating together. Because the guide is usually a large ship and uses the same amount of rudder or standard rudder for all speeds, it is necessary to know what rudder for the ship involved will match the turning circle of the guide ship for the speed at which any turn is made.

At speeds approaching bare steerageway, a decrease in speed results in a larger turning circle. This is because the rudder acting against the inertia of the ship has less effect and tends to keep the ship moving in a straight line. For a turn at low speeds, therefore, more rudder is needed. The minimum speed at which a ship will still have steerageway should be known.

Effect of Shallow Water

The less space there is between the ship's hull and the bottom, the less freely the screw currents flow and act upon the hull and rudder. When that space is very small, the ship may be sluggish or erratic in answering the rudder, a great deal of power is wasted, and the speed through the water is less than indicated by the propeller revolutions. Additionally, high speed in shallow water may create an effect known as squatting: the bow rides upon the bow wave and the stern sits deeper in the water.

Time Lag in Response to Orders

There is a noticeable lag between the time an order is given to the wheel or engines and the time the effect of the response is felt. For example, to have the rudder go over at the same spot as that of the ship ahead so that the turn is made in her wake, the order to turn must be given when the kick of the preceding ship's rudder is near the bridge of the following ship.

Backing Power Available

In some ships, particularly steam propulsion plants, backing power may be considerably less than the power for going ahead. There are two reasons: first, because a backing turbine has fewer impeller blades, it produces less power; and, second, propellers are less efficient when turning astern. "Back one-third" and "back two-thirds" normally call for one-third and two-thirds, respectively, of the power available for backing. The turns for "ahead one-third" and "ahead two-thirds" are based upon one-third and two-thirds, respectively, of standard speed. There is no "back standard" speed. "Ahead one-third (two-thirds)" and "back one-third (two-thirds)" probably do not have equal effect. Consequently, besides twisting when one engine is backing and the other is going ahead (both at one-third or two-thirds), a ship can be expected to pick up a slight amount of way in the direction of the stronger force. In a ship with controllable-pitch propellers or water jets, however, backing power is considerably enhanced because it is the pitch of the propeller blade or direction of the propulsion bucket that determines the direction of the propulsion force. The force generated by the propulsion plant in this instance remains nearly constant.

Factors That Affect Acceleration and Deceleration

The manner in which ships gain and lose headway, carry their way, and respond to changes of engine speed varies with the size of the ship, her propulsion system, her underwater lines, the condition of her bottom, the wind, and the state of the sea. A clean-bottomed, heavy ship or a ship with full lines tends to hold her way. A foul-bottomed, heavy ship with full lines tends to pick up headway slowly in response to changes of engine speed. Gas-turbine ships are more responsive than steamships to speed changes. Waterjet engines, as used in LCSs, provide even more responsiveness both accelerating and decelerating.

Factors That Affect Turning

An OOD should know not only how to make a normal turn but also how to turn a ship in the shortest time and in the shortest possible space. A ship turns in the *shortest time* by going ahead with full power and her rudder hard over just short of the stops. The procedure for turning a ship in the *shortest possible space* depends upon the ship herself and, sometimes, upon wind conditions.

A ship with twin rudders and screws is the easiest and probably the quickest to turn as well as the least affected by wind conditions. Her rudders should simply be put over full or hard in the direction of the desired turn and kept there. "Ahead two-thirds" on the outboard engine and "back two-thirds" on the inboard engine should be rung up. The speed of the inboard engine can be adjusted to keep the ship from going ahead or astern as she turns on her heel.

A ship with a single rudder and twin screws is slightly more difficult to turn in a short space. If the screws are set well off from the centerline and if the turn is not adversely affected by the wind, the turn can be made by going ahead on the outboard engine and backing on the inboard engine. When the wind does adversely affect the turn, or when the screws are not sufficiently offset for a good, powerful couple, motion ahead and astern may be necessary to supplement the effect of the rudder. As a general rule, when a ship is going ahead with steerageway, her rudder should be put over in the direction of the desired turn; when a ship is going astern with steerageway, her rudder should be put in the opposite direction; when a ship has no way on or less than steerageway, her rudder should be put amidships. The amount of way on and the position of the rudder should be carefully watched. Some ships with large single rudders show a tendency somewhat similar to that of a twin-rudder ship to answer to the effect of an ahead-turning screw on the rudder even when they have a small amount of sternway. The OOD must know the characteristics of his or her own ship in this regard.

A ship with a single screw is the most difficult to turn in a short space. Most ships of this type have right-handed propellers and need to have some way on. Therefore, to turn them in a short space, headway and sternway have to be alternated. Whenever the engine is going ahead, the rudder should be thrown in the direction of the desired turn. Knowing when to shift the rudder after starting the engines backing is a matter of knowing the ship. It should usually be done shortly after the ship loses headway and then kept there until the engine is put ahead.

LCS, both FREEDOM and INDEPENDENCE variants, are controlled using steerable waterjets with independent drive trains. They do not have rudders like most other ships although the power and adaptability of the waterjets and drive trains make them more maneuverable than ships of similar size. Handling each of the LCS variants is unique and thoroughly detailed in Gagliano's *Shiphandling Fundamentals for Littoral Combat Ships and the New Frigates.*

HANDLING IN FORMATION

Handling a ship in company with others requires a sound knowledge of the effective tactical instructions and a thorough understanding of the relative motion of ships. Information on the first essential is found in ATP-1, volumes 1 and 2. Every officer standing deck watches at sea should be so familiar with these important directives that he or she can find at once the proper guidance for any circumstance that may arise involving the movements of the ship. The opening chapters of both these volumes are particularly important because they provide the basic concepts and definitions upon which all subsequent instructions are based. A few additional primary source documents that one should be familiar with include International Code of Signals (Pub 102), Multinational Maritime Tactical Signal and Maneuvering Book (MTP 1), and Code for Unplanned Encounters at Sea (CUES).

The second essential for efficient shiphandling in formation, an understanding of relative motion, can be attained by studying and practicing problems on a maneuvering board.

An important by-product of skill in the maneuvering board is the ability to visualize problems and to mentally solve them. For a complicated evolution such as taking a distant station in a formation, a mental solution would of course be approximate and subject to modification by the CIC or a JOOD who actually worked out the problem. Nevertheless, a mental solution permits an instant change of course and speed, which expedites the maneuver, demonstrates a ship's smartness, and gets her "on the way." For simple problems such as gaining 10 degrees in bearing on the guide while maintaining distance, a mental solution is sufficient because it is subject to confirmation by periodic bearings and ranges.

Developing a good "seaman's eye" should be one of a shiphandler's most important goals. Although some people have more natural ability than others in this regard, a true seaman's eye is developed only by experience, practice, and close observation of every maneuver. A shiphandler should learn to visualize and retain a picture of what is happening during a maneuver. He or she should practice correlating what is seen from the bridge wing and the bird's-eye view of the surface-search radar. Perfection of this skill not only sharpens the eye but also renders a reliable means of checking the maneuvering-board solution against what is actually seen.

When a tactical signal for maneuvering is executed, the shiphandler should be able to come to the required speed immediately and, even if there is not a complete maneuvering-board solution, put the rudder over and head in roughly the right direction, as long as it is a navigationally safe course. Course corrections made en route to a station do not cause major problems; being the only ship to remain on the old course and speed does.

Maneuvering signals in formation are likely to require simultaneous actions by a number of ships. It is a shiphandler's responsibility, in addition to getting to the new station, to avoid interfering with or embarrassing other units and to make his or her own movements and intentions clearly understood. The shiphandler should make it a habit to always have an escape route when maneuvering with other ships and to know in advance what to do and in which direction to turn if he or she suddenly has to avoid more than one ship at a time. A common failing of inexperienced shiphandlers is to forget that there are ships around them and to fail to anticipate their maneuvers. This can be disastrous. A ship that is one thousand yards on another ship's quarter and on a parallel course can become a major problem if the latter is forced to cross her bow in order to avoid a third ship.

Operating in formation with aircraft carriers places additional responsibility on the OOD. Most carriers establish a safety "box" around themselves—an area that other ships must avoid. At a minimum, the box is known by the "3:2:1 rule": Other ships must never be closer than three thousand yards off the carrier's bow, two thousand yards off her beam, and one thousand yards astern, unless ordered closer or with notification to the aircraft carrier. Some carriers prescribe even larger boxes, and each establishes a different-size area in her Plane Guard and Horizon Reference Unit Instructions to Escorts notice or SOP. Not only does a carrier's size impose maneuvering limitations on her, but also the amount of rudder-induced heel is likely to be restricted if aircraft are spotted on her deck. A ship that is forward of an aircraft carrier should never turn toward her except in an emergency. If it is absolutely necessary to do so, she should indicate her intentions to the carrier. An officer (either the OOD or JOOD) should constantly have the carrier under observation. Most carriers publish a set of SOPs (noted above); these should be studied by the watch officers on ships in company.

Close Station-Keeping

Visualizing simple problems in relative motion is the key to proficient station-keeping in close formation. Although ships do not now steam in close formation as often as formerly, proficiency in this area is still an important requirement. Surface ships still must be able to steam in column, or in line of bearing, at standard distance, and in circular formation darkened at night and at high speed, sometimes while not radiating radars. Steaming in close column, which is largely a matter of speed adjustment, demands a keen appreciation of speed and how a ship carries her way.

The stadimeter and laser range finder are essential instruments for ships in close formation. Every watch officer should be familiar with their use and know the capabilities and limitations. At close ranges, these tools are more accurate than most radars and particularly helpful in providing quick and accurate information about distance—whether it is opening, closing, or being held steady. Laser range finders can be installed or handheld systems.

Distance reports should state whether distance is closing, opening, or steady. The terms "increasing" and "decreasing" should not be used because there is a chance of confusing distance reports with reports concerning bearings.

It may not be possible to take visual or handheld stadimeter readings on dark nights when there is not enough light, when the ship is too close for radar ranges, or when radar silence is imposed. At such times binoculars can be used to obtain a fair estimate of distance if, during the day, when the exact distance to a ship can be measured, the extent of the binocular field that she fills has been noted. (See the quick reference guide at the end of this chapter for estimates.) The first ship in a column, or the guide ship, should make every effort to ensure good steering and steady speed. The OOD should see that the proper revolutions are being made. The OOD on the ship astern will appreciate such efforts.

The keeping of proper distance between ships in column depends largely on the OOD's ability to detect early indications of opening or closing motion and to make proper speed adjustments to counteract that motion. In this regard the OOD should remember that when a ship is following in the wake of another, she requires a few more revolutions than she would in still water to make good the same speed as the ship ahead; this is because she has to overcome the wake turbulence or "kick" of the preceding ship. An erratic helmsman who takes the ship in and out of another ship's wake complicates the problem of speed adjustment. The helmsman should be watched closely. Speed should be corrected with care; it must be remembered that there is a time lag before the effect of change is felt. If this lag is not allowed for, the same error may be corrected twice, requiring another correction, probably larger, in the opposite direction. Once such surging starts, it is hard to stop. An OOD would be well advised to intently study the time lag of the ship until it is known. The effect of one correction should be carefully observed before another correction is applied.

Excessive use of the rudder acts as a brake. Therefore, steering should always be corrected before speed is increased.

In general, it is safer for a ship in column to be inside, rather than outside, the prescribed distance; it is easier to drop back than to close up. An OOD ought to know the allowable tolerances (usually 10 percent of the prescribed range and 1 degree of bearing) and keep within them because it is also easy to hit the ship ahead if she slows without the OOD noticing. He or she should remember the fellow next astern and keep course and speed as steady as possible. The reputation of being a good ship to follow is a difficult one to earn, but it is worth trying for.

The OOD must keep in mind his or her ship's number in the column and to which side she is to sheer out in an emergency. This is the same side as that of her position when in column open order, and it follows the standard pattern— odd-numbered ships to starboard, even-numbered ships to port. When for any reason the ship gets uncomfortably close to the ship ahead, the thing to do is to ease her bow out very slightly on the side to which she would sheer out in an emergency.

Course changes for a formation in column may be made in two ways: by individual ships turning together or by wheeling, that is, changing course in succession, each ship following the ship ahead. When change of course is made by turning together, the rudder must be put over the proper amount promptly on the execution of the signal. The OOD must inform the helmsman of the new course and see that the latter does not swing past it or use an excessive amount of rudder in meeting the swing. Either of these errors will cause the ship to end up behind bearing in the line of bearing resulting from the maneuver. The OOD should keep the nearest ship toward which the turn is being made under constant visual observation, checking the bearing of the guide as the turn progresses with a view to detecting promptly any tendency to gain or lose bearing.

In practice, ships do not maintain perfect position, particularly when making frequent simultaneous turns, and the OOD must know how to adjust a turn to improve position. This knowledge comes mostly from experience in visualizing the situation and looking ahead. Of course, any such adjustments must consider adjacent ships on both sides.

Assuming that a ship has turned properly, the one astern will turn in the same water. The knuckle of the first ship's wake should be slightly on the second ship's bow, in the direction of the turn. Slick water inboard of the wake is caused by the stern of the ship sliding in the turn; the inboard edge of the slick marks the path of the ship's bow, the outboard edge, that of her stern.

Conning can be performed from both the centerline and the wing of the bridge in order to keep awareness of the ship ahead, and the one astern, if any, can be seen. Knowing exactly when to start a turn takes experience, but the OOD usually orders the rudder put over when the knuckle is abreast the bridge. If the turn is correctly timed, the bow of the ship will follow around at the inboard edge of the slick.

If the turn is made late, the ship will go outside the proper turning circle and the wake of the ship ahead may hold her there. If this happens, the OOD should not swing beyond the new course but should remain steadied and parallel to the column on the new course. When the ship next astern has completed her wheel, the OOD's ship should gradually regain station; it is almost always necessary to increase speed to regain station.

If the turn is made too early, the ship will go inside the proper circle. A slight easing of the rudder will correct this, but speed will probably have to be reduced to avoid dangerous proximity to the ship ahead. A common error in such a situation is to ease the rudder too much so that the ship crosses the wake ahead and is outside after all.

The danger of turns lies in a substantial change of course being started when a ship is too close to the ship ahead. The choice then is between making a large rudder angle to stay inside the turn while slowing, stopping, or backing, and easing the rudder and going outside. It is safer to continue the turn inside; hesitation before easing the rudder to go outside may send the ship forging ahead while her bow is still inside the turn of the ship ahead, putting them in danger of collision.

A ship astern of one that turns too soon or too late should not attempt to follow her but should turn in the wake of the guide. If she is slightly out of position when a turn is ordered, she can maneuver to correct; if she is behind station, she can cut the corner; if too close, she can turn a bit later with full rudder.

At night or in fog, it may not be possible to see the knuckle. If the OOD keeps track of the time elapsed after the signal to execute, he or she can, on the basis of speed and distance from the guide, determine when the point of turn has been reached. This is done by using the "three-minute rule," which states that in three minutes a ship travels as many hundreds of yards as the number of knots she is making. That is, a ship doing fifteen knots travels fifteen hundred yards in three minutes. Therefore, a ship that is one thousand yards astern of the guide at a speed of fifteen knots turns two minutes after the guide executes her turn.

Line of Bearing

In line of bearing, station-keeping is somewhat complicated, because both distance and bearing are involved. A thorough understanding of the relative motion of ships is helpful. When the ship is in close formation, the OOD rarely has time to plot bearings and distances and obtain a solution. The problem has to be visualized and then the course and speed changed properly and promptly as soon as the OOD detects a deviation from the correct bearing and distance. The OOD can quickly determine whether the ship is ahead or behind bearing by lining up an alidade on the prescribed bearing of the guide and then sighting through it. If the line of sight falls ahead of the guide, she is ahead; if astern, she is behind.

When ships are in line abreast, a speed that is greater or less than that of the guide causes a bearing to be advanced or retarded with negligible variation in range. A slight change of course toward or away from the guide causes a closing or opening of range with a slight loss of bearing. A small temporary increase of speed, normally only a few turns, can be used to counteract this small bearing change.

When the line of bearing is a column, a speed differential causes a closing or opening of distance. A change of course causes a change of bearing with a slight opening of distance. A small temporary increase of speed can be used to counteract this small change in range.

For lines of bearing between these two extremes—line abreast and column—the effects of a course or speed differential are a little more complex. A combination of changing course and speed is usually required to maintain station.

When simultaneous turns are made in line or bearing, it is important to watch the ship toward which the turn is made for a sign that she might be turning in the wrong direction.

In close station-keeping it is a good idea to have a handheld VHF radio nearby for instant use in emergency maneuvering situations. An agreed-upon safety (or working) channel is a must as well. Use of these radios is subject, of course, to emissions control (EMCON) conditions in effect, but their value in preventing a potential collision cannot be overstated.

Station-Keeping in Formation

Handling a ship in the main body of a circular formation is slightly easier than handling a ship in close formation because the distance between ships is usually greater. However, because station has to be kept on a definite bearing from the guide and at a definite distance, the problems of station-keeping are similar to those in line of bearing. The only additional determination to be made is what the range and bearing from the guide should be when a ship is moving to a new station. The CIC can be of great assistance to the OOD in these matters.

To determine the ship's range and bearing from the guide, the OOD must be familiar with the system for plotting formations by using polar coordinates. Once the formation has been plotted, the OOD can easily pick the range and bearing of the guide off the plot. A continuous plot of the formation should be kept so that ordered changes can be quickly translated into new range and bearing from the guide. The plot should be kept manually on a maneuvering board as well as electronically on the ship systems available.

It should be kept in mind that the guide is not always at the center of a formation and that, as soon as a signal has been executed, the guide is automatically on station, regardless of where she might be. This situation sometimes results in the center of the formation moving around the guide, and when it does, the other ships move a like amount in the same direction.

For any maneuver, when required range and bearing from the guide have been determined from a plot, actual range and bearing from the guide should be worked out. These figures can be used to determine the course and speed required to bring the ship to her proper station. Except for when a ship is ordered to a new station, a change of formation axis and a change in the formation itself are the only maneuvers that change either her range or her bearing, or both, in relation to the guide.

Screening

Handling a ship in a screen is quite similar to handling a ship in the main body of a circular formation. Station-keeping procedures are the same. Determining range and bearing is, however, more complex, because the distance from the guide is greater. The OOD of a destroyer-type ship must be familiar with the maneuvering rules that govern screening ships as well as those that govern maneuvers in the various formations.

A continuous, up-to-the-minute plot of the entire formation should be kept, just as for a circular formation, so that any ordered change can be quickly translated into a new range and bearing from the guide.

To keep the plot of the screen, the OOD must know where the center of the screen is and the direction of its axis. He or she must be able to distinguish the signals that cause the screen center to shift and those that do not. He or she must also know how to determine the amount and direction of such a shift and how to allow for it in the maneuver, whether or not a reorientation of the screen is required.

An OOD must know under what conditions a screen axis changes without a specific signal and how to determine its new direction in such cases. He or she should make every effort to start for the new station promptly. A little forehandedness will help. After each maneuver, the OOD should start anticipating the next one. He or she should check the plot and then determine the minimum change of formation course in each direction that would cause a reorientation requiring a change of station. When it is appropriate, the OOD should determine the minimum change of course that would require an initial turn to be made in the direction opposite to that of the course change. With these figures firmly in mind, the OOD can quickly translate a signal into action and start the initial turn before the final solution has been worked out.

In working solutions, the OOD must be sure to use the course and speed for the guide that will actually be followed en route to the station. This policy is particularly applicable when the ship starts for her station before the signal that changes the guide's course or speed or both has been executed.

There are two final points to be made about screening. The first is that station-keeping should be *exact*, with the OOD ensuring that the ship is where she is supposed to be at all times. If the screen plan requires the ship to patrol a sector as opposed to maintaining a continuous, exact range and bearing from the guide, the patrolling courses and speeds should be controlled exactly. Then the OOD can afford to devote more time to other matters, perhaps delegating, under supervision, the duty of station-keeping to the JOOD.

The second point is that when a screen is being reoriented or its station changed, the OOD must keep an alert watch over the whole formation, using his or her own eyes and ship systems to the maximum extent. Others can work out maneuvering-board solutions to check the OOD's quick calculations; his or her primary job under many conditions is that of chief safety officer.

Range to the Guide

When the ship is steaming in formation, the OOD must always know the range to the guide. However, to obtain this information, he or she should not put such a burden on the surface-search radar operator in the CIC that the operator is forced to keep the radar on a short range scale and concentrate exclusively on giving range-to-the-guide information to the deck. At night or in low visibility, when the surface-search radar is relied upon more heavily for detecting and tracking ships to prevent collision, this practice can be dangerous. The OOD should use a stadimeter or laser range finder whenever possible; they can be used at night, in good visibility, with running lights as targets. The bridge radar repeaters, of course, should also be used to provide this information, freeing the CIC from the necessity of supplying continuous ranges although forceful backup between the CIC and the bridge is always required.

MAN OVERBOARD

The first requirement in case of a man overboard is prompt action. An alert OOD will see that the people in his or her watch know what their duties are in such an emergency and will be prepared, depending on weather and operating conditions, to

1. Put the rudder over to the side the person went over, to kick the stern away from him or her.
2. Immediately throw over the side a life ring with a strobe light and a smoke float or "rescue ball" to mark the spot as closely as possible.
3. Tell the JOOD, lookout, or anyone available to point at the person, if possible, and continue pointing until he or she is alongside the ship.
4. Have the word passed twice: "Man overboard, port (starboard) side."
5. Sound six or more short blasts on the ship's whistle, and make appropriate visual signals as specified in ATP-1, vol. 1: "By day hoist OSCAR and at night (in peacetime) display two pulsating red lights or fire one white rocket (very light)."
6. Notify the CIC so that it can provide continual ranges and bearings to the person in the water.
7. Notify ships in company and the OTC.
8. Inform the CO, XO, and flag duty officer, if appropriate.
9. Determine recovery method and pass the word. Shipboard, small boat (employing the ship's rigid hulled inflatable boat—RHIB), or helicopter recoveries are all options. Establish communication with the recovery detail.
10. Keep the recovery detail informed as to whether the recovery is to be made from the port or the starboard side of the ship.

As soon as the word "man overboard" has been passed, the CIC should automatically mark the spot, shift the ship's displays to the most effective range scale, and begin passing ranges and bearings to the bridge.

A helicopter provides the quickest rescue, with the advantage that it can pick up a helpless person. If a helicopter is not available, a small boat may be used.

There are a number of methods of recovering a man overboard (see table 6.1 and descriptions following). The four most common are the Anderson turn, which is the fastest but requires skillful shiphandling; the Williamson turn, for night or low visibility; the racetrack turn, for fastest recovery when a ship is proceeding at high speed in clear weather or with a towed array trailing the ship; and the Y-backing, for ships with large turning circles and great backing power proceeding at slow speeds. Very large ships often use a small boat to recover a person. Small vessels also use a boat when the sea is rough and there is little chance of getting the ship close alongside the person. Under any conditions, the OOD should see to it that swimmers with life jackets and tending lines are ready to go into the water. Regardless of which recovery method is used, the same basic principles apply. Full rudder should be used to swing the stern away from the person.

Man-overboard maneuvering for naval vessels involved in tactical evolutions can be found in ATP-1, volume 1, chapter 5. Of specific importance are the instructions for column formation. In this situation, the ship that loses the person takes action to avoid him or her, as do the others, with odd-numbered ships in the column clearing to starboard and even-numbered ships clearing to port. The ship in the best position to recover the person does so, and she keeps the other vessels informed of her actions.

The person should be recovered in the shortest possible time. Large ships usually use the Williamson method. Small ships, in good weather, use the racetrack or Anderson methods. At night or in low visibility, the Williamson turn, though not the fastest recovery method, must be used to bring the ship back along her track. No matter what the method, the best final position is beam to the wind slightly to windward of the person, with all way off. When in this position, the ship provides a lee for the person, and because she will make more leeway, she will drift toward rather than away from the person. For steam-powered ships, it is important that the person be kept *forward* of the main condenser injection intakes, particularly if there is a possibility that he or she still has a parachute attached; a parachute can clog the intakes, which are ordinarily aft of the midship's section on either side. In her final position, the ship should have the person just off her leeward bow.

TABLE 6-1 Methods of Recovering a Sailor Overboard

METHOD AND PRIMARY CONDITIONS FOR USE	DIAGRAM OF SHIP ON COURSE 090 (NUMBERS REFER TO THE EXPLANATION)	EXPLANATION	EXPLANATION	
			ADVANTAGE	DISADVANTAGE
Anderson Turn. Used by ships that have considerable power and relatively tight turning characteristics	1 2 3 4 ⊗ =MAN	1. Put the rudder over full to the side from which the person fell. Stop the inboard engine. 2. When clear of the person, go ahead full on the outboard engine only. Continue using full rudder. 3. When about two-thirds of the way around, back the inboard engine two-thirds or full. Order all engines stopped when the person is within 15° of the bow, then ease the rudder and back the engines as required to attain the proper final position. 4. Many variations of this method are used, differing primarily in respect to the use of one or both engines and the time when they are stopped and backed to return to the person. The variation used should reflect individual ship's characteristics, sea conditions, personal preferences, etc.	Speed	Requires proficiency in shiphandling because the approach to the person is not straightaway. Often impossible for a single-propeller ship.

(continued on next page)

METHOD AND PRIMARY CONDITIONS FOR USE	ON COURSE 090 (NUMBERS REFER TO THE EXPLANATION)	EXPLANATION	EXPLANATION	
			ADVANTAGE	DISADVANTAGE
Williamson Turn. Used in low visibility because it makes good the original track. Used when it is believed that a person fell overboard some time previously and is not in sight.		1. Put the rudder over full to the side from which the person fell. Stop the inboard engine. 2. When clear of the person go ahead full on all engines. Continue using full rudder. 3. When 60° beyond the original course, shift the rudder without having steadied on a course; 60° is proper for many ships. However, the exact amount must be determined through trial and error. Come to the reciprocal of the original course, using full rudder. 4. Use the engines and rudder to attain the proper final position (ship upwind to the person and dead in the water with the person alongside, well forward of the propellers).	Simplicity. Makes good the original tract.	Slowness. Takes the ship relatively far from the person, when sight of him or her may be lost.
Racetrack Turn. (two 180° turns) Used in good visibility when a straight final approach leg is desired. A variation of the one-turn method that provides a desirable straight final approach to the person		1. Put the rudder over full to the side corresponding to the direction from which the person fell. Stop the inboard engine. 2. When clear of the person, go ahead full on all engines. Continue using full rudder to turn to the reciprocal of the original course. 3. Steady for a distance that will give the desired run for a final straight approach. 4. Use full rudder to turn to the person. Use the engines and rudder to attain the proper final position (ship upwind of the person and dead in the water with the person alongside, well forward of the propellers).	Straight final-approach leg facilitates a calculable approach. Ship will return to the person if he or she is lost from sight. Reasonably fast. Effective when wind was from a beam on original course.	Slower than one-turn methods.

(continued on next page)

METHOD AND PRIMARY CONDITIONS FOR USE	DIAGRAM OF SHIP ON COURSE 090 (NUMBERS REFER TO THE EXPLANATION)	EXPLANATION	EXPLANATION	
			ADVANTAGE	DISADVANTAGE
Y-Backing. Used by submarines because of their low height of eye.		1. Put the rudder over full to the side from which the person fell. Stop the inboard engine. 2. When clear of the person, back the engines with full power, using opposite rudder. 3. Go ahead. Use the engines and rudder to attain the proper final position (ship upwind of the person and dead in the water with the person alongside, well forward of the propellers).	The ship remains comparatively close to the person.	Most ships back into the wind or seas, causing poor control.
Delayed Turn. Used when word is received that a person fell overboard, is in sight, and is clear astern of the ship.		1. Put the rudder over full to the side from which the person fell. Go ahead full on all engines. 2. Ahead toward the person. 3. Use the engines and rudder to attain the proper final position (ship upwind of the person and dead in the water with the person alongside, well forward of the propellers).	Fastest method when person is in sight and already clear astern of the ship. Provides a straight run in the critical final phase. Effective when wind was from ahead or astern of ship on original course.	Does not ensure return to the person. Requires good visibility. Takes the ship farther from the person than other methods.

(continued on next page)

METHOD AND PRIMARY CONDITIONS FOR USE	DIAGRAM OF SHIP ON COURSE 090 (NUMBERS REFER TO THE EXPLANATION)	EXPLANATION	EXPLANATION	
			ADVANTAGE	DISADVANTAGE
Boat Recovery. Used by ships that do not have maneuverability to make a good approach to the person. Used when the ship is dead in the water and the person is close aboard but not alongside. Can be used in conjunction with any of the methods shown above.		1. Put the rudder over full to the side from which the person fell. Stop the inboard engine. 2. When the person is clear, back all engines full almost to stop the ship. Use the rudder full to the side of the ready lifeboat to provide a slick in which the boat can be lowered. Stop the engines while the ship still has very slight headway to permit better control of the boat and keep it out of the propeller wash.	Simple. The ship remains close to the person. Does not require that a particular final position be attained.	The person must be in sight. Sea and weather conditions must be satisfactory for small boat operators.

REPLENISHMENT AT SEA (RAS)

The Navy's ability to project sea power over long ocean distances depends on its ability to sustain itself at sea for long periods without direct land-based support. It is the mission of the Combat Logistics Force (CLF) to provide this support with fuel, stores, provisions, and ammunition. In addition to the naval vessels that constitute the CLF, many ships of the Military Sealift Command (MSC) have been designated to provide underway logistic support.

RAS is a commonly encountered evolution, and the manner in which it is executed is one of the basic yardsticks by which a ship's performance is measured. It presents one of the most challenging, exciting, and satisfying opportunities for shiphandling that a watch officer will be given. It can teach more about seamanship and shiphandling than almost any other evolution. Standard doctrine for RAS is outlined in Underway Replenishment (NWP 4-01.4), which also contains a tabulation of the locations and functions of the replenishment stations on all CLF ships. ATP-16 provides the same kind of information for the North Atlantic Treaty Organization's (NATO) replenishment ships. NSTM 571 provides technical details on underway replenishment.

To begin RAS, a replenishment ship comes to a steady course and speed, which are usually dictated by wind and seas or, if the weather is calm, by the course the formation wants made good. The receiving ship takes station astern of the delivering ship and waits for her to signal her readiness to replenish.

Weather conditions permitting, the normal speed of the guide ship is around thirteen knots. Speeds less than eight knots are not advisable because they reduce rudder effect. At speeds greater than fifteen knots, Venturi effect (the pressure differential created around the hull of a moving ship) calls for greater lateral separation. See J. A. Barber's *Naval Shiphandler's Guide* (chapter 9) for a detailed description of how to bring a ship alongside a delivery ship.

The delivery ship indicates preparations for receiving a ship alongside by flying Romeo at the dip on her rigged side. The receiving ship replies that she is ready to come alongside by flying Romeo at the dip on her rigged side. When the delivery ship is ready for the approach, she hoists Romeo close up. The receiving ship hoists Romeo close up and increases speed by three to ten knots over signaled underway-replenishment (UNREP) speed. She slows down so as to be moving at replenishment speed when in position. When the ships are in proper relative position, transfer rigs are passed and hooked up; when the first line is secured, both ships haul down Romeo. They both fly Bravo if fuel or ammunition is being transferred.

Fifteen minutes before the receiving ship expects to complete replenishment, her OOD orders Prep hoisted at the dip to notify the next ship scheduled to replenish. On completion of the replenishment, all nets, slings, lines, and hoses are returned to the delivery ship.

Just before disengaging, when the fuel transfer is complete, the receiving ship hoists Prep close up, and when the last line is clear she hauls it down. When the side has been cleared, the conning officer increases speed by five to ten knots, depending on ship type, and clears ahead, gradually changing course outboard. Propeller wash caused by radical changes in speed and course is likely to have a bad effect on the steering of the delivery ship, and a dangerous situation might develop if a ship is on her other side. The most important tasks of the OOD during an UNREP are the coordination of the multitude of preparations and the management of the bridge team while the ship's focus (and the captain's) is on the evolution itself. The OOD must have the crew on station on time but should avoid wasting the crew's time with needless waiting. Two hundred people waiting thirty minutes on station equals one hundred hours that could be better spent. Coordination with the first lieutenant, department heads, and the XO and watching the progress of other ships conducting UNREP at the same time will help the OOD to call the right time. During the process the OOD must make sure that critical functions such as navigation and communication are being correctly carried out. Of utmost importance also is a plan for the ship's movement following UNREP. The OOD should be alert for hints of problems in the areas of steering and propulsion. Anticipating possibilities is just as important as technical knowledge. In an emergency, all watchstanders must clearly understand their duties. Should there be a requirement to terminate an UNREP abruptly, an emergency breakaway can be conducted. The steps for this procedure are identical to a normal breakaway, but they are conducted in an accelerated manner. In the case of a RAS, the basic steps are:

1. Delivery ship ceases pumping.
2. Receiving ship releases probe.
3. Delivery ship retrieves probe.
4. Delivery ship de-tensions span wire.
5. Receiving ship trips the span wire *on delivery ship's signal.*

Safety note: A tensioned span wire must never be tripped—this could result in serious injury to personnel and damage to equipment.

PILOTS

> A pilot is merely an advisor to the commanding officer. The presence of a pilot on board shall not relieve the commanding officer or any subordinates from their responsibility for the proper performance of the duties with which they may be charged concerning the navigation and handling of the ship.
>
> NAVY REGULATIONS, ARTICLE 0856

Only in the following special circumstances does the presence of a pilot, even if he or she has the conn, relieve the CO of any responsibility for the safety of the ship: when a ship is entering a dry dock; when a ship is traversing the Panama Canal with a licensed canal pilot on board; and when a ship is required by the harbor master to move within a harbor while not under her own propulsion, using only tugs (dead stick). When a pilot is taken on board, the OOD should be sure that the bridge watch understands who has the conn and whose orders to the engine and the helm should be obeyed. Most pilots are accustomed to handling merchant ships, and frequently their commands to the helm and engines differ from standard naval commands. When this is the case, the CO should direct the OOD to relay the pilot's orders to the helm, using proper naval terminology. If possible, the pilot should be advised of the difference in power and speed between his or her orders and the OOD's. When ordering ahead dead slow, for example, the OOD rings up a one-third bell and advises the pilot how many knots the bell was for. As long as the captain, the pilot, and the OOD know how much power is being asked for, differences in terminology can be overcome. The same holds true for orders to the helm. Although pilots usually give orders in degrees of rudder, they often call for "hard rudder." The proper procedure in this case is to call on the helmsman for "full rudder" because this is the naval term for what the pilot means. It is a good idea to ensure the pilot understands how much rudder each standard command equates to. Additionally, ensuring the pilot is aware of the locations of the rudder angle indicators on the bridge will go a long way in reducing confusion as there will usually be a desire to monitor these frequently.

Most pilots are superb seamen and shiphandlers, and the best of them are only too pleased to share their knowledge. Often the CO leaves the conn with the OOD or JOOD and asks the pilot to act as an advisor to the OOD for the purpose of training. An OOD who is fortunate enough to be in this situation should take that opportunity to learn all he or she can.

Occasionally, especially in out-of-the-way places, a ship finds herself with a pilot who does not understand her characteristics or who simply does not come up to the professional standards the ship is accustomed to. In this case, the captain will normally take the conn and either modify the pilot's instructions or politely ignore them. The OOD must pay particular attention to what the helmsman and lee helmsman are doing because they can easily be confused as to which orders they should follow.

To avoid confusion or misunderstanding, a placard or pictures depicting the ship's physical characteristics and dimensions is an invaluable tool to help ensure the pilot completely understands the ship's overall length, beam, draft, masthead height, and configuration of running gear.

QUICK REFERENCE FOR THE WATCH OFFICER

Every watch officer needs to do a little mental arithmetic to get through a watch. While the maneuvering board, naval tactical data system, and whole CIC watch team are there to back the OOD up with detailed maneuvering solutions, it is useful to have a quick way to obtain initial courses, speeds, and distances, and to check solutions from other means. A few of the more common tricks include the following:

Three-Minute Rule. A ship will travel a distance equal to her speed in knots times one hundred yards every three minutes. Example: A ship going fifteen knots will cover fifteen hundred yards every three minutes.

Radian Rule. Every degree difference in bearing divided by sixty and multiplied by the range equals the horizontal separation. Example: A contact, dead in the water or on a reciprocal course, is three degrees off the bow of your ship at a range of two miles. You want to determine your CPA (horizontal separation) quickly. Multiply 3/60 times the range of two miles (four thousand yards) to obtain the CPA of two hundred yards.

Sliding-into-Station Rule. To slide into station, multiply the speed differential in knots times fifty yards for a steam plant and times twenty-five yards for a gas turbine. Example: You want to end up parallel to an oiler going sixteen knots. Your approach speed is twenty-three knots, or seven knots overspeed. For a steamship, you would want to cut engines and slide into station at seven times 50 yards, or about 350 yards short of her position. For a gas turbine, with its quicker response, multiply by twenty-five, or 175 yards. This value (50 yards per knot for a steamship and 25 yards per knot for gas-turbine ship) is the surge factor as defined at the beginning of the chapter.

Stopping the Ship. To stop within one length at five knots, back two-thirds; in two lengths at ten knots, back full. In all cases, if the objective is to get the way off the ship, go to back emergency/flank immediately.

Rule of Binoculars. A beam aspect frigate (FFG/FF) will fill the field of standard (7 × 50) binoculars at about three hundred yards, a cruiser/destroyer (CG/DDG) at about 350, and a carrier at about 450 yards.

Rule for Underway Replenishment. To make an approach at 120 feet (standard) or 150 feet (wide, in the case of a difficult course or inclement weather), bearing offset from the base course to the tangent of the side of the replenishment ship should be as follows at the given distances:

Range to Replenishment

Ship (yards)	120 feet	150 feet	180 feet
600	4 degrees	5 degrees	6 degrees
500	5 degrees	6 degrees	7.5 degrees

400	6 degrees	7.5 degrees	9 degrees
300	8 degrees	10 degrees	12 degrees
200	12 degrees	15 degrees	18 degrees

In other words, when six hundred yards from the replenishment ship with a course of 150 degrees as Romeo corpen (replenishment course), the starboard side of the replenishment ship should bear 146 degrees to effect a 120-foot approach, and 145 degrees to effect a 150-foot approach.

Distance to the Horizon. The distance to the horizon in nautical miles is 1.14 times the square root of the height of eye in feet. A few representative calculations include:

Height of Eye (feet)	Horizon (nautical miles)
50	8.1
75	9.9
85	10.5
100	11.4
110	12.0

Rule of Anchoring. A simple chart to cover the stopping times upon approaching an anchorage is as follows:

Yards to Berth	Steam	Gas Turbine
1,000	5 knots	10 knots
800	All stop	
500		5 knots
250	Back 1/3	All stop
100		Back 1/3
When backing	Drop	Drop

Scope Guide. The scope of chain required to be veered for winds at a level of less than force seven is as follows:

Water Depth (fathoms)	Chain (fathoms)
7	30
7 to 12	45
12 to 20	60

Also, a long-standing rule of thumb for the amount of chain to veer is five to seven times the depth of water. In the end, the more chain veered, the better the holding force, but the greater the swing and drag circles.

SOME QUICK RULES OF SHIPHANDLING

1. All conning orders must be given in a loud, clear, authoritative voice.
2. The conning officer should always be looking forward, not immersed in the administration of the watch or tied to a communications circuit.

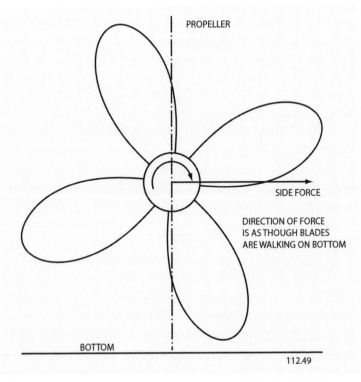

PROPELLER

SIDE FORCE

DIRECTION OF FORCE
IS AS THOUGH BLADES
ARE WALKING ON BOTTOM

BOTTOM

112.49

FIGURE 6-2. Side Force

3. Develop a practiced seaman's eye and strive to conn with rudder commands, not by giving courses. Remember, when the conning officer gives a rudder order, *he or she* controls the rudder; when the conning officer gives a course to steady on, the *helmsman* controls the rudder.

4. When approaching a pier, anchorage, or another ship, the conning officer should have both a plan to complete the evolution and an alternate plan.

5. Always be aware of the forces operating on the ship. One knot of current is the equivalent of thirty knots of wind.

6. Know how to use the anchor. It can save the ship in many difficult situations.

7. The ship's bow will turn into the wind if making way; if not making way, it may end up broadside to the wind. If backing, the ship, especially if she is single-screwed, will back into the wind.

8. Here are a few shiphandling points for UNREP:

    —A bow overtaking a stern will push the bow out.

    —While alongside, ships tend to move laterally toward each other.

    —When two sterns cross, they attract.

9. Engines have relative responsiveness; gas turbines are by far the fastest to respond to orders because the throttles in the pilothouse are directly connected to the engines. Diesels are fairly responsive. Steam plants are slow in responding.

10. When giving rudder/engine commands, generally follow the rule of thirty: The sum of rudder and engine speed should not exceed thirty unless you are willing to have the ship heel over hard—that is, 15 degrees rudder plus fifteen knots. At twenty-five knots, use only 5 degrees, and so forth.

11. Propellers will move the stern laterally as though they were touching the ground—that is, clockwise screw motion will turn the stern to starboard when viewed from astern. See figure 6.2.

12. Never take a chance with a ship for the sake of showmanship.

13. Ships do not back with precision.

14. Always bear in mind the direction to fair water when under way.

15. The conning officer should always physically sight the rudder angle indicator to make sure the helmsman puts the rudder over in the right direction. Likewise, the side of the turn should always be physically checked prior to the turn.

16. In a maneuver with another ship, the conning officer on the other vessel should be absolutely certain of any impending turn your vessel makes.

17. When you first sight a vessel on the horizon, immediately begin to take visual bearings to determine if there is bearing drift. If it appears to be slight, start a maneuvering board and compare solutions with the CIC.

18. Wind can help or hurt the problem. Think through the consequences of the wind's effect.

19. The most sensitive part of many modern ships is the bow, where the sonar dome is located.

20. When a ship is going ahead close to a bank or a seawall, the bow will be forced out and the stern sucked in. When the ship backs down, this tendency is reversed.

21. Never depend on a line, particularly for maneuvering a larger ship near a pier.

22. Before undertaking a demanding situation as a conning officer, review the applicable sections of standard shiphandling references. *Knight's Modern Seamanship* and Barber's *Naval Shiphandler's Guide* are some of the best.

23. Make up a file or a series of index cards with tactical data, ship's characteristics, engine orders, and the like for ready reference until you are fully familiar with the ship. Seek such information from the more senior officers.

24. When tugs are made up, take care not to overpower them with the ship's engines and rudder. Be careful of tugs' lines, and be aware of the time lag often required for a tug to position itself.

25. Enjoy having the conn and handle your ship with confidence and pleasure, always seeking to learn more.

7

SAFE NAVIGATION

The commanding officer is responsible for the safe navigation of his or her ship or aircraft, except as prescribed otherwise in these regulations for ships at a naval shipyard or station, in dry dock, or in the Panama Canal.

NAVY REGULATIONS, ARTICLE 0857

The winds and waves are always on the side of the ablest navigator.

EDWARD GIBBON

The officer of the deck shall be aware of the tactical situation and geographic factors which may affect safe navigation and take action to avoid the danger of grounding or collision in accordance with tactical doctrine, the U.S. Coast Guard Navigation Rules of the Road, and the orders of the Commanding Officer or other proper authority.

OPNAVINST 3120.32D

The naval profession is built upon a foundation of safe navigation at sea. Prudent mariners use multiple methods to fix the ship's position, cross-checking each to establish and validate where the ship has been. The meticulous process of accumulating positional information and plotting it on a chart (electronic or paper) is useful but of secondary importance. The primary responsibility of the navigator and OOD is to understand where the ship is going, to always be "one step ahead," understanding its expected travel and those forces that affect its movement.

Professional mariners develop practical experience through the application of fundamentals learned in the classroom to the tasks they perform at sea and, to a lesser extent, in simulators ashore. There is no substitute for the steady and deliberate growth of experience across a wide variety of environments. Young officers are well served by seeking assignments that offer extensive opportunity to develop depth and breadth of mariner experience. Nowadays it is common practice to account for practical hours gained by documenting watchstanding experiences in logbooks. Such tools provide an accounting for accreditation and licensure as well as establish a benchmark for building additional skills.

GROUNDINGS, ALLISIONS, AND COLLISIONS

Young officers are inclined to look upon accidents at sea as abstract events from which they personally are far removed. The attitude that "it can't happen to me" is particularly dangerous and misplaced, even in today's modern environment with the assistance of advanced tools and resources. On the contrary, the danger of collision, allision, and grounding is very real, a fact that has been painfully and tragically relearned over time. Such tragedies can usually be avoided by the intelligent application of the fundamental principles of good seamanship combined with good judgment and common sense.

Most collisions, allisions, and groundings are attributable to human error. The inescapable conclusion is that disaster results from carelessness, lack of good judgment, or ignorance. Most of the common errors listed below involve duties that are the responsibility of the navigator but of which the OOD should be cognizant. All too often the OOD gives in to the temptation to take a chance, to slop through the watch instead of expending energy in doing the job correctly. It does not take a master mariner to slow, stop, change course, or notify the captain and navigator whenever the ship's position is in doubt.

In response to several mishaps at sea, the U.S. Navy conducted a comprehensive review of incidents involving groundings, allisions, and collisions that occurred between 2007 and 2017. The analysis revealed numerous causal and contributing factors and underscored the importance of five broad themes:

Fundamentals. Maintaining basic skills in seamanship and navigation as well as rigor in individual qualification processes, proficiency, and adherence to existing standards.

Teamwork. The extent to which the surface force deliberately builds and sustains teams, and whether they are tested with realistic and challenging scenarios.

Operational safety. The processes and tools by which ships are made ready for tasking and are employed, and by which technology is used to safely operate at sea.

Assessment. The extent to which ships and headquarters plan, critically self-assess, generate actionable lessons learned, and share knowledge across the force.

Culture. The sum of the values, goals, attitudes, customs, and beliefs that define identity and influence the conduct of work.

Analysis of collisions, allisions, and groundings show that one or more of the thirteen causal and contributing factors were made.

1. Noncompliance with safe navigational practices (fundamentals).
   - Failure of the OOD to notify the captain and the navigator as soon as he or she doubts safety or position.
   - Improper application of known gyro error.
   - Failure to use dead-reckoning plot effectively.
   - Failure to take fixes frequently enough.
   - Failure to fix position by distance run between successive bearings when only one landmark was identified.
   - Failure to use Fathometer and line of soundings.
   - Failure to adjust course to remain on the dead-reckoning track.
   - Poor judgment in evaluating the effects of wind and tide.
   - Failure to account for set and drift and to apply the proper course correction.
   - Making a radical change in course (deliberate or accidental) without informing ships in the vicinity.
   - Too much reliance on nonfixed aids to navigation, such as buoys.
2. Incorrect action in extremis (fundamentals).
   - Failure of crews and commanders to quickly recognize and respond to unfolding risks of collision.

- Failure to stop and assess the situation or take emergency action when doubt of safe position first arose.
- Failure to respond deliberately and effectively when in extremis.
- Injudicious use of the ship's power.
- Failure to understand the tactical characteristics of the ship.

3. Substandard proficiency of bridge and CIC watchstanders (fundamentals).

    - Failure to adequately train personnel for the task.
    - Failure of watchstanders to perform a specific required action or protocol that they had been trained, qualified, and certified to perform.

4. Substandard risk management and planning (operational safety, assessment).

    - Failure to plan for safety and recognize the risks associated with operations in demanding environments.
    - Laying down the ship's intended track too close to known shoal water or over water too shallow for the ship's draft.
    - Failure to plot danger and turn bearings on the chart ahead of time.
    - Failure to have available the latest Notice to Mariners concerning temporary dislocation of aids to navigation.

5. Substandard bridge and CIC coordination (teamwork).

    - Failure to realize in time that there was a risk of collision.
    - Reliance on the CIC and consequent failure to make a sound evaluation of the situation on the bridge.
    - Failure of the CIC and the bridge to ensure that the conning officer understood tactical signals.

6. Substandard CIC performance (fundamentals).

    - Reliance on the CIC and consequent failure to make a sound evaluation of the situation on the bridge.

7. Inadequate use and understanding of technology (fundamentals).

    - Insufficient level of knowledge and failure to use navigation tools.
    - Reliance on radar navigation alone.
    - Failure to adjust radar settings for environmental conditions.
    - Failure to use installed automatic radar plotting aids (ARPA) effectively.

8. Practice of not using AIS (operational safety, assessment).
   - Failure to activate AIS in congested waterways as a means to share position, course, and speed information with ships operating in close vicinity.

9. Substandard use of lookouts (fundamentals, operational safety).
   - Failure of bridge personnel to keep a sharp visual lookout.
   - Failure to use visible aids to navigation properly.
   - Failure to check for steady bearing (visually or electronically) in a closing situation until too late.
   - Failure to use maneuvering boards, alidades, or bearing circles.
   - Misidentification of lights and other fixed aids to navigation.

10. Watch bill execution (culture).
    - Failure to comply with approved watch bills.
    - Inadequate watchstanding procedures for accommodating temporary reliefs resulting in key personnel not being on station or unapproved personnel on watch.

11. Poor log keeping (fundamentals).
    - Nonstard use of terminology, indicative of poor watchstanding formality and the erosion of discipline.
    - Failure of leadership to conduct formal reviews of log keeping information that could have prevented issues before they emerged.

12. Ineffective shipboard training programs (operational safety, assessment).
    - Failure to maintain a rigorous training regimen that establishes and maintains high standards.
    - Failure to maintain adequate level of knowledge among watchstanders.
    - Failure to train individuals on unique equipment configurations on the bridge and CIC.
    - Inadequate oversight and approval of training.
    - The absence of documentation of training conducted.

13. Inadequate fatigue management (culture).
    - Failure to manage fatigue when transitioning from ashore to at-sea watch rotations.
    - Failure to implement circadian watch bills or to align shipboard routines when implementing circadian watch rotations.

In addition to identifying broad areas for improvement and causal and contributing factors, six traits were identified as common among each of the mishap ships:

1. Someone decided not to or did not perform a specific required action or protocol that they had been trained, qualified, and certified to perform.
2. The ship, crew, or watch team had a previous near miss in often similar circumstances, but no explicit action was taken to correct potential causes.
3. Poor log keeping for the entire duration of the period examined by investigators.
4. Ineffective risk identification and mitigation in operational and daily planning.
5. Lack of watch team coordination.
6. Mishap ships were generally regarded as above average performers prior to the mishap.

Most of these mistakes are elementary and—although it is hard to believe that able, intelligent officers would make them—discouragingly common. It does not require genius to stand a proficient deck watch, but it does require vigilance, alertness, a highly developed sense of responsibility, and good judgment.

Most of these mistakes are discussed further along in this book; the others need little elaboration.

NAVIGATION IN THE ELECTRONIC AND INFORMATION AGE

There are many new electronic navigation systems entering the fleet. Most are built around the global positioning system (GPS), which takes highly accurate input from a constellation of satellites and provides precise positioning data to ships. The set of standards adopted by the International Maritime Organization to baseline electronic charting developments and their integration with GPS is generically termed Electronic Chart Display and Information System (ECDIS). The concept is based on the use of a direct feed from GPS and the ship's inertial systems (gyros) to display position, course, and speed on an electronically displayed "chart." The ECDIS-Navy or ECDIS-N includes additional requirements for Navy ships and is widely used across the fleet. The Voyage Management System (VMS) is the U.S. Navy's system for ECDIS-N. VMS is one of the latest specific automated navigation systems in use, and it is employed in most U.S. Navy ships. As mentioned above, it incorporates a chart database with both GPS and ship's gyros as inputs. The software also includes a variety of drop-down menus and options for system monitoring, navigation, chart features, and track-related calculations. Many variants of VMS also incorporate radar feeds and surface contact track data to assist with shipping information. When using these systems, however, it is imperative to fully understand how they receive their position data, from what sources, and the reliability of that data. Monitoring system inputs and understanding the "quality of the fix" is critical to safe navigation. A prudent mariner will always seek additional sources of information to either reinforce or reject automated positional information. There are also inexpensive, small versions of these electronic chart systems available through commercial outlets, costing from a few hundred to a few thousand dollars, and functional on laptop computers. Many ships are installing such systems and using them as a "back check" to the traditional paper, pencil, and charts that have now been used for centuries on ships at sea.

GPS is a powerful tool that provides accuracy from two to seven meters in most cases, although there are still some areas of the world where accuracy is reduced. They are annotated in the publications accompanying the GPS systems. The accuracy of GPS is measured as GPS figure of merit (FOM) on a scale between 1 (the most accurate) and 9 (the least accurate). GPS is easy to use, extremely reliable, and readily accessible. Backups, in the form of emergency navigation laptops (ENL) and handheld GPS receivers, are also common on all U.S. Navy ships as well. All in all, GPS and the associated electronic navigation systems have much to recommend them.

However, as a result of the electronic aids, it is increasingly easy to overlook some of the real essentials of navigation and piloting, such as the geometry behind the visual fix, the correct use of dead reckoning (DR), and close coordination between the bridge and the CIC. The basics—use of the radian rule, calculation and understanding of gyro error, using celestial navigation, teamwork, and communications—cannot be replaced by a new GPS system and a set of electronic charts.

DEAD-RECKONING PLOT

In the days before electronics, when good fixes were rare, hard to get, and highly valued, the dead-reckoning plot was one of a navigator's most important aids. It still is, despite the conveniences of technology.

When a ship's actual position is in doubt, a DR plot (modified, if necessary, by known factors, such as the current) is the best estimate of that position. A good navigator has either the actual or the DR position of the ship instantly available at all times. The mechanics of navigating—the accumulation of fixes that show where the ship has been—is of secondary importance. A navigator's primary duty is to know where the ship is going, not where she has been. A DR plot should cover at least the next two fix intervals and always be maintained on the chart in use. If ECDIS-N is in use, vectors from ownship are automatically generated, but the display must be properly set up based on the desired fix interval.

The "Six Rules of DR" state when a DR position must be plotted:

1. Every hour on the hour.
2. Every course change.
3. Every speed change.
4. Every fix or running fix.
5. Every line of position.
6. From each fix or running fix (plot a new course).

SUMMARY OF FIX ACCURACIES AND INTERVALS

Area	Distance from Land	Accuracy	Recommended Interval
Restricted waters	< 2 NM	50 yds	3 min
Piloting waters	2–10 NM	100 yds	3–15 min
Coastal waters	10–30 NM	500 yds	15 min
En route navigation	> 30 NM	1500 yds	30 min

RADAR NAVIGATION

Radar has become internationally accepted as a primary means of fixing a ship's position in restricted and coastal waters. Properly used, radar permits ships to

SYMBOL	DESCRIPTIVE LABLE	MEANING
⊙	FIX	An accurate position determined without reference to any previous position. Established by visual or celestial observations.
△ (with dot)	FIX	A relatively accurate position, determined by electronic means. This symbol is also used for a fix when simultaneously fixing by two means, e.g., visual and radar/navigation fixes, without reference to any former position.
⌒•	DR	Dead reckon position. Advanced from a previous position or fix. Course and speed are reckoned without allowance for wind or current.
▢•	EP	Estimated position. Is the most probable position of a vessel, determined from data of questionable accuracy, such as applying estimated current and wind corrections to a DR position.

FIGURE 7-1. Navigation Plotting Symbols

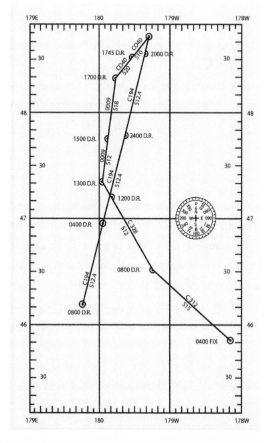

FIGURE 7-2.
Plotting DR Position

navigate safely at greater distances from land and under worse weather conditions than traditional visual methods. The danger is that it is so easy to navigate by radar that a false sense of security, a precursor to disaster, is likely to be created.

The OOD's responsibility for safe navigation is in no way lessened by the fact that the CIC or the quartermaster is navigating by radar. The clear radar pictures that some topographies provide can be deceptive; radar sometimes yields fixes that look accurate but are in fact miles wide of the ship's position. This is especially so in areas where the shoreline is low and sandy and the terrain behind it rises gradually. Furthermore, the clarity of a radar picture can change as a ship's position changes, and a feature that stands out clearly from one angle may begin to "break up" or disappear altogether when seen from another angle. If this happens when a ship is approaching a turn bearing and no dead-reckoning plot or other navigational tools have been applied, she can easily lose her bearings and get into trouble.

When radar is being used in close or restricted waters, it should be cross-checked with whatever other aid to navigation is available. The bridge and the CIC should always lay out the same track, take fixes at the same time, and constantly compare fixes. In this way differences in the ship's position can be discovered and action taken before it is too late. The importance of the relationship between the CIC and the bridge can never be overstressed, especially regarding navigation.

CELESTIAL NAVIGATION

Since the introduction of GPS for commercial use in the 1980s, the use of celestial navigation by mariners has decreased. GPS technology continues to be relied upon for military as well as commercial use and is available in a wide range of products from complex shipboard weapons systems to small, wearable technology. A discussion on the use of celestial bodies such as the sun, moon, and stars for navigation in the age of information may seem antiquated. However, the reliability and availability of GPS is not assured particularly in a casualty environment.

Ample reference material is readily available online, in books, and in curricula designed to teach celestial navigation, and the topic is included in many

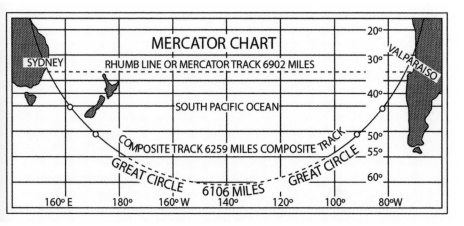

FIGURE 7-3. Rhumb Line and Great Circle Course on a Mercator Chart

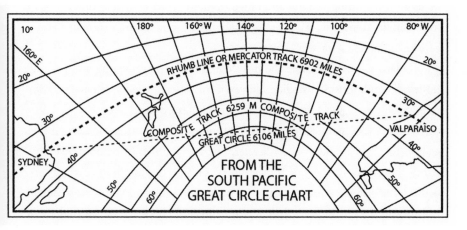

FIGURE 7-4. Rhumb Line and Great Circle Course on a Great Circle Chart

navigation courses. The basic premise relies on the use of a sextant to measure the observed angle of a celestial body in order to derive the altitude, then comparing that sight with a known benchmark reference typically derived from the *Nautical Almanac*, which lists the geographical position for the sun, moon, and many other celestial bodies by hour, day, and year. Additional calculations are necessary to compensate for errors such as declination, altitude, and refraction index.

Celestial navigation skill is an important tool to have in your navigation arsenal and one that should be exercised regularly in order to maintain proficiency. If the need arises to fall back on celestial navigation skills due to unavailability of GPS, you will want to be able to fall back comfortably and reliably.

PILOTING

Piloting is the act of navigating in restricted waters using existing geographic or hydrographic features to frequently fix the ship's position. Land features and navigation aids such as buoys, day shapes, range markers, and lights are marked visually by recording bearings from multiple objects or points of land and plotting those bearing lines on a chart. The intersection of the bearing lines constitutes a fix. Radar navigation is also used in piloting, which provides the added benefits of providing bearing and range from an object as well as operations in low visibility. However, weather, radar sensitivity, and shifting shoreline structure are potential detractors.

Radar has made possible the most complicated maneuvering and piloting under all conditions of visibility. However, this does not reduce in any way the responsibilities of a CO. Extensive use of radar has led many inexperienced officers to think they can neglect the older and more reliable means of safeguarding a ship. Radar is an aid against disaster, not a guarantee. In reduced visibility, either the OOD or the JOOD should be outside the pilothouse, using binoculars and listening for fog signals. "Radarscope fixation" must be avoided. Aviators are taught to scan their instruments and check the air around them constantly. They are warned never to become fixed on one instrument for too long. The OOD should develop the same habits. Rather than become anchored at a radar repeater or at the centerline pelorus, he or she should be constantly on the move, checking both bridge wings and the area astern of the ship and periodically scanning the radar repeaters.

The timely use of navigational lights in low visibility or during uncertain or dangerous maneuvering, whether during exercises or actual operations, is also proper. Running-light switch panels should be kept set up, and bridge personnel should be drilled in turning them on quickly.

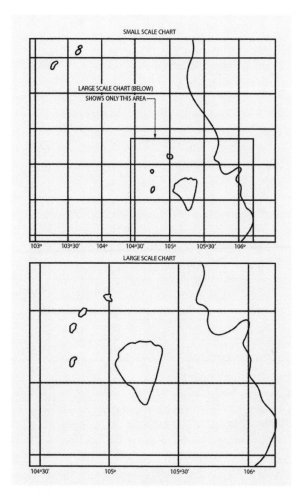

FIGURE 7-5. Small- and Large-Scale Charts

An OOD must understand the capabilities, limitations, and settings of the ship's radars. He or she should know how to operate all the remote-control gear, who is responsible for the maintenance of radar, and how to reach them in a hurry. The OOD should ensure the radars are fully functional, set up as the environmental condition and navigation situation dictates, and available for use consistent with the established emissions-control (EMCON) condition in effect. This is especially important before dark, in higher sea states, when fog descends, and when it begins to rain or snow.

TABLE 7-1 Distance of Visibility of Objects at Various Elevations above Sea Level

HEIGHT IN FEET	DISTANCE IN GEOGRAPHIC OR NAUTICAL MILES	HEIGHT IN FEET	DISTANCE IN GEOGRAPHIC OR NAUTICAL MILES	HEIGHT IN FEET	DISTANCE IN GEOGRAPHIC OR NAUTICAL MILES
1	1.1	31	6.4	100	11.4
2	1.6	32	6.5	105	11.7
3	2.0	33	6.6	110	12.0
4	2.3	34	6.7	115	12.3
5	2.6	35	6.8	120	12.5
6	2.8	36	6.9	125	12.8
7	3.0	37	7.0	130	13.0
8	3.2	38	7.1	135	13.3
9	3.4	39	7.1	140	13.5
10	3.6	40	7.2	145	13.8
11	3.8	41	7.3	150	14.0
12	4.0	42	7.4	160	14.5
13	4.1	43	7.5	170	14.9
14	4.3	44	7.6	180	15.3
15	4.4	45	7.7	190	15.8
16	4.6	46	7.8	200	16.2
17	4.7	47	7.8	210	16.6
18	4.9	48	7.9	220	17.0
19	5.0	49	8.0	230	17.3
20	5.1	50	8.1	240	17.7
21	5.2	55	8.5	250	18.1
22	5.4	60	8.9	260	18.4
23	5.5	65	9.2	270	18.8
24	5.6	70	9.6	280	19.1
25	5.7	75	9.9	290	19.5
26	5.8	80	10.2	300	19.8
27	5.9	85	10.5	310	20.1
28	6.1	90	10.9	320	20.5
29	6.2	95	11.5	330	20.8
30	6.3				

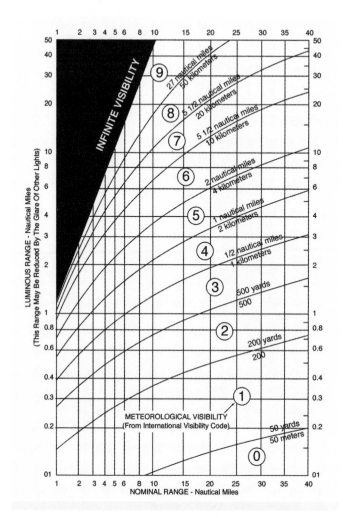

FIGURE 7-6.
Luminous Range
Diagram

It is important to use surface-search radar in poor visibility. At night and when visibility is reduced, radar repeaters on the bridge and in the CIC should generally be on different ranges. Toggling between range scales in order to identify small contacts close-in as well as contacts farther ahead is often necessary in high density shipping environments. Surface-search radars should be kept energized when a ship is under way (but not necessarily emitting when operating under restrictive EMCON conditions), and they should be checked and calibrated at intervals. Keeping all radar repeaters, both in the CIC and on the bridge, on the same range is dangerous because it can lead to concentration on the immediate area at the expense of detecting contacts in the distance, or vice versa. It should be noted that the courts have held the failure of a government vessel to make use of radar while under way in low visibility to have contributed directly to a collision. This philosophy appears in rule 2 of the International Regulations for Preventing Collisions at Sea, which states: "Nothing in these rules shall exonerate any vessel, or the owner, master, or crew thereof, from the consequences of any neglect to comply with these rules or of the neglect of any precaution which may be required by the ordinary practice of seamen, or by the special circumstances of the case."

LOOKOUTS

> Every vessel shall at all times maintain a proper lookout by sight and hearing as well as by all available means appropriate in the prevailing circumstances and conditions so as to make a full appraisal of the situation and the risk of collision.
>
> INTERNATIONAL REGULATIONS FOR PREVENTING COLLISIONS AT SEA, RULE 5

International Regulations for Preventing Collisions at Sea, commonly known as the rules of the road, specifies clearly that a lookout must be both looking and listening. This is an important point because many lookouts are not aware that, even under normal steaming conditions, they have a responsibility to maintain a watch by sight and sound. In low visibility, the duty of the lookout to report what he or she hears is especially important; the lookout should be provided with a telephone talker so that he or she can concentrate on listening for fog signals. A lookout who is wearing headphones when charged with listening for signals is *not* standing a proper watch.

Lookouts should not be trained by casual instruction from their peers or by a so-called break-in watch. They should be included in a formal qualification program that includes training in reporting procedures, recognition and identification, and the use of sound-powered telephones. A lookout should be encouraged to report everything seen, even floating material, and his or her reports should always be acknowledged. If they are not acknowledged, the lookout may begin to think that his or her efforts are wasted and subsequently not report anything. Lookouts should be rotated as frequently as possible, at least hourly. When the weather is bad, they should be the first members of the watch to be issued foul-weather gear, and they should be relieved as often as necessary. In extremely cold or windy weather, a lookout's efficiency drops to almost zero after half an hour of duty. Of note, bridge watch officers have the added responsibility of functioning as additional lookouts in the performance of their duties on the bridge.

Frequent compass checks of the bearings of all closing ships are essential. They are the best and most important means of preventing collisions at sea. In low visibility, bearings should be checked by radar. A steady bearing with decreasing range means that collision is imminent. Even a slowly changing bearing is warning of a dangerous situation. Action must be taken. This means notifying the captain if time permits, changing course, or stopping and backing.

MANEUVERING BOARDS

One skill the capable watch officer must polish is processing contact information via the maneuvering board, or "mo board." Despite the increasing use of combat system and computer-generated maneuvering solutions, the use of the maneuvering board and dividers will not disappear, nor should it be allowed to. Whenever a contact is perceived to pose a risk of collision, the competent watch officer will see that a maneuvering board solution is prepared both in the pilothouse and in the CIC, should the ship be manned for that.

In fact, many COs order that a maneuvering board solution be worked on any contact with a closest point of approach (CPA) of less than some set distance, perhaps five thousand yards. The reasons for doing so are plain. When the watch officer has to plot position and calculate true course and speed, CPA, and all the other information available on the maneuvering board, he or she is paying full attention to contact situations. In an age of machine-generated solutions on cathode-ray tubes, large-screen and flat-screen displays, a maneuvering board solution gives a comforting sense of indispensable human input.

The intent in this brief section is not to provide a detailed description of how to do the "mo board." Those skills are well taught in precommissioning programs and in the qualification process the typical watch officer undergoes after earning a commission. Rather, the objective is to provide a few salient examples in maneuvering board format of the most common problems faced by the watchstander: the true course or speed and CPA of a nonmaneuvering contact, true wind, stationing, and maneuvering to adjust CPA, among others. For the watch officer who already has a basic understanding of the maneuvering board, these examples serve as a quick reference.

Whenever working a maneuvering board, it is important to be precise and consistent with measurements taken from both the radar and the dividers on the maneuvering board itself. Here are a few general pointers:

1. Use the largest scale possible for speed and distance and try to use the same scale for both. Use the same scales throughout each problem.
2. Be careful and double-check yourself.
3. Work in true bearings, not relative.
4. Label all points and use arrowheads to indicate direction.
5. At least three "cuts" are required on each contact before an accurate solution can be determined.

THE NAVIGATOR AND THE OOD

In addition to those duties prescribed by regulation for the head of a department, he or she will be responsible, under the Commanding Officer, for the safe navigation and piloting of the ship. The navigator will receive all orders relating to his or her navigational duties directly from the Commanding Officer and will make all reports in connection therewith directly with the Commanding Officer. . . . The duties of the navigator will include advising the Commanding Officer and the Officer of the Deck as to the ship's movements, and if the ship is running into danger, as to the safe course to be steered.

OPNAVINST 3120.32D

The navigator and the OOD share responsibility for knowing the navigational situation of a ship. When the navigator is on the bridge, he or she is usually doing the actual navigation and recommending to the OOD changes in course and speed to make good a track or to keep the ship out of danger. Nevertheless, the OOD has the responsibility, in the words of the regulation, to "take appropriate

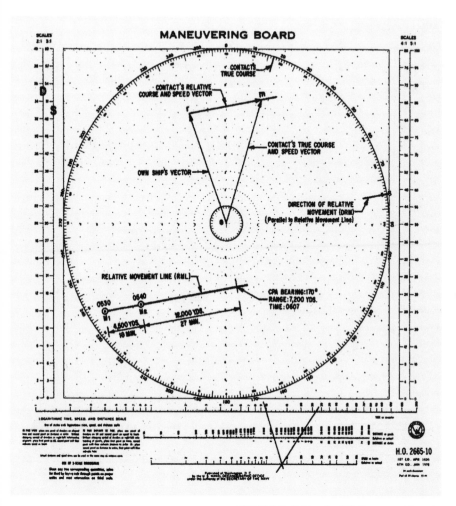

FIGURE 7-7. Solving for CPA Course and Speed
(Source: QM2, Navy Rate Training Manual, 1986, pp. 5–8)

action" to ensure the safety of the ship. When the navigator and the OOD do not agree on the course of action to be taken, the navigator may, if authorized in writing to do so, relieve the OOD. The navigator must, however, immediately inform the CO that he or she has done so. This very rare situation is not likely to develop if both the navigator and the OOD understand and are paying attention to the navigation of the ship. It is likely to arise if the OOD is taking

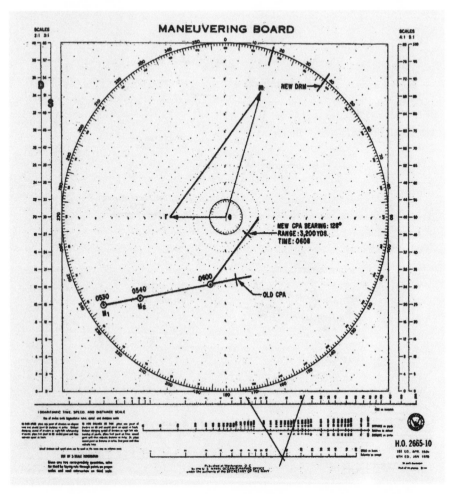

FIGURE 7-8. Solving for CPA Course and Speed
(Source: QM2, Navy Rate Training Manual, 1986, pp. 5–11)

little interest in the navigation because the navigator or an assistant is on the bridge and doing the navigating. The navigator's position as the authoritative advisor on the safe navigation of the ship does not relieve the OOD of any responsibility.

Additionally, because of the navigator's unique responsibility for safe navigation at all times, the OOD should keep that person informed of anything that may be pertinent. The OOD should never hesitate to consult the navigator, day or night, on questions about safe navigation.

Checking the gyro should be the concern of the OOD and navigator. Gyrocompasses, while increasingly precise and reliable, can develop large errors, and the only way to detect them quickly is to be aware at all times of the relationship between the gyro and the magnetic compass. The QMOW logs the readings of both in a compass record book. He or she should know the importance of this routine chore. When a gyro error has been detected and measured, it must be applied to the course to be steered *in the right direction.* A useful mnemonic device is, "Compass least, error east, and compass best, error west." When converting from gyro to true, add easterly and [subtract] westerly, that is, $G + E = T$.

When a ship is in formation, the OOD routinely makes the course and speed changes dictated by the tactical situation and not directly related to the safe navigation of the ship. The OOD should nevertheless inform the navigator of any such changes other than minor alterations necessary to maintain station. He or she should also ensure that the ECDIS vectors (or DR plot, if on paper charts) reflect accurate course and speed changes. This should be done even when a ship changes station. A ship's change of station from one side to the other of a large formation can have a significant effect on her geographical position.

BRIDGE RESOURCE MANAGEMENT

OODs are managers of systems and processes, both machine and human. There are numerous systems onboard a modern bridge: radar, electronic navigation tools, communications gear, Fathometer, lights, flags and day shapes, maneuvering boards, and many other tools of the trade. Each ship is configured and outfitted with a unique fingerprint of equipment and gear. Even among ship of the same class, there will be considerable variation in equipment onboard. The navigator and OODs must be implicitly familiar with the settings and operation of all equipment on the bridge. In addition to proficiency on systems, the human element—the orchestration of individuals among the team—must also be actively managed.

For these and many other reasons, bridge watch team members periodically participate in mandatory bridge resource management (BRM) training, which is usually conducted in both a classroom and a simulator. BRM is the study of all the resources (tools, systems, processes) available to the navigator and OOD as well as of the use of those tools in an optimum manner. BRM training focuses on reviewing the rules of the road, key watch team responsibilities, and the effective interaction of all team members in safely piloting a ship factoring traffic and environmental conditions (wind, current, visibility). Whenever possible, BRM training should include elements from the CIC team as well as bridge watchstanders. The purpose is to ensure that bridge and CIC watch teams function as a cohesive unit. Key elements of BRM training can vary but generally include the following:

Human Factors

Most mishaps are attributed to human error. BRM includes an emphasis on those human factors that influence an individual's ability to perform. These factors can range from the psychological issues to physiological medical conditions such as being "under the weather" to social stressors such as interpersonal relationships. Training proficiency, currency, and experience are also factors that influence human performance. Every seasoned OOD can recall their first watch and how they carried the heavy burden of responsibility incumbent in their new position.

Individual risk management tools to account for rest, experience, and complexity (such as weather and nonstandard equipment configurations) are in use across the fleet. In addition, some ships implement "human factors councils" to address organizational concerns. BRM training on human factors enables teams to be more aware of how human factors impact performance.

Voyage Planning

A safe voyage begins long before leaving the pier. Effective planning involves the collection of pertinent information about the transit, building a plan, and briefing it prior to execution. Unit characteristics such as—draft, length, beam, and vessel height as well as handling characteristics such as advance and transfer at various speeds should be considered in the voyage plan. Aids to navigation should be considered and validated against the latest Notice to Mariners. Expected conditions, weather, tides and currents, wind, and visibility each should be factored into the plan. Contingency plans that provide expected actions in the event of an emergency should also be discussed. Safe anchorage areas, water depth, bottom type, and channel widths are but a few of the many considerations that go into an effective voyage plan.

Once a plan is built, particularly those involving special evolutions, it should be briefed to all the individuals who will be on watch during the evolution. Special evolutions briefs are an important mechanism for developing a shared mental model of what is expected to happen. Often young officers tend to view pre-evolution briefs as meant for the CO and senior leadership. On the contrary, these briefs are meant for those in the audience in order to establish a common reference for what is going to happen and when. This way all personnel will know where and when key activity will take place, such as when the tugs will be made up, where the pilot will embark, or when small boats will be recovered. The shared mental model generated by the brief has the additional benefit of helping prevent single-point failures and empowering forceful backup among watchstanders. A strong plan that is well briefed will create a team more readily able to respond to changes and identify emerging safety concerns.

Standardized Procedures

Standardized procedures provide a framework for accomplishing tasks the same way every time. The Convention on the International Regulations for Preventing Collisions at Sea (COLREGS), or "rules of the road," are essentially a set of standardized procedures that govern the conduct of vessels at sea. There are numerous other standardized procedures that govern conduct onboard ships. For example, the CO's standing orders establish the circumstances under which the CO must be notified or specific permissions obtained. The CO's night orders supplement the CO's standing orders by providing additional guidance and special instructions. Checklists are also used extensively on board ships to ensure completeness and correctness of action. Checklists exist for entering port or getting under way, prior to conducting underway replenishment and taking on fuel, conducting wet well-deck operations, entering conditions of low visibility, or even simple inventories of equipment. Each are a form of standardized procedures that help ships operate effectively every time. The OOD should be very familiar with each of the checklists that pertain to navigation and seamanship.

USS VALLEY FORGE (CG-50) NIGHT ORDERS

FROM:_____ TO: _____ TIME ZONE:_____

OTC/XB _____	XV _____
XW _____	XC_____
XX_____	XY _____
XS _____	XT_____
XN_____	XD _____
XL _____	XH _____
XP _____	XK _____
XR _____	XU _____
XJ_____	SQ_____
FOTC_____	AFOTC_____

TACTICAL DATA

FORMATION _____ GUIDE_____

BASE COURSE_____ SPEED _____

STATION ASSIGNMENT _____

_____

PLANT STATUS

1A 1B	1 2 3		2A 2B
2A 2B	4 5 6	1 2 3	3A 3B
ENGINES	FIRE PUMPS	GENERATORS	400HZ CONV.

SUNRISE_____ SUNSET _____ MOONRISE_____ MOONSET_____

FORECAST: _____

_____

MANUEVERING INSTRUCTIONS: _____

_____

_____

_____

_____

_____

_____

FIGURE 7-9. Captain's night orders

Situational Awareness and Voyage Monitoring

Situational awareness is the state of knowing what is happening around you. Because the maritime environment is constantly changing, maintaining situational awareness throughout a watch or voyage requires continuous effort. As time passes, so too does your situational awareness. Thus, bridge watchstanders as well as those in the CIC must continuously gather and process information to re-establish situational awareness. Are we fully aware of all contacts and navigation hazards in our vicinity? Do we know the current status of our systems and settings, and are they appropriate for the environmental conditions? Is my radar on the appropriate range and environmental setting? Have the weather, currents, or tides changed? What is the set and drift, and is the ship's heading appropriate? Each of these questions and more contribute to continuously maintaining situational awareness at sea. BRM study focuses on developing effective processes for gathering and assessing information in order to establish a clear picture of what is happening within and around the ship.

Stress, Complacency, and Distraction

Psychological factors such as stress, complacency, and distraction can affect watchstanding performance. Ensuring that you and your shipmates are mentally prepared, trained, and ready for the task is part of your responsibility as OOD. Periods of stress should be expected. What is important is not simply that stress will occur but how your team acknowledges and copes with it. Workload sharing is one method to ensure that no single individual is overwhelmed. This might include bringing additional personnel to the bridge or CIC in order to further share workload when tasks become more complex. One caution is appropriate here, as having too many personnel on the bridge or other control station can be a dangerous distraction as well.

During World War II, Fleet ADM Chester W. Nimitz, in a letter to the Pacific Fleet, stressed the impact that psychological factors can have on safe navigation:

> There are certain psychological factors which have fully as much to do with safety at sea as any of the more strictly technical ones. A large proportion of the disasters in tactics and maneuvers comes from concentrating too much on one objective or urgency, at the cost of not being

sufficiently alert for others. Thus, absorption with enemy craft already under fire has led to being torpedoed by others not looked for or not given attention; while preoccupation with navigation, with carrying out the particular job in hand, or with avoiding some particular vessel or hazard, has resulted in collision with ships to whose presence we were temporarily oblivious. There is no rule that can cover this except the ancient one that eternal vigilance is the price of safety, no matter what the immediate distractions.

No officer, whatever his rank and experience, should flatter himself that he is immune to the inexplicable lapses in judgment, calculation, and memory, or to the slips of the tongue in giving orders, which throughout seagoing history have so often brought disaster to men of the highest reputation and ability. Where a mistake in maneuvering or navigating can spell calamity, an officer shows rashness and conceit, rather than admirable self-confidence, in not checking his plan with someone else before starting it, if time permits. This is not yielding to another's judgment; it is merely making sure that one's own has not "blown a fuse" somewhere, as the best mental and mechanical equipment in the world has sometimes done.

Communications

Communication entails the effective and complete transfer of information from one person or group to another. Communications as it pertains to BRM involves the proper use of communications tools and the sharing of critical information both within and outside the lifelines of the ship. For example, BRM offers a training environment to practice effective and timely VHF radio communications with other vessels to establish agreement on maneuvering. Similarly, using standardized commands for shiphandling, establishing formality of reports within a watch team, and practicing verbatim repeat-backs are each important focus areas of BRM training.

Fatigue

Fatigue is often listed as one of many contributing factors in mishaps at sea. Numerous scientific studies have established that sleep deprivation results in poor decision making, impaired judgment, and decreased communication. The U.S. Navy has implemented the use of circadian watchbills (outlined in chapter 5) to combat the effects of cumulative fatigue on board U.S. Navy ships. BRM training focuses on recognizing the signs of sleep deficit as well as offering tools and processes to mitigate the negative effects of fatigue.

Pilot Integration

The use of a harbor pilot is now mandatory for many ships. BRM training on pilot integration ensures that bridge teams are able to quickly and effectively integrate the expertise of harbor pilots who have extensive training and knowledge of the local area. OODs should ensure that pilots are provided general information on ship specifications, maneuverability capabilities and constraints, and engineering configuration. In addition, the CO will establish with the pilot how maneuvering orders will be carried out. Training also reinforces the role of the pilot as a consultant to the CO, who retains responsibility and accountability for the safety of the vessel (except in special circumstances such as dry-docking).

Teamwork

The importance of teamwork cannot be overstated. One of the most significant overall causes of collisions is the failure of the bridge and the CIC to check each other's actions through a systematic approach to comparing maneuvering board solutions, fixes, and tactical signals. If the CIC and the bridge work together and check each other, very few problems emerge.

Error Chains

Mishaps typically involve numerous errors that each contributed to a failure. In most circumstances, just eliminating one error would have broken the error chain and prevented a disaster. The study of error chains using case studies is a vital part of BRM training. By heightening awareness of how failures emerged in the past, BRM training offers a path to prevent future failures. All bridge watchstanders benefit from the careful study of the conditions under which mishaps and failures have occurred. In this way, teams are better equipped to break the error chain and prevent disasters before they occur.

As a watch officer, you must use all the tools at your disposal. You will find that in most situations you will be able to navigate your ship safely and easily with GPS and electronic charts. There will be many times, however, when you will be proud of your rigorous training program with high standards; you will be thankful your team participated in BRM training; you will be glad for the excellence of your piloting team and their visual fixes; you will be happy to have a written record of your track through a difficult channel; and you will understand that to stand a safe watch you must navigate using a wide variety of systems. Possessing a thorough understanding of navigation principles and the tools and skills to sail safely is a mariner's responsibility. Cutler's *Dutton's Nautical Navigation* is an outstanding comprehensive reference for naval officers as are many others. The text has been continuously updated to ensure currency with recent advances in navigation practices.

8

STANDARD COMMANDS

Each person on watch will . . . use phraseology customary to the service when issuing orders and taking reports.

OPNAVINST 3120.32D CH 1

Nowhere in the Navy are terminology and phraseology as important as in commands given by the conning officer to the helmsman or the lee helmsman. Because misunderstanding or ambiguity can so quickly lead to disaster, there must be no possibility of a command being misunderstood, and the formal use of widely understood standard terminology and phraseology is meant to prevent confusion. Shortcuts and individual variations are to be discouraged; all personnel who man ship-control stations should become accustomed to receiving their commands in the same format no matter the watch officer.

MANNER OF GIVING COMMANDS

Commands should be given in a clear voice, loud enough to be heard, and the tone should be incisive.

The word "helm" should not be used in any command relating to the operation of the rudder. Commands to the helmsman are given in a logical sequence. The first word is "right" or "left," which indicates the direction in which the helmsman is to put the wheel over. The second word indicates how far it is to be put over, for example, "Right *standard* rudder." The purpose of giving a command in this manner is to ensure quick and accurate compliance by the helmsman, who starts turning the wheel instantly upon hearing "right" or "left." By the time the amount of rudder has been specified, he or she can bring the rudder-angle indicator to rest on the exact number of degrees. One exception is when ordering hard rudder. In that case, the sequence is, "*Hard* right (left) rudder," indicating that the maximum rudder should be applied as rapidly as possible in the indicated direction.

Similarly, in a command to control the ship's propulsion, given to the lee helm, the first term, "port (starboard) engine" or "all engines," indicates to the operator which handles or knobs to move. The next word, "ahead" or "back," tells in which direction to move them. The last part of the command, "one-third," "full," and so on, gives the amount of the speed change and tells the operator where to stop his or her instrument. Standard commands to the engines are these:

1. "All engines ahead one-third (two-thirds, standard, full, flank)" or "All engines back one-third (two-thirds, full)."
2. "Starboard (port) engine, ahead one-third (two-thirds, standard, full)" or "Starboard (port) engine, back one-third (two-thirds, full)."

In an emergency, normal acceleration and deceleration tables are sometimes abandoned and orders are given for the ship to go ahead or back with all available power as quickly as possible. In such instances, the proper command is, "All engines ahead (back), emergency." On a steam-powered ship using an EOT, the operator should then ring up "ahead flank" (or "back full") three or more times in rapid succession.

The exact number of revolutions per minute to be made on each engine should be indicated to the engine room by the revolution indicator. If the number of revolutions desired is not the exact number for the speed ordered, the former must be specified: "*Indicate* one one seven revolutions (or rpm)." The word "revolutions" (or "rpm") should always be included in this order to prevent confusion with orders concerning course or bearings. When increasing or decreasing revolutions in small increments, the exact number of revolutions desired should also be stated, for instance, "Indicate one one seven revolutions," rather than "Up two" or "Take off three."

When practical, the number of revolutions desired should be ordered rather than the speed desired. This would not be practical if, for instance, the conning officer were on the wing of the bridge, unable to see or remember the revolutions required, and felt that he or she should not move. In such a situation, the conning officer should say, "Indicate turns for _____ knots," and require a report of the turns rung up as well as a repetition of the command. The turns-per-knot table should be memorized as soon as possible. The method of ordering speed may vary from ship to ship, even within a class so check the CO's standing orders upon reporting aboard and before conning.

One-third speed and two-thirds speed are one-third and two-thirds of the prescribed standard speed. The revolutions for these speeds are the number of revolutions per minute required to achieve those fractions of standard speed. Full speed and flank speed are greater than standard speed. They are usually based on fractional increments of standard speed. The rpm for these speeds are also those actually required to achieve them. When small adjustments in speed are desired, the only command usually necessary is the one ordering the change in revolutions. However, when revolutions are ordered that will result in a speed within a different increment, that increment should also be rung up on the EOT.

Most gas-turbine ships make use of an "integrated throttle control" or "programmed control lever" providing direct commands to the engines with the proper rpm and pitch combinations automatically factored for a given desired speed. On these ships, during normal underway operations, the helm and lee helm watch stations are often combined. During special evolutions, however, such as RAS, during sea and anchor detail, or during maneuvering drills, the watch stations are assigned to separate individuals for increased safety.

It is important that all commands be repeated loud and clear, just as they were given by the officer at the conn, by the helmsman, or by lee helmsman. This practice serves as a check on the officer who originated the command and provides an opportunity for correction of any slip of the tongue, such as "left" when "right" was meant.

It is equally important to require the person at the helm or lee helm to report when he or she has complied with the command. The conning officer must acknowledge this final report with, "Very well."

STEERING COMMANDS TO THE HELM

When a specific amount of rudder is desired:

Command: "Right full rudder (or right standard rudder)."

Reply: "Right full (standard) rudder, aye, sir (or ma'am)."

Report: "My rudder is right full (standard), sir (or ma'am)."

When the rudder order is given in degrees:

Command: "Left 10 degrees rudder."

Reply: "Left 10 degrees rudder, aye, sir (or ma'am)."

Report: "My rudder is left 10 degrees, sir (or ma'am)."

When the helmsman is to steady on a specific course:

Command: "Steady on course ___."

Reply: "Steady on course ___, sir (or ma'am)."

Report: "Steady on course ___, sir (or ma'am). Checking ___ magnetic."

When maximum possible rudder is required:

Command: "Hard right rudder."

Reply: "Hard right rudder, aye, sir (or ma'am)."

Report: "Rudder is hard right, sir (or ma'am)."

> *Note:* On some older rudder systems, the danger in using hard rudder lies in the possibility of jamming the rudder into the stops. For this reason, it is rarely used except in emergencies. If hard rudder is chosen when there is no emergency, the conning officer may reduce the possibility of jamming the rudder by first ordering full rudder and then increasing the rudder to hard, allowing the helmsman more control of the rudder's movement. On newer computer-assisted systems, the danger of jamming the rudder as a result of ordering the helm hard right (left) is minimal.

When the amount of rudder is to be increased:

Command: "Increase your rudder to (right full, right 10 degrees, etc.)."

Reply: "Increase my rudder to, sir (or ma'am)."

Report: "My rudder is (right full, right 10 degrees, etc.)."

When the amount of rudder is to be decreased:

Command: "Ease your rudder to _____ (standard, left 10 degrees, etc.)."

Reply: "Ease my rudder to _____, sir (or ma'am)."

Report: "My rudder is _____ (standard, left 10 degrees, etc.)."

When the rudder is increased or decreased while the ship is turning to an ordered course:

Command: "Right standard rudder, steady on course 270."

Reply: "Right standard rudder, steady on course 270, aye, sir (or ma'am)."

Command: "Increase your rudder to right full, steady on course 270."

> *Note:* When the rudder is increased or decreased, the conning officer must restate the desired course.

Reply: "Increase my rudder to right full, steady on course 270, aye, sir (or ma'am)."

Report: "My rudder is right full, coming to course 270, sir (or ma'am)."

When course change is less than 10 degrees:

Command: "Come right, steer course _____."

Reply: "Come right, steer course _____, aye, sir (or ma'am)."

Report: "Steady course, checking course ___ magnetic, sir (or ma'am)."

When the rudder angle is to be reduced to zero:

Command: "Rudder amidships."

Reply: "Rudder amidships, aye, sir (or ma'am)."

Report: "My rudder is amidships, sir (or ma'am)."

When the course to be steered is that which the ship is on at the instant the command is given:

Command: "Steady as she goes."

Reply: "Steady as she goes, aye. Course ___, sir (or ma'am)."

Report: "Steady on course ___, sir (or ma'am). Checking course _____ magnetic."

> *Note:* Injudicious use of this order could cause momentary loss of control over the ship's swing if the helmsman is required to use a large rudder angle to carry out the order. To prevent this, the order may be preceded by, "Rudder amidships." This, of course, requires anticipation on the conning officer's part to ensure a correct heading. In this situation, the conning officer should always maintain positive control of the rudder.

When the swing of the ship is to be stopped without steadying on any specific course:

Command: "Meet her."

Reply: "Meet her, aye, sir (or ma'am)."

Note: Immediately after the reply is given, the conning officer must order a course to be steered.

Command: "Steady on course ___."

Reply: "Steady on course ___, aye, sir (or ma'am)."

Report: "Steady on course ___, sir (or ma'am). Checking course ___ magnetic."

When equal and *opposite* rudder is desired relative to that previously ordered:

Command: "Shift your rudder."

Reply: "Shift my rudder, aye, sir (or ma'am)."

Report: "Rudder is ___ (an angle equal but opposite to that previously ordered)."

When the heading of the ship is to be determined at a given moment:

Command: "Mark your head."

Report: "Head is (exact heading at that moment), sir (or ma'am)."

Note: If the helmsman appears to be steering properly but the ship is not on her correct heading, the conning officer should use this command to compare the helmsman's compass repeater with other repeaters on the bridge.

When the helmsman appears to be steering badly or is continually allowing the ship to drift from the ordered course:

Command: "Mind your helm."

Reply: "Mind my helm, aye, sir (or ma'am)."

Note: No report necessary.

When the ship is in a situation where minor deviation from an ordered course may be permitted to one side but none may be permitted to the other side (for example, when alongside another ship for refueling):

Command: "Steer nothing to the left (right) of course ___."

Reply: "Steer nothing to the left (right) of course___, aye, sir (or ma'am)."

Note: No report necessary.

Whenever ordering a course change, the conning officer should perform the following activities:

1. Check the side to which he or she intends to turn to make sure that it is safe to turn in that direction.
2. The ship's speed determines how quickly her head will swing. At very low speeds, a large angle of rudder may be required to bring about a course change; at very high speeds, a large rudder angle may cause her to swing so rapidly that she cannot be safely controlled. All conning officers should be familiar with the tables of turning speeds and turning diameters for their ship. This information is contained in the ship's tactical data book. Generally, the sum of rudder order plus speed in knots should not exceed thirty or else there will be a probability of fairly heavy rolls.
3. After giving a rudder order, the conning officer should always monitor its execution by checking the rudder-angle indicator to ensure there was no misinterpretation of the command. A quick glance at the rudder-angle order indicator upon giving an order can provide the conning officer quick feedback that the initial direction of rudder movement is as ordered.
4. In a turn without an ordered course, the helmsman should call out the ship's head for each 10 degrees that the ship swings. If the conning officer does not want the helmsman to do this, he or she should give the helmsman the order, "Belay your headings." The helm should reply, "Belay my headings, aye, sir (or ma'am)."

ENGINE-ORDER COMMANDS TO THE LEE HELM

Engine orders are always given in the following order:

1. *Engine.* Which engine is to be used. If both engines are to be used, the command is, "All engines."
2. *Direction.* Ahead, back, or stop.
3. *Amount.* Ahead one-third, two-thirds, full, flank. Back one-third, two-thirds, full.

4. *Shaft revolutions desired.* Number of revolutions in three digits for the desired speed in knots. Shaft revolutions are not used for backing orders.

Examples

When a twin-screw ship is to go ahead on both engines to come to a speed of six knots:

Command: "All engines ahead one-third. Indicate zero eight eight revolutions for six knots."

Reply: "All engines ahead one-third. Indicate zero eight eight revolutions for six knots, aye, sir (or ma'am)."

Report: "All engines are ahead one-third. Indicating zero eight eight revolutions for six knots, sir (or ma'am)."

When different orders are given to port and starboard engines, revolutions should not be specified:

Command: "Port engine ahead one-third, starboard engine back one-third."

Reply: "Port engine ahead one-third, starboard engine back one-third, aye, sir (or ma'am)."

Report: "Port engine is ahead one-third, starboard engine is back one-third, sir (or ma'am)."

When the order is to only one engine, the report must include the status of both engines:

Command: "Starboard engine ahead one-third, port engine back one-third."

Reply: "Starboard engine ahead one-third, port engine back one-third, aye, sir (or ma'am)."

Report: "Starboard engine is ahead one-third, port engine is back one-third, sir (or ma'am)."

Command: "Starboard engine stop."

Reply: "Starboard engine stop, aye, sir (or ma'am)."

Report: "Starboard engine is stopped. Port engine is back one-third, sir (or ma'am)."

When there are to be small changes of speed, for example, when the ship is along-side another for refueling or to keep station on the formation guide, the conning officer may order:

Command: "Indicate one zero zero revolutions."

Reply: "Indicate one zero zero revolutions, aye, sir (or ma'am)."

Report: "One zero zero revolutions indicated for three revolutions over eleven knots, sir (or ma'am)."

On many gas-turbine ships with controllable reversible-pitch propellers, at speeds below twelve knots, the ship's speed is controlled by varying the pitch of the propeller blade, measured as a percentage. This requires additional orders at lower speeds, as in:

Command: "All engines ahead one-third. Indicate ___ rpms, ___ percent pitch for ___ knots."

Reply: "All engines ahead one-third. Indicate pitch and turns for ___ knots, aye, sir (or ma'am)."

Report: "All engines are ahead one-third, indicating pitch and turns for ___ knots."

Note: This may vary from ship to ship, even within a class.
Check the captain's standing orders.

When maneuvering in restricted waters, getting under way, docking, or mooring, ships usually use what are known as maneuvering bells. Under these circumstances, only engine, direction, and amount are given. Revolutions are not specified. Depending on the type of ship, each engine amount is equivalent to a standard number of knots; for example, one-third equals five knots, two-thirds equals ten knots, and so on. When maneuvering bells (or "maneuvering combination") are desired, the conning officer must order the helmsman as follows:

Command: "Indicate maneuvering combination (bells)." (By convention, this is usually an engine order for nine nine nine revolutions.)

Reply: "Indicate (nine nine nine) revolutions for maneuvering combination (bells), sir (or ma'am)."

Report: "Engine room answers (nine nine nine) revolutions for maneuvering combination (bells), sir (or ma'am)."

Note: This order is not used on many ships although still is in use on older steam- and some diesel-powered ships.

Some COs develop variations in the maneuvering bells to indicate one-half of the power increment, often by indicating seven seven seven or eight eight eight. This tells the throttleman to cut standard acceleration and deceleration and power levels in half for more explicit shiphandling around the pier. The watch officer should consult the CO's standing orders to see if this practice is acceptable on the ship.

COMMANDS TO LINE HANDLERS

Many a good approach to landing is offset by the improper use of mooring lines. Using lines properly requires knowledge of the standard commands to line handlers. The following examples and definitions are in common use in the fleet and form the basis of all orders to lines. Orders should state the number of the line, when appropriate, and telephone talkers should be used for transmitting them.

Mooring lines are numbered from bow to stern in the order in which they are run out (or tend) from the ship: 1, bow line; 2, after bow spring; 3, forward bow spring; 4, after quarter spring; 5, forward quarter spring; 6, stern line. The breast line amidships is not numbered. There are other alternative mooring line patterns used, but the above pattern is the most widely used configuration.

Command	*Meaning*
"Stand by your lines."	Man the lines, ready to put them over, cast them off, or take them in.
"Let go" or "Let go all lines."	Slack off to permit people tending lines on the pier or on another ship to cast off.
"Over all lines."	Pass the lines to the pier, place the eye of each over the appropriate bollard, but take no strain.
"Take a strain on (line 3)."	Put the line under tension.
"Slack (line 3)."	Take tension off the line and let it hang slack.
"Ease (line 3)."	Let out enough of the line to lessen tension.
"Take (line 3) to the capstan" or to "power."	Lead the end of the line to the capstan, take the slack out of it, but put no strain on it.

"Heave around on (line 3)."	Apply tension on the line with the capstan.
"Avast heaving."	Stop the capstan.
"Hold what you've got on (line 3)."	Hold the line as it is.
"Hold (line 3)."	Do not allow any more line to go out. ("Hold" commands should be used with extreme caution because they require the lines to be held even to parting.)
"Check."	Hold heavy tension on line but let it slip as necessary to prevent it from parting.
"Surge."	Hold moderate tension on the line but let it slip enough to permit the ship to move.
"Double up."	Pass additional bights on all mooring lines so that there are three parts of each line to the pier.
"Single up."	Take in all bights and extra lines, leaving only a single part of each of the normal mooring lines.
"Take in all lines."	Have the ends of all lines cast off from the pier and brought on board.
"Cast off all lines."	Used when secured with *another* ship's lines in a nest. Cast off the ends of the lines and allow the other ship to retrieve her lines.
"Shift."	Used when moving a line along a pier. Followed by specification of the line and where it is to go: "Shift number 3 from the bollard to the cleat."

When a ship's auxiliary deck machinery is to be used to haul in a line, the command given is, "Take one (number 1) to the winch (capstan or to power)." This may be followed by, "Heave around on one (number 1)," and then, "Avast heaving on one (number 1)."

The proper naval term for the line-handling drum on the anchor windlass is "warping head." Usage, however, has given authority to the synonyms "winch," "capstan," and "power."

COMMANDS TO TUGS

Tugs are normally handled by two-way VHF radio. However, the following whistle and hand signals are still in use. They may be transmitted to tugs by flashing lights, but only when whistle or hand signals cannot be used.

Whistle Signals

A blast lasts two to three seconds. A prolonged blast lasts four to five seconds. A short blast lasts about one second. Care must be exercised to ensure that whistle signals are directed to and received by the tug for which they are intended. Whistles of different tones have been used successfully to handle more than one tug.

Signal	Meaning
One blast	From stop to half-speed ahead
One blast	From half-speed ahead to stop
Four short blasts	From half-speed ahead to full-speed ahead
One blast	From full-speed ahead to half-speed ahead
Two blasts	From stop to half-speed ahead
Four short blasts	From half-speed astern to full-speed astern
One blast	From half-speed or full-speed astern to stop
One prolonged blast	Cast off, stand clear two short blasts

Whistle signals are usually augmented by hand signals.

Hand Signals

Signal	Meaning
Arm pointed in direction desired	Half speed (ahead or astern)
Fist describing arc	Full speed (ahead or astern)
Undulating movement of open hand, with palm down	Dead slow (ahead or astern)
Open hand held aloft, with palm facing the tug	Stop

Closed fist with thumbs extended, swung up and down	Cast off, stand clear
Hand describing circle as if turning wheel to the right (clockwise), facing in the same direction as the tug	Tug to use right rudder
Hand describing circle as if turning wheel to the left (counterclockwise), facing in the same direction as the tug	Tug to use left rudder
Arm at side of body with hand extended, swung back and forth	Tug to use rudder amidships

A tug must acknowledge all whistle and hand signals with one short toot (one second or less) from her whistle. The exceptions are the backing signal, which must be acknowledged with two short toots, and the cast-off signal, which must be acknowledged by one prolonged and two short toots.

AUXILIARY POWER UNITS

Auxiliary power units (APUs) on some classes of naval vessels give an increased maneuvering capability in close quarters. APUs are electrically driven, trainable motors positioned near the bow of the ship.

Command	Meaning
Train port APU 90 degrees	Position port APU to push the ship toward 090 degrees relative
Energize port (starboard) APU	Port (starboard) APU on
Stop port (starboard) APU	Port (starboard) APU off

BOW THRUSTERS

Bow thrusters on ships are used to move the ship's bow, many times used in amphibious ships to maneuver with a causeway for amphibious landings. Additionally, they improve maneuverability near the pier or in close quarters. The bow thruster is an electrically driven, controllable-pitch propeller located near the bow inside a traverse hull tube.

HALF SPEED AHEAD OR ASTERN

Arm pointed in direction desired

FULL SPEED (either)

Fist describing arc (as if "bouncing" an engine telegraph)

DEAD SLOW (either)

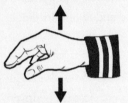

Undulating movement of open hand (palm down)

STOP

Open palm held aloft facing tug

TUG TO USE RIGHT RUDDER

Hand describing circle as if turning wheel to right (clockwise, facing in the same direction as the tug)

TUG TO USE LEFT RUDDER

Hand describing circle as if turning wheel to left (counterclockwise, facing in the same direction as the tug)

TUG TO PUT RUDDER AMIDSHIP

Arm at side of body with hand extended and swung back and forth

CAST OFF, STAND CLEAR

Closed fist with thumb extended, swung up and down

FIGURE 8-1. Tugboat Hand Signals

Command	Meaning
Bow thruster starboard	Bow thruster will move the ship to starboard. The controllable-pitch propeller will slew to 50 percent.
Bow thruster stop	Bow thruster will slew to 9 percent pitch.

LITTORAL COMBAT SHIPS AND FRIGATES

Littoral combat ships have proliferated in the fleet and their unique standard commands and engine configurations are also unique to U.S. Navy standards. The U.S. Naval Institute book *Shiphandling Fundamentals for Littoral Combat Ships and the New Frigates* by CAPT Joseph Gagliano provides a detailed review of maneuvering these ships. The following description is offered to provide the watch officer an introduction to the unique commands used in the LCS class. You should review the standing orders of your specific ship to understand how orders should be communicated on board. LCS do not have conventional propellers and rudders as all other ships in the Navy. Instead they are controlled with a combination of diesel engines, gas turbines, water jets, and hydraulically actuated reversing plates (commonly referred to as "buckets"). The ship is propelled by water being drawn through hull intakes that travels through the water jets by an impeller. The thrust of the buckets can be controlled from 0 percent to 100 percent in both the forward and astern directions. Instead of one-third to flank orders, the watch officer may order a "T-Setting" from T-0 to T-10 ahead or astern. Instead of rudder orders, the combinators can be controlled to move the water jets from centerline to up to 30 degrees port or starboard. With numerous combinations to control the water jets and combinators, LCS are highly maneuverable but require an in depth understanding of the ship's engineering plant and maneuvering characteristics.

Examples

When an LCS is to go ahead, speed is ordered by T-Setting once 100 percent bucket is reached:

Command: "Diesel water jets back 30 percent bucket."

Reply: "Diesel water jets back 30 percent bucket, aye, sir (or ma'am)."

Report: "Diesel water jets are back 30 percent bucket, sir (or ma'am)."

Command: "All ahead, T4."

Reply: "All ahead T4, aye, sir (or ma'am)."

Report: "All ahead T4, sir (or ma'am)."

When different orders are given to port and starboard engines:

Command: "Port ahead T1, starboard back T1."

Reply: "Port ahead T1, starboard back T1, aye, sir (or ma'am)."

Report: "Port is ahead T1, starboard engine is back T1, sir (or ma'am)."

When the order is to only one engine, the report must include the status of both engines:

Command: "Starboard ahead T1, port back T1."

Reply: "Starboard ahead T1, port back T1, aye, sir (or ma'am)."

Report: "Starboard is ahead T1, port is back T1, sir (or ma'am)."

Command: "Starboard T0."

Reply: "Starboard T0, aye, sir (or ma'am)."

Report: "Starboard is T0. Port is back T1, sir (or ma'am)."

Steering Commands to the Helm

When a specific amount of water jet is desired:

Command: "Right 10 degrees (or standard, full, etc.) water jet."

Reply: "Right 10 degrees (or standard, full, etc.) water jet, aye, sir (or ma'am)."

Report: "Water jet is 10 degrees (or standard, full, etc.) right, sir (or ma'am)."

When the course change is less than 10 degrees:

Command: "Come right/left to course ___."

Reply: "Come right/left to course ___, sir (or ma'am)."

Report: "Steady on course ___, sir (or ma'am). Checking ___ magnetic."

When the helmsman is to steady on a specific course:

Command: "Steady on course ___."

Reply: "Steady on course ___, sir (or ma'am)."
Report: "Steady on course, sir (or ma'am). Checking magnetic."

When the helmsman is to place water jets at 0 angle:
    Command: "Centerline water jets."
    Reply: "Centerline water jets, aye, sir (or ma'am)."
    Report: "Water jets are centerline, sir (or ma'am)."

When the amount of water jet is to be increased:
    Command: "Increase your water jet to (right full, right 10 degrees, etc.)."
    Reply: "Increase my water jet to ____, aye, sir (or ma'am)."
    Report: "My water jet is (right full, right 10 degrees, etc.), sir (or ma'am)."

When the amount of water jet is to be decreased:
    Command: "Decrease your water jet to (right full, right 10 degrees, etc.)."
    Reply: "Decrease my water jet to _____, aye, sir (or ma'am)."
    Report: "My water jet is (right full, right 10 degrees, etc.), sir (or ma'am)."

ZUMWALT-CLASS DESTROYERS AND FUTURE SURFACE COMBATANT

ZUMWALT-class destroyers were introduced to the fleet in 2016 and have a unique propulsion system. Future surface combatants may be designed with this propulsion system as well, so gaining familiarity with it is useful. Using gas turbines only for electric power generation, propulsion through the water is achieved by massive induction motors that drive two fixed-pitch propellers, a design also used in the Royal Navy. This efficient lash up between turbine-generated power and electromotive force applied to propellers requires watch officers to have specific knowledge of electric drive propulsion and the respective capabilities and limitations on maneuverability. Steering commands are the same as other rudder-controlled ships, and although thrust commands are similar, maneuvering with electric drives and fixed-pitch propellers demands a more specifically technical application of standard commands.

9

WEATHER

If you don't like the weather, . . . wait a minute and it'll change.

WILL ROGERS

The coldest winter I ever spent was a summer in San Francisco.

POPULARLY ATTRIBUTED TO MARK TWAIN

The weather—we are surrounded by it, discuss it endlessly, and spend millions of dollars attempting to predict it. Understanding the weather is essential if a professional watch officer is to effectively stand his or her watch. Not only is weather important from a safety and navigation perspective, it can have significant tactical impacts, and the benefits and drawbacks of certain weather conditions or effects should be recognized and understood. Yet weather receives little attention in traditional commissioning programs and navy schools, and we generally don't know enough about it when knowledge is what we most need.

CLOUDS

The first and most obvious feature of the weather at sea is the clouds. There is much to be learned from each cloud layer, and each represents different aspects of the interaction of wind and waves. A capable watch officer has at least a nodding acquaintance with the major cloud formations and can give a general indication of what each portends. The following are some of the key cloud formations:

Cirrus. These delicate white clouds commonly make feather-like plumes across the sky. They have little shading, occur at very high altitude, and are generally composed of ice crystals. They can indicate the direction of a storm.

Cirrocumulus. Also called mackerel sky, these clouds look like thousands of cotton balls pasted together. They generally indicate the approach of a storm.

Cirrostratus. These faint veils of cloud can cause halos to appear around the sun and the moon. They are often a precursor of rain.

Altocumulus. These clouds look like flat globes arranged in lines or waves. They differ from cirrocumulus clouds in casting shadows.

Altostratus. Thick cirrostratus clouds without any halo, these appear as part of a thin veil or sheet and can completely obscure the sun and the moon. Either heavy snow or light rain can fall from altostratus clouds.

Nimbostratus. These covered, shapeless clouds are slightly illuminated from behind. When precipitation occurs, it is normally continuous, although it does not always reach the ocean.

Stratocumulus. These layers or patches of clouds are composed of rolls, generally soft gray. They occasionally have dark spots.

Stratus. These low, even clouds assemble just above the earth. Their presence can give the sky a hazy appearance. Drizzle is the precipitation normally associated with stratus clouds.

Cumulus. These dense clouds rise from a horizontal base into gently rounded projections. They can create strong and unpredictable updrafts.

Cumulonimbus. These heavy cloud masses resemble towers or mountains, and their upper levels have a full appearance. They are associated with heavy rain, snow showers, violent hail, and thunderstorms.

FOG

Fog can be the mariner's worst enemy, particularly when a ship enters or leaves port. Fog is formed when warmer air moves over colder water. Great fog banks can develop just offshore, particularly in the north Atlantic and the Aleutians. Fog generally forms at night and lingers until morning, when heat from the sun evaporates the droplets or an offshore wind drives them away.

One way to predict the formation of fog is to determine the difference between the wet- and dry-bulb temperatures. Fog generally forms when the wet-bulb depression is 4 degrees or less. Keeping a continuous record of the depression will serve the watch officer well by helping to predict dangerous conditions.

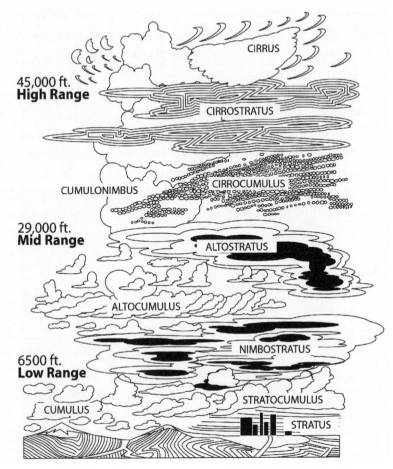

FIGURE 9-1. The Ten-Cloud Genera

FRONTS

The seam where one air mass or weather system meets another is a front. The colder mass, which is heavier, forces the warmer mass aloft, usually forming clouds and inclement weather. When fronts converge, the front on the surface is occluded.

Cold fronts are usually fifteen to fifty miles wide; warm fronts can be as wide as three hundred miles. The area where a warm and cold front meet is normally low pressure.

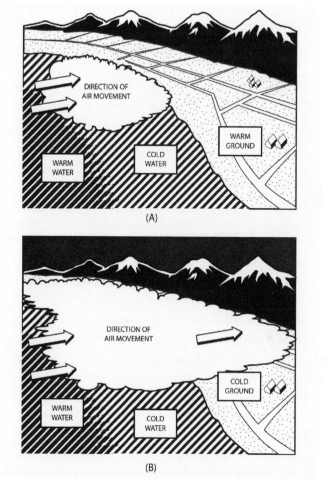

FIGURE 9-2.
Coastal Fog. This shows how it is formed and dissipated: (A) by day when the ground is warm, and (B) by night when the ground is cold.

When a cold front is approaching, the horizon will darken in the direction of the front. A fast cold front, with cumulonimbus clouds, can cause violent and sudden thunderstorms or showers. When the cold front passes, the temperature drops, pressure rises, and the sky clears rapidly.

The appearance of a warm front, usually preceded by cirrus clouds, brings a variety of cloud formations, including (in rough order) cirrostratus, altostratus, nimbostratus, and stratus. Visibility is poor, generally because of fog, rain, or drizzle. Thunderstorms can develop ahead of a front.

A stationary front, as the name implies, is a region where two air masses abut each other without much movement. As a general rule, the weather and clouds along a stationary front are similar in character to those founded along a warm front.

An occluded front occurs when a cold front overtakes a warm front, forcing warm air up and leaving a front on the surface that may be either cool or warm. An occluded front generally displays characteristics similar to those of a warm front.

ATMOSPHERIC PRESSURE AND ISOBARS

Every watch officer must understand atmospheric pressure, as it is one of the best indicators of weather activity. With the ship's barometer, variations in atmospheric pressure can be measured accurately. Pressure readings are given in inches of mercury, and at the earth's surface the baseline reading is 29.92 inches. As a general rule, a high barometer (more than 30 inches) portends fair weather. The bridge quartermaster, who is trained in weather observation, will report the barometric pressure to the watch officer every hour, also indicating whether the barometer is rising or falling and giving the amount in hundredths of an inch: "Sir (or ma'am), the barometer has fallen two-hundredths in the past hour." Because an air mass moves from a high-pressure region to a lower-pressure one, knowledge of barometric pressure in different regions provides clues about the direction and movement of frontal systems and the air masses that form the weather (wind, precipitation, etc.). More important than a single "snapshot" reading is an understanding of the *relative* changes in the barometer from hour to hour and of any deviation in the expected reading for a given geographical area during the season of the measurement. The watch officer should notify the CO and navigator, and probably the first lieutenant and operations officer, of changes in the barometer that seem excessive or out of the ordinary.

As a general rule, a steady barometer means good weather. A falling barometer (either below normal for the region or time of year or simply declining in the immediate region) normally presages wind and rain, especially when coupled with increasing temperature and moisture. A sudden fall (more than four-hundredths of an inch in an hour) can mean heavy winds. A rising barometer, especially with decreasing moisture and temperature, generally portends milder, drier weather. A rapid rise can mean unsettled conditions with a variety of weather shifts.

A map of pressure areas and the movement of air masses depicts frontal systems and lines of equal pressure called isobars. Isobars do not join or cross, and by studying them, you can obtain a fairly good idea of weather in a given region. The difference in pressure between isobars gives an indication of wind strength (the greater the difference between high and low pressure over a given distance, the stronger the wind). If isobars are close to each other, the wind generated by the pressure differential will generally be stronger. Conversely, when there is more room between the isobars, winds will be lighter. On a map or chart, an elongated area of low pressure is referred to as a trough or trough line. Troughs are associated with strong weather and occasionally violent wind shifts.

In areas of high pressure the wind blows outward, while in areas of low pressure it blows inward. In the Northern Hemisphere, the combination of the earth's rotation and the structure of the isobars causes the air to circulate in a clockwise direction around high-pressure centers and in a counterclockwise direction around low-pressure centers. The opposite is true in the Southern Hemisphere.

WEATHER PROVERBS

Often the best person to predict the weather is the experienced watchstander or member of the bridge team. The chief or first-class quartermaster on most ships will have a "feel" for the weather. Here are a few of the phrases and proverbs they often utter:

- Red sky at night, sailors delight (good weather coming).
- Red sky at morning, sailors take warning (weather deteriorating, generally in the afternoon).
- Greenish tint to the sky (a deep low-pressure area to the north or west).
- Yellow sunset (coming strong winds).
- Sunrise low in the sky (light winds and fair weather).
- Sunrise high in the sky (winds and cloudiness).
- Mares' tails and mackerel scales make tall ships carry low sails (cirrus clouds [mares' tails] and cirrocumulus clouds [mackerel scales] often indicate pressure lows and possible warm fronts).

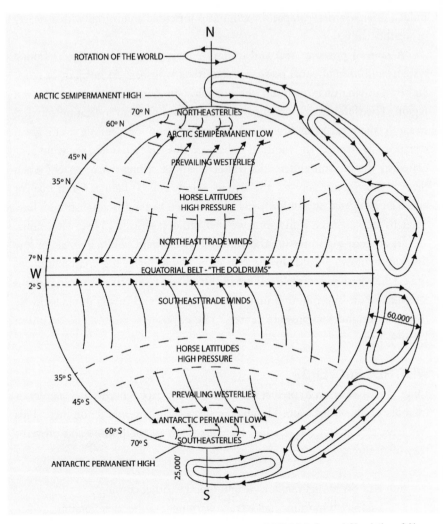

FIGURE 9-3. General Circulation of Air

NAVY WEATHER FORECASTING AND RESOURCES

For the watch officer on a naval vessel, many excellent weather and environmental information services and products are available. The point of contact is generally the ship's navigator (occasionally the operations officer), with the specific point of contact often being the QMOW on the bridge.

TABLE 9-1 Apparent Wind Speed

KNOTS	INDICATION
less than 1	Calm, smoke rises vertically
1–3	Smoke drifts slowly
4–6	Wind felt on face
7–10	Wind extends light flag
11–16	Wind raises dust, cinders, etc.
17–21	Wind waves and snaps flags briskly
22–27	Wind whistles through rigging
28–33	Walking into the wind becomes difficult
34–40	Wind generally impedes walking

The best overall information on the Navy's oceanographic support system is Commander, Naval Meteorology and Oceanography Command (CNMOC), Instruction 3140.1M, the U.S. Navy Meteorological and Oceanographic Support System Manual. This comprehensive publication details all the support services available, including tropical cyclone warnings, tsunami warnings, daily forecasts, warnings of destructive extratropical weather systems, high-sea warnings, ice conditions, storm tide or surge warnings, area analysis and prognostic charts, severe local weather, satellite environmental data, and acoustic range predictions. These are available to the watch officer by a variety of means, including fleet broadcast and via the internet using both secure and nonsecure internet protocol routing paths. Additionally, specialized support services for specific operations, including optimum track ship routing (OTSR), route weather forecasts (WEAX), oceanic fronts and eddy positions, and fleet operating area forecasts, are available upon request via record message traffic. Specific support is also available for the Great Lakes.

Links to CNMOC products may be found through the National Oceanographic Portal: https:www.metoc.navy.mil.

- Naval Oceanography Operations Command (NOOC): http://www .metoc.navy.mil/nooc/nooc.html

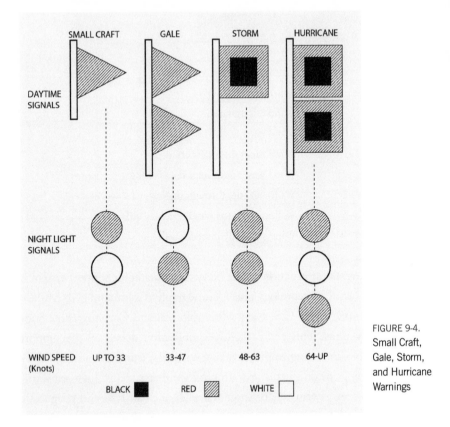

FIGURE 9-4. Small Craft, Gale, Storm, and Hurricane Warnings

- Joint Typhoon Warning Center (JTWC): http://www.metoc.navy.mil/jtwc/jtwc.html
- Fleet Numerical Meteorology and Oceanography Center (FNMOC): http://www.metoc.navy.mil/fnmoc/fnmoc.html
- Naval Oceanographic Office (NAVOCEANO): http://www.metoc.navy.mil/navo/navo.html
- Fleet Weather Center San Diego (FWC-SD): http://www.metoc.navy.mil/fwcsd/fwc-sd.html
- Fleet Weather Center Norfolk (FWC-N): http://www.metoc.navy.mil/fwcn/fwcn.html
- Naval Oceanography Antisubmarine Warfare Center Yokosuka (NOAC-Y): http://www.metoc.navy.mil/noacy/

TABLE 9-2 Beaufort Scale and Estimating True Wind by Sea Conditions

KNOTS	BEAUFORT NUMBER	WAVE HEIGHT (FEET)	DESCRIPTION	SEA CONDITIONS
0	0	0	Calm	Sea smooth and mirrorlike.
1–3	1	¼	Light air	Scale-like ripples without foam crests.
4–6	1	½	Light breeze	Small, short wavelets; crests glassy and do not break.
7–10	3	1	Gentle breeze	Large wavelets; some crests begin to break; occasional white foam crests.
11–16	4	3	Moderate breeze	Small waves, becoming longer; fairly frequent white foam crests.
17–21	5	6	Fresh breeze	Moderate waves, taking a more pronounced long form; many white foam crests; there may be some spray.
22–27	6	12	Strong breeze	Large waves form; white foam crests more extensive everywhere; there may be some spray.
28–33	7	15*	Near gale	Sea heaps up, and white foam from breaking waves blown in streaks in the direction of the wind.
34–40	8	20†	Gale	Moderately high waves of greater length; edges of crests break; foam blown in well-marked streaks in the direction of the wind.
41–47	9	30‡	Strong gale	High waves; dense streaks of foam in the direction of the wind; crests of waves begin to roll over; spray may reduce visibility.
48–55	10	40‡	Storm	Very high waves with long overhanging crests; foam in great patches blown in dense white streaks in the direction of the wind; visibility reduced.
56–63	11	50‡	Violent storm	Exceptionally high waves; sea completely covered with long white patches of foam lying in the direction of the wind; visibility reduced.
64 and over	12	60‡	Hurricane	Air is filled with foam and spray; sea completely white with driving spray; visibility very much reduced.

* Duration of sixteen hours, not fully arisen.
† Duration of twenty hours, not fully arisen.
‡ Duration of twenty-four hours, not fully arisen.

On many ships, a meteorology detachment is assigned for forward deployments or for periodic embarkations. In addition, tremendous analytical reach-back capability is available via official Navy websites offering a variety of tailored products.

STORMY WEATHER

Shiphandling in a storm is a required skill for any watch officer. Knowing how to predict storm paths and how to escape them are equally important. A sound knowledge of weather greatly reduces the chance that a watch officer will place the ship in danger.

A cyclone is a violent windstorm that results from the presence of areas of dramatically low pressure. A tropical cyclone is also called a typhoon in the western Pacific or a hurricane in the Atlantic and eastern Pacific. Cyclones have well-defined areas and paths that are difficult to predict. These storms are extremely dangerous to both shipping and—when they make landfall—populated areas. A few clarifying definitions follow:

- *Tropical Disturbance.* This is a system of wind, generally one hundred to three hundred miles in diameter, that originates in the tropics and has maintained a distinct character for at least twenty-four hours.
- *Tropical Depression.* This consists of one or more closed isobars beginning to rotate in a pattern, with wind speeds no higher than thirty-three knots.
- *Tropical Storm.* This has closed isobars and wind speeds from thirty-four to sixty-three knots.
- *Typhoon or Hurricane.* This is a mature storm with winds over sixty-four knots and a distinct eye.

Rainfall in a tropical storm is heavy, particularly in the center, and winds are forceful. Wind circulates counterclockwise in northern latitudes and clockwise in southern latitudes. The eye of the storm is usually five to thirty miles in diameter and winds are calm, although the seas remain heavy. Interestingly, the South Atlantic is generally free of tropical storms because of the proximity of the African and South American landmasses.

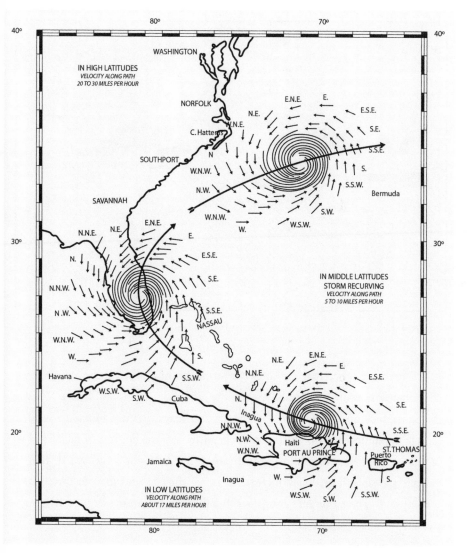

FIGURE 9-5. Track of a Tropical Cyclone Originating in the West Indies

Despite the sophisticated weather-tracking and prognostication devices available to the watch officer, a tropical cyclone can form with extreme rapidity and overtake an unsuspecting ship with ease. The watch officer should learn and heed the signs discussed above, particularly during hurricane or typhoon season.

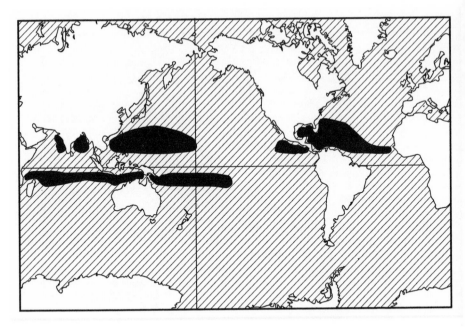

FIGURE 9-6. Source Regions of Tropical Cyclones

The basic device that indicates the formation of a storm is the barometer. Barometric pressure falls steadily when the air is hot, moist, and heavy. Wind begins to pick up. In advance of heavy winds, the sea rises in a long, low swell, and light plumes of cirrus clouds appear in an arc over the horizon. Some observers have reported a humming sound caused by increasing wind speed. Rain squalls appear and gradually increase to heavy showers and then to torrential downpours. The barometer continues to fall as the sea churns with ever-larger waves.

Determining the bearing of a storm is a simple matter. In the Northern Hemisphere, where the storm whirls counterclockwise, the center will be about 110–112 degrees to the right of a watch officer facing the wind. The wind hauls in one direction or the other, depending on the semicircle in which the ship finds herself. The next step in the problem, determining distance to the storm center, is more difficult. The following scale presents a rough idea:

Average Fall of Barometer	Distance from Center
2/100 to 6/100	250 to 150 miles
6/100 to 8/100	150 to 100 miles
8/100 to 12/100	100 to 80 miles
12/100 to 15/100	80 to 50 miles

A storm can move up to fifty miles per hour, although speeds of five to twenty miles per hour are far more common.

After determining range and bearing to the center, the watch officer has to ascertain the track of the storm. The basic track can be determined by taking three to five bearings on the center, roughly two hours apart. If the wind hauls to the right, the ship is in the dangerous semicircle; if it hauls to the left, the ship is in the navigable semicircle. If the wind continues from the same direction and the barometer continues to fall, the storm is headed directly for the ship. The eye of the storm is a fairly good radar target, and the storm can be tracked on radar.

As a general rule, the best method for maneuvering in a storm in the Northern Hemisphere is as follows:

1. If the ship is in the right (dangerous) semicircle, put the wind on the starboard bow and make as much headway as possible without subjecting the ship to danger. If it is necessary to heave to, face into the sea.

2. If the ship is in the left (navigable) semicircle, put the wind on the starboard quarter and hold on that heading. If it is necessary to heave to, proceed stern into the sea.

3. If the ship is ahead of the storm center, bring the wind two points on the starboard quarter and maintain that heading to make for the left (navigable) semicircle.

4. If the ship is behind the storm center, avoid the center by the most practical route, keeping in mind that the storm will eventually curve northeastward.

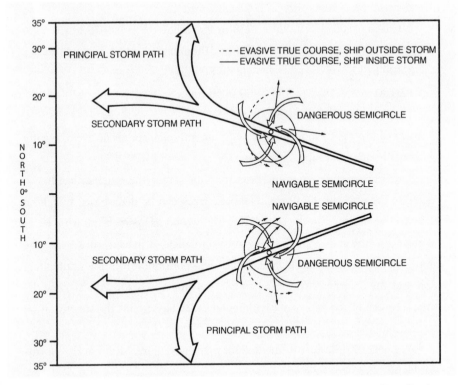

FIGURE 9-7. Storm Evasion

Attempting to outrun the storm by "crossing the T" is problematic because of the heavy swells that build rapidly ahead of the storm. Additionally, unpredictability makes it dangerous to approach the storm closely from ahead. The storm may follow the path toward the warmest waters, although this will have little influence over its path if the storm is moving fast.

As noted previously, two excellent texts providing a thorough treatment of weather for those at sea are Kotsch's *Weather for the Mariner* and Kotsch and Henderson's *Heavy Weather Guide*.

10

THE RULES OF THE ROAD

Without the rule of law, civilization soon turns to barbarism.

TACITUS, ROMAN ORATOR AND HISTORIAN

The intent of this brief chapter is not to present a detailed analysis of the international and inland navigation rules and regulations but rather to provide the watch officer with a handy reference summarizing these rules so that they may be accurately and professionally followed.

This chapter discusses the International Regulations for Prevention of Collisions at Sea, 1972 (72 COLREGS). It also discusses the Inland Navigation Rules, which were enacted by law on 24 December 1980 and became effective for all inland waters except the Great Lakes on 24 December 1981. The inland rules became effective on the Great Lakes on 1 March 1983. Some differences do remain between the international and inland rules, although they are fairly similar.

On 19 November 1989, nine amendments to the 72 COLREGS became effective. These nine amendments are technical in nature and are reflected in this discussion. The Coast Guard has adopted several amendments to the inland and international rules and annexes, which are also reflected.

The best source for studying the rules of the road is the U.S. Department of Homeland Security and U.S. Coast Guard publication Navigation Rules and Regulations Handbook. This handy and well-illustrated publication is available on your ship (check with the navigator, CIC officer, or senior watch officer) from any Coast Guard station, and online at www.navcen.uscg.gov; it contains the actual text of the rules. If you want additional interpretation, the Naval Institute Press published *Farwell's Rules of the Nautical Road*, by Craig Allen, which is considered the classic of the profession on this subject. In addition to these, there are numerous computer-based question banks as well as mobile phone–based apps ideal for continual study and testing one's knowledge.

While the resources mentioned above are quite good, there is simply no substitute for studying and reading the rules of the road directly from the Coast Guard text. It doesn't take very long to read through the rules, and you should set aside some time to do this every couple of months while you are assigned to sea duty and standing watch. The U.S. Coast Guard website contains the latest developments in navigation systems in use, along with links to the navigation rules, the text of the specific regulations, and frequently asked questions. This information is downloadable for study aboard ship.

What follows is a summary of the rules, with emphasis on sections that are more difficult to remember on short notice. This is for quick reference only; every watch officer should have a complete understanding of the rules based on reading, study, testing, and seminar discussion with other members of the wardroom:

Rule 1: Application. This sets out areas in which the rules apply. International rules apply to all vessels upon the high seas and all waters navigable by seagoing vessels. Inland rules apply to all vessels on the inland waters of the United States. Rule 1, both international and inland, also contains a permit for submarines to display an intermittent flashing amber (yellow beacon) with a sequence as follows: one flash per second for three seconds followed by a three-second off period.

Rule 2: Responsibility. Nothing in the rules shall exonerate any vessel from the consequences of any neglect to comply with the rules, or of the neglect of any precaution that may be required by the ordinary practice of seamen or by the special circumstances of the case. Due regard shall be had to all dangers of navigation and collision and to any special circumstances, including the limitations of the vessels involved, which may make a departure from these rules necessary to avoid immediate danger.

Rule 3: General Definitions. Key definitions include the following.

- Vessel: Any craft, including nondisplacement craft, wing-in-ground (WIG) craft, and seaplanes, used or capable of being used as a means of transportation on water.
- Power-driven vessel: Any vessel propelled by machinery.
- Sailing vessel: Any vessel under sail, provided that propelling machinery is not being used.
- Vessel engaged in fishing: A craft fishing with nets, lines, trawls, or any other apparatus that restricts maneuverability. This does not include vessels with fishing apparatus that does not restrict maneuverability, such as trolling lines.
- Seaplane: Any aircraft designed to maneuver on the water.
- Vessel not under command: A craft unable to maneuver as required by the rules and that cannot keep out of the way of another vessel.
- Vessel restricted in its ability to maneuver: A craft whose maneuverability is restricted because of work such as underway replenishment, air operations, mine clearance, towing, working navigation marks, or laying submarine cable or pipeline.
- Vessel constrained by draft: A power-driven vessel severely restricted in its ability to maneuver because of the relation between draft and depth of water (international rules only).
- Underway vessel: A vessel not at anchor, made fast to the shore, or aground. Length and breadth of a vessel mean her length overall and greatest breadth.
- Restricted visibility: Any condition in which visibility is restricted by fog, mist, falling snow, heavy rainstorms, sandstorms, or any other similar causes.
- Wing-in-Ground: A multimodeal craft that, in its main operational mode, flies in close proximity to the surface by using surface-effect action.

Rule 4: Application. The steering and sailing rules apply to any condition of visibility.

Rule 5: Lookout. Every vessel shall at all times maintain a proper lookout by sight and hearing as well as by all available means appropriate in the prevailing circumstances and conditions so as to make a full appraisal of the situation and the risk of collision.

Rule 6: Safe Speed. All vessels shall travel at a safe speed to enable them to "take proper and effective action to avoid collision and be stopped within a distance appropriate to the prevailing circumstances and conditions." The factors that should be taken into account in determining safe speed include visibility; traffic density; the maneuverability of the vessel; background light at night; the state of the wind, sea, and current; the proximity of navigational hazards; and draft in relation to the depth of water. If there is radar aboard, factors relating to radar shall be taken into account.

Rule 7: Risk of Collision. All vessels shall use "all means available . . . to determine if risk of collision exists." If there is any doubt, risk is deemed to exist. Radar shall be properly used. A factor that shall be considered is whether the compass bearing of an approaching vessel changes appreciably. Risk sometimes exists even when an appreciable bearing change is evident, particularly when one vessel is approaching a very large vessel or tow or a vessel at close range.

Rule 8: Action to Avoid Collision. Any action shall be positive; made in ample time; and with due regard to the observance of good seamanship. Any alteration of course and/or speed shall be readily apparent to another vessel observing visually or by radar. A succession of small alterations of course and/or speed should be avoided. The effectiveness of such action shall be carefully checked until the other vessel is finally past and clear. To avoid collision or allow more time to assess the situation, a vessel shall slacken speed or take all way off by stopping or reversing her means of propulsion.

Rule 9: Narrow Channels. Keep to starboard. Smaller ships shall not impede the passage of larger ones constrained to the channel. Fishing and crossing vessels shall not impede a channel. Overtaking vessels still give way. Avoid anchoring in a narrow channel.

Rule 10: Traffic Separation Schemes. These specific rules should be reviewed prior to entering such waters. You shall remain in assigned lanes, join or leave at a slight angle, and cross at a right angle. Avoid separation zones altogether.

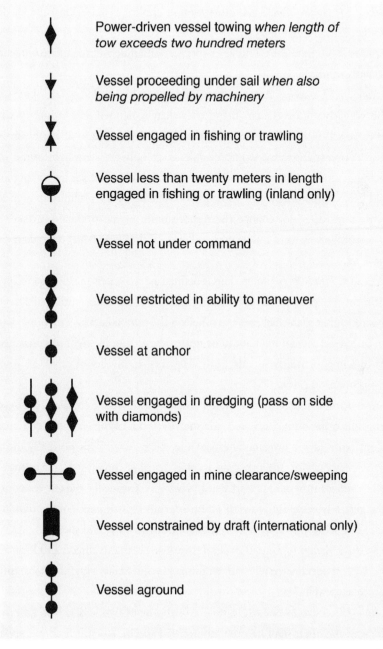

Power-driven vessel towing *when length of tow exceeds two hundred meters*

Vessel proceeding under sail *when also being propelled by machinery*

Vessel engaged in fishing or trawling

Vessel less than twenty meters in length engaged in fishing or trawling (inland only)

Vessel not under command

Vessel restricted in ability to maneuver

Vessel at anchor

Vessel engaged in dredging (pass on side with diamonds)

Vessel engaged in mine clearance/sweeping

Vessel constrained by draft (international only)

Vessel aground

FIGURE 10-1. Day Shapes. These are international and inland, unless otherwise indicated.

Rule 11: Application. This entire section applies to vessels in sight of one another.

Rule 12: Sailing Vessels. This gives specifics of sailing rules of the road having to do with wind.

Rule 13: Overtaking. Any vessel overtaking another shall keep out of the way of the vessel being overtaken. Being overtaken is defined as coming up with another vessel from a direction more than 22.5 degrees abaft of her beam. At night, the overtaking vessel would be able to see only the stern light of the vessel being overtaken and not the sidelights. If in doubt, you are overtaking and should behave accordingly. Any subsequent alteration of the relationship between the two ships does not change the responsibility of the original overtaker to keep out of the way until finally past and clear of the vessel being overtaken. See figure 10.2.

Rule 14: Head-On Situation. This is defined as two vessels meeting on reciprocal or nearly reciprocal courses involving the risk of collision. Both shall alter to starboard so that each shall pass the other on the port side. The situation occurs when one vessel sees another ahead or nearly ahead, and by night sees masthead lights in a line, or nearly so, and both sidelights. If any doubt exists, assume a head-on situation exists.

Rule 15: Crossing Situation. When crossing with risk of collision, the vessel that has the other on its starboard side shall keep out of the way and, if circumstances permit, avoid crossing ahead of the other vessel. This normally means that the vessel having the other on its port hand is "privileged" ("stand on"). This is a simple mnemonic: Port hand privileged. Generally, the correct course for the give-way vessel is to turn to starboard, thus passing astern of the stand-on vessel. (The stand-on vessel is the one maintaining course and speed.)

Rule 16: Action by Give-Way Vessel. Every vessel that is directed to keep out of the way of another vessel shall, so far as possible, take early and substantial action to keep well clear.

Rule 17: Action by Stand-On Vessel. When one of two vessels is to keep out of the way, the other shall keep her course and speed. When it becomes apparent that the give-way vessel isn't getting out of the way, the stand-on vessel *may*

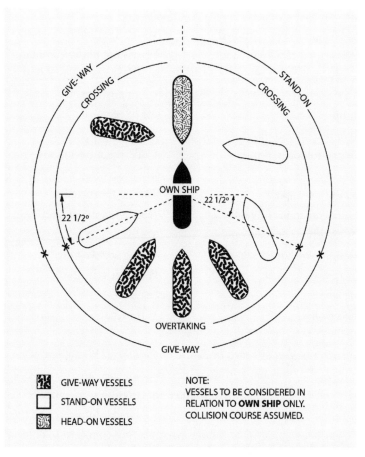

FIGURE 10-2. Head-on, Crossing, and Overtaking Situations

take action to avoid collision by its maneuver alone. The stand-on vessel *shall* take action when the situation reaches a stage where the give-way vessel's action alone cannot avoid collision. To avoid collision in a crossing situation, a craft shouldn't alter course to port for a vessel on its port side. Nothing in this rule relieves the give-way vessel of the obligation to keep out of the way.

Rule 18: Responsibilities between Vessels. The simplest means of understanding the relative responsibilities of vessels is a list going from the most privileged vessel (gives way to no other) to the least privileged (gives way to all others).

International	*Inland*
Vessels aground or anchored	Vessels aground or anchored
Vessels not under command	Vessels not under command
Vessels restricted in ability to maneuver	Vessels restricted in ability to maneuver
Air operations	Air operations
Alongside operations	Alongside operations
Underwater operations	Underwater operations
Minesweeping	Minesweeping
Towing (restricted)	Towing (restricted)
Vessels constrained by draft	Does not apply inland
Vessels fishing or trawling	Vessels fishing or trawling
Sailing vessels under sail	Sailing vessels under sail
Power-driven vessels	Power-driven vessels
Seaplane	Seaplane
WIG Craft	WIG Craft

Rule 19: Conduct of Vessels in Restricted Visibility. This applies when vessels are not in sight of one another when in or near an area of restricted visibility. A vessel shall proceed at a safe speed adapted for conditions of restricted visibility, with engines ready for immediate maneuver; use radar to determine the risk of collision and take appropriate action; avoid altering course to port for a vessel forward of the beam, except when overtaking; and avoid altering course toward a vessel abeam or abaft the beam. Whenever a fog signal is heard forward of the beam, the vessel shall reduce speed to bare steerageway and if necessary take all way off.

Rule 20: Application. This covers lights and shapes and discusses the application period for them. Lights are on sunset to sunrise only, except in restricted visibility. Shapes shall be displayed during the day.

Rule 21: Definition. This defines lights as follows.

- Masthead light: white, 225 degrees (that is, covered by the light), 22.5 degrees abaft the beam each side.

- Sidelights: red or green, 112.5 degrees, 22.5 degrees abaft the beam each side.
- Stern light: white, 135 degrees, 67.5 degrees forward each side.
- Towing light: yellow, 135 degrees, 67.5 degrees forward each side.
- All round: white, 360 degrees.
- Flashing: yellow, 120 flashes per minute.
- Special flashing (inland only): yellow, 50 to 70 flashes per minute.

Rule 22: Visibility of Lights. This gives ranges of lights as follows.

Vessels greater than fifty meters

Masthead	6 miles
Sidelight	3 miles
Stern light	3 miles
Towing	3 miles
White, red, green, or yellow (as required)	3 miles
Special flash (as required, inland only)	2 miles

Vessels greater than twelve meters but less than fifty meters

Masthead	5 miles
Vessel less than twenty meters	3 miles
Sidelight	2 miles
Stern light	2 miles
Towing light	2 miles
White, red, green, or yellow (as required)	2 miles
Special flash (as required, inland only)	2 miles

Vessels less than twelve meters

Masthead	2 miles
Sidelight	1 mile
Stern light	2 miles
Towing light	2 miles
White, red, green, or yellow (as required)	2 miles

Inconspicuous, partly submerged, or objects being towed

White all-round light	3 miles

Rule 23: Power-Driven Vessels Under Way. While the best method of studying the rules of lights is to use a well-illustrated guide such as *Farwell's Rules of the Nautical Road,* some basic guidelines are set out here and in the rules that follow.

- Power-driven vessel: A larger power-driven vessel (greater than fifty meters) shall have sidelights, a stern light, and a second masthead light abaft of and higher than the forward one.
- Air-cushion vessel: This craft shall show the all-round flashing yellow light where it can best be seen.
- Small vessel: Generally, a small vessel may show a single all-round white light and sidelights if possible.

Rule 24: Towing and Pushing Vessels. A towing vessel shall have two white lights with a diamond day shape and a yellow towing light astern. In inland waters, two yellow stern lights are added.

Rule 25: Sailing Vessels Under Way and Vessels Under Oars. The mnemonic for sailing lights is, "Red over green, sailing machine." The red over green, however, is optional. The day shape (when a sailboat is under power) is a small cone pointing down at the engine.

Rule 26: Fishing Vessels. "Green over white, trawling at night; red over white, fishing at night"—so the mnemonic goes. The day shape is two black cones with their points together, or a basket for vessels under twenty meters (sixty feet).

Rule 27: Vessels Not Under Command or Restricted in Their Ability to Maneuver. Not under command: "Red over red, the captain is dead" is the operative mnemonic, with two black balls as the corresponding day shape.

Restricted ability to maneuver: Red over white over red for lights, with a corresponding day shape or ball-diamond-ball. If a dredge is working, the side to pass on has two green lights, the fouled side two red. There are two diamonds on the good side and two balls on the fouled side ("diamonds are better than pearls"). A vessel towing or conducting aviation or alongside operations exhibits the same lights and day shapes. Minesweeping operations require three green lights, one masthead light, and one light on each side of the operation area, with black balls for day shapes.

Rule 28: Vessels Constrained by Draft. These require three red lights in a vertical display by night, or a single blank cylinder or can by day (shown only in international waters).

Rule 29: Pilot Vessels. "White over red, pilot ahead" is the mnemonic. If at anchor, the vessel displays a single black ball.

Rule 30: Anchored Vessels and Vessels Aground. Anchored vessels display a single white light forward and high in the ship, unless they are greater than fifty meters, in which case they display a second light aft and lower than the after white light. The day shape for a vessel at anchor is a single black ball. Aground vessels display "red over red, navigator's dead," with three black balls ("one for the captain, one for the XO, and one for the navigator") for the day shape.

Rule 31: Seaplanes. Do the best you can; exhibit lights and day shapes as similar in characteristics and position as possible.

Rule 32: Definitions. This rule defines a few terms for sound and light signals.

- Whistle: Any sound-signaling appliance that meets certain technical specifications.
- Short blast: One second.
- Prolonged blast: Four to six seconds.

Rule 33: Equipment for Sound Signals. A vessel longer than twelve meters requires a whistle; one longer than twenty meters requires a whistle and a bell; one longer than one hundred meters also requires a gong. A craft less than twelve meters requires some means of signaling.

Rule 34: Maneuvering and Warning Signals. This rule marks the greatest point of divergence between the international and inland rules. In international rules, the signals demonstrate immediate action; in inland rules, the signals demonstrate intent and shall be agreed on by the parties involved. Briefly, the international rules are as follows:

One short: "I am altering my course to starboard."
Two short: "I am altering my course to port."
Three short: "I am operating astern propulsion."
Five or more short: "Danger."
One prolonged: "Blind bend."

The international overtaking sequence when in a narrow channel of fairway is as follows:

> Two prolonged, one short: "I intend to overtake you on your starboard side."
> Two prolonged, two short: "I intend to overtake you on your port side."
> One prolonged, one short, one prolonged, one short: "Agreement."

The inland rules for vessels within sight of one another and meeting or crossing within half a mile of each other are briefly as follows:

> One short: "I intend to leave you on my port side."
> Two short: "I intend to leave you on my starboard side."
> Three short: "I am operating astern propulsion."
> Same signal in return: "Agreement."

For overtaking situations:

> One short: "I intend to overtake you on your starboard side."
> Two short: "I intend to overtake you on your port side."
> Same signal in return: "Agreement."
> Five short: "Danger."
> One prolonged: "Blind bend."

Rule 35: Sound Signals in Restricted Visibility.

Vessel	*Signal (interval)*
Power-driven, making way	One prolonged (intervals not more than two minutes)
Power-driven, under way, not making way	Two prolonged (intervals not more than two minutes)
Not under command, restricted sailing, fishing, towing	One prolonged, two short (intervals not more than two minutes)
Towed vessel, if manned	One prolonged, three short (intervals not more than two minutes)

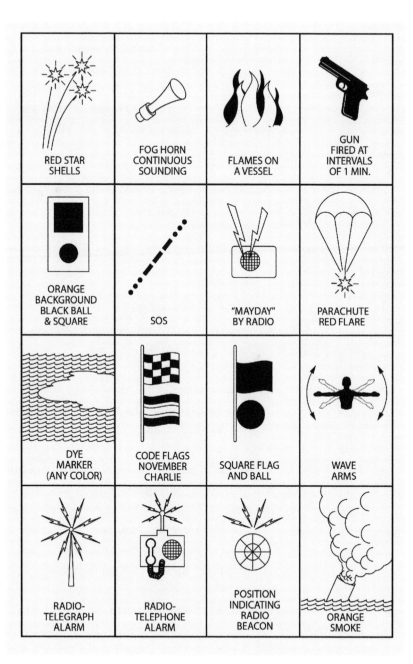

FIGURE 10-3. Distress Signals (Source: 72 COLREGS)

Anchored	Bell forward, gong aft (intervals not more than one minute)
	Optional short-prolonged-short
Aground	Anchored signal plus three strokes on the bell before and after the rapid ringing of the bell
Piloting	Four short

Rule 36: Signals to Attract Attention. Vessels should make a sound or light signal, to attract attention and not embarrass any vessel in the process.

Rule 37: Distress Signals. See figure 10.3.

Rule 38: Exemptions. This sets out a few exemptions to light requirements for older vessels.

- *Annex I: Positioning and Technical Details of Lights and Shapes.*
- *Annex II: Additional Signals for Fishing Vessels Fishing in Close Proximity.*
- *Annex III: Technical Details of Sound-Signal Appliances.*
- *Annex IV: Distress Signals.* See figure 10.3.
- *Annex V: Pilot Rules.* These are inland rules only.
- *COLREGS Demarcation Lines.* These lay out the exact lines between international and inland rules based on geographic points in the United States.
- *Vessel Bridge-to-Bridge Radiotelephone.* This gives details of operating bridge-to-bridge radiotelephones. As a general rule, in U.S. waters, a radiotelephone set on channel 13 is required for most vessels, particularly power-driven ones more than three hundred tons, passenger vessels more than one hundred tons, and towing vessels more than twenty-six tons. Dredges and floating plants likewise have radiotelephones.

Lastly, other administrative information (penalty provisions, duties related to casualty assistance, injunctions) is also included in the COLREG publication.

11

ENGINEERING

At the heart of any ship is an engineering plant that moves the hull through the water, makes fresh water from the sea, provides electrical power and hotel services, and in general permits the ship to perform her mission and support her crew. Over the past twenty years, an increasing number of frontline U.S. Navy warships and Coast Guard cutters have been commissioned with gas-turbine, diesel, and hybrid propulsion plants. Additionally, steam-propulsion plants are still in service in a number of U.S. ships. A smaller number are nuclear powered or all electric.

While it is impractical and unnecessary to elaborate in this small volume on the details of running each type of engineering plant, it is useful for the deck watch officer to have solid knowledge of the plants as well as broad knowledge of engineering, casualty control, damage control, and general propulsion and auxiliary issues. The discussion that follows is aimed at the non-EOOW. Volumes that offer more detail for the watch officer include Blank and Bock's *Introduction to Naval Engineering*, Felger's *Engineering for the Officer of the Deck*, and Bruhn, Saulnier, and Whittington's *Ready to Answer All Bells: A Blueprint for Successful Naval Engineering*—a particularly good reference work on engineering (all from Naval Institute Press). The intent here is to provide quick reference on basic engineering issues as they pertain to the topside watch.

RELATIONSHIP OF THE OOD AND
THE ENGINEERING OFFICER OF THE WATCH

The EOOW is one of the principal assistants to the OOD. He or she reports directly to the watch officer, generally via an intercommunications voice unit (MC) circuit—that is, the "growler," "squawkbox," or telephone. The EOOW is also responsible to the engineering officer for the safe operation of the plant and the execution of the engineer's and captain's standing orders for propulsion and auxiliary systems. In the course of a normal watch the OOD and EOOW converse several times, generally about routine shifts in equipment status in the plant, minor problems or concerns, and routine reports. The requirements vary from ship to ship and plant to plant. The documents that shape the routine reports flowing between the EOOW and OOD are the standing orders of the CO, the engineer's standing orders, the night orders of the CO and the engineer, and the Standard Ship's Organization and Regulations Manual (SORM).

In an emergency, the EOOW normally makes his or her first report of a casualty or problem to the watch officer, and it is the responsibility of the OOD to pass the information to the CO and take whatever action is necessary from the bridge. The EOOW is generally responsible for informing the chief engineer of the problem; the engineer then informs the captain in far greater detail as to the nature of and solution to the problem. As an example:

> The EOOW of a cruiser is informed that there is a hot line shaft bearing on the No. 2 shaft. The EOOW informs the OOD of the casualty and begins Engineering Operational Sequencing System (EOSS) casualty control (EOCC) procedures. The OOD calls the CO and informs him or her of the casualty and the impact on the ship's maneuverability. The OOD takes maneuvering action to slow the ship if necessary, informs the officer in tactical command (OTC) and other ships in company if necessary, and avoids shipping if necessary. The EOOW then calls the engineer, who generally proceeds either to the central control station (central, or CCS) or to the vicinity of the casualty to assess the situation. The engineer subsequently calls the CO to explain the cause

of the problem (faulty temperature sensor, replacing sensor, estimated time of repair twenty minutes, etc.) and its impact on the ship's ability to maneuver. The EOOW then calls the OOD to give a more detailed explanation of the casualty and to mention any constraints on the plant.

Communications between the EOOW and the watch officer must be concise and clearly understood. They should be repeated over the circuit so that both watch stations are in full agreement as to the information that was passed. As an example, The EOOW informs the OOD, "Bridge, Central, I have a hot line shaft bearing; bearing number 2A, request you slow to standard." The OOD replies, "Central, Bridge, hot line shaft bearing number 2A, slowing to standard, aye." And the EOOW confirms: "Central, aye."

By constantly practicing the repeat-back method, even during routine conversations, the OOD and the EOOW see to it that during an emergency the information will be accurate and quickly passed.

The watch officer must also learn to let the EOOW handle a crisis as it occurs and to avoid demanding an excessive amount of information during the critical early seconds of a casualty. At that time the EOOW is focused on keeping the plant stable, and the last thing he or she needs is a constant drumbeat of questions and comments from the pilothouse. The watch officer who falls into this may be trying to keep the captain informed, but he or she needs to realize that when the situation has stabilized, the EOOW will be calling the CO with a full explanation. Far better than badgering is to let the EOOW conduct initial responses and begin casualty control.

The watch officer's real concerns in the event of a casualty are simple: to gather enough information to give the captain a quick report, recognizing that more detail will shortly be coming from the engineer; to understand any maneuvering implications of the casualty, for example, a locked shaft or the loss of an engine on a shaft; and to foresee anything that could suddenly affect the routine of the ship, for example, a fuel leak. Beyond this, the EOOW must be permitted to correct the casualty and restore the plant to full readiness.

If the watch officer has a problem with an EOOW who he or she believes is not forthcoming with information or is uncooperative, the situation should be discussed with the senior watch officer or engineering officer upon conclusion of the watch. The wrong thing is to enter into prolonged confrontation with the EOOW during the watch.

BASIC ENGINEERING KNOWLEDGE

There is a body of basic knowledge that each watch officer should have about the plant over which he or she is ultimately responsible. In the Navy, this is the knowledge a junior engineering officer of the watch should have as part of the personnel qualification standards (PQS), and it is fundamental to the proper execution of the watch. Watch officers are generally tested by a qualification board prior to assuming the watch. While not extensive or all-inclusive (because, after all, an EOOW is always on duty as a reference source for the OOD), this knowledge must be mastered by the watch officer. Until it is fully committed to memory, the watch officer may want to jot down particulars on index cards, which can be carried in a pocket for referral and study. In particular, the OOD must have a complete knowledge of the casualty control procedures for major engineering systems as well as actions to take to support damage control.

While this information varies, as a baseline each watch officer should be well versed in the following:

- *Propulsion.* The basic method of propulsion, amount of shaft horse-power generated, number of engines or boilers, basic drive train, basic thermodynamic cycle, steering system, main lubricating-oil system, shafting and bearing supports for the main shafts, fuel-oil filling and distribution system, and aviation-fuel filling and distribution system.

- *Electrical.* The number of generators, the specifications for generators, the basic configuration of the electrical distribution system, the layout of load centers, the power source for critical loads (steering, vital combat systems, propulsion systems, etc.), the special frequency systems (400-Hz generators, distribution), the emergency power supply (emergency diesels, uninterruptible power supply, etc.), the casualty power-distribution system, and the degaussing system.

- *Auxiliaries.* The number of evaporators, the reverse-osmosis units and their ratings, the amount of feed and fresh, the air conditioners, the dry air, the chill water, the air compressors (high pressure and low pressure), and the main and secondary drainage systems.

- *Damage Control.* Major systems (HALON, installed carbon dioxide, AFFF/FP180, HICAP, etc.), the capabilities of each, the use of portable firefighting systems, the fire-main layout, the number of fire pumps, the normal pressure, the installed eductors, the ventilation, and the countermeasure washdown system.

- *Engineering Control.* The layout of the CCS, the location of control mechanisms for most major engineering systems, and a basic understanding of controls for key equipment.

In addition to or in place of index cards, many ships publish an engineering department handbook that includes the information indicated above. Similarly, many ships have a damage-control handbook with a great deal of essential information.

THE GAS-TURBINE PLANT

The advantages of a gas-turbine plant include its light weight and compact structure, extremely quick start-up times, relative quietness, minimal manpower requirements, easily replaceable engines, reliability, efficiency at high rates of speed, and cleanliness. Some of the disadvantages include the requirement for a lot of fuel storage, inefficiency when there are small or partial loads, huge consumption of air (which can be dangerous in a nuclear/biological/chemical [NBC] environment), and complexity of the controllable reversible-pitch propeller system and clutches.

From the perspective of the watch officer, the major advantages of the gas-turbine plant are rapidity of response and operations that are almost casualty-free. Because the throttle control for propulsion gas-turbine engines is normally on the bridge, response to engineering commands is virtually instantaneous. The ship moves ahead and astern within seconds of the throttle movement on the bridge. The engineering plant is unusually reliable. The OOD will encounter a few basic casualties, but the likelihood of major shaft-stopping problems is minimal. With two engines available on each of twin shafts in most plants, it takes only moments to start one engine if there is a problem with the other.

THE CONVENTIONAL STEAM PLANT

The advantages of a steam plant include efficiency at cruising speed, reliability, reasonable efficiency at partial loading, and the usefulness of steam for auxiliary systems (heating, distilling, etc.). Disadvantages include the size of the plant, its start-up time, the requirement for large fuel tanks, low endurance at high speeds, inefficiency at lower speeds, and, above all, the manpower requirement.

Steam, dependable and effective as a means of propulsion, will be used in the foreseeable future on many older ships and some new warships. In the nuclear variant (discussed below), steam propulsion will be used for the largest surface combatants (aircraft carriers) and submarines. Some of the casualties associated with steam plants require a watch officer to slow the ship considerably. The watch officer provides permission for the EOOW to conduct blow-downs, light off and secure boilers and generators, pump bilges, and place vital machinery or equipment out of commission for preventive maintenance.

THE NUCLEAR STEAM PLANT

The advantages of a nuclear steam plant include, above all, endurance, the lack of requirement for air during combustion (rendering it safe during NBC warfare), and reliability. Disadvantages include the cost of construction, maintenance, and training of the workforce to maintain the plant; weight; start-up time; added radiological and environmental procedures and protocols; and the length of overhauls.

The nuclear steam plant is reliable and run by specialists. The relationship between the watch officer and the EOOW is similar to that associated with other plants.

THE DIESEL PLANT

The advantages of a diesel plant include exceptional efficiency at all loads, low cost, smaller reduction gears, reliability, low manning levels, and simplicity of adaptation. Disadvantages include the amount of maintenance and the frequency of overhauls, the consumption of an inordinate amount of lubricating oil, noise (especially disadvantageous for ships involved in ASW or escort duty), and problems resulting from the need to drive a single shaft with three or more diesels.

THE COMBINED DIESEL–GAS-TURBINE PLANT

The combined diesel and gas-turbine engineering plant offers the benefits of both systems. The fuel efficiency of a diesel at lower speeds is combined with gas-turbine propulsion when higher speeds are necessary. Disadvantages include added transition time when shifting between propulsion modes as well as those noted above.

THE ALL-ELECTRIC PLANT

The ZUMWALT class of destroyer uses an all-electric plant that integrates the use of power between propulsion and the combat system. The integrated power system provides optimum efficiency by redirecting power to combat systems and sensors only when needed. Power is generated by two main and two auxiliary turbine generators and made available for propulsion, combat systems, or other uses through an integrated power distribution system. Benefits of all-electric population include eliminating the need for extensive drive shafting and reduction gears and beneficial acoustic properties.

THE ENGINEERING OPERATIONAL SEQUENCING SYSTEM (EOSS)

The watch officer needs a basic appreciation of the concept of EOSS. The complexity of the modern plant requires standardized guidelines for normal operations and casualties. Watchstanders in the engineering plant are provided with specific checklists and step-by-step procedures to deal with every conceivable situation.

The two parts of EOSS that the watch officer may hear about from the engineer are engineering operational procedure (EOP), which covers normal activities such as starting a main engine, switching duplex strainers, and bringing a forced-draft blower on the line, and, of equal importance to the watch officer, engineering operational casualty control (EOCC). EOCC refers to actions watchstanders take in the event of a casualty in the plant. Engineering watchstanders memorize the immediate actions required and, in the event of a casualty, immediately inform the watch officer on the bridge of any actions required there. Once the casualty is under control, specific recovery steps outlined in the EOCC are followed.

UNDERSTANDING THE ENGINEERING OFFICER OF THE WATCH

A quick review of this excerpt from OpNavInst 3120.32D is always useful for the OOD. It provides an excellent overview of what your counterpart in engineering is doing. Because most OODs go on to become EOOWs, and the EOOW qualification is an essential milestone, it is also helpful from a professional perspective.

BASIC FUNCTION. The Engineering Officer of the Watch (EOOW) is the officer or petty officer on watch designated by the Engineer Officer to be in charge of an Engineering Department watch section. They are responsible for safe and proper performance of engineering department watches following the orders of the Engineer Officer, the Commanding Officer, and higher authority.

a. DUTIES, RESPONSIBILITIES, AND AUTHORITY. The Engineering Officer of the Watch shall:

(1) Supervise personnel on watch in the Engineering Department (except damage control), ensuring that machinery is operated according to instructions, required logs are maintained, machinery and controls are properly manned, and all applicable inspections and safety precautions are carried out.

(2) Ensure that interior communications circuits are properly manned and that circuit discipline is maintained and correct procedures and terminology are followed.

(3) Ensure that orders from the OOD concerning the speed and direction of rotation of the main engines are executed promptly and properly.

(4) Immediately execute all emergency orders concerning the speed and direction of rotation of the screws.

(5) Immediately inform the OOD and the Engineering Officer of any casualty which would prevent the execution of engine speed orders or would affect the operational capability of the ship.

(6) Ensure that directives and procedures issued by higher authority concerning the operation of machinery in the Engineering Department are followed.

(7) Keep informed of the power requirements for operations. Ensure that the propulsion and auxiliary machinery combinations will effectively meet operational requirements. Advise the OOD and the Engineering Officer when any modification of the propulsion plant or major auxiliaries is required.

(8) Supervise and coordinate on-the-job training for engineering personnel on watch.

(9) Assume such other responsibilities as the Engineering Officer may direct.

(10) In addition, on nuclear-powered ships, the EOOW is also governed by the requirements of OpNavInst 9210.2 (Series).

(11) On ships that do not station a damage control watch officer, supervise the maintenance of a log of all fittings which are in violation of the material condition of readiness prescribed. Entries shall show the name and rate of the person requesting permission to open a fitting, approximate length of time to be open, and time closed. Anyone, without permission, who violates the material condition of readiness in effect shall be the subject of an official report.

12

THE WATCH OFFICER IN PORT

The Command Duty Officer is that officer or authorized Petty Officer designated by the Commanding Officer to carry out the routine of the unit in port and to supervise the Officer of the Deck in the safety and general duties of the unit. In the temporary absence of the Executive Officer, the duties of the Executive Officer will be carried out by the Command Duty Officer.

OPNAVINST 3120.32D

THE COMMAND DUTY OFFICER

Security of ships in port has always been paramount. The 12 October 2000 attack on USS COLE (DDG 67) during a brief refueling stop in Aden, Yemen; the events of 11 September 2001; and the 2014 shooting onboard USS MAHAN (DDG 72) underline the potential threats facing our forces—whether overseas or at home. Force protection is a serious undertaking and a constant responsibility that must always be factored during in-port operations. There is no substitute for proper training and vigilance

The primary responsibility of the in-port duty section is the safety and security of the ship. The command duty officer (CDO), designated by the CO, must lead watchstanders in discharging this responsibility. He or she customarily stands duty for a twenty-four-hour period and sets the tone for the duty section's performance. The CDO reports to the XO or, in that person's absence, the CO. Routine reports made to the CO by the OOD should also be made to the CDO. If the XO is temporarily absent, the heads of departments or their designated representatives report to the CDO concerning matters affecting the operation and administration of their departments. The CDO should conduct frequent inspections to ensure the safety and security of the ship. Additionally, he or she has the responsibility of drilling duty emergency parties.

Clearly, this is a critical position that requires a great deal of preparation. Navy Regulations state that the CDO is an officer eligible for command. In fact, the CDO may be required to get the ship under way on a moment's notice; although he or she rarely takes this action, the possibility shows how well prepared a CDO must be to accept the responsibilities of the watch. A good CDO does not execute responsibilities from the confines of the wardroom or stateroom but rather makes frequent rounds of the ship and keeps informed as to her status. COs and XOs have specific guidelines for the CDO, usually written in detail in the ship's in-port standing orders, which should be reviewed at least monthly. The following suggestions can help any CDO maintain high standards for the duty section:

1. The CDO should conduct frequent and random inspections throughout the ship, keeping an eye out for hazards, cleanliness, crew appearance, work in progress, material condition, and ship-wide security.

2. The CDO should always inform the quarterdeck of his or her whereabouts and how he or she may be contacted.

3. The CDO should attempt to be on the quarterdeck for the arrival and departure of the CO and XO so that they can pass along any necessary information.

4. The CDO should pay close attention to drills by emergency response teams and critique them. He or she should be creative, vary the scenario to cover common contingencies, and remember to have the rescue-and-assistance team train.

5. The CDO should inform the CO and XO if a drill will be conducted while they are on board. This courtesy goes a long way to alleviating their anxiety when a training environment and drill is called away.

6. The CDO should be on deck to observe special evolutions such as colors and sunrise. These evolutions are a sign of a ship's pride and professionalism, and the CDO's personal interest always helps to make them run smoothly and efficiently.

7. The CDO should watch for sudden and unexpected changes in weather (particularly a change in barometric pressure readings of .04 or more in any one hour). This is critical if boat operations are being conducted.

8. The CDO should know the status of the ship's boats at all times and ensure that the OOD is logging the status correctly.

9. The CDO should frequently spot-check hazardous storage areas to ensure proper storage of volatile material.

10. The CDO should always know the status of the engineering plant and frequently check it.

11. The CDO should require the quarterdeck to inform him or her immediately of any changes in fire-main pressure or any unusual readings observed by sounding-and-security or roving patrols.

12. The CDO should mentally prepare to respond to emergencies and should have emergency telephone numbers—such as those of the base fire department, ambulance, security, and chaplain—within reach.

13. The CDO should ensure that preparations are made for upcoming events. For example, if the ship expects to get under way the following day, he or she should ensure the getting underway check-off list is on track, which entails making sure that arrangements have been made to clear away paint floats, waste oil barges, and so on. The CDO should think at least one day ahead of the duty day.

14. If in doubt, the CDO should call the CO or XO for assistance.

The CDO sets the standards for the duty section. Slovenly appearance, lack of interest in drills and exercises, or a lethargic attitude toward duty will be reflected by the watch team. On the other hand, an exuberant, visible, and concerned CDO will lead the way to a taut and safe watch.

THE ANTITERRORISM TACTICAL WATCH OFFICER (ATTWO)

The ATTWO coordinates integration of waterborne and shoreside Anti-Terrorism/Force Protection (ATFP) assets and reports to the CDO for the defense of the unit against terrorist attack.

OPNAVINST 3120.32D

Normally stood up in non-Navy ports of call or during force protection conditions that require additional tactical level leadership, the ATTWO is responsible for coordinating the ship-wide response to threats, ensuring clear communications, and keeping the command duty officer updated on the status of the response. The ship's in-port standing orders and antiterrorism plan will normally provide details that direct immediately and controlling actions of the ATTWO. The ATTWO reports to the command duty officer and coordinates with the OOD.

THE OFFICER OF THE DECK

> The officer of the deck is that officer or petty officer on watch designated by the Commanding Officer to be in charge of the unit. They are primarily responsible for the safety, security, and proper operation of the unit.
>
> OPNAVINST 3120.32D

When a ship is in port, the OOD's responsibilities are considerably less complex than when she is at sea. This does not mean, however, that the job is any less demanding. Although not faced with maneuvering or signals, the OOD in port is occupied with a seemingly endless series of things to supervise, inspect, and control. He or she is expected to make timely and sound decisions on matters that are, in their own way, nearly as important as anything that happens at sea. If the OOD is to stand watch properly, he or she must be at least as well prepared as at sea and must be ready to respond quickly to a variety of situations.

A chief petty officer or petty officer who is assigned as OOD in port has the same status as a commissioned or warrant officer so assigned, and his or her orders have the same force. This person is designated in writing by the CO and in most ships is required to complete the section of the surface warfare officer's PQS test that relates to the OOD in port. The person must also pass an oral board.

PREPARING FOR THE WATCH

Considerable preparation in the form of reviewing ship's routine, receiving instructions from local commanders and from the senior officer present afloat

(SOPA), and learning policy concerning special situations is necessary before taking over a deck watch in port. The basic information and checklists that the OOD needs are usually kept in a notebook on the quarterdeck and in the unit's in-port standing orders. Some of the most important things that OODs in port must consider are listed below; experience or special circumstances will suggest others.

If the ship is pierside, the OOD should know:

1. Evolutions that may occur during the watch.
2. The status of visitors.
3. Quarterdeck search procedures in effect.
4. The local security climate, including the force protection condition (FPCON) in effect.
5. The last time security watches reported.
6. The status of the ship's propulsion machinery.
7. Current material condition of readiness.
8. Who the SOPA is and what other commanders and flagships are present.
9. What flags and pennants are flying.
10. The status of crew aloft, crew over the side, or divers in the water.
11. What guard ships (military, medical, etc.) are present, what radio circuits are guarded, and whether visual guards are posted.
12. What services the ship is receiving from the pier.
13. The status of all boats in the water, in skids, out of commission, away on trips, scheduled for trips, and so forth, and the status of fuel in boats.
14. The status of ship's vehicles—location, drivers, trips planned, fuel, and so forth.
15. The weather, and changes anticipated.
16. The amount of rise and fall of the tide, the state of the tide, and the time of the next change in the tide.
17. The status of aircraft.
18. Who the CDO is and how he or she may be reached.
19. The status of ship's restricted crew, prisoners, or medical cases.

20. What orders are currently in effect or unexecuted.
21. The location of the CO and XO.

If the ship is at anchor, the OOD should also know:

1. The anchorage bearings.
2. The nature of the holding ground (i.e., mud, sand, rock), the depth of water, and the scope of chain on deck (typically five to seven times the water depth or in accordance with ship-specific guidance).
3. The position of the ship on the chart and how frequently fixes are being taken.
4. Anchor(s) in use.
5. Anchor(s) ready for letting go.
6. Frequency of anchor watch reports.
7. Steaming notice required.
8. Other ships present and their location.
9. When the ship is moored to a buoy or buoys, the amount of chain or wire used.

SMART APPEARANCE

In port, more than at any other time, the initial impression a visitor receives is based almost solely on the appearance and smartness of the quarterdeck and the watch. This impression is all encompassing: It is created by crew, officers, and captain. Thus, the appearance of a ship, her boats, and her crew is a major responsibility of the OOD. He or she must not only know the proper standards of cleanliness and smartness but also enforce them. It takes little practice to note such things as loose bits of line, slack halyards, and sloppy execution of the colors ceremony. But it takes energy, initiative, and patience to correct them. Junior officers vary in their powers of observation and in their attitude about action. The better an officer's reputation for standing a taut watch and for being intolerant of anything that downgrades the ship, the more readily the crew will respond. An officer with such a reputation is not likely to have watchstanders on the quarterdeck in frayed or soiled uniforms, or to allow crew on liberty that are not properly groomed or in proper attire. He or she will, in short, find high standards easy to maintain. On the other hand, an officer who is slovenly and does not have the pride to stand a proper watch will be continually beset. Superiors will be constantly calling him or her on the appearance of the ship or the quarterdeck's response to unique circumstances and the crew will not be responsive. Every officer should resolve early on to run a taut and efficient watch, complying with procedures and with an expert level of knowledge. People respect an officer who knows his or her job and performs it fairly and pleasantly, but in accordance with directives and the traditionally high standards of the Navy.

WATCH ORGANIZATION

Prior to taking over a watch, the OOD must find out what watches are being manned, who is manning them, and to whom each watchstander reports. Because few watch teams are centered in one place, as they are when the ship is under way, this information is important for getting the watch started smoothly. The oncoming OOD should be informed of any changes to the watch bill that have been authorized, of watches posted for special evolutions, and of watch conditions that differ from those promulgated in the plan of the day.

The Petty Officer of the Watch

> The petty officer of the watch is the primary enlisted assistant to the officer of the deck in port of large ships.
>
> OPNAVINST 3120.32D

The petty officer of the watch (POOW) is the OOD's right-hand watchstander and should be given responsibility for overall supervision of the watch team. The POOW is usually the person closest to the OOD in qualification and experience (sometimes the POOW is a qualified OOD) and is specifically responsible for assisting him or her in training and inspecting the watch. If properly trained and briefed by the OOD, the POOW can serve as a second pair of eyes and can double-check the ship's routine. In addition to the duties required by naval and ship's policy, such as log keeping and supervising boats, he or she should be, under the OOD, the leader of the watch team. The POOW is normally armed with a 9-mm pistol.

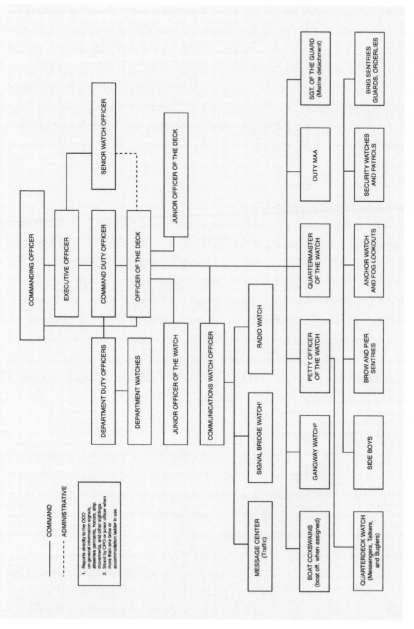

FIGURE 12-1. Watch Organization in Port

The Messenger of the Watch

Normally nonrated, the messenger of the watch is detailed by the OOD and the POOW to perform various routine duties, such as waking watch reliefs, escorting visitors, and periodically sprucing up the quarterdeck. Messengers should not be considered qualified until they have been aboard a ship long enough to know the location of all major working spaces, offices, staterooms, and other frequently visited areas. A sure way to give the impression of a sloppy ship is to provide a visitor with a messenger escort who does not know his or her way around. When a watch is expected to be unusually active, two messengers should be assigned.

The Sounding-and-Security Watch

The sounding-and-security watch is required to make his or her rounds in a random fashion and to report to the OOD hourly. The small size of the average in-port duty section makes this duty particularly important. With most of the crew ashore on liberty, this watchstander is likely to be the only person in a position to discover flooding, fire, or a breach of the ship's security. Therefore, his or her performance should be closely monitored by the OOD and, whenever possible, double-checked by the POOW. It is a good practice for the OOD periodically to quiz the sounding-and-security watch to ensure that he or she is actually checking the spaces assigned. Failure of this watchstander to make a report to the quarterdeck must be immediately investigated.

The Master-at-Arms

The duty master-at-arms is normally a petty officer first or second class who stands no other watches during the duty day. He or she is responsible for conducting periodic musters of restricted crew, supervising the performance of extra duty, and conducting a number of routine inspections of various spaces to check for cleanliness. When a working party is called away, the duty master-at-arms should be placed in charge of mustering and supervising it.

One of this person's most important duties is to enforce standards of order and discipline. When a disciplinary problem is discovered or suspected, the duty master-at-arms should be called away at once, given instructions by the OOD, and charged with investigating the situation. In cases of drunken or disorderly conduct, the duty master-at-arms may be empowered to obtain assistance from other senior petty officers in the duty section.

Cold-Iron Watch

In ships whose main machinery is inactive or that have no auxiliary watch on duty below, a "cold-iron watch" is stationed. This consists of members of the engineering watch who, at regular intervals, inspect all machinery spaces for violations of watertight integrity and for fire hazards.

EXTERNAL SECURITY

In port, the security of the ship is one of the most important duties of the OOD and CDO. Threats to her security may be natural, may be caused by fire and heavy weather, or they may arise from an almost infinite range of deliberate human actions. Tight security is a necessity at all times, and no matter how quiet and uneventful a watch may seem, the OOD should never allow it to be relaxed. Of specific concern is the physical threat to U.S. naval vessels from terrorists as well as the cyber threat that can impact the ship at any time. No ship is ever immune to these threats, which can be carried out in a variety of unconventional ways. From the physical security standpoint, suicide attackers are particularly challenging as they are willing to die for their cause. The quarterdeck watch team must always assume that the danger of terrorism is present and must not allow lax security procedures. FPCONs will be promulgated by senior commanders to aid in scaling our defense levels based on information from all sources. It is important to note, however, that there is always some level of threat.

If a breach in security is discovered, the OOD has a trained self-defense force. The type of ship and her mission determine who constitutes this force. Members are specifically designated and trained in security procedures, which the OOD should know and fully understand. The OOD should call away the security force if the ship or crew is in any way threatened. The team follows established procedures to ensure the security of the ship. The OOD should never hesitate to initiate a security alert; if there is any doubt, he or she should call it away. The OOD should also periodically drill this team at the discretion of the CDO.

Control of Visitors

> Commanding Officers are responsible for the control of visitors to their commands and shall comply with the relevant provisions of the Department of the Navy directives concerning classified Information and physical security.
>
> NAVY REGULATIONS

Almost every naval vessel in commission must be prepared for the control, identification, and supervision of visitors. Depending on the security requirements in force, the OOD may be required to issue passes for visitors, check whether there is written authorization for them to come aboard, and provide them with escorts. No matter how busy the quarterdeck gets, the OOD must always maintain control over visitors. They should not be allowed to wander from the quarterdeck or to proceed without escort simply because they claim to know the way.

In general, dealers and tradespeople or their agents are admitted only as authorized by the CO for the following purposes:

1. To conduct public business.
2. To transact private business with individuals at the request of the captain.
3. To furnish services and supplies that are not available to the personnel of the command or are not available in sufficient quantity.

Fleet and force regulations that restrict casual visiting and the approach of bumboats should be followed with great care. Persons with a legitimate reason to come on board must be received politely. Every person coming on board, even those in uniform or professing official or business connections, should present proper identification. The harder it is to screen visitors, the more important it is to observe precautions.

Inspection of Packages and Personal Effects

The OOD is authorized to inspect all parcels, briefcases, and other items carried on board by both visitors and ship's company and, under some circumstances, to inspect those being carried off the ship. The OOD's authority is backed by federal regulation, and there are no exceptions to it. Personal effects should be inspected for classified material, contraband, drugs, liquor, and weapons as well as government property being removed from the ship without authorization. When circumstances dictate, body searches of all or randomly chosen persons may be carried out. If many people are to be inspected at one time, the duty master-at-arms should be called away to assist and to prevent congestion on the quarterdeck. Security technology such as metal detectors (both fixed and hand-held wands), X-ray machines, and explosive detection devices are available for use on most ships. These devices improve the efficiency and effectiveness of searches prior to individuals boarding ships. It is important to note that the location for screening individuals and parcels is prior to their crossing the ship's brow. In this manner, security is maintained at a perimeter removed from the ship.

Sentries and Guards

Sentries and armed guards will always be employed, although their numbers may vary, and the OOD needs only to implement existing command procedures covering the use of forecastle, fantail, roving, and pier sentries to effect a change in their posture or presence. This will normally be conducted by a duty section chief of the guard in coordination with the CDO. Navy Doctrine for Antiterrorism/Force Protection is NWP 3-07.2. It contains detailed procedures and SOP for naval force protection. Pier sentries control flow of personnel and traffic on the pier. It is absolutely essential that sentries clearly understand their duties and stand a taut watch. They constitute the first line of defense for units in port. The "11 General Orders of a Sentry" are

1. To take charge of this post and all government property in view.
2. To walk my post in a military manner, keeping always on the alert, and observing everything that takes place within sight or hearing.
3. To report all violations of orders I am instructed to enforce.
4. To repeat all calls from posts more distant from the guard house than my own.
5. To quit my post only when properly relieved.
6. To receive, obey, and pass on to the sentry who relieves me, all orders from the commanding officer, command duty officer, officer of the deck, and officers and petty officers of the watch only.

7. To talk to no one except in the line of duty.

8. To give the alarm in case of fire or disorder.

9. To call the officer of the deck in any case not covered by instructions.

10. To salute all officers and all colors and standards not cased.

11. To be especially watchful at night, and, during the time for challenging, to challenge all persons on or near my post and to allow no one to pass without proper authority.

All sentries may be armed when the situation demands. The OOD must be certain that armed sentries or guards are proficient in the use of their weapons and fully qualified in terms of PQS and all other shipboard requirements. Navy Tactical Reference Publication (NTRP) 3-07.2.2 (January 2015), Force Protection Weapons Handling Standard Procedures and Guidelines, spells out Navy SOP for handling a variety of force protection weapons, also known as "Guard Mount Procedures." The procedures included in this document are required to be posted at weapons handling points and shall be followed every time that weapons turnovers occur.

Sneak Attack and Sabotage

Particularly during darkness, ships at anchor or moored are vulnerable to various forms of sneak attack and sabotage conducted by swimmers, people in small boats, or submarines. Limpet mines can be attached to the hull of the ship, explosive charges can be placed below the ship, and mobile limpets can be used. Saboteurs may pose as bumboat crews or visitors, or they may mingle with a returning liberty party. Surreptitious boarding from the shore is possible when ships are moored to a pier. Attack may also consist of contamination of food and water supplies, a chemical or biological attack, or destruction of vital equipment by explosives or other means.

Where such dangers exist, normal security measures must be increased. The OOD should maintain gangway security by considering all approaching boats, persons, and packages suspect until they have been identified and inspected. All unnecessary lines, fenders, and sea ladders should be taken in. Boats not in use should be hoisted in, and booms should be rigged out of reach of swimmers and boats. Guards should be posted at all topside openings and a party identified to be ready to repel boarders. Automatic weapons can be manned and additional watchstanders armed. Unnecessary noise should be avoided. Swimmers and explosive-ordnance-disposal teams may be assigned to inspect the ship's bottom, but only after sonar has been secured and all sentries and boats have been advised so as to prevent the dropping of explosive charges.

In case of attack, the highest degree of material readiness should be set, the rail manned with armed personnel, the SOPA and all ships present notified, and the ship made ready for getting under way immediately. In any case, the secure ship is the one that remains vigilant, has researched all threat indicators, and employs a well-trained watch organization.

INTERNAL SECURITY

The safety of a ship may be threatened by persons or forces within as well. The OOD should make sure that required patrols are carried out and reports made in person and on time. In addition to making routine checks of watertight closures and other safety devices, patrols should be alert to fire hazards and to the presence of combustibles that have not been properly stowed.

Shipyard Security

> It shall be the responsibility of the commanding officer of a ship in commission which is undergoing overhaul, or which is otherwise immobilized at a naval station or naval shipyard, to request such services as are necessary to ensure the safety of the ship.
>
> NAVY REGULATIONS

A ship under repair and overhaul in a shipyard has particular security problems. All workers coming on board must be identified. If their tools are stowed in racks on deck, they should be safeguarded by ship's sentries. Most shipyard workers are honest, but a small percentage might not be able to resist a souvenir or two, particularly if tools are left adrift. It must be the duty of the watch on deck to see that theft, by both ship and shipyard personnel, is prevented.

Compartments containing classified matter must be secured, either by lock or by sentry. There are times when yard workers have to enter locked spaces, and the OOD can anticipate such occasions by keeping reasonably well informed about the nature and location of the work being done. Fire watches are normally assigned to every welder and person performing hot work on the ship. Another precaution that should be taken during shipyard work is the inspection of spaces after each shift for rubbish and any other material that may create a fire hazard.

Custody of Keys

Custody of a ship's keys is carefully organized, and the OOD must fully understand how it works. Designated duty personnel have custody of some of the keys to their spaces. Department heads must maintain a locker containing all the keys to their spaces and make them available to the OOD at all times for use in an emergency. The OOD must know who the duty keyholders are and what procedures to follow to gain access to secured spaces.

ANCHORAGE AND MOORINGS

When the ship is anchored, moored, or secured to a pier or wharf, the OOD's greatest responsibilities concern the weather. At sea, the CO makes the big decisions; in port, the OOD must often take action before the CO can be advised of a situation.

It is advisable for the OOD to know what sort of weather can be expected in a certain area at a certain time of year. Meteorological forecasts, although often accessible via the internet, are not always available, nor are they always 100 percent accurate. They may even lull inexperienced officers into a false sense of security. The *actual* weather at the ship's position is the important factor, not just the weather that is *forecast* for that position. Pilot charts are another source of this information. There may be little possibility of winds more than forty knots in San Diego Bay at any time, but at Adak, in the Aleutians, the wind can whip up to sixty knots almost any afternoon. Thus, the OOD should inspect anchor chains or mooring lines as often as the weather dictates and take appropriate action to avert problems.

Dragging

The most certain indication of dragging is a change in anchorage bearings, particularly those near the beam. These bearings should be checked at regular intervals even in good weather. The ship's standing orders will normally contain a specific order on anchoring, detailing the requirements for watchstanders, fix intervals, and actions in the event of dragging anchor. A dragging anchor can be detected by watching the chain or by feeling it on deck. The chain pulsates or jumps when the anchor is dragging because the flukes are alternately taking hold and being pulled loose.

The major safeguards against collision or grounding caused by dragging are having (1) a second anchor ready to go, and (2) steam at the throttle or a gas-turbine engine ready to start, the steering gear ready for use, and the engine room ready to answer bells. The latter course is expensive in personnel hours and fuel and should be ordered if necessary. The OOD should not hesitate to inform the CO of the possibility of dragging. The CO will decide what precautionary measures to take.

A ship secured to a well-anchored mooring buoy by an anchor chain is not likely to be in danger unless the wind or current is exceedingly high. In severe weather, vessels as big as destroyers have been known to carry away from a mooring, generally because too little scope of chain was allowed. When the scope of chain is not long enough to provide a catenary, the sudden strain as the bow of the ship pitches is sufficient to part the chain or the chain stopper on deck. To counter the yaw that results from a long scope to the buoy, an additional safety is to drop an anchor straight down (underfoot).

Heavy Weather

A ship alongside a pier or a wharf, with the standard mooring lines doubled up, is in little danger from high winds except in extreme cases. When heavy seas and high winds are anticipated, the OOD should do the following:

1. Request permission to hoist in all boats in the water, to trice up gangways, and to order boat-pool boats to return to their base or be secured astern on long painters.
2. Establish a special boat watch.
3. Call away the anchor detail and prepare to drop the anchor underfoot if directed. *Note:* This practice is now performed with regularity as a normal in-port procedure during typhoon and hurricane seasons.

4. Put over storm wires, spring lays, or the anchor chain to augment mooring lines.

5. Try to get any camels that might be holding the ship off the pier removed (if this will improve the stability and security of the moor).

6. Have all loose gear on deck secured and, if the ship is beginning to surge, be prepared to take in the brow.

7. Be prepared to disconnect shore power and shift to ship's power. Shore power cables placed under strain are liable to part, causing fires and explosions.

8. If extreme conditions are forecast, be prepared to light off one or more boilers to get under way when directed.

9. Police the pier thoroughly for any loose debris that may become airborne in high winds.

HURRICANES AND TYPHOONS

When a hurricane or typhoon is moving into the area, the ship must either put to sea to avoid the storm or remain in port and ride it out. If the ship is to remain in port, she may move to a sheltered anchorage, in which case all preparations for getting under way should be made and the precautions listed above be carried out.

Preparations for riding out a storm, normally prescribed in the SOPA's instructions, include the following:

1. Double up the mooring lines, employ storm lines and spring lays, and inspect them frequently.

2. Recall personnel to the ship and place the engineering plant and sea detail on standby.

3. Maintain radio and signal watches, man the radar, and keep a plot of the storm in the CIC.

4. Police the dock area, secure topside gear, break out heavy-weather gear and flashlights, and inventory rescue-assistance lockers.

5. Maintain a plot of the storm's movements and brief the crew on them.

The anchorage should allow room for the ship to swing with the longest scope of chain available. Main engines should be used to offset the wind, with revolutions per minute from three to five knots as required.

Bearings on shore, radar, drift lead, continuous echo soundings, and a continuous watch on the chain should all be used to detect signs of a dragging anchor. The Hurricane Havens Handbook and Typhoon Havens Handbook are excellent references that contain a wealth of information on these destructive systems. These resources are regularly updated and available online through the Naval Research Laboratory (www.nrlmry.navy.mil) under Research Products, Fleet Applications and Handbook Projects.

STORES AND FUEL

When stores are to be loaded, the OOD must make certain that the right people have been notified and are in charge. The deck force is responsible for operating gear and tackle, and the OOD should check to see that a competent boatswain's mate is on the job. The supply officer or that person's representative should check the stores aboard and direct their stowage.

When a ship is refueling in port, the OOD has clearly defined responsibilities for both safety and the prevention of spills. In coordination with the engineering officer, he or she should see that the required stations are manned for the detection of spills and that oil-recovery materials are available for use on short notice should a spill occur. The reports required and the telephone numbers to call in case of a fuel spill should be at hand on the quarterdeck. During fueling, the OOD is also responsible for displaying proper signals and passing the word restricting smoking.

LIBERTY

Crews are granted liberty by sections. When a ship is in a foreign port, forward deployed, or in a high state of readiness, her crew is normally divided into three to four duty sections. This practice is followed because experience has taught that the minimum number of people required to get a ship under way is about one-third of her crew. In home port and when no special conditions of readiness are in effect, many ships have their crews divided into six duty sections, five of which may be on liberty at a given time. The six-section construct also provides the opportunity to readily collapse into three sections should it be required for additional force protection or other readiness reasons. Regardless of prevailing conditions, the duty section left on board should always be big enough to fight fires, deal with emergencies, and carry out the ship's routine. The CDO should always question if there are enough personnel on board to combat the most stressing expected situation and not just routine operations. If the OOD feels that this condition is not being met, the CDO should be informed immediately.

Inspection of Liberty Parties

The OOD and the watch team have the primary responsibility for enforcing the Navy's and the ship's standards of dress and grooming. The OOD in port must continually inspect individuals going ashore and judge, using common sense and knowledge of the rules, whether someone should be permitted to go ashore or be turned back. Ensuring these standards are properly enforced is a continuous process, requiring constant monitoring.

Fashions and styles of dress change and, considering the range of age groups and interests represented in most ships, it is challenging to lay down definitive standards for dress and grooming. However, it is reasonable to assume that the majority of any crew will respect reasonable standards, especially if they are equitably enforced by all deck watchstanders.

In foreign ports, the situation is slightly different. Because a sailor ashore represents his or her country, navy, and ship, the command has every right to expect that he or she will present an appearance that is a credit and not an embarrassment. This requires an extra degree of attention.

The return of liberty parties may be a routine matter or it may be a lively occasion. The OOD usually has only to identify the crew members by visual inspection of their military identification card. If the ship has just made port after a long voyage or is sailing the next day for an extended absence, there may be a few individuals who overconsume alcohol and are less than orderly in their deportment. A master-at-arms should be detailed to get them off the quarterdeck and to their berthing safely. While maintaining complete control of the quarterdeck and the conduct of the watch, the OOD must let experienced assistants handle most such matters directly. However, persistent troublemakers may require special attention, and direct orders may be needed to control them. Physical contact should be avoided, and enlisted watchstanders should be left to handle those who will not go below peacefully.

The people most in need of attention are those who are brought aboard apparently drunk. They should be taken to sick bay and examined; they may have head injuries or be under the influence of drugs instead of, or in addition to, being drunk. If necessary, the duty medical officer should be called to examine them. Matters of this sort are recorded fully in the log, together with a written medical report. An extremely drunk sailor should not be sent below without a watch.

In the end, ships must know their personnel intimately. They must know who among them is "low risk" and who is "high risk" with regard to personal conduct ashore. The quarterdeck becomes a last check in this process.

Loading Liberty Boats

While juniors in the Navy generally embark in boats and vehicles before their seniors, the procedure is sometimes reversed. When liberty parties are being loaded into boats or buses, the chief petty officers sometimes go first, followed by the other petty officers in descending order of rank. This practice enhances the prestige of the petty officers and provides them with a convenience that they well deserve. When many officers are waiting to go ashore, some junior officers may have to wait for the next boat to leave room for the senior officers. During periods of high winds and sea states, particular care should be given to loading the boats in use. During these occasions, it is prudent to reduce normal boat loading by one-half. If winds and seas increase further, boat operations may be suspended completely in the interests of personnel safety.

CREW'S MESS

> Each meal served in the general mess shall be sampled by an officer detailed by the Commanding Officer for that purpose. Should he or she find the quality or quantity of food unsatisfactory or should any member of the mess object to the quality or quantity of the food, the Commanding Officer shall be notified and shall take appropriate action.
>
> NAVY REGULATIONS

It is normal procedure, when in port, for the CDO or the OOD to eat at least one meal in the crew's mess during the duty day. When under way, one of the watch officers should eat a meal with the crew daily. When an officer eats with the crew, he or she should note not only the quantity and quality of food being served but also, equally important, the cleanliness and adequacy of mess gear, the manner in which food is served, and the cleanliness of food handlers. It is not unusual for a CO to make an unannounced visit to the crew's mess and personally check these matters.

Night Rations

It is customary to serve a night ration ("midrats") to the persons who have the midwatch. This helps them to stay awake and sustains them during tasks that are often just as demanding as those of the day. In cold weather, a warm ration is especially welcome to those going on or coming off watch topside as well as to those standing watch in the engineering spaces. This is sometimes only offered during underway routine but can be added in port if deemed impactful.

EIGHT O'CLOCK REPORTS

Eight o'clock reports are an important part of a ship's routine. They serve two functions: they confirm that security and damage-control inspections have been made and they furnish the XO with information to make a report to the CO on the condition of the ship at 2000. The reports made to the XO or the CDO by the heads of departments at 2000 are known as eight o'clock reports, *not* twenty hundred reports. On many ships, they are taken at 1930 or even earlier.

WORKING PARTIES

A ship's schedule often requires large working parties to complete an evolution such as provisioning ship. The necessity is normally accepted by the crew with reasonable understanding. Many times, when only small groups are involved, the OOD can contribute to the well-being of the crew by considering their comfort. Leisure time and meal hours should be respected as much as possible. Crew members whose work is interrupted by a meal should not be required to change into another uniform just to eat, and those who miss a regular meal should have a complete hot meal saved for them. Working parties leaving the ship should be provided with such comforts as rain gear and drinking water if circumstances warrant.

When crew members are required to do work that results in their losing sleep or missing regular meals, it is incumbent upon the officer to see that they get compensatory rest and meals. This is the essence of *taking care of your people.*

APPREHENSION AND RESTRAINT

An OOD must know the difference between apprehension and the three degrees of restraint: confinement, arrest, and restriction in lieu of arrest. He or she will have occasion to take custody of crew members charged with misconduct. They may be delivered by the shore patrol, base police or security, or an officer or petty officer aboard ship, and they may even deliver themselves for such minor offenses as being out of uniform. It is important that the OOD know the legal meanings of the terms involved and also know what action to take. All officers, petty officers, and noncommissioned officers of any service have authority to apprehend offenders subject to the Uniform Code of Military Justice (UCMJ). Enlisted persons have the same authority when they are assigned such duties as shore patrol and military police.

Apprehension means clearly informing a person that he or she is being taken into custody and for what reason. It should be noted that apprehension in the services means the same thing as arrest in civilian life. A police officer informs a citizen that he or she is "under arrest," while a naval officer says that the person is being "apprehended," or taken into custody.

Custody is control over the person apprehended until he or she is delivered to the proper authority, who, on board ship, is the OOD. In general, persons who have authority to apprehend may exercise only that force that is necessary. Petty officers should apprehend officers only in unusual circumstances, for example, when an officer is doing something that disgraces the service.

Restraint involves some deprivation of free movement. It is never imposed as a punishment, and the degree to which it is imposed should be no greater than what is necessary to ensure the presence of the offender at further proceedings in the case. A suspect need not be restrained at all if his or her presence at future proceedings is ensured.

Only the CO may impose restraint on a commissioned officer or a warrant officer. If an officer should be restrained, the CO must be notified. Ordinarily only officers impose restraint on enlisted persons. However, the CO may delegate this authority to warrant officers and enlisted persons.

Confinement is physical restraint imposed on a serious offender to ensure the presence of the person at future proceedings.

Arrest is the restraint of a person, by oral or written order, to certain specified limits, pending the disposition of charges. It is not imposed as punishment. It is imposed only for probable cause based on facts concerning an alleged offense.

One of the disadvantages of placing the accused under arrest is that he or she may no longer be required to perform military duties. Should the accused be required to perform military duties, arrest is automatically terminated and a lesser form of restraint, "restriction in lieu of arrest," can be imposed.

A person apprehended on board ship is delivered, together with a misconduct report, into the custody of the OOD. The latter advises the XO (or CDO) of the situation and receives instructions regarding the nature of the restraint to be imposed, which depends on the gravity of the offense. If formal restraint, such as arrest, is ordered, the OOD notifies the offender, making sure the offender understands the nature of the restraint and the penalties for violating it. The OOD confirms that the offender has been so notified by having that person sign the misconduct report slip. The OOD then turns the offender over to the master-at-arms. The whole affair must, of course, be entered in the log with full details.

When the offense is relatively minor and it can be assumed that the accused will not attempt to leave the area to avoid trial, no restraint is necessary. Arrest and restriction in lieu of arrest may be lifted only by the authority who ordered the restraint or by that person's superior. Once a person has been confined, he or she can be released only by order of the CO of the activity where the confinement takes place. On board ship, of course, the authority ordering confinement is usually the CO.

ASYLUM AND TEMPORARY REFUGE

Under the conventions of international law and as a matter of U.S. government policy, certain persons may, in certain circumstances, be granted asylum or temporary refuge on board a naval vessel. The terms and conditions under which asylum or temporary refuge is granted are specified in the Navy Regulations cited below:

1. If an official of the Department of the Navy is requested to provide asylum or temporary refuge, the following procedures shall apply:

   a. On the high seas or in territories under exclusive United States jurisdiction (including territorial seas, the Commonwealth of Puerto Rico, territories under United States administration, and possessions):

      (1) At his or her request, an applicant for asylum will be received on board any naval aircraft or water-borne craft, Navy, or Marine Corps activity or station.

      (2) Under no circumstances shall the person seeking asylum be surrendered to foreign jurisdiction or control, unless at the personal direction of the Secretary of the Navy or higher authority. Persons seeking political asylum should be afforded every reasonable care and protection permitted by the circumstances.

   b. In territories under foreign jurisdiction (including foreign territorial seas, territories, and possessions):

      (1) Temporary refuge shall be granted for humanitarian reasons on board a naval aircraft or water-borne craft, Navy, or Marine Corps activity or station, only in extreme or exceptional circumstances wherein life or safety of a person is put in imminent danger, such as pursuit by a mob. When temporary refuge is granted, such protection shall be terminated only when directed by the Secretary of the Navy or higher authority.

      (2) A request by foreign authorities for return of custody of a person under the protection of temporary refuge will be reported to the CNO or Commandant of the Marine Corps. The requesting foreign authorities will be informed that the case has been referred to higher authorities for instructions.

(3) Persons whose temporary refuge is terminated will be released to the protection of the authorities designated in the message authorizing release.

(4) While temporary refuge can be granted in the circumstances set forth above, permanent asylum will not be granted.

(5) Foreign nationals who request assistance in forwarding requests for political asylum in the United States will not be received on board but will be advised to apply in person at the nearest American Embassy or Consulate. If a foreign national is already on board, however, such person will not be surrendered to foreign jurisdiction or control unless at the personal direction of the Secretary of the Navy or higher authority.

c. The Chief of Naval Operations or Commandant of the Marine Corps, as appropriate, will be informed by the most expeditious means of all action taken pursuant to subparagraphs 1a and 1b above, as well as the attendant circumstances. Telephone or voice communications will be used where possible, but must be confirmed as soon as possible with an immediate precedence message, information to the Secretary of State (for actions taken pursuant to subparagraphs 1b[1] and 1b[5] of this article, also make the appropriate American Embassy or Consular Office an information addressee). If communication by telephone or voice is not possible, notification will be effected by an immediate precedence message, as described above. The Chief of Naval Operations or Commandant of the Marine Corps will cause the Secretary of the Navy and the Deputy Director for Operations of the National Military Command Center to be notified without delay.

2. Personnel of the Department of the Navy shall neither directly nor indirectly invite persons to seek asylum or temporary refuge.

Operational commanders usually require, in addition to the above, a report of the circumstances surrounding a request for asylum or temporary refuge, generally under the operational reporting system.

REPORTING AND DETACHMENT OF PERSONNEL

An OOD should appreciate that first impressions are important. When new people are being received on board, the provisions of the ship's organization manual should always be followed and every effort made so that a new officer or enlisted person feels at ease. New people, especially those reporting to their first ship from boot camp or school, are likely to be overwhelmed by their surroundings. Their apprehension will be lifted considerably by the knowledge that the ship is interested in their welfare. If a sponsor has not been assigned or is not on board, the OOD and the duty master-at-arms should see that a temporary escort is assigned to give a new crew member help in finding his or her compartment, the mess decks, and the offices into which he or she will have to check. This escort should be well versed in the ship's procedures and policies and know the specifics of the new shipmate's division or department if possible. Remember, there is only one opportunity to get a first impression right.

People being detached should be processed on the quarterdeck as expeditiously as possible because they may have transportation arrangements to make. If there is to be any sort of departure ceremony, those taking part in it should be standing by on the quarterdeck before the people departing arrive.

RECEIVING GUESTS AND VISITORS

The OOD is responsible for welcoming all guests and visitors to the ship. He or she usually has advance information as to who is expected, who will meet them on the quarterdeck, and what sort of assistance the watch is to provide. Exercise observers and ship riders are generally met by the cognizant department head or a representative, and VIPs by the CO. When the ship is open to general visiting or to tours by special groups, the OOD should check in advance arrangements prescribed by the ship's visiting bill. Areas of the ship should be roped off as required and tour guides mustered and inspected before the visitors arrive. When large numbers of visitors are expected, arrangements must be made in advance for the provision of local police or guard forces.

As mentioned in the beginning of this chapter, the safety and security of the ship remain the primary responsibility for the in-port duty section. A major part of this includes force protection. When receiving guests and visitors, or when hosting tours, positive control and the appropriate level of screening must always be in place.

13

SAFETY

The Commanding Officer shall require that persons concerned are instructed and drilled in all applicable safety precautions and procedures, that these are complied with, and that applicable safety precautions, or extracts therefrom, are posted in appropriate places. In any instance where safety precautions have not been issued or are incomplete, the Commanding Officer shall issue or augment such safety precautions as are deemed necessary, notifying, when appropriate, higher authorities concerned.

NAVY REGULATIONS, ARTICLE 0825

Safety must be practiced twenty-four hours a day because the operation of a naval vessel is dangerous. It involves powerful machinery, high-speed equipment, steam under intensely high temperature and pressure, volatile fuels and propellants, heavy lifts, high explosives, stepped-up electrical voltages, and the elemental forces of wind and wave, which are unpredictable. Inexperienced sailors are inclined to be careless, if not downright reckless. It is a watch officer's responsibility to see that all precautions are observed to protect the lives of the crew and the safety of the ship.

Precautions ensure the safe operation of all equipment. The Naval Ships Technical Manuals contain safety precautions, as do manuals put out by the various bureaus and the SORM (OpNavInst 3120.32). As new equipment is introduced into the fleet, new safety procedures are generated and old ones modified. Accidents and injuries also lead to a continual updating of precautions, the general trend being toward more detailed descriptions of procedures, checks, and inspections.

Every accident that occurs in a ship should be reported in standard form to the appropriate safety center so that the condition that caused it can be investigated and corrective action taken. OODs should always be on the alert for dangerous conditions and violations of safety rules and prompt about correcting them.

The OOD, both in port and under way, should see that the following safety regulations and procedures, compiled from OpNavInst 3120.32D, are adhered to. Most ship, fleet, and type commanders supplement these regulations to fit specific situations or requirements. For example, detailed procedures are issued for the guidance of personnel who handle nuclear weapons. The watch officer is also directed to the Navy Occupational Safety and Health Program Manual for Forces Afloat, NavShips technical manuals, and planned maintenance system (PMS) maintenance requirement cards (MRCs) for detailed guidelines and precautions applicable to their specific situations.

The Navy Safety Center is an invaluable source of safety-related information across the spectrum of naval activities—afloat and ashore. Training materials, instructions, checklists, news, articles, and best practices are all available via the Navy Safety Center website (http://www.public.navy.mil/navsafecen). This site offers many downloadable resources for shipboard training, including a "safety toolbox" to help build a robust shipboard safety program stressing proper practices and procedures—essential elements an alert watch officer is always ready to enforce.

AMMUNITION

1. All personnel required to handle ammunition must be carefully and frequently instructed in the safety regulations, methods of handling, storage, and uses of all kinds of ammunition and explosive ordnance with which the ship, aircraft unit, or station is supplied.

2. No one is permitted to inspect, prepare, or adjust live ammunition and explosives until he or she thoroughly understands the duties, precautions, and hazards involved and has been properly qualified.

3. Only careful, reliable, mentally sound, and physically fit persons are permitted to work with or use explosives or ammunition.

4. All persons who supervise the inspection, care, preparation, handling, use, or disposal of ammunition or explosives must do the following:

   a. Exercise the utmost care that all regulations and instructions are observed and remain vigilant throughout the operation.

   b. Carefully instruct and frequently warn those under them of the need for constant vigilance.

   c. Before beginning the operation, ensure that all subordinates are familiar with the characteristics of explosive materials and equipment involved, safety regulations to be observed, and the hazards of fire, explosion, or other catastrophe that safety regulations are intended to prevent.

   d. Be alert for hazardous procedures or symptoms of a deteriorating mental attitude and take immediate action when such are detected.

5. Smoking is not permitted in magazines or in the vicinity of operations involving explosives or ammunition. Matches, lighters, and spark- or flame-producing devices are not permitted in spaces where ammunition or explosives are present.

6. Personnel working with explosives or ammunition are limited to the minimum number required to perform the operation properly. Unauthorized personnel are not permitted in magazines or in the vicinity of operations involving explosives or ammunition. Authorized visitors must always be properly escorted.

7. When fused or assembled with firing mechanisms, mines, depth charges, rockets, projector charges, missiles, and aircraft bombs must be treated as if armed.

8. Live ammunition, rockets, or missiles are loaded into guns or on launchers only for firing purposes, unless personnel are otherwise notified.

9. Supervisors must enforce good housekeeping in explosives spaces. Nothing should be stored in such spaces except explosives, their containers, and authorized handling equipment.

10. No detonator is to be assembled in a warhead in or near a magazine containing explosives. Fusing is to be done at a designated fusing area.

BOATS

1. Operating ship's boats such as rigid-hulled inflatable boats (RHIB) deployed in various sizes throughout the fleet, requires constant vigilance and strict observance of standard safety practices.

2. Boat crews must keep their stations, especially when weather conditions are unpleasant, for it is usually during these times that vigilance is most needed.

3. Boats must always be properly loaded for the sea state. In heavy weather, the boat is loaded slightly down by the stern with all passengers and crew in life jackets. Boat passengers must remain seated when a boat is under way and keep arms inboard of gunwales.

4. The coxswain, or boat officer when assigned, is responsible to the CO for the enforcement of these regulations.

5. No boat is to be loaded beyond the capacities established by the CO and published in the boat bill.

6. Smoking is forbidden in boats.

7. No persons other than those specifically designated by the engineering officer should operate or attempt to operate a boat engine; test, remove, or charge a boat's battery, or tamper in any way with a boat's electrical system; or fuel a ship's boat.

8. No person is to be assigned as a member of a boat crew unless he or she is a qualified swimmer; has demonstrated a practical knowledge of boat seamanship, the rules of the road, and boat safety regulations; and has duly qualified for his or her particular assignment.

9. All persons in boats being hoisted in or out, or hung in the davits, must wear vest-type, inherently buoyant life preservers properly secured and safety helmets with chin straps.

10. Boats must not be boarded from a boat boom unless someone is standing by on deck or in a boat at the same boom.

11. Fueling instructions must be posted in all power boats, and passengers must be kept clear of a boat that is being refueled.

12. Maximum operating speeds must be posted permanently on the engine cover of all boats.

13. Standard equipment listed in the allowance list must be in boats at all times.

14. Prescribed lights must be displayed by all boats under way between sunset and daylight or in poor visibility.

15. Life buoys must be carried forward and aft in each boat and secured in such a manner that they can be easily broken out for use.

16. All boats leaving the ship should have local charts or chartlets with courses to and from their destination recorded thereon. Compasses, fog-signaling and communications equipment must be carried on boats.

17. All boats must have life preservers on board to accommodate all persons embarked and should be used at all times.

18. No boat should be dispatched or permitted to proceed unless released by the OOD. Release should not be given unless it has been determined that the boat crew and passengers are wearing life preservers and that weather and sea conditions are suitable for small-boat operations.

19. Recall and lifeboat signals must be posted in boats where they can be easily read by the coxswain.

20. A set of standing orders to the coxswain must be prepared and kept in each boat.

CARGO

1. Open hatches in use should be cleared of any adjacent loose equipment that might fall into them and injure personnel below.

2. Traffic about a hatch is restricted to the side where cargo is not being worked. The area over which loads are traveling is roped off to traffic.

3. Hatch beams or other structures in the way of hatches where cargo is being worked are secured by bolts or removed. Personnel moving hatch beams must wear a safety line, which should be tended at all times.

4. Qualified personnel must always supervise the topping and lowering of booms. Before any repairs are made or any gear is replaced, booms should always be lowered on deck. When lifelines are removed for any purpose, officers and petty officers must see that emergency or temporary lines are rigged and that everyone is cautioned to keep clear.

CLOSED COMPARTMENTS

A ship has many confined spaces (especially tanks and voids) in which both toxic and nontoxic gas may be present. Some hazardous atmospheres are not detectable by smell and must be tested to ensure they are safe for personnel. The danger of explosion, poisoning, and suffocation exists in closed compartments or poorly ventilated spaces such as tanks, cofferdams, voids, and bilges. To address these hazards, the shipboard Gas-Free Engineering Program establishes procedures and specialized training to test for hazards and establish safe conditions. No person should enter any such compartment or space until the space has been declared safe by a qualified gas-free engineer. The following precautions should be observed:

1. The seal around the manhole or other opening should be broken before all hold-down bolts or other fastenings are completely removed, to allow dissipation of pressure that may have built up inside or to make it possible to quickly secure the cover again if gas or water is present.

2. No person should enter any such space without permission from the commanding officer and after having the space certified as safe by the ship's gas-free engineer.

3. No naked light or spark-producing electrical apparatus should be carried into a closed space.

4. Safety lamps used in closed compartments must be in good operating condition. If a lamp fades or flares up, the space should not be entered.

5. No person should work in such a compartment without a lifeline attached and a responsible person stationed outside the compartment to tend the line and maintain communications.

COMPRESSED GAS

Compressed gases used aboard ship include oxygen, acetylene, carbon dioxide (CO_2), and plain compressed air. Helium, nitrogen, ammonia, and certain insecticide fogs may also be used. All cylinders are identified in stenciled letters and by color as follows:

- *Yellow.* Flammable materials, such as acetylene, hydrogen, and petroleum gases.
- *Brown.* Poisonous materials, such as chlorine, carbon monoxide, and sulfur dioxide.
- *Green.* Oxidizing material, particularly pure oxygen.
- *Blue.* Anesthetics and materials with similarly harmful fumes.
- *Gray.* Physically dangerous materials: inert gas under high pressure or gas that would asphyxiate if breathed in confined areas, such as CO_2, nitrogen, and helium.
- *Red.* Fire-protection materials, especially CO_2 and nitrogen.
- *Black with Green Striping.* Compressed air and helium-oxygen and oxygen-CO_2 mixtures.

All flammable gases, such as acetylene, become highly explosive when mixed in certain proportions with air. Even an inert gas like CO_2 can cause an explosion if its cylinder becomes too hot or cracks because of rough handling. The following rules should be obeyed without exception.

1. Gas cylinders and air cylinders must be kept away from high-temperature areas. Oil should never be allowed to come in contact with oxygen cylinder valves because a violent explosion could result.
2. Gas cylinders must not be handled roughly, dropped, or clanked against each other. They should not be handled or transported without their valve caps in place.
3. Flames or sparks should not be permitted in any closed spaces where acetylene or oxygen tanks are stored; seepage from the tanks may have filled the compartment with a dangerous level of gas or pure oxygen.
4. Caution should be used around cylinders of poisonous gas. There is always the possibility that gas is leaking from a loose valve or seeping through a defective connection.
5. In case of fire or other disaster, gas cylinders should be moved immediately from the danger area and, if necessary, thrown overboard.

DIVERS

Divers may go below the ship only with the permission of the OOD. The OOD is responsible for seeing that the following safety precautions are observed before granting permission:

1. The location and status of all ship's machinery that might affect a diving area must be determined before diving operations begin. The status of this equipment must not be altered without prior notification by the engineering duty officer and the concurrence of the diving officer.

2. Divers must not enter the water until permission is granted by the OOD and the international signal Code Alfa is flying from the ship and the diving boat.

3. Without the specific knowledge and concurrence of the diving officer,

    a. No suctions from or discharge to the sea is authorized without concurrence by the diving officer. For example, main ballast tanks will not be flooded or blown, firemain and seawater cooling systems may need to be secured.

    b. Stern planes will not be moved.*

    c. The rudder will not be moved.*

    d. The screw will not be turned. With the concurrence of the diving officer, screws may be turned at minimum jacking speed. In this case, the OOD, via the engineering duty officer, must ensure that screws are turning no faster than the minimum jacking speed.

    e. The mooring will not be adjusted.

    f. Secondary propulsion motors will not be rigged out or trained, nor will the screw be turned except as noted above.*

    g. The main space drainage system will not be operated.

    h. The anchor and anchor chain will not be manipulated in any way.*

    i. The torpedo tubes will not be exercised.*

    j. Active sonar systems will be secured.

    *System must be properly tagged out.

4. All boats must stay at least fifty yards from the diving area.

5. Except in an extreme emergency, no diving operation will commence unless four qualified divers are present.

6. Divers must always dive with one standby diver in a ready condition.

7. Divers are checked for sickness and injury immediately upon leaving the water.

8. All ships in a nest must be informed of the presence of divers on any ship in the nest.

9. When divers are over the side, the word is passed every thirty minutes.

10. Active sonar must not be operated if divers are anywhere in the nest.

11. When divers are working in the vicinity of adjacent ships, the regulations set forth in this article apply. The duty officer must clear with the duty officer of the ship in which divers are working before undertaking any evolution prohibited by this article.

ELECTRICAL AND ELECTRONIC EQUIPMENT

This includes generators, electrically powered machinery and mechanisms, power cables, controllers, transformers and associated equipment, radars, radios, power amplifiers, antennas, electronic warfare equipment, computers, and associated controls.

1. No person is to operate, repair, adjust, or otherwise tamper with any electrical or electronic equipment (unless it is within his or her assignment in the department organization manual to perform a specific function on certain equipment) except in emergencies, and then only when no qualified operator is available.

2. No person is to be assigned to operate, repair, or adjust electrical or electronic equipment unless he or she has demonstrated practical knowledge of its operation and repair and of all applicable safety regulations, and then only when duly qualified by the head of the department.

3. No person is to paint over or otherwise mutilate markings, name plates, cable tags, or other identification on any electrical or electronic equipment.

4. No person is to hang anything on, or secure a line to, any power cable, antenna, wave guide, or other piece of electrical or electronic equipment.

USS _____

1. Diving will be conducted over the side, commencing at _____
   (time/date).

2. The following work is to be accomplished by the divers:_____
   _____

3. Diving will be in the following location(s): _____
   _____

4. Prior to a diver entering the water, accomplish the following:

Initials

_____ a. Notify the engineer officer/engineering duty officer of the diving operation. Determine the operating status of sea water systems within the diving area. Direct no alterations of this status (except as described in f. below) without the permission of the engineering duty officer. Inform diving supervisor of systems in operation.

_____ b. Notify reactor officer/radiation control officer (nuclear powered ships only). Ensure divers have radiological protection specified by the reactor officer.

_____ c. DANGER tag-out rudder to ensure no movement and secure and tag-out the cathodic protective source.

_____ d. Ensure that screws are on the jacking gear and locked (screws may be turned at minimum jacking speed with the concurrence of the diving supervisor).

_____ e. Do not permit mooring line adjustment.

_____ f. Do not permit main circulating water system components to be operated.

_____ g. DANGER tag-out anchor windlass and brake to ensure no manipulation in any way.

_____ h. Do not conduct boiler/steam generator blow downs or if a nuclear powered ship, permit no discharge of radioactive effluent.

_____ i. Keep all small boats outside a 50-yard radius of the diving operations.

_____ j. Do not permit diving unless the required number of qualified divers in ___ accordance with the U.S. Navy Diving Manual are present with one diver out of the water in a ready condition as a standby diver.

_____ k. If equipped with thrusters or electric propulsion motors, tag them out ___ to ensure they are not operated.

_____ l. Do not permit any active sonar to be operated.

_____ m. Notify adjacent ships or other ships in a nest of the diving _____ operations. Request the command duty officers of these ships to not permit active sonar operation.

_____ n. Fly CODE ALPHA. Ensure this signal is flying from the diving boat.

_____ o. Pass the following word prior to the divers entering the water: "Divers _ are over the side in the vicinity of _____", and every 30 minutes ___ thereafter.

5. Conditions have been established to permit diving operations.

_____
                              Command Duty Officer/Time

Diving Commenced _____

Diving Completed _____

Note: Initials certify completion of an item. If an item is not applicable, indicate "NA" on initial line.

FIGURE 13-1.
Check Sheet
for Divers over
the Side

5. Only authorized and portable electrical equipment that has been tested by the electric shop is to be used.

6. Electrical equipment must be de-energized (and, if possible, checked with a voltage tester or voltmeter to ensure it is de-energized) before being serviced or repaired. Circuit breakers and switches of de-energized circuits are to be locked or placed in the "off" position while work is in progress, and a suitable warning tag should be attached.

7. Every effort must be made to insulate a person working on live circuits or equipment, and all other related safety measures should be observed. If possible, rubber gloves should be worn. Another person should be standing by to de-energize the circuit and to render first aid. The CO must approve working on live circuits.

8. No personal electrical or electronic equipment should be used aboard ship until it has been inspected for electrical safety by authorized shipboard personnel and approved for use.

9. No person should intentionally receive a shock from any voltage whatsoever. Any person who is shocked shall report the shock to the ship's medical officer or corpsman.

10. Bare lamps or fixtures with exposed lamps must not be installed in machinery spaces. To minimize the hazard of fire caused by flammable fuels making contact with exposed lamps, only enclosed fixtures are to be installed in such spaces.

11. Personnel are not permitted aloft near energized antennas unless it has been determined that no danger exists. If there is any danger from rotating antennas, induced voltages in rigging and superstructure, or high-power radiation that could cause direct biological injury, equipment should be secured and a suitable warning tag should be attached to the main supply switches. These precautions are also observed if any other antenna is in the vicinity, as on an adjacent ship.

12. Department heads must see that electrical and electronic safety precautions are conspicuously posted in appropriate spaces and that personnel are frequently and thoroughly instructed and drilled in their observance.

13. Department heads must ensure that all electrical and electronics personnel are qualified in the administration of first-aid treatment for shock and that emergency resuscitation procedures are posted in all spaces containing electronic equipment.

14. Department heads must make sure that rubber matting is installed in front and in back of propulsion-control cubicles, power and lighting switchboards, interior communications (IC) switchboards, test switchboards, fire-control switchboards, announcing-system amplifiers, and control panels; areas in and around radio, radar, sonar, and countermeasures equipment spaces that may be entered by personnel servicing or tuning energized equipment; and around workbenches in electrical and electronics shops where equipment is tested or repaired.

FIRE AND EXPLOSION PREVENTION

The reduction of fire and explosion hazards is the responsibility of every person on board, both individually and collectively. The gravity of these hazards is increased by the configuration of machinery spaces and the presence on board of fuel and heat. The following steps are essential:

1. To the extent possible, eliminate all fire and explosion hazards, including nonessential combustibles.

2. Wherever possible, replace highly combustible materials with less combustible ones.

3. Keep only the minimum required amount of essential combustibles.

4. Stow and protect all combustibles in designated lockers.

5. Avoid the accumulation of oil and other flammable materials in bilges and inaccessible areas. Any excess must be flushed out or removed at the first opportunity.

6. Stow oily rags in airtight metal containers.

7. Stow paint, paintbrushes, rags, paint thinner, and solvents in authorized locations.

8. Do not use compressed air to accelerate the flow from containers of oil, gasoline, or other combustible fluids.

9. Make regular and frequent inspections for fire hazards.

10. Train all personnel in fire prevention and firefighting.

11. Enforce sound fire-prevention policies and practices.

12. Maintain damage-control equipment in a state of readiness for any emergency.

FUEL OIL

1. While oil is being received on board, no naked light, lighted cigarette, electrical apparatus, or anything else likely to spark should be permitted within fifty feet of an oil hose, tank, or compartment containing the tank or a vent. No one may carry matches or cigarette lighters while loading or unloading oil.

2. No naked light, lighted cigarette, electrical fuse, switch (except the enclosed type), steel tool, or other apparatus liable to cause sparks should be permitted at any time in a compartment that contains fuel-oil tanks, pumps, or piping. Electric lamps used in such a compartment must have gaslight globes. The term "naked light" includes oil lanterns as well as open lanterns, lighted candles, and lighted matches. Flashlights must not be turned on or off inside a fuel compartment lest a spark ignite vapors.

3. No person should be allowed to enter a fuel-oil tank until the tank has been freed of vapor, the person has obtained permission from the safety officer or CO, and the required precautions have been taken. No one should ever enter a fuel-oil tank without wearing a lifeline attended by someone outside the tank.

4. Compartments and tanks used for the storage of fuel oil should not be painted on the inside.

5. Whenever a fuel-oil tank is to be entered, work is to be done in it, or lights other than portable explosion-proof electric lights are to be used, and whenever work is to be done in the vicinity of an open tank or of pipes, all such tanks and pipes must first be cleared of vapor after the fuel oil has been removed. No person should enter a fuel-oil tank for any purpose without obtaining permission from the safety officer or CO.

6. Oil fires can be extinguished by smothering and cutting off oxygen. CO_2 extinguishers and chemicals or water in the form of fog may be used.

HAZARDOUS MATERIAL

To attain and maintain operational effectiveness, Navy ships require specified types and quantities of hazardous material (HM). Great care must be taken in handling, using, and storing HM to prevent injury to personnel, damage to equipment, or harm to the environment. Risks associated with HM are greater aboard ship than ashore because of the limited number, confined nature, and "at sea" environment of shipboard spaces. Consequently, special precautions and an effective program to manage HM are both needed. The maintenance of safe and healthful working conditions for HM is a chain of command responsibility. Implementation begins with the CO and extends to the individual sailor. The OOD, particularly in port, has a key role in ensuring HM does not enter or leave the ship in an unauthorized fashion.

HM is material that, because of its quantity, concentration, or physical or chemical characteristics, may pose a substantial hazard to human health or the environment when incorrectly used, purposefully released, or accidentally spilled. Subcategories of HM include

- Flammable or combustible materials
- Toxic materials
- Corrosive materials (including acids and bases)
- Oxidizing materials
- Aerosol containers
- Compressed gases

Not included in this definition are ammunition, weapons, explosives, explosive actuated devices, propellants, pyrotechnics, chemical and biological warfare materials, pharmaceutical supplies (if not considered hazardous based on composition, physical form, and review of procedures, which may involve handling and dispensing of the materials), medical waste and infectious materials, bulk fuels, and radioactive materials. Asbestos, mercury, lead, and polychlorinated biphenyls are HM that require special guidance for their handling and control.

Ships are required to transfer used or excess HM to a Navy shore activity to determine if it is suitable for further use. Navy shore activities possess trained personnel who can determine, working with ship's personnel, whether shipboard HM is usable, reusable, or should be disposed of as hazardous waste (HW). The shore activity will act as the HW generator if they determine that the material has no further use and will dispose of it as required by federal, state, and local regulations.

Ships shall develop a spill contingency plan in preparation for possible HM spills or releases to the environment. This plan shall include information on spill response team makeup, spill cleanup equipment location, and internal and external spill reporting criteria. The OOD must be well acquainted with this plan, which will be outlined in the ship's SORM.

The hazard characteristic code (HCC) is a two-digit alphanumeric code that is used to provide a means of categorizing HM. HCCs are assigned by trained scientific or engineering personnel, thereby uniformly identifying HM that is managed by all government activities. HCCs allow personnel to properly receive, handle, store, and process HM. In particular, the HCC allows the user to determine which materials are compatible for storage with other materials. In addition, HCCs can be used to simplify spill response and cleanup, processing of HM during recoupment operations, and assist in the identification of potential HW. The HCC serves as an identifier for automated processing of HM transactions and space utilization management. The HCCs can be found in OpNavInst 5100.19E.

HEAVY WEATHER

Safety requires the following precautions in heavy weather:

1. Decks exposed to the sea should be kept clear of all personnel except those on urgent duty. Word to this effect and concerning any other area to which entry is forbidden should be passed periodically.
2. Extra lifelines and snaking should be in place, particularly in areas where there are ongoing evolutions such as replenishment or recovery of a person overboard.

HELICOPTERS

Helicopters on ships are operated with permission from the OOD. A primary responsibility of the OOD is to position the ship in accordance with established guidance for winds and seas. Thresholds for winds and seas vary by ship class and reference material should be readily available to the OOD. The OOD is responsible for ensuring the ship is ready to conduct flight operations. Because preparation for flight operations involves numerous controlling stations' discrete actions, ship-specific checklists are used. These procedures should be followed closely and progress communicated among the controlling stations. The following are examples of precautions and checklist items that must be observed before conducting helicopter operations:

1. All helicopter safety crews (firefighting, pilot rescue, boat, etc.) must be fully manned, briefed, on station, and ready.

2. Adequate communications between controlling stations and aircraft should be established.

3. Engineering and combat systems equipment must be configured to support flight operations. This may require starting or securing specific equipment based on ship class such as engines, radars, and fuel pumps.

4. Only those involved are allowed in the vicinity of helicopter operations, and they must wear required safety gear, such as flight deck boots, helmets, goggles, and life vests.

5. A complete and thorough check must be made of the helicopter area for loose gear or objects (foreign object debris or FOD) that could cause injury or damage.

6. All hands topside must remain uncovered.

7. Passengers are led to and from a helicopter by a member of the handling crew or flight crew.

8. Lights are secured topside for night flight operations.

Ships with low freeboard flight decks deserve special mention due to the issue of pitch, roll, sea state, and swell direction and the requirement to maintain all parameters "within the envelope" during flight deck operations, whether launching, recovering, traversing, or engaging/disengaging rotors. Incidents of wave run-up and taking water over the flight deck have resulted in catastrophic mishaps and loss of life when flight deck envelopes were exceeded. NATOPS addresses this danger through the use of "polar plots" to graphically display the risk of water intrusion on the flight deck based on sea conditions, swell direction, ship's heading, and ship's speed. Such tools are useful in establishing safe conditions for operations; however, environmental conditions are constantly changing and the hydrodynamic effects of maneuvering in turbulent seas are difficult to predict. Thus, watchstanders must be ever vigilant in assessing the prevailing conditions as well as their intended maneuvers even while operating within prescribed envelopes.

HELM SAFETY OFFICER

The helm safety officer is a bridge watchstander when transiting in restricted waters, conducting special evolutions, or at any other time deemed necessary by the CO or OOD. The helm safety officer is a commissioned officer who is PQS qualified and proficient. The helm safety officer monitors the steering control station personnel (typically helmsman and lee helmsman), ensuring that all orders from the conning officer are acknowledged and complied with. In the event of a casualty, the helm safety officer also monitors EOCC actions conducted by the helmsman and lee helmsman and will assist if necessary. The helm safety officer shall have no other duties while assigned.

HOT WORK

Hot work involves welding, flame-cutting, open-flame supplement, and the manipulation of metal with temperatures over 400 degrees. No person should engage in hot work until the gas-free engineer (or an authorized representative) has inspected the place where it is to be done and indicated that it is free of the danger of poisoning, suffocation, fire, and explosion.

1. No hot work shall be undertaken without the permission of the CO under way or the duty officer in port.

2. When flammable or explosive materials are to be exposed to welding or cutting, a fire watch should be posted in the vicinity. If fire hazards exist

on both sides of a deck or bulkhead being worked on, a watch should be posted on each side. Fire watches should remain on station for at least thirty minutes after a job has been completed to ensure that no smoldering fires have started. Suitable fire-extinguishing equipment should be kept near all welding and cutting operations.

3. No welding or burning is permitted in compartments where explosives are stored.

4. Various synthetic materials yield toxic gases when burned or heated. Suitable warning signs must be placed in areas where dangerous vapors can accumulate.

5. Only qualified personnel may operate welding equipment.

LIFE JACKETS

Life jackets must be worn whenever there is a possibility of personnel slipping, falling, or being carried into the water. The safest life jacket, when properly worn, is the Navy's standard buoyant vest, although several adequate life jackets are in use throughout the fleet. Each jacket must be properly maintained and fitted appropriately to the user. Life jackets must be worn by the following persons:

1. Those working over the side, in port and at sea, on stages and in boatswain's chairs, boats, or punts. "Over the side" means any part of the ship outside the lifelines or bulwarks.

2. Those going out on weather decks during heavy weather, even if they are to be exposed only long enough to go from one station to another.

3. Those handling lines or other deck equipment during such evolutions as transfers between ships, fueling under way, and towing.

4. Those in boats being raised or lowered, entering boats from a boom or Jacob's ladder, in boats under way, and on the ship in rough water or low visibility. Ring buoys with a line and light attached must be available when a sea ladder or a Jacob's ladder is being used.

5. Those being transferred by highline or helicopter. They must don life jackets before they get into the transfer seat or sling.

LIFELINES

1. No person is to lean on, sit on, stand on, or climb over any lifeline, either in port or at sea. Personnel working over the side in port may climb over lifelines when necessary, but only if they are wearing life preservers.

2. No lifeline is to be dismantled or removed without the permission of the first lieutenant, and even then temporary lifelines must be promptly rigged.

3. No person shall hang or secure any weight or line to any lifelines unless authorized by the CO.

LIGHTS

When a ship is in port at night, weather decks, accommodation ladders, gangways, and brows must be well lighted.

LINES AND RIGGING

When work with lines and rigging is being done, the following precautions should be observed:

1. Lines or rigging under heavy strain should be eased to prevent overstress or parting. Personnel must keep clear of heavily stressed line or wire and must under no circumstance stand in the bight of a line or on a taut fall.

2. Heavy loads should not ordinarily be hoisted overhead, but if it is essential, the person responsible must warn everyone away from the area directly below.

3. Boat falls and highlines should be replaced at the first indication of wear or stress.

4. Lines not in use should be carefully made up and stowed clear of walkways and passages.

5. Lines must be made fast not to capstans or gypsy heads but only to fittings provided for that purpose, such as cleats or bitts.

6. Steadying or frapping lines should be used on boat falls and on large lifts to prevent uncontrolled swinging or twisting.

LINE-THROWING GUN

A line-throwing gun is used in the opening phase of replenishment operations, during which the following safety precautions must always be observed:

1. Members of the line-throwing crew must wear red helmets and highly visible red jackets so that they can be easily identified.

2. The bolo heaver and line-throwing gunner must be thoroughly trained to place the line within easy reach of the receiving ship's crew, no matter what the conditions of range, wind, and relative motion may be.

3. Bolos and gun lines must be properly prepared for running.

4. When the receiving ship reaches the proper position, both ships pass the word over the bullhorn and topside loudspeaker: "Stand by for shot line—all hands take cover."

5. The officer in charge at each replenishment station in the firing ship sounds a one-blast signal on a mouth whistle or passes the word "stand by" on the electric megaphone. When he or she is ready to receive the shot line and all personnel in the vicinity have taken cover, the officer in charge of the corresponding station in the receiving ship replies with a two-blast signal on a mouth whistle and passes the word "ready" on the electric megaphone. After ascertaining that all hands in the vicinity of the target area are under cover, the officer in charge on the firing ship gives the order to fire. The bolo is thrown or the gun is fired only by order of the officer in charge.

6. Only those members of each replenishment station designated by the officer in charge may leave cover to retrieve the bolo or shot line. No one else in the receiving ship may leave cover until all bolos or shot lines are on board and word has been passed on the topside loudspeaker that shot (bolo) lines are secure.

7. The receiving ship, unless she is an aircraft carrier, does not normally fire her line-throwing guns unless ordered or requested by the delivering ship.

8. All hands must take cover immediately on receipt of the word to do so.

MACHINERY

Machinery refers to every engine, motor, generator, hydraulic system, and other apparatus that supplies power or motive force.

1. Except in emergencies, and then only when no qualified operator is present, no person should operate, repair, adjust, or otherwise tamper with any machinery unless assigned by the department head to perform a specific function on that machinery.
2. No person should be assigned to operate, repair, or adjust any machinery unless he or she has demonstrated practical knowledge of its operation and repair and of all applicable safety regulations, and then only when certified by the head of the department responsible for such machinery.
3. The power or activation source of machinery undergoing repair should be tagged to that effect to prevent the accidental application of power.

OPERATIONAL RISK MANAGEMENT (ORM)

ORM is a term with which the OOD should be very familiar, both in port and at sea. It means identifying and assessing hazards, evaluating control options, and supervising all activities with an eye toward controlling those hazards. It is discussed in OpNavInst 3120.32D, Article 604.7, and in a dedicated instruction, Operational Risk Management, OpNavInst 3500.39D. It is a systematic method of thinking that should be applied to everything under the control of the OOD. It increases awareness of hazards and risks involved in operations.

ORM is a closed loop process following five sequential steps:

1. Identify hazards.
2. Assess hazards.
3. Make risk decisions.
4. Implement controls.
5. Supervise (watch for changes).

ORM assessments apply at one of three levels, depending on the situation and how much time is available for planning and preparation. Each level incurs additional rigor:

DO NOT ACCEPT ANY UNNECESSARY RISK and ensure DECISIONS ARE MADE AT THE APPROPRIATE LEVEL

HAZARD SEVERITY

SEVERITY	The expected consequences of an event in terms of degree of injury, property damage or other mission-impairing factors.
CATASTROPHIC	Loss of the ability to accomplish the mission. Death or permanent total disability. Loss of a mission-critical system or equipment. Major facility damage. Severe environmental damage. Mission-critical security failure. Unacceptable collateral damage.
CRITICAL	Significantly degraded mission capability or unit readiness. Permanent partial disability or severe injury or illness. Extensive damage to equipment or systems. Significant damage to property or the environment. Security failure. Significant collateral damage.
MODERATE	Degraded mission capability or unit readiness. Minor damage to equipment, systems, property, or the environment. Minor injury or illness.
NEGLIGIBLE	Little or no adverse impact on mission capability or unit readiness. Minimal threat to personnel, safety or health. Slight equipment or systems damage, but fully functional and serviceable. Little or no property or environmental damage.

HAZARD PROBABILITY

PROBABILITY
The likelihood an event will occur.

FREQUENT
Occurs often or continuously experienced.

LIKELY
Occurs several times.

OCCASIONAL
Occasionally will occur in time.

SELDOM
Seldom may occur in time.

UNLIKELY
Unlikely it will occur in time.

RISK MANAGEMENT AT A GLANCE

Risk management identifies and controls hazards before they become accidents. Risk Management applies to all missions at all times. The following FIVE STEPS are applied:

1. Identify the Hazard/Risk: What is or is not risky? Consider all aspects of current and future missions, environment and known risks.

2. Assess the Hazards: How big is the risk? Label is from "low" to "extremely high". How likely will the hazard occur? If the hazard does happen, how bad will it be?

3. Make Risk Decisions: What can stop or reduce the hazard? Identify control options to reduce the hazard until the lower risk outweighs the potential damage.

4. Implement Controls: Make sure everyone knows—and uses— the controls you created.

5. Supervise: Visit the troops doing the work. Do the controls work? Supervise and revise until they do!

FIGURE 13-2. Operational Risk Management

1. Time-critical ORM (on the spot—no written record).

2. Deliberate ORM (written records are made and most often applied for many shipboard evolutions).

3. In-depth ORM (provides an even deeper analysis than deliberate ORM).

Risk Assessment Matrix			PROBABILITY				
			Frequency of Occurrence Over Time				
			A Frequent (Continuously experienced)	B Likely (Will occur frequently)	C Occasional (Will occur several times)	D Seldom (Unlikely; can be expected to occur)	E Unlikely (Improbable; but possible to occur)
SEVERITY Effect of Hazard	Catastrophic (Death, Loss of Asset, Mission Capability or Unit Readiness)	I	EH 1	EH 1	H 2	H 2	M 3
	Critical (Severe Injury or Damage, Significantly Degraded Mission Capability or Unit Readiness)	II	EH 1	H 2	H 2	M 3	L 4
	Moderate (Minor Injury or Damage, Degraded Mission Capability or Unit Readiness)	III	H 2	M 3	M 3	L 4	L 4
	Negligible (Minimal Injury or Damage, Little or No Impact to Mission Readiness or Unit Readiness)	IV	M 3	L 4	L 4	L 4	L 4
			Risk Assessment Levels				
			EH=Extremely High 1; H=High 2; M=Medium 3; L=Low 4				

FIGURE 13-3. Risk Assessment Matrix

ORM is guided by four basic principles:

1. Accept risk where the benefit is greater than the risk.
2. Accept no unnecessary risk.
3. Accept and manage risk by planning.
4. Make risk decisions at the right level.

An excellent Naval Safety Center website addressing ORM is http://www .public.navy.mil/navsafecen/. This comprehensive site includes ORM instructions, checklists, presentations, articles, and instructional aids. Pocket reference cards outlining the basic ORM process may be downloaded for individual use. Samples from the site follow below.

PAINTING

Poisoning from paint may be produced by either the vehicle or the pigment. The vehicle is a volatile solvent. Excessive exposure to a vaporized solvent produces irritation of the nose and throat, headache, dizziness, loud or boisterous conversation, loss of memory, and a staggering gait. A person exhibiting such symptoms must be quickly removed from exposure to paint fumes.

The pigment in some paints contains lead or other high solids that may be absorbed through the skin or inhaled as particles, particularly if a spray gun is used. The following precautions should be observed:

1. A painter should wear a respirator and change its filter frequently. (Respirators offer no protection against paint fumes.)
2. After painting, workers should wash their hands and clean under their fingernails to protect against pigment poisoning.
3. Soiled clothing should be changed as soon as possible.
4. Personnel regularly employed or around spray guns should wear face masks.

PERSONNEL PROTECTION

1. Personnel working on or near rotating machinery must not wear clothing with loose ends or loops that might be caught by moving equipment.
2. Personnel working on steam valves or other hot units must wear leather or other heavy gloves.
3. Personnel working in the vicinity of steam equipment must keep their bodies well covered to reduce the danger of steam burns.
4. Personnel brazing, welding, or cutting must wear protective goggles, a helmet, and leather welding jackets.
5. Personnel must wear goggles whenever they are working with substances corrosive to the eyes.
6. Personnel must wear respirators when working in areas with excessive dust.

PERSONNEL TRANSFER

Although proficiency is no longer evaluated as a basic phase training requirement, personnel highline transfer equipment is still inventoried aboard most ships. If required, personnel transfer at sea is performed as outlined in applicable NSTM and NWP references to ensure the safety of those being transferred.

1. The highline is a four-inch synthetic, double-braided spun polyester (Dacron) line.

2. The highline used for personnel transfer is tensioned by a minimum of twenty-five people. The highline is hand-tended to prevent its parting as a result of ship's movement.

3. A highline that has been tended by a capstan may not be used for personnel transfers.

4. Persons being transferred must wear orange-colored, inherently buoyant life preservers.

5. Boatswain's chairs used in personnel transfers must have a quick-release seat belt. They should also be fitted with a flotation device.

6. Stretchers used to transfer patients must be equipped with flotation gear.

RADIATION

Radioactive material is present in a nuclear reactor core, in contaminants in the primary coolant, in the sources used for calibration of radiation-monitoring equipment, and in certain electronic tubes.

1. Radiation sources must remain installed in radiation-detection equipment or be stowed in shipping containers in locked storage.

2. Spare radioactive electronic tubes and fission chambers are to be stored in clearly marked containers and locked storage.

3. All hands must scrupulously obey radiation warning signs and remain clear of radiation barriers.

SAFETY DEVICES

1. Mechanical, electrical, and electronic safety devices must be inspected at regular intervals and whenever unusual circumstances or conditions warrant. When practical, such devices should be inspected while the equipment or unit to which they apply is in operation. Machinery or equipment must not be operated when their safety devices are not in proper working condition.

2. No person is to tamper with any safety device, interlock, ground strap, or similar device intended to protect operators or their equipment.

SEMISAFE AND DANGEROUS MATERIALS

Semisafe materials are materials considered safe as long as they are in unopened containers that do not leak—but it is understood that, should leakage occur, any spilled material will be cleaned up promptly and the leaking container disposed of. Some common semisafe materials are diesel oil, grease, lubricating oil, metal polish, paint, safety matches, and wax.

Dangerous materials may or may not be in sealed containers. Some common dangerous materials are acids, alcohol, anticorrosive paint, bleaching powder (chlorinated lime), calcium hypochlorite, compressed gases, gasoline, kerosene, lacquer, paint thinner, paint-stripping compound, paint drier, rust-prevention compound, storage-battery electrolyte, turpentine, and varnish.

All semisafe and dangerous materials should be stowed in storerooms specifically designed for paint and flammable liquids, unless another designated stowage area is provided. Naked lights and spark-emitting devices must not be used in compartments that contain semisafe or dangerous materials.

Calcium hypochlorite and bleaching powder must be stowed in a clean, cool, dry compartment or storeroom not adjacent to a magazine; they must be isolated from flammable materials, acids, and other chemicals. Their containers should be inspected periodically for tight sealing and rust. The contents of defective containers must be used immediately or otherwise disposed of. Bleach in plastic containers must be stowed in a covered metal container.

SHOES

All persons must wear rubber-soled shoes. Safety shoes must be worn onboard ships and in areas designated for foot hazards. Shoes with taps, cleats, or any other metal device on the heels or soles may not be worn on board ship or in ship's boats.

SMALL ARMS

Small arms are handheld pistols, rifles, machine guns, line-throwing guns, and flare guns of less than .50-caliber bore diameter.

1. No one is to be issued a small arm unless he or she has demonstrated to the department head or division officer full knowledge of its operation

and safety regulations that pertain to it. This includes applicable PQS and classroom instruction, familiarization firing, and qualification firing. A list of qualified individuals is normally maintained at the ship's armory.

2. No one is allowed to insert a clip or otherwise load any small arm unless he or she intends and is required to use the weapon in the performance of duty.

3. Clearing barrels are in use aboard all U.S. Navy ships for the safe, orderly transfer of weapons between armed sentries and watchstanders. These procedures are discussed in chapter 12 and appendix I.

4. Only designated persons may clean, disassemble, adjust, or repair small arms.

5. A small arm must never be pointed at anyone unless its bearer intends to shoot, or in any direction where accidental discharge could do harm.

SMOKING

Smoking is strictly prohibited in the following areas and during the following evolutions:

1. Holds, storerooms, gasoline tank compartments, gasoline pump rooms, voids, trunks, any shop or space where flammable liquids are being handled, ship's boats, bunks or berths, magazines, handling rooms, ready-service rooms, gun mounts or turrets, gasoline-control stations, oil-relay tank rooms, battery and charging rooms, film-projection rooms and the vicinity of motion-picture stowage, photography laboratories, and areas where vinyl or saran paint is being applied.

2. Any area of the ship where ammunition is being handled.

3. When ammunition is being either loaded or unloaded.

4. When fuel oil, diesel oil, aviation gasoline, or other volatile fuel is being received or transferred.

5. During general quarters, general drills, and emergencies, except as authorized by the CO.

6. When word is passed that the smoking lamp is out.

Most ships now limit the areas where smoking is permitted to only a few select locations—and then only when those designated areas are declared "open."

SPECIAL EQUIPMENT

All personnel concerned with the operation of such equipment as davits, winches, and booms must be thoroughly familiar with the safety precautions peculiar to its use. Applicable safety precautions must be posted in the vicinity of the equipment. Only personnel who have been instructed in the relevant duties and have been authorized by the first lieutenant are permitted to operate cranes, capstans, winches, and windlasses. Except in an emergency, operation of such machinery must be supervised by a responsible officer.

SYNTHETIC LINES

Know the types of lines your ship is using and their general characteristics. Not all synthetic lines respond the same under tension. Standard nylon and polyester synthetic lines for mooring and rigging (whether three-strand, plaited, or double-braided) have relatively high elasticity and a low coefficient of friction. Therefore, persons working with them should take the following precautions:

1. Give an extra turn when securing synthetic line to bitts, cleats, capstans, and other holding devices.
2. Exercise extreme care when easing out synthetic lines from bitts, cleats, and other holding devices.
3. Make sure no one is standing in the direct line of pull when heavy loads are applied to nylon line. Nylon line stretches to one-and-one-half times its original length, and when it parts, it snaps back with lethal effect.

Aramid lines, also synthetic, exhibit significantly different characteristics (less than 6 percent stretch at breaking strength, compared to 30–65 percent stretch for the nylon and polyester lines mentioned above). The aramid lines store less energy under tension and as a result are less prone to snapback. Aramid lines are extremely strong for their size, very similar to wire rope. For these reasons, they are smaller in diameter, lighter, easier to handle, and take up less storage space than corresponding nylon lines rated for the same breaking strength. Drawbacks include the fact that aramid lines do not show indications of strain under tension as well as nylon, and tattletale lines are ineffective due to the low stretch characteristics. As a result, four-strand aramid lines are designed with one strand to purposely fail first—as a warning—before the breaking strength of the remaining three strands is reached. An additional consideration is the fact that the aramid outer jacket appears to be more susceptible to chaffing than its nylon counterpart. Last, due to the reduced elasticity of aramid, the lines are more difficult to balance in a moor—requiring more precise adjustment. Despite these considerations, the high strength, smaller size, reduced weight, and diminished threat of snapback from aramid lines make them especially attractive for shipboard use.

TAG OUT

The proper tag out of equipment and instruments greatly enhances the safety of both crew and ship. Once a piece of equipment has been tagged, it cannot be untagged, operated, or used without specific directions from a competent authority. General practice is as follows:

1. All tags must be filled out completely, dated, and signed.
2. A proper entry must be made in the tag-out log whenever machinery is tagged in or out.
3. The individual who tags equipment must be notified before any change is made to its status.

Both "danger" tags and "caution" tags can be used (see figures 13-4 and 13-5). Tag out is a fairly complicated process with many built-in safeguards. Details are contained in the SORM and the Tag-Out Users Manual (TUM).

TOOLS

Danger from electric shock, electric shorts, and flying particles accompanies the use of pneumatic or electrically powered tools.

1. No person is to use an electric or pneumatic tool unless specifically authorized to do so by the division officer, and then only after demonstrating that he or she knows how to use it and what safety measures to follow.

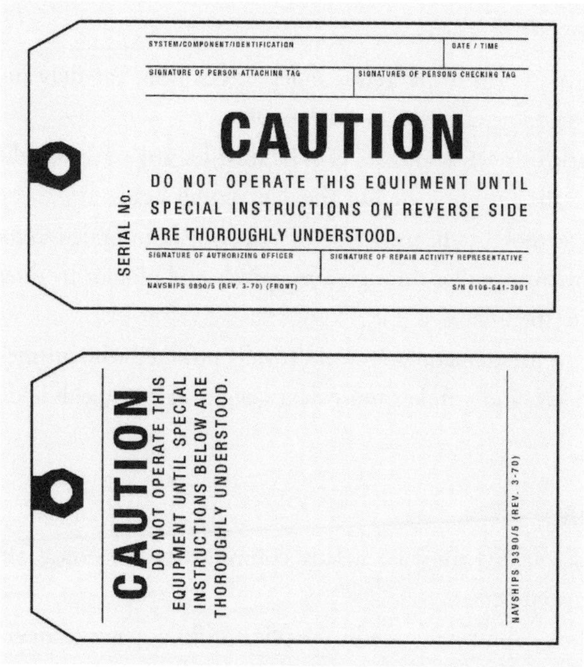

SYSTEM/COMPONENT/IDENTIFICATION — DATE / TIME

SIGNATURE OF PERSON ATTACHING TAG — SIGNATURES OF PERSONS CHECKING TAG

CAUTION

DO NOT OPERATE THIS EQUIPMENT UNTIL
SPECIAL INSTRUCTIONS ON REVERSE SIDE
ARE THOROUGHLY UNDERSTOOD.

SIGNATURE OF AUTHORIZING OFFICER — SIGNATURE OF REPAIR ACTIVITY REPRESENTATIVE

SERIAL No.

NAVSHIPS 9890/5 (REV. 3-70) (FRONT) — S/N 0105-541-3901

CAUTION

DO NOT OPERATE THIS
EQUIPMENT UNTIL SPECIAL
INSTRUCTIONS BELOW ARE
THOROUGHLY UNDERSTOOD.

NAVSHIPS 9390/5 (REV. 3-70)

FIGURE 13-4.
Caution Tags

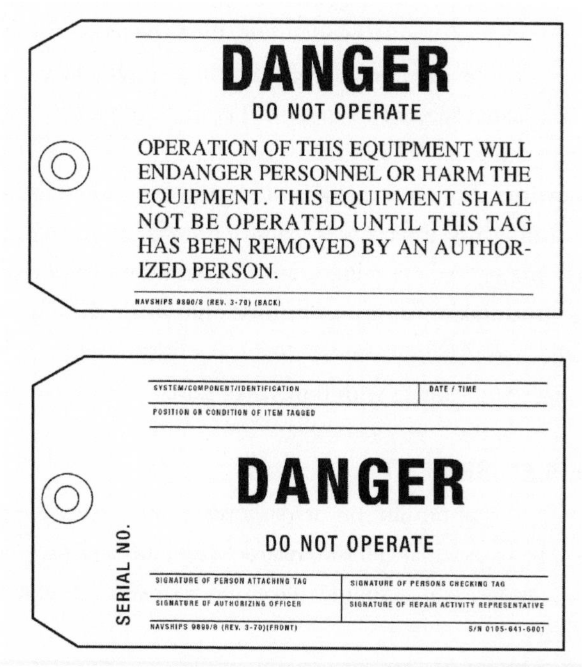

DANGER

DO NOT OPERATE

OPERATION OF THIS EQUIPMENT WILL
ENDANGER PERSONNEL OR HARM THE
EQUIPMENT. THIS EQUIPMENT SHALL
NOT BE OPERATED UNTIL THIS TAG
HAS BEEN REMOVED BY AN AUTHOR-
IZED PERSON.

NAVSHIPS 9890/8 (REV. 3-70) (BACK)

FIGURE 13-5.
Danger Tags

SYSTEM/COMPONENT/IDENTIFICATION — DATE / TIME

POSITION OR CONDITION OF ITEM TAGGED

DANGER

DO NOT OPERATE

SIGNATURE OF PERSON ATTACHING TAG — SIGNATURE OF PERSONS CHECKING TAG

SIGNATURE OF AUTHORIZING OFFICER — SIGNATURE OF REPAIR ACTIVITY REPRESENTATIVE

SERIAL NO.

NAVSHIPS 9890/8 (REV. 3-70)(FRONT) — S/N 0105-541-6901

2. No electric tool is to be issued unless it has been carefully inspected and checked for resistance to insulation.

3. No electric or pneumatic tool is to be used for any purpose other than those specifically authorized by the department head.

4. No electric tool is to be used unless its housing is grounded to the ship's metal structure, either through a receptacle and plug or by direct connection to the hull.

5. All persons using pneumatic or electrically powered wire brushes, chippers, sanders, and grinders must wear goggles or eye shields and rubber gloves.

TOXIC MATERIAL

The issue and use of HM must be strictly controlled by a medical officer or some other designated person.

Methyl alcohol—commonly used in duplicator fluid, paint thinner, cleaners, and antifreeze—is hazardous if inhaled, absorbed through the skin, or swallowed. The swallowing of even small amounts can cause permanent blindness or death. Methyl alcohol and products containing it may be released only in the amount required and at the time needed to perform a specific job. It may be used only in well-ventilated spaces and in a manner that prevents it from coming into contact with the skin.

Halogenated hydrocarbons, normally used in gaseous or liquid form as solvents, refrigerants, fumigants, insecticides, paint removers, dry-cleaning fluids, and propellants for pressurized containers, are also hazardous if inhaled, swallowed, or absorbed by the skin. They may be used only where there is adequate ventilation, by authorized personnel under close supervision, and in such a way that they do not come into contact with the eyes or skin.

UNDERWAY REPLENISHMENT

In this operation, speed is important but must never be attained at the price of safety. It is impossible to anticipate all the hazardous situations that could arise. The following precautions, which should always be reviewed before an operation begins, are a start:

1. Only essential personnel should be allowed in the vicinity of a transfer station.

2. Lifelines should be lowered only when absolutely necessary, and if they are, temporary ones must be rigged.

3. When line-throwing guns or bolos are used, all hands on the receiving ship must take cover.

4. Topside personnel engaged in handling stores and lines must wear safety helmets and orange-colored, inherently buoyant, vest-type life preservers. If safety helmets have quick-acting breakaway devices, the chinstrap must be fastened and worn under the chin. If helmets are not so equipped, the chin strap must be fastened behind the head or worn unbuckled. Between-ship phone talkers must not secure neck straps around their necks lest they be dragged over the side by the telephone lines.

5. Line-handlers must use the hand-over-hand method of hauling in a line. They should not hold a line and run with it to provide extra pull.

6. Cargo-handlers must wear safety shoes, and those handling wire-bound or banded cases must wear work gloves.

7. All hands must keep clear of bights and handle lines from the inboard side and stay at least six feet away from any block through which lines pass. Personnel must also keep clear of suspended loads and rig-attachment points until loads have been landed on deck.

8. Care must be taken to prevent the shifting of cargo. No one should get between any load and the rail.

9. Deck space in the vicinity of transfer stations must be covered with a slip-resistant material.

10. A life-buoy watch must be stationed well aft on the engaged side and provisions made for rescuing anyone who falls overboard. If a lifeguard ship is not available, a boat must be kept ready.

11. Prior to making the approach on the delivery ship, suitable measures must be taken to avoid the hazards associated with high-energy radio and radar transmissions. This is especially important when ammunition, gasoline, and other petroleum products are handled.

12. Dangerous materials, such as acids, compressed gases, and hypochlorites, must be transferred separately from one another and from other cargo. The delivery ship must notify the receiving ship of the type of dangerous material in each load before transferring it. The receiving ship must keep dangerous materials separated and stow them in designated storerooms as soon as possible.

13. When fuel oil is being received or transferred, naked lights and electrical or mechanical apparatus likely to spark may not be within fifty feet of an oil hose in use, an open fuel tank, the vent terminal from a fuel tank, or an area where fuel oil or fuel-oil vapors are or may be present. The term "naked light" includes all oil and gas lanterns, lighted candles, matches, cigars, cigarettes, cigarette lighters, and apparatus for flame welding or arc welding and cutting. Portable electric lights for fueling must have explosion-proof protected globes, be thoroughly inspected for proper insulation, and be tested before they are used. When a ship is being fueled, portholes on the side where she is being fueled must be closed and secured. Fuel-tank overboard discharges must be monitored by personnel in direct communication with the fuel-control station. All scuppers and deck drains around the fueling station should be blocked to prevent fuel spills.

VOLATILE FUELS

Aviation gasoline, motor gasoline, JP-4, and JP-5 are highly volatile liquids. They give off a vapor that, when combined with the proper proportion of air, forms an explosive mixture that can be set off by a slight spark or flame. Furthermore, the vapor can travel along an air current for a considerable distance and then be ignited, the flash traveling back to the source of supply and causing an explosion or fire.

1. All spaces into which the vapors of volatile fuel issue must be constantly and thoroughly ventilated.

2. No smoking and no naked lights (see number 13 above) are permitted in the vicinity of volatile-fuel tanks or filling connections, drums, cans, stowage, piping, or spaces through which such piping passes.

3. Care must be taken to prevent the striking of sparks in places where the vapors of volatile fuels may collect. Only spark-proof tools should be used.

4. When gasoline is carried in cans for a ship's use, it must be stowed in the storeroom for paint and flammable liquids. If there is no such storeroom, it should be stowed on the weather deck so that the containers may be readily jettisoned overboard.

5. Gasoline may be issued only under the supervision of a reliable person who must make sure that all containers are securely closed and all safety regulations observed.

6. The metal nozzle at the end of a fuel hose must be properly grounded to prevent sparks from static electricity (see number 13 under "Underway Replenishment," above).

7. Gasoline may not be used for cleaning purposes under any circumstances.

8. Upon completion of loading or delivery, piping and hoses must be carefully drained back into the ship's tanks or into containers that can be closed and sealed.

WHALES AND MARINE MAMMALS

An emerging area of safety concern is protecting whales and mammals in the marine environment. OpNavInst 5090.1D, Environmental Readiness Program Manual, contains the important references. The quiet submarine threat and safe navigation makes active sonar training vital for national security. The Navy's policy is to operate in compliance with environmental laws and to work effectively with regulatory agencies to balance active sonar use with the protection of marine life. The Navy therefore goes to great lengths to mitigate the potential effects of active sonar on marine life. The Commander, U.S. Fleet Forces Command issued guidance in 2004 implementing the use of Protective Measures Assessment Protocol (PMAP) software for the purpose of aiding ships in planning training events involving the use of ordnance or acoustic transmissions. In the Atlantic Ocean, there is particular concern about the calving season of the whales, from December through March. The critical habitat is located off the Atlantic coast, from Georgia to Florida. For the Pacific Ocean, there is particular concern during the gray whale's migration season, from January through

April. In both cases, if a whale strike occurs, there are specific reports that must be made. While transiting through the key areas during the whale season, it is required from a safety standpoint to brief watch teams, proceed at a safe speed, and, if sighting a whale, slow to five to eight knots. You should never approach a whale head-on or come closer than five hundred yards. Specific procedures are in place to report whale sightings to local operation area (OPAREA) authorities.

NAVY MARINE MAMMAL PROTECTION EFFORTS

The U.S. Navy exercises caution when operating in areas likely to contain marine mammals. Efforts to minimize potential effects on marine mammals include the following:

- Tracking historical trends of marine mammal populations in geographic areas where our ships operate.
- Using software tools that help operators determine if an operating area has any particular aspects that could lead to harming a marine mammal. This allows ships and aircraft to analyze the training area where a specific exercise will take place and then use protective measures as appropriate.
- Scanning for animals with passive sonar, trained shipboard lookouts, and available airborne assets prior to commencing an exercise. Navy lookouts are skilled in spotting small objects at sea under all conditions.
- Reducing sonar levels to 25 percent of operating power if whales or dolphins are detected within 450 yards of a Navy vessel's sonar dome.
- Ceasing use of active sonar if a marine mammal is detected within two hundred yards of an active source.

WORKING ALOFT

Personnel may go aloft only to perform work or duty, and then only with the permission of the OOD. Before granting permission, the OOD is responsible for seeing that the following safety precautions are observed:

1. The power on all radio-transmitting antennas and radar antennas in the vicinity has been secured, and power switches have been tagged out.

USS_____
Time/Date_____

1. Personnel will be going aloft at (location) _____ for accomplishing
   the following work_____

   _____

2. Prior to allowing personnel to go aloft, accomplish the following:

Initials

_____ a. If underway, obtain the commanding officer's permission.

_____ b. DANGER tag-out all rotating equipment, such as radar antennas, in the vicin-
          ity of the work area.

_____ c. Place a sign on all HF, MF, and LF transmitters and all radars whose danger
          zone encompasses the work area. The sign should read:
          SECURED. PERSONNEL ALOFT
          DATE_____ TIME_____ INITIALS_____

_____ d. Ensure personnel going aloft are wearing a parachute type safety harness
          with a Dyna-Brake(r) safety lanyard, working lanyard, and climber safety
          device (if a climber safety rail is installed).
          Ensure that PMS has been accomplished on all equipment prior to use.

_____ e. Notify the engineering officer of the watch/engineering duty officer to
          ensure that safety valves are lifted only in an emergency when personnel
          are aloft (main control should notify the officer of the deck of an impending
          emergency as soon as possible to permit warning of personnel aloft).

_____ f. If work is to be accomplished on or in the vicinity of the whistle, secure
          power to the whistle (steam, air, electricity) and DANGER tag out.

_____ g. Ensure that personnel are briefed on safety prior to going aloft. This should
          include, as a minimum, keeping the lanyard attached with a minimum of
          slack to a fixed structure at all times; changing the lanyard connection point
          as work progresses; keeping good footing and grasp at all times.

_____ h. Ensure all tools are attached to personnel with preventer lines; or, if passed
          up, have lanyards attached which are firmly secured before removal from the
          bucket.

_____ i. Ensure that assistance is provided to keep areas below the working area clear
          and for passing tools or performing rigging.

_____ j. Ensure that personnel working in the vicinity of stacks, or other areas where
          they may be subjected to exhaust fumes, are wearing proper respiratory
          protection equipment.

_____ k. Do not permit work aloft, except in an emergency, if wind speed is greater
          than 30 knots, roll is in excess of 10°, pitch is in excess of 6°, or if ice or
          thunderstorms threaten.

_____ l. If in port, notify officers of the deck/command duty officers of adjacent
          ship(s) to ensure that high-powered radio and radar transmitters will not be
          energized and endanger personnel going aloft.

FIGURE 13-6. Check Sheet for Working Aloft
(*continued on next page*)

_____ m. Fly the KILO or KILO THREE flag, as appropriate, if in port.

_____ n. Prior to personnel going aloft, have the following passed over the IMC: "DO NOT ROTATE OR RADIATE ANY ELECTRICAL OR ELECTRONIC EQUIPMENT WHILE PERSONNEL ARE WORKING ALOFT".

_____ o. If a crane in used to suspend personnel, ensure that the crane has a current certification and the work platform is approved by NAVSEA for handling personnel.

3. Conditions have been established to permit personnel working aloft.

_____

Command Duty Officer/Officer of the Deck/Time

Working Aloft Commenced _____

Working Aloft Completed _____

Note: Initials certify completion of an item. If an item is not applicable, indicate "NA" on initial line.

FIGURE 13-6. *Continued*

2. The engineering officer has been instructed not to lift safety valves and, if personnel are to work in the vicinity of the whistle, to secure steam to the whistle.

3. Personnel, if they are to work in the vicinity of stack gases, have protective breathing masks and have been instructed to remain there for only a brief time.

4. Personnel have an approved safety harness, which should be attached to the ship's structure at the level where they will be working.

5. All tools, buckets, paint pots, and brushes have lanyards with which they can be secured when used for work on masts, stacks, upper catwalks, weather decks, or sponsons that overhang areas where other personnel may be.

6. An announcement has been made over the 1MC concerning the operation aloft and any applicable restrictions, to prevent inadvertent changes in the status aloft.

7. The OODs of adjacent ships have been alerted so that high-powered radio and radar equipment in their ships will not be energized or present a danger to personnel going aloft.

8. If the ship is in port, the "kilo" flag has been hoisted to indicate personnel working aloft.

USS_____
Time/Date_____

1. Personnel (number) _____ will be going over the side at (location) _____ for accomplishing the following work _____

2. Prior to allowing personnel to work over the side, accomplish the following:

Initials

_____ a. If underway or in dry dock, obtain the commanding officer's permission.

_____ b. Ensure that personnel working over the side wear a parachute type safety harness with Dyna-Brake® safety lanyard and working lanyard, wear an inherently buoyant lifejacket modified with a button hole in the back to wear with the safety harness, and wear a hard-hat with a chin strap. Appropriate PMS shall be performed on harness, safety lanyard, and lifejacket prior to use. (Note: If working from a float or punt in the water, safety harness and safety lanyard are not required. Lifejackets and hard hat shall be worn. If in a dry deck without water, the life jacket is not required.)

_____ c. Each person working over the side has an assistant to tend lines. (Note: If working from a punt or float, at least one assistant shall be provided on the deck or pier. If in a dry dock without water, a tending line is not required.)

_____ d. Ship's propellers are stopped and overboard discharges in the area of personnel working over the side are secured and DANGER tagged.

_____ e. If work is to be accomplished in port between the ship and a pier or between the ship and other ships, a camel is in place.

_____ f. Power tools, if in use, are pneumatic. NO electric powered tools shall be used.

_____ g. Ensure that an experienced, senior person has checked the rigging of the bosun chair or staging prior to use.

_____ h. Ensure that personnel working over the side are briefed on safety prior to working over the side.

_____ i. Do not permit working over the side, except in an emergency, if wind speed is greater than 30 knots, roll is in excess of 10°, pitch is in excess of 6°, or if ice or thunderstorms threaten.

_____ j. Ensure that a petty officer in charge of work is stationed. Ensure PO in charge is alert for anything which would cause an increase in ship's motion or for the possibility of a collision.

_____ k. If in port, notify officers of the deck/command duty officers of ships alongside.

_____ l. Fly the KILO ONE or KILO THREE flag, as appropriate, if in port.

_____ m. If a crane is used to suspend personnel over the side, ensure that the crane has current certification and that the work platform is approved by NAVSEA for handling personnel.

3. Conditions have been established to permit personnel working over the side.

_____
Command Duty Officer/Officer of the Deck/Time

Working Over the Side Commenced _____

Working Over the Side Completed _____

Note: Initials certify completion of an item. If an item is not applicable, indicate "NA" on initial line.

FIGURE 13-7.
Check Sheet
for Working
over the Side

WORKING OVER THE SIDE

Personnel assigned to work over the side must be instructed in all safety precautions by their division officers before they can be permitted on scaffolding or stages or in boatswain's chairs. The following precautions must be observed:

1. Personnel working over the side must be supervised by a competent petty officer, and only qualified personnel should be assigned to tend safety lines.

2. All personnel working on stages, in boatswain's chairs, or in boats alongside the ship must wear inherently buoyant life preservers. With the exception of personnel in boats, they must also wear approved safety harnesses with shock-absorbing inertial attachment points and be equipped with safety lines tended from the deck above.

3. All tools, buckets, paint pots, and brushes used by personnel working over the side must be secured by lanyards to prevent their loss overboard and injury to personnel below.

4. Any person assigned to do work over the side of the ship while she is under way must have the permission of the CO.

14

BOATS AND VEHICLES

Small-boat operations require particular attention from the watch officer. Today's sleek and powerful boats are valuable assets to their parent ships. They provide the means of immediate response to emergency situations at sea and in port as well and may serve as the primary connection with the beach, especially in some foreign ports. It is as true now as it was in the past—a ship is judged by its communications off the ship and the appearance and performance of her boats, vehicles, and crew.

The watch officer should always remember that boat operations have the potential for catastrophe. Improper watchstanding and monitoring, preparation, loading, and poor handling of boats have caused many accidents and loss of life. Responsibility for the safety of a ship's boats and embarked passengers cannot be taken lightly. The complex coordination required to ensure safe, smart performance dictates that boat operations be carefully supervised by both the CDO and the OOD.

UNDER WAY

During operations at sea, the OOD must be concerned with the readiness and security of the boats. OpNavInst 3120.32D requires that at least one boat, if available, be prepared for lowering at all times and that at least one complete boat crew be assigned to rescue and assistance. The operations department and engineering department should conduct an inspection of the rescue boat daily and provide the boat report to the OOD on its readiness for service. The OOD should know the duty boat crew's qualifications as well as how long it would take to assemble them. He or she should also know which personnel will lower the boats in an emergency, who will be in charge of the operation, and how long it will take to lower the boats. The first lieutenant is responsible for providing qualified individuals for boat crews and ensuring that all personnel engaged in small-boat operations are adequately trained for this duty.

The readiness of boat engines, the amount of fuel in boats, and rescue equipment are other matters of interest to the OOD. In cold weather, precautions must be taken to keep the engines warm, either with heaters or by starting them frequently. It goes without saying that, at sea, boats should be fueled to capacity and refueled upon returning to the ship from a mission.

When lowering and recovering a boat, the OOD must be particularly concerned with safety. A boat should not be lowered in a trough or in waters too rough for recovery, and the ship should not exceed five knots even under the calmest of conditions, although a slight amount of headway is desirable during recovery for ease in hooking the boat to the davit or crane. A course should be selected that gives the ship a minimum roll and provides a lee on the side of the ship where the evolution is taking place. Usually a sufficient lee is gained by placing the wind and seas 30 to 50 degrees off the bow on the opposite side of the ship from where the boat will be recovered. The OOD should also try not to pick up a boat with sternway on the ship; if this is absolutely necessary, he or she should ensure that the falls are hooked or unhooked in reverse of normal order. A boat should not be lowered or hoisted with nonessential personnel on board. Everyone in the boat during its raising or lowering must wear a hard hat with chin strap fastened, safety shoes, and a life jacket. They must grip the lines as the boat goes up or down. If practical, personnel other than the regular crew should enter or leave the boat only while it is waterborne. When not conducting boat operations, the OOD must be concerned with the security of the boat in its stowage. It is prudent to have a designated watchstander check boats once a watch, more often during heavy weather. When heavy weather is expected, the OOD should inform the first lieutenant so that he or she may take extra precautions to ensure the security of the boats. Any deficiencies in the condition of the boats, their readiness for operation, or the readiness of their crew should be brought to the attention of the first lieutenant and the CO immediately.

All these matters are part of the routine of a well-run ship, but the OOD cannot afford to assume that all is well. If a lifeboat is not ready when needed or is launched with a green crew, the OOD is certain to be held responsible.

IN PORT

In port, the operation, appearance, and security of boats and vehicles are the responsibility of the OOD. OpNavInst 3120.32D, Article 6.3.1 (Boat Bill), directs the OOD to perform the following duties:

1. Directly supervise ship's boats, and comply with the boat schedules published by the XO and other proper authority.
2. Ensure that boats are operated safely and that all boat safety regulations are observed.
3. Ensure that boats are not overloaded, and that loading capacity is reduced to a safe margin when weather conditions require.
4. Use boat officers under such conditions as:
   a. Foul weather or reduced visibility (existing or expected) and on long trips.
   b. First boat trips in foreign or unfamiliar harbors and when required by local regulations.
   c. Returning large liberty parties after sunset, especially prior to sailing.
5. Notify the CDO when weather conditions make the suspension or resumption of boating advisable.
6. Inspect boats secured alongside hourly. If weather or sea conditions hinder safety, hoist boats in or send them to a safe haven.
7. Ensure the coxswain, or qualified boat crew designated by cognizant department head, inspects and reports readiness of the lifeboat(s):
   a. Daily at sunset while in port.
   b. At the beginning of each watch while under way.

Calling away, dispatching, fueling, and receiving boats and vehicles can be complicated and overwhelming for an OOD who has not organized the watch. A manual status sheet or electronic tracking system is mandatory to keep track of the boats and vehicles on so many missions. Even when an assistant is maintaining a record of missions and conditions of readiness, intelligent supervision by the OOD is still needed. Boats and vehicles should be inspected for appearance, and their equipment should be checked. If the instructions to be given a coxswain or driver are complicated, it is best to send for that person and discuss them. If there is any doubt about a person's memory, he or she should be given instructions in writing, and they should be short, complete, and reasonable. The coxswain must be given, and must review with the navigator or quartermaster, a section of the harbor chart showing the ship's berth, other occupied anchorages, all commonly used landings and compass courses thereto, and a copy of local traffic rules and navigational dangers and aids. Tracks to and from the boat's destination should also be clearly marked. A boat or vehicle should never be sent to wait for someone indefinitely; if the passenger or passengers should fail to show up, the services of the boat or vehicle are lost until word can be gotten to the coxswain or driver, and that might take hours. The proper procedure for all boats and vehicles, except, of course, an admiral's barge or captain's gig or some equivalent vehicle, is to direct them to wait for someone a certain length of time or until a specified hour.

APPEARANCE

The appearance and smartness of a ship's boats and vehicles are important to officers and enlisted personnel who take pride in their ship and in their service. A smart boat is a criterion by which a ship and her crew are evaluated. Fresh, neat paintwork and fancy knotwork make a good impression, but the manner in which a boat is handled and how it accomplishes tasking is even more significant. The OOD is responsible for ensuring that coxswains have good sea manners, which includes rendering proper courtesies to passing boats and avoiding hot-rod landings and excessive wake.

The OOD can be a major factor in maintaining high standards for a ship's boats. His or her critical appraisal of a boat and its crew as it comes alongside is the first step. If the OOD then corrects any deficiencies, he or she will have done much to ensure that the ship is well represented by her boats.

BOAT GONGS

Ships use boat gongs to indicate that liberty boats will soon depart. Gongs are sounded over the ship's general announcing circuit, their meaning varying as follows:

Number of Gongs	Meaning
3	Boat departs in ten minutes.
2	Boat departs in five minutes.
1	Boat departs in one minute.

CAPACITY AND LOADING

The capacity of a naval boat is indicated on a label plate affixed to it during construction. The figure shown on the plate indicates maximum capacity under good conditions; capacity is always reduced in rough weather or when cargo is carried along with passengers.

It is worth an OOD's time to learn the technique of loading a large liberty boat because doing it properly is one of those small but significant signs that a ship is smartly run and has an efficient and effective OOD. After the chief petty officers have embarked, other personnel should load from fore to aft. A little supervision may be required to prevent the center section from filling up first, which results in people climbing over each other or walking along the gunwales, a dangerous practice.

CREWS

The first lieutenant is responsible for training the boat crews, but it is the OOD's responsibility to ensure that those who operate boats during his or her watch are qualified and proficient. The OOD must be especially diligent in this because the potential for disaster is proportional to the crew's inexperience. The OOD's responsibility for safety dictates that he or she allow only fully qualified crew members to operate the boat. Inexperienced personnel may be allowed to go along for instruction if they wish but never as substitutes for fully qualified people. There can be no compromise when safety is involved.

EQUIPMENT

Compasses, life jackets, and other pieces of equipment must be checked by the OOD as circumstances warrant. When a long boat passage is to be taken or visibility is likely to be low, a chart, electronic navigation or mapping system, or compass-book entry showing heading and time on each course should be presented for guidance and reference. Life jackets, foul-weather clothing, harbor charts, and firefighting equipment are other items with which the OOD should be concerned. Life jackets should be checked and crews and passengers directed to wear them when weather or sea conditions warrant. The number of people allowed in a boat should not exceed the number of life jackets in the boat. It should never be assumed that boats belonging to other units are properly equipped; the OOD should have them inspected if they are to be used by his or her ship.

INSPECTION

The engineering officer designates a qualified petty officer to make a daily check of boats' engines, and the first lieutenant makes periodic checks on the condition of each boat and the equipment it carries. While these inspections are usually thorough, they do not guarantee that certain equipment will be in a certain boat at a particular time, nor do they relieve the OOD of exercising the prudence and foresight expected of a good seaman.

ORDERS

Orders to the coxswain of a boat should be given in a seamanlike and explicit manner. An unseamanlike order might be, "All right, coxswain, shove off and get the navigator at the Dock Street landing." A seamanlike and explicit order would be, "Coxswain! When told to shove off, go to the Dock Street landing and pick up the navigator, LCDR Jones. If he does not show up by 1800, return to the ship. Do you understand?" If the coxswain answers in the affirmative, the OOD would say, "Shove off and carry out your orders."

It should be remembered that a boat "hauls out" to the boom, it does not "tie up" or "secure" to the boom. A ship "makes fast" to a pier, while a boat "makes fast" to the accommodation ladder (not to the gangway). A boat may be "secured," but this means a longer-lasting fastening than "made fast."

SAFETY

The safest way to secure boats is to hoist them in at night or in bad weather. When this procedure is not practical, they should be hauled out to the boom and kept under surveillance. Boats usually ride well at the boom, but the practice of making fast astern is risky in bad weather. Boatkeepers or boat sentries are usually posted when the weather threatens ship's boats. Boats should never lie unattended at the accommodation ladder or other locations where they may be exposed to open wind and sea conditions.

If a boat is to be left in the water for a long time, the OOD should make a visual inspection of it at least once an hour and should direct all roving security patrols to check it as well by embarking the boat and using a flashlight to inspect the boat, including the bilge. This is to prevent unauthorized use or theft or to discover a flooding problem quickly. (For detailed safety precautions governing boat operations, see chapter 13.)

SCHEDULES

The XO generally prescribes boat schedules, and they should be followed meticulously by the OOD. Only the most unusual circumstances should be allowed to cause cancellation of a scheduled boat, particularly at night when people ashore may be planning to return to the ship in that boat. If a scheduled boat trip must be canceled, permission for the cancellation is obtained from the XO or CDO, and the word must be passed.

When, as often happens, officers and enlisted personnel waiting to leave the ship are going to the same destination as the senior officer, that person usually allows them to embark in his or her gig or barge. The OOD should find out whether the senior officer concerned follows this practice and, if so, embark the people before he or she comes onto the quarterdeck. If doubt exists, there is nothing wrong with asking the senior officer whether he or she is willing to take crew members along. If the answer is affirmative, as is almost always the case, every effort must be made to expedite the loading of the boat. Juniors normally enter boats (and vehicles) first and leave them last.

SECURITY

One way to ensure the safe and effective operation of boats is to provide a boat officer. This is true, of course, only if the officer is qualified.

A boat officer can wear a web belt, which is a badge of authority and distinguishes him or her from passengers who are officers. When there are not enough commissioned or warrant officers to act as boat officers, it is customary to assign chief petty officers of deck ratings.

For a more thorough study of small boat operations, the reader is referred to OpNavInst 3120.32D, Article 6.3.1 and NSTM 583 (Boats and Small Craft).

VEHICLES

Ships in port are assigned vehicles to assist in carrying out daily business. The OOD is usually tasked with keeping track of these vehicles and seeing that they are always ready for use. Losing track of the status of a ship's vehicles can significantly hamper a ship's in-port operation and is certain to ruin the OOD's day. The wise OOD will have direct control of all vehicle keys. He or she will give them only to authorized users and require that they be returned. Ship's vehicles should normally be parked within sight of the quarterdeck to prevent theft or damage. The OOD should keep notes on who is using vehicles, who will require them and why, and how long trips will take. Priorities must be established, and the OOD may end up making unpopular decisions. Common sense is usually the rule. Often the consolidation of several trips can make for more efficient use of a vehicle. The name and whereabouts of the duty driver are also of concern to the OOD. The OOD must make sure that the duty driver is on station, in the correct uniform, and ready for an appointment ahead of schedule. Upon return of a vehicle's keys, the OOD should ascertain the fuel status of the vehicle and have it refueled if necessary.

Any number of things can go wrong with ship's vehicles, all of which spell trouble for the OOD. He or she can avoid most of this trouble by requiring a face-to-face turnover of keys before and after each use. The OOD should not lose track of a vehicle and should ensure that every vehicle is used for ship's business only. It is helpful to keep a separate logbook to record the status of each vehicle.

Vehicle Security

Marked government vehicles or vehicles carrying uniformed passengers are possible targets for terrorists. The OOD must always be alert to the possibility of a local terrorist threat and must take appropriate precautions. He or she must always consult the CDO for special precautions and instructions.

WASTE, FRAUD, AND ABUSE

Ship's vehicles and boats should be used only for official purposes. They should not make unofficial stops, for example, at a restaurant or shopping mall, while conducting official business. Misuse will rightfully lead to complaints against the command, especially when a vehicle or boat carries official Navy or command-specific markings. Always check any questionable requests for vehicles or boats with the CDO or XO. Review OpNavInst 3120.32D, Article 5.1.32.

15

HONORS AND CEREMONIES

Honors and ceremonies are based on customs and a long-established code of agreements and regulations, most of which are common to all navies. With some exceptions, honors and ceremonies take place in port, and the manner in which they are rendered or carried out under the supervision of the OOD does much to give a ship a reputation for smartness. It is important that they be conducted in a manner that also reflects credit on the U.S. Navy and the United States.

The governing source for appropriate honors is U.S. Navy Regulations (1990). The OOD need not commit regulations to memory. For convenience, allow time for preparation. To aid the OOD, some ships keep a table of honors posted on the quarterdeck for ready reference.

With honors and ceremonies, as with nearly all other activities, an OOD must look ahead. He or she should be able to estimate the degree of readiness required at any given time. For example, if the ship is anchored at an advanced base, the weather is bad, and there is a possibility of air attack, the OOD is not likely to need side boys standing by. On the other hand, circumstances might be such that the OOD should have the full guard ready at a moment's notice.

The following pages contain enough information from Navy Regulations to enable the OOD, under normal conditions, to discharge his or her duties. On special occasions, such as the death of an important person, the OOD will have to refer to Navy Regulations.

THE QUARTERDECK

> The Commanding Officer of a ship shall establish the limits of the quarterdeck and the restrictions as to its use. The quarterdeck shall embrace so much of the main or other appropriate deck as may be necessary for the proper conduct of official ceremonial functions.
>
> NAVY REGULATIONS, ARTICLE 1256

The quarterdeck functions as the command and control center for a ship's daily administrative activities and for the conduct of the ship's in-port routine. It is whatever part of the ship the CO designates. It is normally on the main deck near the brow, making it the first line of security for the ship. It may be marked off by appropriate lines, deck markings, cartridge cases decoratively arranged, or fancy work. It is always kept clean and shipshape. Personnel not on duty should not be allowed on or near the quarterdeck. The dignity and appearance of the quarterdeck reflect the professional and seamanlike attitude of a ship and her crew. The OOD should be zealous in upholding this dignity and appearance, together with the highest standards of smartness on the part of the personnel.

The brow should always be tended by the OOD or an assistant for reasons of both security and courtesy. Every person who comes aboard should be greeted immediately by a member of the watch. His or her business should then be ascertained and credentials examined. If all is in order, appropriate steps must be taken to have the guest escorted below or to send for the person he or she wishes to see. Officers' guests should be taken to the wardroom.

When an officer comes aboard by boat, his or her boat usually lies alongside the accommodation ladder until it receives its orders. The OOD should ask the visitor or an aide what orders are desired for his or her boat, gig, or barge.

SIDE BOYS

Side boys, being the first members of the crew to come under the observation of an important visitor, should be particularly smart, their shoes polished and their uniforms immaculate. They should be kept together under the eye of a petty officer and not employed in any activity that might spoil their appearance or remove them from the quarterdeck. The OOD should see that they are properly instructed and can fall in without confusion. Similar care should be taken with the guard and band, if appropriate for the occasion. Generally, side boys are not paraded or required on any occasion other than a prearranged visit by a flag officer or a VIP.

PIPING THE SIDE

The call "Alongside" is timed to finish just as a visitor's boat reaches the accommodation ladder. During this call, the side boys and the boatswain's mate stand at attention but do not salute.

For a visitor approaching by way of an accommodation ladder, the call "Over the side" starts just as his or her head appears at quarterdeck level. For a visitor approaching over a brow, it starts when he or she arrives at a designated point at the outboard end of the brow. Side boys and the boatswain's mate salute on the first note and drop their hands from salute on the last note. The boatswain's mate may salute with the left hand. The saluting and piping procedure is reversed when a visitor leaves.

OFFICIAL VISITS

When the OOD is notified that an official visit is to be paid to the ship, he or she should take these steps:

1. Consult the table of honors in Navy Regulations.
2. Notify the admiral, chief of staff, CO, XO, CDO, navigator, senior watch officer, flag lieutenant, and CO of the marine detachment.
3. Have on deck a qualified boatswain's mate and a quartermaster.
4. Inspect and rehearse the side boys.
5. Inspect the quarterdeck for appearance.
6. Station an alert lookout, notify the signal bridge to be prepared, and have the visitor's personal flag ready.
7. Notify the band if appropriate.
8. If a gun salute is required, notify the combat systems officer.

SALUTES AND HONORS

The following extracts from Navy Regulations provide a ready reference for the OOD:

Morning and Evening Colors

1. The ceremonial hoisting and lowering of the national ensign at 0800 and sunset at a naval command ashore or aboard a ship of the Navy not under way shall be known as Morning Colors and Evening Colors, respectively, and shall be carried out as prescribed in this article.

2. The guard of the day and the band shall be paraded in the vicinity of the point of hoist of the ensign.

3. "Attention" shall be sounded, followed by the playing of the national anthem by the band.

4. At Morning Colors, the ensign shall be started up at the beginning of the music and hoisted smartly to the peak or truck. At Evening Colors, the ensign shall be started from the peak or truck at the beginning of the music and the lowering so regulated as to be completed at the last note.

5. At the completion of the music, "Carry on" shall be sounded.

6. In the absence of a band, an appropriate recording shall be played over a public address system. "To the Colors" shall be played by the bugle at Morning Colors and "Retreat" at Evening Colors and the salute shall be rendered as prescribed for the national anthem.

7. In the absence of music, "Attention" and "Carry on" shall be the signals for rendering and terminating the salute. "Carry on" shall be sounded as soon as the ensign is completely lowered.

8. During colors, a boat under way within sight or hearing of the ceremony shall lie to, or shall proceed at the lowest safe speed. The boat officer, or in his absence the coxswain, shall stand and salute except when dangerous to do so. Other persons in the boat shall remain seated or standing and shall not salute.

9. During colors, vehicles within sight or hearing of the ceremony shall be stopped. Persons riding in such vehicles shall remain seated at attention.

10. After Morning Colors, if foreign warships are present, the national anthem of each nation so represented shall be played in the order in which a gun salute would be fired to, or exchanged with, the senior officer or officer present of each such nation, provide that, when in a foreign port, the national anthem of the port shall be played immediately after Morning Colors, followed by the national anthem of other foreign nations represented.   ARTICLE 1206

Salutes to the National Ensign

1. Each person in the naval service, upon coming on board a ship of the Navy, shall salute the national ensign if it is flying. He or she shall stop on reaching the upper platform of the accommodation ladder, or the shipboard end of the brow, face the national ensign, and render the salute, after which he or he shall salute the officer of the deck. On leaving the ship, he or she shall render the salutes in inverse order. The officer of the deck shall return both salutes in each case.

   a. After rendering the appropriate salute to the national ensign, an officer coming on board a ship to which he or she is attached shall report his or her return. An officer coming on board a ship to which he or she is not attached shall request permission to come on board and shall state his or her business. An enlisted person shall request permission to come on board, and shall state his or her business if the ship is not the one to which he or she is attached.

   b. After rendering the appropriate salute to the officer of the deck, an officer shall state that he or she has permission to leave. An enlisted person shall request permission to leave.

2. A member not in uniform shall render appropriate honors to the national ensign by facing the flag and standing at attention with the right hand over the heart. If covered, men shall remove their headdress with the right hand and hold it at the left shoulder, the hand being over the heart.

3. Each person in the naval service in uniform, upon being passed by or passing a military formation carrying the national ensign uncased shall

render the hand salute. A member not in uniform being passed by or passing such a formation shall face the flag and stand at attention with the right hand over the heart. If covered, men shall remove the head-dress and hold it at the left shoulder, the hand being over the heart. Persons in vehicles or boats shall follow the procedure prescribed for such persons during colors.

4. The salutes prescribed in this article shall also be rendered to foreign national flags and ensigns and aboard foreign men-of-war, unless to do so would cause embarrassment or misunderstanding. Aboard foreign men-of-war, the practice of the host nation may be followed, if known.

ARTICLE 1207

Saluting Ships and Stations

Saluting ships and stations of the naval service are those designated as such by the Secretary of the Navy or by the Secretary's duly authorized representative. The gun salute prescribed in these regulations shall be fired by such ships and stations. Other ships and stations shall not fire gun salutes, unless directed to do so by the senior officer present on exceptional occasions when courtesy requires.

ARTICLE 1212

"Passing Honors" and "Close Aboard" Defined

"Passing honors" are those honors, other than gun salutes, rendered on occasions when ships of embarked officials or officers pass, or are passed, close aboard. "Close aboard" shall mean passing within six hundred yards for ships and four hundred yards for boats. These rules shall be interpreted liberally, to insure that appropriate honors are rendered.

ARTICLE 1227

Passing Honors between Ships

1. Passing honors, consisting of sounding "Attention" and rendering the hand salute by all persons in view on deck and not in ranks, shall be exchanged between ships of the Navy and between ships of the Navy and the Coast Guard, passing close aboard. [See table 15.1 for correct sequence.]

2. In addition, the honors prescribed in [table 15.2] shall be rendered by a ship of the Navy passing close aboard a ship or naval station displaying

the flag of the official indicated therein; and by naval stations, insofar as practicable, when a ship displaying such flag passes close aboard. These honors shall be acknowledged by rendering the same honors in return.
ARTICLE 1228

Passing Honors to Officials and Officers Embarked in Boats

1. The honors prescribed in [table 15.3] shall be rendered by a ship of the Navy being passed close aboard by a boat displaying the flag or pennant of the . . . officials and officers listed [in table].

2. Persons on the quarterdeck shall salute when a boat passes close aboard in which a flag officer, a unit commander, or a commanding officer is embarked as indicated by a display of a personal flag, command pennant, commission pennant, or a miniature thereof.
ARTICLE 1229

Passing Honors to Foreign Dignitaries and Warships

1. The honors prescribed for the President of the United States shall be rendered by a ship of the Navy being passed close aboard by a ship or boat displaying the flag or standard of a foreign president, sovereign, or member of a reigning royal family, except that the foreign national anthem shall be played in lieu of the national anthem of the United States.

2. Passing honors shall be exchanged with foreign warships passed close aboard and shall consist of parading the guard of the day, sounding "Attention," rendering the salute by all persons in view on deck, and playing the foreign national anthem.
ARTICLE 1230

Sequence in Rendering Passing Honors

1. "Attention" shall be sounded by the junior when the bow of one ship passes the bow or stern of the other, or, a senior is embarked in a boat, before the boat is abreast, or nearest to abreast, the quarterdeck.

2. The guard, if required, shall present arms, and all persons in view on deck shall salute.

3. The music, if required, shall sound off.

4. "Carry on" shall be sounded when the prescribed honors have been rendered and acknowledged. ARTICLE 1231

Dispensing with Passing Honors

1. Passing honors shall not be rendered after sunset or before 0800 except when international courtesy requires.

2. Passing honors shall not be exchanged between ships of the Navy engaged in tactical evolutions outside port.

3. The senior officer present may direct that passing honors be dispensed with in whole or in part.

4. Passing honors shall not be required by nor required of ships with small bridge areas, such as submarines, particularly in restricted waters.

ARTICLE 1232

TABLE 15-1 Passing Honors between Ships, Sequence

OOD OF JUNIOR SHIP	OOD OF SENIOR SHIP	BUGLE CALL	BATTERY WHISTLE
1. Sounds "Attention" starboard (port)		"Attention" starboard (port)	1 whistle starboard, 2 whistles (port)
	2. Sounds "Attention" starboard (port)		
3. Sounds "Hand salute" (guard presents arms and band sounds off if required)		1 short note	1 short whistle
	4. Sounds "Hand salute" (guard presents arms and band sounds off)		
	5. Sounds "TWO" (in 3 seconds or after band sounds off)	2 short notes	2 short whistles
6. Sounds "TWO"			
	7. Sounds "Carry on"	"Carry on"	3 short whistles
8. Sounds "Carry on"			

TABLE 15-2 Passing Honors between Ships, Protocol

OFFICIAL	UNIFORM	RUFFLES AND FLOURISHES	MUSIC	GUARD	REMARKS
President	As prescribed by senior officer present	4	National Anthem	Full	Man rail, unless otherwise directed by senior officer present
Secretary of state when special foreign representative of the president	As prescribed by senior officer present	4	National Anthem	Full	Crew at quarters
Vice president	Of the day	—	"Hail Columbia"	Full	Crew at quarters
Secretary of defense, deputy secretary of defense, secretary of the Navy, or under-secretary of defense	Of the day	—	National Anthem	Full	Crew at quarters
Assistant secretary of defense, under-secretary or assistant secretary of the Navy	Of the day	—	National Anthem	Full	Crew at quarters

Crew at Quarters on Entering or Leaving Port

The crew shall be paraded at quarters during daylight on entering or leaving port on occasions of ceremony except when weather or other circumstances make it impracticable or undesirable to do so. Ordinarily occasions of ceremony shall be construed as visits that are not operational; at homeport when departing for or returning from a lengthy deployment; and visits to foreign ports not visited recently; and other special occasions so determined by a superior. In lieu of parading the entire crew at quarters, an honor guard may be paraded in a conspicuous place on weather decks. ARTICLE 1233

TABLE 15-3 Passing Honors to Officials and Officers Embarked on Boats

OFFICIAL	RUFFLES AND FLOURISHES	MUSIC	GUARD	REMARKS
President	4	National Anthem	Full	"Attention" sounded, and salute by all persons in view on deck; if directed by the senior officer present, man rail*
Secretary of state when special foreign representative of president	4	National Anthem	Full	"Attention" sounded, and salute by all persons in view on deck
Vice president	4	"Hail Columbia"	Full	"Attention" sounded, and salute by all persons in view on deck
Secretary of defense, deputy secretary of defense, secretary of the Navy, undersecretary of defense, an assistant secretary of defense, undersecretary or assistant secretary of the Navy	4	Admiral's march	Full	"Attention" sounded, and salute by all persons in view on deck
Other civil officials entitled to honors on official visit	—	—	—	

* Those who man the rail salute on signal

Side Honors

1. On the arrival and departure of civil officials and foreign officers, and of United States officers when so directed by the senior officer present, the side shall be piped and the appropriate number of side boys paraded.

2. Officers appropriate to the occasion shall attend the side on the arrival and departure of officials and officers. ARTICLE 1249

Dispensing with Side Boys, Guard, and Band

1. Side boys shall not be paraded on Sunday, or on other days between sunset and 0800, or during meal hours of the crew, general drills and evolutions, and period of regular overhaul; except in honor of civil officials or foreign officers, when they must be paraded at any time during daylight. Side boys shall be paraded only for scheduled visits.

2. Except for official visits and other formal occasions, side boys shall not be paraded in honor of officers of the armed services of the United States, unless otherwise directed by the senior officer present.

3. Side boys shall not be paraded in honor of an officer of the armed services in civilian clothes, unless such officer is at the same time acting in an official civil capacity.

4. The side shall be piped when side boys are paraded, but not at other times.

5. The guard and band shall not be paraded in honor of the arrival or departure of an individual at times when side boys in his or her honor are dispensed with, except at naval shore installations. ARTICLE 1250

Honors at Official Inspection

1. When a flag officer or unit commander boards a ship of the Navy to make an official inspection, honors shall be rendered as for an official visit, except that the uniform shall be as prescribed by the inspection officer. The inspecting officer's flag or command pennant shall be broken upon his arrival, unless otherwise prescribed in these regulations, and shall be hauled down on his departure.

2. The provisions of this article shall apply, insofar as practicable and appropriate, when a flag or general officer, in command ashore, makes an official inspection of a unit of the command.

16

FLAGS, PENNANTS, AND BOAT HAILS

The watch officer should be aware that the displaying of flags and pennants, like execution of honors and ceremonies, represents a highly visible evolution that will either enhance or detract from a ship's reputation for smartness. This is not an area to be given only cursory attention. The watch officer should see that each action is carried out in a precise, professional manner. This chapter contains the most basic information on the usage of flags and pennants. It is derived from Flags, Pennants, and Customs (NTP-13b) and U.S. Navy Regulations. The former publication should be studied by every officer who stands deck watches.

Many countries have variations of their national flag authorized for specific uses. The national flag used by men-of-war is the ensign; that used by merchant ships is the merchant flag. The United States of America has only one flag, the colors, which is used for all purposes and may properly be called the ensign when used in the Navy. A union jack is the union, or inner upper corner of a national flag. The U.S. union is, of course, a blue field with fifty white stars on it. Beginning in 2002 U.S. ships were authorized to fly the First Navy Jack in lieu of the union jack. The First Navy Jack is thirteen red and white alternating stripes emblazoned with a rattlesnake and the phrase "Don't Tread on Me." In 2019 the Navy returned to using the union jack.

GENERAL RULES FOR DISPLAY

The distinctive mark of a naval ship or craft in commission is an officer's personal flag, a command pennant, or a commission pennant. The distinctive mark of a naval hospital ship, such as the COMFORT or the MERCY, is the Red Cross flag. Not more than one distinctive mark is displayed at the same time. Except as prescribed in Navy Regulations for certain occasions of ceremony and when civil officials are embarked, one of the distinctive marks mentioned above is displayed day and night at the after masthead or, in a mastless ship, from the most conspicuous hoist.

When a ship is not under way, the ensign and the union jack are displayed from 0800 until sunset from the flagstaff and the jackstaff, respectively. When a ship has entered port at night, at daylight she displays the ensign from the gaff, if appropriate, for a time sufficient to establish her nationality. It is customary for other ships of war to display their ensigns in return. When mooring or unmooring, the colors are shifted from the gaff to the flagstaff on the stern or the other way around, and the jack is raised or lowered on the bow. The instant the last mooring line leaves the pier or the anchor is aweigh between 0800 and sunset, the BMOW sounds a blast on a handheld whistle and passes the word over the 1MC: "Under way, shift colors." This enables the lowering and raising of the flags to occur simultaneously. The jack on the jackstaff forward and the national ensign on the flagstaff aft, if flying, are hauled down smartly. At the same instant, the steaming ensign is hoisted on the gaff and the ship's international call sign and other pertinent signal flags are hoisted or broken. On mooring, the instant the anchor is let go or the first line is made fast to the pier, the boatswain's mate performs the same actions as for unmooring. At this signal, the ship's call sign and steaming ensign are hauled down smartly, and the jack and national ensign are run up.

Unless otherwise directed by the senior officer present, a ship displays the ensign during daylight from her gaff under the following circumstances:

1. Getting under way and coming to anchor.
2. Falling in with other ships.
3. Cruising near land.
4. In battle (when a special, larger battle ensign is displayed).

RULES FOR THE U.S. ENSIGN
During Gun Salutes

A ship of the U.S. Navy displays the ensign at a masthead while firing a salute in honor of a U.S. official or national anniversary, as follows:

1. At the main during the national salute prescribed for the third Monday in February and the 4th of July.
2. At the main during a 21-gun salute to a United States civil official, except by a ship displaying the personal flag of the official being saluted.
3. At the fore during a salute to any other United States civil official, except by a ship which is displaying the personal flag of the official being saluted. NAVY REGULATIONS, ARTICLE 1261

During a gun salute, the ensign must also remain displayed from the gaff or the flagstaff.

In Boats

The national ensign is displayed from waterborne boats of the naval service as follows:

1. When under way during daylight in a foreign port.
2. When ships are required to be dressed or full-dressed.
3. When going alongside a foreign vessel.
4. When an officer or official is embarked on an official occasion.
5. When a flag or general officer, a unit commander, a commanding officer, or a chief of staff, in uniform, is embarked in a boat of the command or in one assigned to the personal use of such an officer.
6. At such other times as may be prescribed by the senior officer present. NAVY REGULATIONS, ARTICLE 1262

Dipping

When a vessel under U.S. registry, or under the registry of a nation formally recognized by the government of the United States, salutes a ship of the U.S. Navy by dipping her ensign, she is answered dip for dip. If the ensign is not already being displayed, it is hoisted, the dip is returned, and after a suitable interval, it is hauled down. An ensign being displayed at half-mast is hoisted to the truck or peak for the purpose of answering a dip.

Ships of the U.S. Navy dip the ensign only in return for such compliment. Submarines are not required to dip the ensign.

Half-Masting

When an ensign that is not already being displayed is to be flown at half-mast, it must be hoisted to the truck or peak before being lowered to half-mast. Similarly, before the ensign is lowered from half-mast, it must be hoisted to the truck or peak.

When the ensign is half-masted, the jack, if displayed from the jackstaff, must also be half-masted.

Because small boats are a part of a vessel, they follow the procedures of the patent vessel as regards the half-masting of colors.

Following Motions of Senior Officer Present

Whenever the ensign is to be hoisted, lowered, or half-masted, the motions of the senior officer present are followed, except as prescribed for answering a dip or firing a salute.

A ship displaying the flag of the president, secretary of defense, deputy secretary of defense, secretary of the Navy, an assistant secretary of defense, an undersecretary of the Navy, or an assistant secretary of the Navy is regarded as the ship of the senior officer present.

DISPLAY OF FOREIGN ENSIGNS DURING GUN SALUTES

When a ship is firing a salute to a foreign nation in one of that nation's ports, returning a salute fired by a warship of that nation, or firing a salute on the occasion of a celebration or ceremony of that nation, she displays the ensign of the foreign nation at the main truck.

When a ship is firing a salute to a foreign dignitary or official entitled to twenty-one guns, she displays the national ensign of that dignitary or official at her main truck. When firing a salute to a foreign official entitled to less than twenty-one guns, or to a foreign officer, or when returning a salute fired by a foreign officer, she displays the national ensign of the foreign official or officer at her fore truck.

DISPLAY OF THE UNITED NATIONS FLAG

The following policy concerns the display of the United Nations flag:

1. The United Nations flag will be displayed at installations of the armed forces of the United States only upon occasion of visits of high dignitaries of the United Nations while in performance of their official duties with the United Nations, or on other special occasions in honor of the United Nations. When so displayed it will be displayed with the United States flag, both flags will be of the same approximate size and on the same level, the flag of the United States in the position of honor on the right (observer's left).

2. The United Nations flag will be carried by troops on occasions when the United Nations or high dignitaries thereof are to be honored. When so carried, the United Nations flag will be carried on the marching left of the United States flag and other United States colors or standards normally carried by such troops.

3. On occasions similar to those referred to in paragraph 2, above, U.S. Naval vessels will display the United Nations flag in the same manner as is prescribed for a foreign ensign during visits of a foreign President or Sovereign.

4. Except as indicated in paragraphs 1, 2, and 3, above, the United Nations flag will be displayed by United States Armed Forces only when so authorized by the President of the United States. NTP-13(B)

U.S. naval vessels authorized to display the United Nations flag display it in the same manner as that prescribed for a foreign ensign during visits of a foreign president or sovereign.

PERSONAL FLAGS AND PENNANTS

Afloat

Except as otherwise prescribed in Naval Regulations, a flag officer or a unit commander afloat displays a personal flag or command pennant from the flagship. It should never be displayed from more than one ship.

When a flag officer eligible for command at sea is embarked for passage in a naval ship, that ship displays his or her personal flag, unless the ship is already displaying the flag of an officer who is senior.

Flags or pennants of officers not eligible for command at sea are not displayed from ships of the U.S. Navy.

Broad and Burgee Command Pennants

Broad and burgee command pennants are the personal pennants of officers, not flag officers, commanding units of ships or aircraft. The broad command pennant indicates command of the following:

1. A division of aircraft carriers or cruisers.
2. A force, flotilla, or squadron of ships or craft of any type.
3. An aircraft wing.

The burgee command pennant indicates command of the following:

1. A division of ships or craft other than aircraft carriers or cruisers.
2. A major subdivision of an aircraft wing.

The broad and burgee command pennants are surcharged with numerals to indicate the organizational number within a ship type. When two commanders within a type are entitled to display the same command pennant and have the same organizational number in different echelons of command, the commander in the higher echelon uses Roman numerals in the surcharge. In all other cases, Arabic numerals are used. Blue numerals are used on board command pennants, red numerals on burgee command pennants.

Burgee command pennants are rarely seen.

Bow and Flagstaff Insignia for Boats

A boat regularly assigned to an officer for personal use must carry insignia on each bow as follows:

1. For a flag or general officer, the stars of rank, as arranged on his or her flag.
2. For a unit commander who is not a flag officer, a replica of his or her command pennant.
3. For a CO or a chief of staff not a flag officer, an arrow.

In a boat assigned to the personal use of a flag or general officer, unit commander, chief of staff, or CO, or in which a civil official is embarked, flagstaffs for the ensign and for a personal flag or pennant must be fitted at the peak with devices as follows:

- *Spread Eagle.* For an official entitled to a salute of nineteen or more guns.
- *Halberd.* For a flag or general officer whose official salute is less than nineteen guns; for a civil official entitled to a salute of eleven or more guns but less than nineteen guns.
- *Ball.* For an officer of the grade, or relative grade, of captain in the Navy; for a career minister, a counselor or first secretary of embassy or legation, or a consul.
- *Star.* For an officer of the grade, or relative grade, of commander in the Navy.
- *Flat Truck.* For an officer below the grade, or relative grade, of commander in the Navy; for a civil official not listed above, and for whom honors are prescribed for an official visit.

Personal Insignia at the Masthead

When the president's flag is displayed at a masthead where an ensign is required to be displayed during an official visit or during periods of dressing or full-dressing ship, it shall remain at that masthead to port of the U.S. ensign and to starboard of a foreign ensign.

Except as provided above, a personal flag or command pennant is not displayed at the same masthead with a national ensign. When both are to be displayed, the personal flag or command pennant should be displayed as follows:

1. During a gun salute, it should be lowered clear of the ensign.
2. During an official visit, it should be shifted to the starboard yardarm in a single-masted ship and to the fore truck in a two-masted ship.
3. During periods of dressing or full-dressing ship:
    a. If displayed from the fore truck or from the masthead of a single-masted ship, it should be shifted to the starboard yardarm.
    b. If displayed from the main truck, it should be shifted to the fore truck in lieu of the ensign at that mast.
    c. If displayed from the after truck of a ship with more than two masts, it should remain at the after truck in lieu of the ensign at that mast.

Flags or Pennants in Boats and on Automobiles

When embarked in a boat of the naval service on an official occasion, an officer in command, or an acting chief of staff, displays a personal flag or command pennant or, if not entitled to either, a commission pennant from the bow.

When embarked in a boat of the naval service on other than official occasions, an officer entitled to display a personal flag or command pennant may display a miniature of the flag or pennant in the vicinity of the coxswain's station.

When riding in an automobile on an official occasion, an officer entitled to display a personal flag or command pennant may display the flag or pennant forward on the vehicle.

All flag officers are authorized to show the stars of their rank on automobiles assigned to them. These stars may be displayed only on six-by-twelve-inch plates attached to or in the vicinity of the license plates. Stars or replicas of personal flags may not be painted on automobiles. Some of these customs have been altered to support antiterrorism/force protection measures.

Half-Masting

Personal flags, command pennants, and commission pennants should be half-masted for deceased officials or officers only as prescribed in Navy Regulations.

Civil Officials in Boats

When a U.S. civil official is embarked in a naval boat on an official occasion, a flag should be displayed in the bow as follows:

1. A union jack for a diplomatic representative of or above the rank of chargé d'affaires, within the waters of the country to which he or she is accredited; and a governor general or governor commissioned by the president, within the area of his or her jurisdiction.
2. A consular flag for a consular representative.
3. A personal flag for other civil officials when they are entitled to the display of a personal flag during an official visit.

Officials of the United Nations and the North Atlantic Treaty Organization

When an official of the United Nations or the North Atlantic Treaty Organization is embarked in a U.S. naval vessel, that person is not entitled to have a personal flag displayed unless he or she is a U.S. Navy flag officer eligible for command at sea.

MISCELLANEOUS FLAGS AND PENNANTS

Absence Indicators

The absence from his or her ship of a flag officer, unit commander, chief of staff, or CO is indicated from sunrise to sunset by the display of an absence indicator, as prescribed in table 16.1. Substitute pennants, as shown in the signal book, are used as follows:

First	Flag officer or unit commander
Second	Chief of staff
Third	Captain
Fourth	Other embarked

When a CO acting as a temporary unit commander is absent from the ship, both absence pennants should be displayed.

TABLE 16-1 Use of Substitute Pennants

SUB.	INDICATION	WHERE NORMALLY DISPLAYED	ABSENTEE
1st	Absence of an official from his or her ship for a period of 72 hours or less	Starboard main yardarm (outboard)	A flag officer or unit commander whose personal flag or command pennant is flying in this ship.
2nd	Same as 1st substitute	Port main yardarm (inboard)	A chief of staff
3rd	Same as 1st substitute	Port main yardarm (outboard)	A captain (executive officer if captain is absent for a period exceeding 72 hours)
4th	Same as 1st substitute	Starboard main yardarm (inboard)	A civil or military official whose flag is flying in this ship

Intention to Depart

The hoisting of the speed pennant where best seen (in port) indicates that the official or officer whose personal flag or command pennant is displayed will leave the ship officially in about five minutes. The hauling down of the speed pennant means that the official or officer is departing.

The following procedure is used when a flag officer shifts his or her flag:

1. Five minutes before departure, the flagship hoists the speed pennant at the main truck, below the personal flag.
2. As the officer departs, the flagship hauls down the speed pennant and hoists the appropriate absence pennant.
3. When the officer arrives in the new flagship, that ship breaks his or her flag at the main truck.
4. During the breaking of a personal flag in a new flagship, the former flagship hoists a commission pennant and hauls down the personal flag and the absentee pennant.

Church Pennant

Public law authorizes the use of the church pennant above the ensign "during church services conducted by naval chaplains at sea." The words "at sea" are interpreted for U.S. Navy purposes as meaning "on board a naval vessel." Shore stations are not authorized to display the church pennant above the ensign, but they may display it separately, if desired.

If divine services are being conducted at the time of morning colors, or if they begin at that time, the ensign is hoisted to the peak at the time prescribed for it. The church pennant is then hoisted and the ensign dipped just clear of it.

Should the time of evening colors occur while divine services are being conducted, the church pennant is hauled down and the ensign hoisted to the peak just before the time for colors; the ensign is then hauled down at the prescribed time.

Should the ensign be displayed at half-mast, the church pennant should be hoisted just above it.

Battle-Efficiency Pennant (Meatball)

The battle-efficiency pennant, known as the "meatball," is flown at the fore truck during the period provided in Awards for Intra-Type Competition when not under way.

When a guard flag, ready-duty flag, or Presidential Unit Citation pennant is displayed at the fore truck with the battle-efficiency pennant, the latter should be flown below the other flag.

Homeward-Bound Pennant

Specifications for the design of and rules for the use of the homeward-bound pennant have never been fully established. The usage set forth in NTP-13 is believed to conform with tradition.

POW/MIA Flag

When prescribed by the senior officer present, the POW/MIA flag shall be flown from 0800 until sunset. The point of display on board ships in port is the inboard halyard, port signal yardarm. The POW/MIA flag flies beneath the national ensign at shore activities. Additionally, shore activities may display the POW/MIA flag indoors to enhance commemoration ceremonies.

PUC, NUC, and MUC Pennants

Ships that have been awarded the Presidential Unit Citation, the Navy Unit Commendation, or the Meritorious Unit Commendation should fly the appropriate pennant, described in NTP-13, at the fore truck from sunrise to sunset when not under way.

Special Flag-Hoist Signals

Instructions from the senior officer present may prescribe certain flag hoists for local use, such as a request for the garbage or trash lighter or the water barge.

DRESSING AND FULL-DRESSING SHIP

Ships not under way are dressed or full-dressed from 0800 until sunset when prescribed or when directed. Ships under way are never dressed or full-dressed.

When full-dressing is prescribed, the senior officer present may order that dressing be substituted for it if, in his or her opinion, the weather makes it advisable. That officer may also, under such circumstances, direct that the ensigns be hauled down from the mastheads after being hoisted. See NTP-13 for details of dressing and full-dressing, including the specified sequence of signal flags and pennants to be hoisted.

BOAT HAILS

Night

All boats approaching a ship at night should be hailed as soon as they are within hearing (or radio) distance. The watch on board ship should call out, "Boat ahoy!," and the coxswain should indicate the rank or rate of the senior person in the boat by replying as follows:

Rank or Rate	Coxswain's Reply
President or vice president of the United States	"United States"
Secretary of defense, deputy or assistant secretary of defense	"Defense"
Secretary, undersecretary, or assistant secretary of the Navy	"Navy"

Chief of naval operations, vice chief of naval operations	"Naval operations"
Fleet or force commander	"Fleet," or abbreviation of administrative title
Rear or vice admiral, not in command	"Flag officer"
General officer	"General officer"
Chief of staff	"Staff"
Squadron commander	"___RON___" (the abbreviation or short title and number of the squadron is used, for example, DESRON 23)
Marine officer commanding a unit, for example, a battalion	"Battalion commander"
CO of a ship	Name of ship
Other commissioned officer	"Aye, aye"
Noncommissioned officer	"No, no"
Enlisted personnel	"Hello"
Boat not intending to come alongside, regardless of rank or rate of senior passenger	"Passing"

Day

During hours when honors are rendered, the OOD should challenge an approaching boat as soon as possible by raising an arm with a closed fist in the direction of the boat and training a long glass or binoculars on the coxswain. The coxswain should reply by holding up the number of fingers corresponding to the number, if any, of side boys standing by to honor the officer in his or her boat. A wave-off from the coxswain indicates that no side boys are required.

SIGNAL FLAGS

The following signals from the International Code of Signals (H0102) are of general interest to the OOD. They may be flown when preceded by the signal flag code as follows:

Code A   I have a diver down; keep well clear at slow speed.

Code B   I am taking in, discharging, or carrying dangerous goods
              (such as explosives or fuel).

Code H   I have a pilot on board.

Code P   All persons should report on board, as the vessel is about
              to get under way.

Code Q   My vessel is "healthy" and I request free pratique.

Other signal flags from ATP-1 should be committed to memory by qualified in-port OODs.

17

THE WATCH IN THE COMBAT INFORMATION CENTER

The Ops Room of a modern warship, with everyone at their computers and controls, is to any visiting stranger one of the weirdest places on earth.

ADMIRAL JOHN "SANDY" WOODWARD, COMMANDER OF THE ROYAL NAVY'S SOUTH
ATLANTIC TASK FORCE DURING THE 1982 FALKLAND ISLAND'S WAR

The CIC Watch Officer is a representative of the CIC Officer and supervises the operation of the CIC during the watch period.

OPNAVINST 3120.1D

Up until this point we have been primarily concerned with standing the watch either on the bridge or on the quarterdeck. In this chapter, we focus on some of the unique aspects of watchstanding in the CIC—also known as the command and decision center (CDC) on some ships or an operations center (OPS CTR) in the commonwealth navies.

The use of secure internet protocol routing of tactically relevant information has enabled near-real-time sharing of almost all tactical data. It has also proliferated multiple chat rooms (each focusing in specific warfare areas with theater-wide subscribers), e-mail exchanges (and the use of secure websites for the posting of guidance, reports, and collaborative planning), and reach-back capability (leveraging the expertise and analytical power of specialists ashore). This access to information can lead to watchstanders not focusing on fulfilling the truly important tasks of controlling the ship's sensors and weapons while maintaining safety of navigation and effective voice communications on and off the ship. Harnessing this vast amount of information, organizing the watch team to leverage it and drive it—*vice letting it overwhelm you*—is a major part of standing a successful watch in the CIC. It has given rise to a new term: *knowledge management*. Those standing watch in leadership positions in the CIC must be effective knowledge managers. To be successful, however, a full understanding of the fundamentals is necessary; everything builds from it.

PREPARING FOR WATCH IN THE CIC

You must be well rested prior to assuming the watch in the CIC, and you should also ensure you are well fed. The use of circadian watch bills for fatigue management, noted in chapter 5, have use for all watchstanders, not just those on the bridge. Many key mistakes are the result of hungry and tired watchstanders. Also, you should take the opportunity to pass through the ship's combat systems maintenance center on your way to taking the watch in the CIC. This will give you the best possible appreciation for the current state of the sensors and weapons systems in the ship. Additionally, you should stop through the ship's intelligence center and have a quick discussion with the ship's intelligence officer or enlisted intelligence specialist prior to assuming the watch. Finally, it is advisable to make a quick stop through the bridge. This gives you an invaluable sense of the environmental conditions facing the bridge team, such as the weather, sea state, and lighting. An additional sound practice is to brief and debrief together as a full watch team prior to and after your watch.

WATCH STATIONS IN THE CIC

The key watch station in the CIC is the combat information center watch officer (CICWO). This officer's job is to back up the bridge watch team in all aspects of navigational safety, maneuvering of the ship, communications, and sensor management. As the name of the watch implies, the CICWO is required to maintain an accurate flow of information from the ship's electronic sensors to the ship's bridge. In this chapter we focus on the work of the CICWO, although it is important to understand some of the other key watchstanders in the CIC.

The CICWO also supports the other watchstanders in combat, including the following:

- *Tactical Action Officer* (TAO). The ship's TAO is the senior watch-stander in the CIC and is the CO's direct representative in the employment of the ship's weapons system. He or she directs the action of all members of the CIC team and further guides the OOD in the overall employment of the ship. The TAO is in charge of the tactical employment and the defense of the ship. When a TAO is not assigned, the CICWO is overall responsible for all information, including navigation recommendations, from CIC during any condition of readiness.

- *Combat Systems Warfare Coordinators.* On many ships, various officers stand watch as warfare coordinators for air, surface, subsurface, and electronic warfare. They work directly for the TAO and interact with the CICWO in the overall operation of the ship. The surface warfare coordinator (SUWC), in addition to their warfare coordinator responsibilities, provides direct support to the OOD as the primary surface contact management and contact avoidance watchstander.

- *Communication Watch Officer.* The communication watch officer is in charge of the radio communications, normally assigned to the area in which the majority of radio receivers and switching equipment is located, that is, radio central. He or she will work closely with the CICWO on all matters related to communications effectiveness.

- *Combat Systems Officer of the Watch* (CSOOW). This individual may be located within the CIC or in a dedicated combat systems maintenance central. He or she is in charge of the overall operation of the ship's combat system, reporting normally to the TAO when that watch is being stood. The CICWO works closely with the CSOOW on all sensors and communications equipment in the CIC.

KEY RESPONSIBILITIES OF THE CICWO

Supervise Personnel

The first and most important responsibility of the CICWO is to supervise the personnel on watch in the CIC, working hard to make sure that all contacts—surface, subsurface, and air—are reported. Performing this important duty effectively means understanding exactly the jobs of all the watchstanders in the CIC.

The best way to gain this appreciation is to stand a series of watches with each of them during your own training period before you begin assuming the watch. Another effective means of gaining an appreciation of their job is to study the qualification books associated with each of the key watch positions in the CIC. Understanding each watchstander's basic console functions is central to understanding their roles. You should also understand the basics of the jobs undertaken by the other senior watch stations in the CIC, for example, the TAO and warfare coordinators. Remember also that supervising these highly trained watchstanders is a distinct leadership challenge—you are very much an example when you walk into the CIC and should be prepared to take charge and act with extreme professionalism from the moment you walk into the space.

Maintaining Situational Awareness

A second key challenge for the CICWO is maintaining accurate summary and geographic plots, status boards, and watch information. Such information is used by all personnel in the CIC to maintain situational awareness so it is imperative this information be correct and available. Housekeeping is also a function of the CICWO. A clean, well-organized, and neatly arranged watch space always outperforms a sloppy space with loose papers lying around. Make your watch team keep everything in organized, tabbed binders; file messages immediately in the appropriate binders. Keep the watch station notebooks updated. Check status boards once an hour and give them a "common sense" readability test. A good policy is that when you leave watch, the entire CIC should have improved in neatness and organization and have all reference information and operational guidance in place for the next watch. This sounds mundane, but it is important.

Communications

The third key function of the CICWO is ensuring that communications circuits are correctly set up and manned by well-trained operators and that correct procedures and terminology are used. This effort begins with understanding the communications plan, which is typically promulgated by naval message and outlines the frequency assignments and channels to be used for all primary and secondary communications circuits. You must be the expert in communications procedures. This can be reviewed quickly prior to each watch until it becomes second nature. A ship is judged by the quality of its communications—it is an obvious measure of effectiveness that will be commented upon by everyone in your strike group.

Evaluation

Evaluating the mass of information received is a fourth key function of the CICWO. You will receive a vast amount of data through the systems that are in place in your ship. These include voice, radio, radar, sonar, electronic-warfare support measures, visual lookouts, intelligence, messages, e-mails, chat, and secure websites—at times, the sheer volume of information can seem overwhelming. Your job is to bring order from the chaos. This is largely a matter of experience, but gradually you will be able to discern patterns and important pieces of the puzzle that can be extracted from the mass of information and fused together for dissemination to your shipmates. Start, obviously, by focusing on anything that relates directly to your ship. Direction will be contained within strike group or warfare commander guidance that establish procedures for distances in which you should focus around your ship; as a rule of thumb, anything within about two hundred nautical miles for air activity, one hundred miles for surface activity, and thirty miles for subsurface activity is germane. These distances will be tailored according to specific circumstances, sensor performance, and the region in which you're operating. Additionally, you should focus on information that relates to the significant mission your ship is executing at any given moment. As an example, if you are charged with undersea defense of the carrier, you should be paying particular attention to the prediction ranges for subsurface contacts generated by sonar control. You will quickly develop a sense of what information is critical, what is important, and what is "nice to know" at any given moment.

Dissemination

Once you have set up the watch properly, gathered the information, and evaluated it, your job is really just beginning. The fifth task before you as CICWO is to disseminate effectively and quickly the evaluated information to appropriate control stations throughout the ship. These include the bridge, flag plot (if a destroyer squadron commander, amphibious squadron commander, or flag officer is embarked), war room, strike operations center, air operations, air intelligence, and weapons-control stations. Dissemination can take a variety of forms, from a phone call to the OOD stationed on the bridge to forwarded e-mail to the battle watch captain. It may be verbal, electronic, or written. Your ship will have set procedures in place to accomplish this dissemination of information, but you should be creative and aggressive in sending information around the ship.

Recommendations

The sixth important function of the CICWO is to keep the OOD informed of the CIC's recommendations for maintaining station, avoiding navigational hazards and collisions, and safely maneuvering the ship. In most situations, this is your single most important duty. The CIC and bridge may be in two different locations, but the watches must work together as a single team that safely and effectively controls the ship. In addition to maintaining an accurate navigation plot in the CIC, a surface contact plot should also be continuously maintained. The bridge and CIC should frequently compare information on navigation and surface contacts. Throughout every watch you stand, you should keep the safety of the ship in the forefront of your mind. Things can get very confusing on the bridge, and your job is to back up the bridge watchstanders at all times. Be proactive in this regard. If there is a disconnection between your team in the CIC and the folks on the bridge, it is up to you to go to the bridge and resolve it. If you ever feel the ship is standing into danger and your recommendations are not being followed, immediately contact the CO, XO, or senior watch officer to help resolve the dispute. Every time the ship maneuvers—whether for changing station, adjusting the position of intended movement (PIM), or any other purpose—you should provide the bridge a coherent recommendation by the fastest clear means. This may be the 21MC, a phone talker, a telephone call from you to the OOD, or any other means appropriate to the configuration of your ship. The key is that you as CICWO and the OOD on the bridge have minute-to-minute access to each other to compare your solutions and achieve concurrence before maneuvering the ship.

Control Sensors

A seventh mission of the CICWO is to control the use of radar, sonar, electronic-warfare support measures, and voice circuits. This is, of course, done through the watchstanders working those particular stations. You cannot simultaneously supervise all of them, but it is a good practice to spend a moment or two with each operator at least once an hour. This gives you the chance to judge their general proficiency, state of alertness, tactical knowledge, and situational awareness. It will also give you a chance to impart some of the "big picture" to them. Try not to focus on a single piece of the puzzle; your job is to cycle from station to station and maintain overall control of the ship's systems.

Operational Administration

There is an eighth requirement for the CICWO: keeping up with what might be termed the "paperwork" of the watch. This means you need to be familiar with the operational plans, orders, tactical publications, directives, and regulations of higher authority that affect the watch or the operation of the CIC. You must also ensure the highest standards are followed in the preparation of the watch logs. This may require substantive off-watch study as well as participation in special evolution briefings.

Operational Tasks

Finally, the CICWO must also be prepared to execute a series of operational tasks, including initiating SAR procedures, assuming duties as a warfare commander if so directed, controlling the combat direction system if no TAO is posted, reporting all landfalls, maintaining a competent navigation track and position record of the ship's movements, and supervising the work of the ship's lookouts. These are all important duties and should receive your attention in the course of the watch.

This is a long list of duties, and the new CICWO may justifiably ask, "Where do I put my emphasis?" The answer to this question is fairly straightforward. Your task is to support the OOD in the safe maneuvering of the ship. If you take as your charter the role of backup to the OOD, you will succeed as the CICWO. Everything falls out from this vital duty. Pay close attention to it, and you will do just fine.

SUPPORTING THE EMBARKED STAFF

As a watch officer in the CIC, you may be very involved in supporting an embarked staff. On a destroyer or cruiser, this may be a destroyer squadron commander, while an amphibious ship may embark an amphibious squadron commander. Larger ships, such as carriers, may embark a flag officer with a rather large staff.

In each case, the duties of the CICWO are usually laid out in an instruction published by the senior officer of the embarked staff. He or she will spell out the necessary support from the flagship. Normally this will consist of several consoles in the CIC, a chart or plot table, a large screen display, one or two status boards, and a few watchstanders to augment the staff. In the case of a larger staff on a carrier or large amphibious ship, there will normally be a dedicated space to support the embarked commander. You will also be required to keep the embarked staff informed of the ship's activity as well as assist in maintaining the situational awareness of the staff as they execute their larger, force-wide responsibilities.

You should endeavor to make the time the embarked staff spends on your ship a very pleasant and tactically successful experience for them. By helping them succeed, your ship will succeed in its mission. As you stand your watches, take the time to stop by the embarked staff module prior to assuming the watch. Try to consider tactical events from the perspective of the embarked staff. For example, if you are steaming in formation with a group of ships, the embarked staff will be interested in an accurate plot of all ships in the force. You should support their requirements with the flagship's sensors and ensure that they can keep track of their entire force. Check in with them every hour or so and inquire as to their general sense of how everything is going and satisfaction with their support from your ship.

A FEW PRINCIPLES FOR CIC WATCH OFFICERS

Here are ten good watchstander rules for CICWOs:

1. *Be in charge.* If you are getting overwhelmed, call for help early. You will know if events are overtaking your ability to sort them out and

provide quality support to the OOD. The first call to make is to the senior watch officer. He or she will be able to provide some additional support to your watch team as required.

2. *Never lose your temper.* It clouds your judgment and increases chaos. Your fundamental job is to bring order out of chaos, not to add more chaos with loud or angry comments or questions. There will be many frustrating moments in the course of some watches you stand in a CIC, and there will be many factors over which you have no control. But you always have the opportunity to keep control of yourself. Remember that your watch team will look at you for their cue when things get hectic. Your reactions will count a great deal. Stay calm and cool on the outside, no matter how high the frustration gets on the inside.

3. *Constantly seek to match problem to resource to plan.* You will face many problems, and your first instinct should be to think, "What resources can I bring to bear to solve this problem?" Next you should consider a plan that will permit you to use the resources to solve the problem. Here is one possible scenario: There is a patrol boat operating somewhere to the east of your ship. You know this because of electronic intercepts from your ship's SLQ-32. Your problem is to refine the location of this potential threat to your ship. Immediately consider where you can obtain resources to work the problem. You need aircraft, which can move rapidly and triangulate the electronic signal. Work to get control of a helicopter from your own ship, a land-based aircraft such as a P-8, or an aircraft from the carrier's air wing if you are operating with a CVN. Before you have control of an aircraft, you need a plan. Fly the aircraft off-axis a sufficient distance from the ship to establish triangulation with the electronic line of bearing from the ship. Your cross-fix should establish the position of the patrol boat. Think "problem to resource to plan" and you will usually resolve whatever issue you face.

4. *Adjust warning condition and weapons posture as required.* It is very easy to forget about making changes to warning conditions and weapons posture. As the CICWO, you must remain attuned to changes to these

extremely important aspects of your ship's operations. While you will not be in a position to direct warning condition and weapons posture without approval from the CO, you should remain informed of the tactical situation and ready to make appropriate recommendations, especially in the absence of a posted TAO.

5. *Keep your status boards updated.* This seems so simple yet is often over-looked or forgotten in the bustle of standing watch in a CIC. Your watch team will need to ensure information of general use is posted and available. Keeping the boards updated will also force your team to stay on top of the entire tactical picture.

6. *Keep your watch station notebooks updated.* Each watch station should have a three-ring binder or notebooks in which general tactical updates and messages can be filed, pass-down information can be posted, and standing direction from the CO can be kept. As CICWO you should take a look at each watch station notebook at least once during each watch.

7. *Minimize communications over the circuits.* The key is ensuring you don't pass superfluous information. Never use a "double call-up," wherein you call another unit and await confirmation from them before passing information. You should simply call up the unit and immediately pass your traffic. Always have a good sense of what you will say whenever you pick up a radio handset, and never transmit in haste.

8. *Be confident, polite, professional, and "can do" on the circuits.* Your tone will translate directly and quickly into your ship's reputation. Be upbeat and try to solve problems for other units, not add to the general confusion of a situation. If you are frustrated or angry, don't pick up a handset. Carefully monitor your more junior watchstanders as well, trying to encourage them to be assertive but pleasant when discussing issues with their opposite numbers on other ships.

9. *Always have a plan, especially when using airplanes.* Don't simply turn fuel into noise without purpose. Ensure your watch personnel brief pilots clearly and with energy. Take their debriefs with enthusiasm and interest. One of the key things you must do in a CIC is to provide pilots with the information they need to have a tactically successful flight.

They will stop through on their way to preflight the aircraft and get the information you provide. Likewise, they will stop through the CIC after the flight and conduct a debrief with you or the antisubmarine tactical air controller (ASTAC) if appropriate. If you come across as too busy to take their debrief or provide inadequate information to them before their flight, they will quickly lose interest in coming back.

10. *Remember to study the rules of engagement.* It is critically important to fully understand all the issues related to rules of engagement, especially how and when the rules of engagement may be modified. In the real world, when ordnance is released, everything changes forever. Remember that.

PUBLICATIONS

As the CICWO, you are essentially the "keeper of the library" for the ship during tactical operations. The bridge watch team is focused on looking out of the bridge windows and will count on you and your watchstanders to constantly review the publications to ensure the ship is in tactical and operational compliance with the rules.

Be sure to familiarize yourself with the ship's tactical library before you find yourself in the middle of a busy watch. You should have a working knowledge of the most frequently used publications as well as a general sense of where to find key information. At the end of this book you will find a fairly complete list of current publications with which a competent CICWO should be familiar. The key types of publications and some of the best-known individual titles are annotated below.

Fleet Exercise Publications

Fleet exercise publications (FXPs) contain the general guidance for conducted exercises. They list the "how-to" aspect of putting together the day-to-day evolutions for watchstanders. Some of the key FXPs with which you should be very familiar are FXP-1, Antisubmarine Warfare Exercises; FXP-2, Antiair Warfare Exercises; and FXP-3, which includes guidance on strike warfare, anti-surface-ship warfare, intelligence, and electronic warfare.

Allied Tactical Publications

NATO uses allied tactical publications (ATPs) for the conduct of exercises involving all the allied nations ascribing to that treaty. They are also used as the basis for exercises with other nations allied to the United States but not in NATO, for example, Australia, Japan, and South Korea. Some of the particularly important or frequently used allied publications include: ATP-1, volumes 1 and 2, Allied Maritime Tactical Instructions and Procedures and the accompanying Signal and Maneuvering Book; ATP-3 and 3(B), Antisubmarine Evasive Steering; AXP-1, Allied Submarine and Antisubmarine Exercise Manual; and ATP-8, Doctrine for Amphibious Operations.

Naval Doctrine Publications

Naval doctrine publications (NDPs) are important publications that talk about the role of the Navy and Marine Corps in joint operations. These publications are growing in number and importance. Some of the key ones that the CICWO should peruse include NDP-1, Naval Warfare; NDP-5, Naval Planning; and NDP-6, Naval Command and Control.

Joint Doctrine Publications

The fastest-growing area of publications in the U.S. military is joint doctrine publications, which constitutes the merging of doctrine that binds the services together. Joint doctrine is emerging every year and is accessible on the World Wide Web at both the unclassified and classified levels. Your ship's operations officer will know how to access these important publications. They are divided into several groups, including personnel and administration, intelligence operations, logistics, plans, and C4 systems. As CICWO, you should have at least a basic familiarity with the operational joint doctrine publications (the 3.0 series) that bear on maritime affairs.

Naval Warfare Publications

Long the backbone of the tactical library, the naval warfare publications (NWPs) are—in effect—written Navy doctrine for the day-to-day conduct of operations at sea. Some of the key ones you should be familiar with as the CICWO include NWP 1-03, Joint Reporting System and the associated series of reporting system publications; NWP 1-10.1, the Tactical Action Officer Handbook; NWP 1-14, Commander's Handbook on the Law of Naval Operations; NWP 3-01, the series on antiair warfare; NWP 3-20, the series on surface ship operations, with a close look at the tactical manual for your specific ship class; and NWP 3-21, the antisubmarine series. You might also find a need for a couple of others for reference, including NWP 3-50 on search and rescue; NWP 3-56 on tactical communications; and NWP 4-01.4 on underway replenishment. Finally, the NWP 3-2 series on aircraft tactical manuals will also provide valuable reference when working with specific aircraft.

MINE WARFARE AND MINE AVOIDANCE

One area of watchstanding that may involve the watch officer both on the bridge and in the CIC is the potentially critical activity of avoiding mines. In the course of qualifying both as an OOD and as a CICWO, you will be involved in the study of how to avoid mines.

It is important to realize that many nations have the ability to lay mines. Several U.S. ships have struck mines over the past decades, including the USS SAMUEL B. ROBERTS (FFG 58), the USS TRIPOLI (LPH 10), and the USS PRINCETON (CG 59)—as well as the tanker BRIDGETON while she was under U.S. escort. All of these mine strikes occurred in the Arabian Gulf.

Mines constitute a psychological deterrent. They are inexpensive and easy to deliver, and they are very time-consuming to remove. They are, in effect, a very valuable force multiplier for poor countries. Worldwide, since 1982, thirty-eight ships of various nations have been sunk or damaged by mines.

While a thorough discussion of types and placement of mines is outside the scope of this work, you should take the time to occasionally review applicable references. Review the various types of mines: bottom, moored, drifting, propelled warhead, and very shallow water.

In terms of mine avoidance, as a watch officer—either on the bridge or in the CIC—you should be aware of the basic material and tactical measures involved in finding and avoiding mines. Some of the key elements of mine avoidance include degaussing, acoustic measures, cathodic protection, sonar (particularly the increasingly available Kingfisher), visual aids, readiness conditions, and plant operations.

Most ships have a standard checklist that should be executed when nearing or entering a suspected minefield. If your ship does not have one, the basic steps include the following:

- Transit during daylight hours where visual detection is possible.
- Energize degaussing, which will protect against magnetic mines.
- Set and maintain watertight integrity (that is, set material condition Zebra).
- Impose silent routine and quiet ship conditions.
- Maintain constant engine rpm.
- Keep speed slow (six knots or below).
- Pass mined area at high tide and deepest point.
- Be ready to maneuver or anchor.
- Post mine lookouts.
- Alter course if necessary.
- Minimize below-deck personnel.
- All hands use head protection and life jackets.
- Use helicopter flying down the intended track to sweep visually.

If you encounter a mine ahead, attempt to pass no closer than three hundred yards and submit an immediate report of the mine's location, maintaining visual contact if possible while marking and plotting the location. You may want to consider exiting a minefield by backing out along the course you made good entering. As a last resort, consider small arms fire, but the preferred method is to contact a higher authority to obtain explosive ordnance disposal assistance. These professionals can be flown to your ship, parachute into the surrounding water, and destroy the mine.

Appendix A

STANDING ORDERS GUIDANCE AND SAMPLE STANDING ORDERS

Each ship's commanding officer produces a unique set of standing orders in accordance with guidance set forth by COMNAVSURFPAC/COMNAVSURF-LANTINST 3120.3, Principles of the Commanding Officer's Standing Orders. Below are those principles and examples of how a ship may implement that guidance (refer to the original reference, above, for a complete description of all engineering-specific guidance). You should review your own ship's standing orders when you arrive and at least monthly thereafter.

GENERAL GUIDELINES AND CONSIDERATIONS

1. Considerations for Commanding Officer's Standing Orders
   a. Warfare publications, operating sequencing systems, and other instructions contain information specific to the operation and employment of ship systems for the accomplishment of assigned missions. However, this doctrine generally does not specifically address the day-to-day management of the ship's routines that form the foundation of safe shipboard operations. The standing orders should provide a compendium of processes and procedures to be followed by the crew on a day-to-day basis.
   b. Ultimately, the standing orders are the responsibility of the Commanding Officer.
   c. Standing orders are effective only if read and understood by the crew. Therefore, as a general rule, shorter standing orders are preferred. Additionally, concise directives should be favored over long,

flowing text. Commanding Officers would be well advised to remember that the target audience for their standing orders is typically petty officers and junior officers, not senior staff.

d. Standing orders must be current and relevant. Standing orders written to support equipment no longer aboard the ship or for missions that no longer apply will quickly cause the crew to assume the Commanding Officer has lost interest in their standing orders. Commanding Officers should establish a process such that the standing orders are regularly reviewed and updated, if necessary. Commanding Officers should take measures to ensure the standing orders do not duplicate or conflict with other ship's instructions, unless specifically desired and carefully considered as a point of emphasis.

e. Standing orders are an appropriate place to promulgate tripwires and expected action. For tripwires to be effective, watch teams must understand the parameter(s) that triggers the tripwire, must have a means by which the parameter(s) can be monitored, and must understand the context and intent of standing order tripwire procedures. Typical errors that reduce the value of tripwire schemes are:

i. Too many tripwires—watch teams simply can't remember and/or monitor desired parameters.

ii. Poorly defined tripwires—watch teams don't understand the Commanding Officer's intent and fail to identify the tripwire.

iii. Watch team-defined tripwires—watch teams pick tripwires on a selective basis, without the advantage of the Commanding Officers' experience and knowledge.

2. Considerations for the Modification of Standing Orders

a. Following modernization of equipment, the Commanding Officer shall address new capabilities, limitations, and processes, and modify Standing Orders as appropriate.

b. User interface preference plays a real role in team performance. Watchstanders have a wide array of information, both processed (e.g., Combat Systems Fire Control Data) and raw (e.g., commercial radar returns). Additionally, most COTS systems offer multiple display options. While system doctrine can provide an explanation of display content and recommendations as to when such displays may be preferred, ultimately, the Commanding Officer shall provide guidance for the employment of those systems.

c. Effective standing orders must be sufficiently specific to be actionable. Increased specificity also demands a higher degree of responsiveness to changes in prevailing conditions. Individual Commanding Officers are best suited to ensure that standing orders are appropriate to the prevailing circumstances and responsive to changing operations, equipment, personnel, etc.

3. Considerations for Additional Topics to Include in Standing Orders

a. Default lineups for systems and communications layout (e.g., standardized communication speaker layout in the pilothouse). Commanding Officers may also wish to specify default tactical decision aid displays (e.g., north up versus heading up displays on navigation radar repeaters).

b. Safety and/or maintenance requirements not otherwise specified but desired by the Commanding Officer.

c. Duties, responsibilities, and expectations of watches not otherwise specified.

d. Items not otherwise specified for which the Commanding Officer's permission is required.

e. Items not otherwise specified for which the Commanding Officer desires a report.

STANDING ORDER NUMBER 1
Responsibilities

1. *Commanding Officers Shall Address:*
   a. Commanding Officer (CO) Responsibility Statement
   b. Executive Officer (XO) Responsibility Statement
   c. Tactical Action Officer (TAO) Responsibility Statement
   d. Officer of the Deck (OOD) Underway Responsibility Statement
   e. Conning Officer (CONN) Responsibility Statement

    f.   Engineering Officer of the Watch (EOOW) Responsibility Statement

    g.   Navigation Officer Responsibility Statement

    h.   Senior Watch Officer (SWO) Responsibility Statement

    i.   Watch position relationships; at a minimum, the relationship between the TAO and the OOD and between the OOD and the EOOW.

    j.   Actions to take if watchstanders are unable to resolve a disagreement or clarify a discrepancy. At a minimum, include how disagreement between the TAO and OOD should be resolved.

    k.   That the presence of the CO or XO at or in the vicinity of a watch station does not relieve any watchstander of his/her responsibility for the proper conduct of that watch unless properly relieved. Watchstanders adhering to the principle of forceful backup make recommendations for the safe operation of the ship regardless of the presence of the CO.

2. *Commanding Officers Should Address:*

    a.   Verbiage of 1MC announcements requesting the Captain's presence in a controlling station and notification of routine reports.

    b.   XO's responsibilities in the CO's absence.

    c.   Department Head (DH) Responsibility Statement(s).

3. *Commanding Officers May Address:*

    a.   OOD underway weapons release authority.

    b.   Which individuals or watch stations have the authority to relieve a watch station. For example, the Navigator has the authority to relieve the OOD (written authority per reference (b)).

    c.   Emphasis on requesting relief from the SWO if any watchstander feels they are unable to stand a proper watch; e.g., too fatigued, illness, or physically/mentally unable.

STANDING ORDER NUMBER 2
The Watch

1. *Commanding Officers Shall Address:*

    a.   How the sound shipboard operating principles will be incorporated into the execution of the watch.

      (1) Formality

      (2) Procedural Compliance

      (3) Level of Knowledge

      (4) Questioning Attitude

      (5) Forceful Backup

      (6) Integrity

  b. The setup of the watch rotation and shipboard routine prioritizing circadian rhythms when feasible.

  c. How turnovers will be staggered when feasible.

  d. TAO, OOD, and EOOW turnover instructions, including what spaces need to be toured and what information the oncoming TAO/OOD/EOOW must review prior to relieving.

  e. The importance of adhering to the Navigation Rules (commonly referred to as the "Rules of the Road"). Particular emphasis shall be placed on requirements for maintaining a proper lookout as well as the requirement to use all available means appropriate to the prevailing circumstances and conditions (i.e., using alidades or bearing circles to check bearing drift, visual lookouts, and surface-search radars).

2. *Commanding Officers Should Address:*

  a. Implementing the Plan, Brief, Execute, Debrief (PBED) process in day-to-day watchstanding and special evolutions.

  b. Emphasizing the importance of appropriate rest prior to turnover.

  c. Ensuring a complete exchange of information with the previous watch and include specifics.

  d. Addressing reasons to decline relieving the watch and to whom to report; for example, SWO, XO, CO. List example reasons.

  e. Establishing standards for watchstanding on the bridge addressing topics such as the importance of a dark bridge at night, running a taut watch, alertness, presence of food and/or drinks, using the 1MC, striking of bells, etc.

  f. Actions for watchstanders during marine mammal encounters.

3. *Commanding Officers May Address:*
   a. Stating when turnovers require CO's permission and how turnovers are announced. Some may be in the space verbally such as the CONN; some may be over the command net such as the TAO.
   b. Establishing a requirement to conduct a formalized watch turnover brief with specified watch stations.

STANDING ORDER NUMBER 3
Conning and Maneuvering

1. *Commanding Officers Shall Address:*
   a. Adherence to and knowledge of actions or conditions that prevent compliance.
   b. Requirements for when maneuvering board solutions are to be calculated by both Bridge and Combat Information Center (CIC) watch teams for surface contacts meeting defined Closest Point of Approach (CPA) criteria.
   c. Standard Commands to the Helm/Lee Helm. Watch officers should know the guiding principles and examples for the development of standard commands. Class-specific standard commands developed at a different echelon of command (i.e., squadron or group) may be incorporated to meet this requirement so long as the class-specific standard commands meet all the requirements in this instruction.
   d. Handling and propulsion characteristics specific to the ship.
   e. Process for the commanding officer to relieve the CONN.
   f. High traffic density situations that prompt the OOD to station additional watchstander(s) in the pilothouse or CIC. The bridge will inform the commanding officer when this additional measure is taken.
2. *Commanding Officers Should Address:*
   a. Providing example handling/propulsion characteristics which may include:
      (1) Turn diameter distances for various rudder angles and speeds.
      (2) Applicable order/speed/RPM/pitch combinations depending on ship class.

(3) Locked shaft and Trail shaft limitations depending on ship class.

(4) Surge rate for deceleration.

b. Relationship with harbor pilots and the use of tugs.

c. Preparing to steer toward "safe water" at any moment, and understanding a break-out plan if in formation.

d. Baseline standoff distances and action in the event they will not be maintained such as the "3-2-1 rule" for maneuvering in the vicinity of a CVN or large deck amphibious ship and minimum standoffs for surfaced submarines.

3. *Commanding Officers May Address:*

a. Procedures or requirements for specified maneuvering considerations, for example visually checking turns, using a formation diagram on a maneuvering board (i.e., in SCREEN KILO formations), and altering course from PIM for contacts.

b. Quick math such as the 1/3/6 minute rules and the radian rule.

c. Providing direction commonly derived from other references such as "Naval Shiphandling," "Knight's Modern Seamanship," "Naval Shiphandler's Guide," etc.

STANDING ORDER NUMBER 4
Required Reports

1. *Commanding Officers Shall Address:*

a. Contact Report format and criteria that require the report. Criteria for the contact report should include the CPA distance that mandates the report, a minimum distance between ownship and the contact, or minimum time to CPA to make the report allowing adequate time for the Commanding Officer to evaluate the situation.

b. Other reports, to promote organization and facilitate watchstander training; e.g., general, navigation, formations, engineering, special evolutions, occurrences.

c. Including a statement about quickly developing situations or late detections of contacts, sometimes referred to as "pop-up" contacts, with the priority to take action and notify the CO as soon as possible with available information.

d. When in doubt notify the Commanding Officer.

2. *Commanding Officers Should Address:*
   a. Format of the report, ensuring it suits the CO without becoming too cumbersome, complicated, or time-consuming to complete. Example elements include:
      (1) Who is making the report
      (2) Time
      (3) Ownship course and speed
      (4) Type of contact (Clarify if this means type per ROR or type of vessel; i.e., fishing boat or vessel engaged in fishing)
      (5) Source of contact information (Hold visual/by RADAR/on AIS)
      (6) Relative position of contact (By numerical relative bearing or port/stbd bow/beam/quarter)
      (7) Range to contact
      (8) Course and speed of contact
      (9) Target angle of contact
      (10) Direction and rate of bearing drift
      (11) CPA range, bearing, time, and source or method of calculation
      (12) Type of situation or evaluation of hierarchy
      (13) Evaluation of risk of collision per USCG Navigation Rules rule 7
      (14) Intentions
      (15) Concurrence with CIC

3. *Commanding Officers May Address:*
   a. The following general reports:
      (1) Any information deemed significant for the CO to know, but not specifically mandated for report.
      (2) 12 O'Clock reports (1200 position, magazine temperatures, fuel and water, draft, boat, muster, etc.).
   b. Navigation reports:
      (1) When passing within (specify range) of shoal water.
      (2) Discrepancies between charted depths and fathometer readings.
      (3) Notification guidelines when off PIM/track by a specified range (ahead/behind/laterally) or time (ahead/behind).
      (4) Casualties, alignment errors, or maintenance discrepancies to navigation equipment (specify equipment).

      (5) Weather changes (wind speed, sea state, visibility, barometric pressure, dew point spread, temperature, etc.) with specific criteria.

  c. Engineering reports:

      (1) Equipment casualty that impacts ship maneuverability or safety of navigation.

  d. Other reports:

      (1) Reason for delays to commencement of an evolution.

      (2) Granting/requesting permission to proceed on duties assigned.

      (3) Detection of other military units (air, surface, or subsurface, regardless of nationality).

      (4) Whenever a watchstander declines to relieve the watch.

      (5) Conflicting interpretation of tactical signals, maneuvers, or situations that are not promptly clarified.

      (6) Injuries.

      (7) Loss of communications.

      (8) When queried, warned, or reprimanded on any communication circuit.

      (9) Formation reporting guidance to include changes in ordered formation composition, inability to maintain station, and the breakdown of units in company.

      (10) Marine mammal sighting.

      (11) Request for assistance from distressed mariners.

  e. Designate when reports shall be made to individuals in addition to the CO. For example, make all Navigation reports to the XO and Navigator, or make all contact reports to embarked Commanders in addition to the CO.

STANDING ORDER NUMBER 5
Commanding Officer Approval Items

1. *Commanding Officers Shall Address:*

  a. Deviating from Standing Orders, Night Orders, or orders from Commanders exercising OPCON/TACON of ownship or any approved procedure such as those contained in EOSS, CSOSS, PMS, Fleet Guidance, etc.

2. *Commanding Officers Should Address:*

   a. General

      (1) Discharging waste over the side.

      (2) Conducting casualty control drills.

      (3) Setting and securing the Restricted Maneuvering Doctrine (RMD).

      (4) Turnover of specified watch stations when the CO is present.

      (5) Securing from General Quarters.

   b. Engineering

      (1) When setting single valve protection to the sea, or any high energy or immediately dangerous to life or health (IDLH) system.

      (2) Main engine / prime mover startup (specify exceptions; for example, permission not required when inherent in another order such as setting maximum engineering reliability).

      (3) Tagging out specified equipment.

      (4) Rolling or stopping shafts.

      (5) Opening reduction gears.

      (6) Aligning installed drainage.

      (7) Transferring flammable liquids.

   c. Weapons/Combat Systems

      (1) Handling/transferring ammunition.

      (2) Testing magazine sprinklers.

      (3) Firing any weapon (reference exceptions granted for self-defense).

   d. Safety

      (1) Entry into IDLH spaces such as tanks, voids, spaces contaminated by toxic gas, etc.

      (2) Working on energized equipment (specify conditions).

      (3) Bypassing equipment interlocks or safety devices.

      (4) Personnel going topside after dark when underway.

      (5) Personnel going aloft or over the side while underway.

      (6) Exceeding heat stress risk stay times.

e. Navigation

(1) Securing navigation equipment (specify equipment; e.g., fathometer, VMS, NAVSSI, GPS, INS, navigation RADAR, fluxgate compass, etc.).

(2) Prior to closing within specified distance of land/shoal or prior to crossing a specified depth curve.

f. Special Evolutions

(1) Launching/recovering small boat.

(2) UNREP permissions such as commencing the approach, tensioning/de-tensioning CONREP rigs, prior to receiving fuel or pumping to a receiving ship, etc.

(3) Permissions associated with anchoring such as removing stoppers and letting go during anchoring.

(4) Permissions associated with flight operations such as granting green deck, moving aircraft elevators, unfolding rotors, lowering nets, etc.

(5) Permissions associated with well deck operations such as granting green well, vehicle movements, ballasting or deballasting, etc.

(6) Permissions associated with mission bay operations such as opening or closing doors, crane and lift operations, vehicle movements, etc.

(7) Permissions associated with streaming towed bodies.

STANDING ORDER NUMBER 6

Navigation

1. *Commanding Officers Shall Address:*

a. Notification requirements and actions any time the watch team experiences a conflict between expected navigation plan information and actual observations; e.g., fathometer readings do not correlate to charted depths, unexpected presence of navaid, or absence of expected navaid, track appears erroneously close to hazard, etc.

b. AIS transmission requirements per Fleet Commander guidance.

c. Fix interval guidance as directed by Navy navigation regulations.

2. *Commanding Officers Should Address:*
   a. Quantifying a high-density traffic area, taking into account ship and mission parameters, training and proficiency, and area of operations.
   b. Equipment-specific guidance. For example:
      (1) Fathometer settings and corrected fathometer soundings to account for hull projections such as rudders or a sonar dome.
      (2) VMS: including review of advisories and settings (e.g., Ownship Safety Zone configuration, fix source precedence, etc.).
      (3) Use of the Emergency Navigation Laptop (ENL).
      (4) Navigation radar setup.

STANDING ORDER NUMBER 7
Restricted Visibility

1. *Commanding Officers Shall Address:* When to implement the provisions of the ship's tailored Low Visibility Bill per reference (c) within XX NM (specify range).
2. *Commanding Officers Should Address:*
   a. Considerations for transmitting position via AIS.
   b. Varying the timing of fog signals randomly (within 2 min intervals) to avoid sounding simultaneously with another ship, especially when closing a contact held on radar.

STANDING ORDER NUMBER 8
Man Overboard

1. *Commanding Officers Shall Address:*
   a. The preferred method of recovery in daytime/nighttime and whether the man overboard is in sight or not.
   b. Initial plotting responsibilities.
   c. Off-ship reporting requirements (to include but not limited to: BTB emergency calls, sound signals, and operational reporting).
   d. Guidance for special circumstances (to include but not limited to: towed body operations, wet well operations, flight operations—as applicable based on ship class).

2. *Commanding Officers Should Address:*

    a. Securing use of fathometer or active sonar (mission dependent).

    b. Guidance on the use of smoke floats and life rings.

STANDING ORDER NUMBER 9
Anchoring

1. *Commanding Officers Shall Address:*

    a. Plotting and fix intervals per Navy navigation regulations.

    b. Required actions when actually dragging anchor or suspecting the ship is dragging anchor.

    c. Use of ship's nomograph for determining the minimum length of chain and the horizontal distance from the ship to the anchor for flat and sloped bottoms.

2. *Commanding Officers Should Address:*

    a. Additional actions in observed or anticipated inclement weather.

    b. Specified equipment configuration.

    c. Required reports while at anchor.

STANDING ORDER NUMBER 10
Restricted Maneuvering Doctrine

1. *Commanding Officers Shall Address:*

    a. Authorities for setting, maintaining, and securing from RMD.

    b. Conditions when RMD is required.

    c. Specific engineering plant deviations from normal operation procedures based on ship technical characteristics and references.

    d. Equipment configuration for RMD, tailored to meet their ship-specific needs.

STANDING ORDER NUMBER 11
Engineering/Maximum Plant Reliability

1. *Commanding Officers Shall Address:* Plant configuration for maximum engineering reliability and the conditions under which it should be set.

STANDING ORDER NUMBER 12
Steering Control
1. *Commanding Officers Shall Address:*
   a. Conditions when a Master Helmsman and Lee Helmsman are required.
   b. Conditions when after steering must be manned, and guidance for when the space is unmanned, regarding which watchstanders shall respond and their condition of readiness.
2. *Commanding Officers Should Address:*
   a. Equipment configurations based on specific operations.
   b. Standard commands for transferring control between the pilothouse and after steering.

STANDING ORDER NUMBER 13
Small Boat Operation
1. *Commanding Officers Shall Address:* Special shiphandling considerations for launching and recovering boats (e.g., creating a lee).
2. *Commanding Officers Should Address:*
   a. Minimum manning for small boats while maintaining requirements listed in references (b), (o), and (p).
   b. Requirements for the Boat Officer to receive a brief from the bridge team prior to launch that covers ensuing operations.
   c. Sequencing and associated permissions for launching and recovering small boats.

STANDING ORDER NUMBER 14
Flight Deck Operations
1. *Commanding Officers Shall Address:*
   a. Shiphandling restrictions based off of approved wind envelopes, polar plots, or other technical guidance based on ship class and aircraft specifications.
   b. Equipment configurations for both day/night and aided/unaided flight operations.

  c. Sequencing and associated permissions for launching and recovering aircraft.

2. *Commanding Officers Should Address:*

  a. Emergency situations and reporting responsibilities.

  b. Conflicts between the OOD and the aircraft commander.

STANDING ORDER NUMBER 15
Well Deck/Mission Bay Operations

1. *Commanding Officers Shall Address:* Delegated authorities and authorizations related to the conduct of well deck/mission bay operations.

2. *Commanding Officers Should Address:*

  a. Emergency considerations where safety of ship may preclude safety concerns of personnel and equipment in well deck or mission bay.

  b. Additional considerations based on the mission package capability and projected operating environment.

STANDING ORDER NUMBER 16
Towed Gear Operations

1. *Commanding Officers Shall Address:*

  a. Restrictions to maneuvering capability when deploying/retrieving or operating towed body (i.e., NIXIE or passive towed array sonar) per appropriate reference documentation.

  b. Emergency considerations for both ship control and towed gear recovery teams.

2. *Commanding Officers May Address:* Additional reporting and coordination instructions between the Bridge, Combat Information Center, and Sonar Control.

RESTRICTED MANEUVERING DOCTRINE GUIDANCE

Ref: (a) Engineering Operational Sequencing System (EOSS)

   (b) COMNAVSURFPAC/COMNAVSURFLANTINST 3540.3 (EDORM)

   (c) OpNavInst 3120.32 (SORM)

(d) COMNAVSURFORINST 3500.5 (Watchstander's Guide)

(e) COMNAVSURFPAC/COMNAVSURFLANTINST 3504.1C (Redlines)

1. *Purpose.* The Restricted Maneuvering Doctrine (RMD) is a risk management tool that places a premium on ship maneuverability and safety at the potential cost of equipment. This established standardized RMD is written for a permissive, non-combat environment and, therefore, minimizes risk of possible equipment damage by setting the minimum requirements necessary to maintain effective ship control. The Commanding Officer retains the authority and responsibility to elevate readiness in light of the current threat environment and mission requirements; the Captain should amend the minimum engineering plant configuration requirements as situationally required to ensure adequate responsiveness to the tactical situation.

2. *Definitions.* RMD is to be set in those situations where ship's speed and maneuverability **must** be maintained for the safety of the ship at the risk of damaging equipment. Once the command decision has been made to set RMD, watchstanders are authorized to deviate from established casualty control procedures to ensure maneuverability is maintained. RMD will be set for the minimum amount of time required, and will normally be set during the following conditions:

a. Sea and Anchor Detail (In Port or Under Way).

b. Operating in restricted waters or a high traffic area.

c. Complex, close-in maneuvering situations or evolutions in close proximity to other vessels; i.e., Connected Replenishments (CONREP).

d. Other Special Evolutions as required per the Commanding Officer's Standing Orders and Battle Orders.

e. Unplanned:

(1) If the Officer of the Deck believes an unsafe or dangerous situation is developing which can be mitigated by setting RMD.

(2) When the tactical situation warrants, the Tactical Action Officer can direct the setting of RMD via the Officer of the Deck. Amplifying requirements and pre-planned responses will be delineated in the Commanding Officer's Battle Orders.

    f. Whenever the Commanding Officer deems it necessary.

3. *Responsibility.*

    a. *Commanding Officer (CO).*

       (1) CO will establish an RMD Policy informed by this appendix.

       (2) Approve any deviations to RMD.

    b. *Chief Engineer (CHENG).*

       (1) Review RMD for technical accuracy when required.

       (2) Advise the CO of any deficiencies of propulsion or ship's service electrical system equipment.

       (3) Incorporate the contents of this instruction into all qualifying boards for engineering supervisory watches, notably the Engineering Officer of the Watch / Readiness Control Officer, Propulsion and Auxiliaries Control Console Operators (PACC / A-EOOW), and Electrical Plant Control Console (EPCC) Operator as applicable.

    c. *Officer of the Deck (OOD).* Set RMD if the prevailing conditions or tactical situation warrant.

    d. *Engineering Officer of the Watch (EOOW) / Readiness Control Officer (RCO).* When in RMD, ensure that all orders from the OOD concerning the speed and direction of the ship are executed.

4. *Setting RMD.*

    a. When RMD is ordered, the OOD will direct all controlling stations (as per SORM) to set RMD:

    b. For Planned RMD, set briefed "Maximum Reliability" plant line-up as determined by the CO prior to setting RMD.

    c. Have the word passed over the 1MC: "SET THE RESTRICTED MANEUVERING DOCTRINE."

    d. Controlling Stations will announce over the controlling circuits: "RESTRICTED MANEUVERING DOCTRINE IS IN EFFECT."

e. Watchstanders will place "RESTRICTED MANEUVERING" placards and electronic status indicators (as applicable) at all ship controlling stations.

f. "RESTRICTED MANEUVERING DOCTRINE IS SET" will be entered in the Deck, CIC/CCC, CSOOW, and Engineering Logs.

g. All controlling stations will report to the OOD once all watchstanders have acknowledged that RMD is set and equipment is aligned per RMD / Maximum reliability plant lineup.

h. Once all controlling stations report RMD is set, pass the word over the 1MC: "RESTRICTED MANEUVERING DOCTRINE IS IN EFFECT. DO NOT START, STOP, OR CHANGE THE STATUS OF ANY EQUIPMENT, OR CONDUCT ANY PREVENTIVE OR CORRECTIVE MAINTENANCE WITHOUT APPROVAL FROM THE COMMANDING OFFICER." And continue to repeat every 30 minutes.

i. NO PMS or corrective maintenance should be conducted during RMD, unless:

    (1) Specific permission is requested from the CO via the OOD.

    (2) Required maintenance in support of a special evolution that is briefed and approved by the CO prior to setting RMD.

j. NO new tag outs will be authorized without CO's specific approval during RMD.

k. NO ground isolation or troubleshooting will be conducted without CO's specific approval during RMD.

5. *RMD is in EFFECT.*

a. A direct verbal order from the CO to the EOOW/RCO takes precedence over any other means of transmitting propulsion orders from the bridge to engineering controlling stations.

b. In the event of a casualty, EOOW will notify the OOD immediately of its effect on ship's speed, shaft revolutions per minute (RPM), electrical distribution and/or steering. If necessary, the OOD will have to compensate for loss of ship's speed by increasing RPM or pitch on the unaffected shaft, particularly when alongside another ship.

(1) CO has authority to direct action during RMD to direct casualty control

c. The EOOW shall report any unusual condition or trend to the CO and OOD as early as practical to allow as much time as possible to maneuver the ship to safety or to prepare mitigation for a possible casualty.

6. *Secure from RMD.*

a. When the special conditions that caused the restricted maneuvering situation to exist have passed, the OOD, with the approval of the CO, will direct all controlling stations to secure from RMD.

b. All controlling stations will report to the OOD once all watchstanders have acknowledged the report.

c. Watchstanders will remove "RESTRICTED MANEUVERING" placards and electronic status indicators (as applicable).

d. The OOD must have the word passed over the 1MC: "SECURE FROM RESTRICTED MANEUVERING DOCTRINE."

e. "SECURE FROM RESTRICTED MANEUVERING DOCTRINE" will be entered in the Deck, CIC/CCC, CSOOW, and Engineering Logs.

7. *Action.* All watchstanders will review this instruction monthly as determined by the CO. The content of this instruction will be prerequisite knowledge for all qualifying controlling stations, including, but not limited to: TAO/CICWO, OOD, EOOW/RCO, PACC, A-EOOW, Engineroom Operators (ERO) / Engineering Plant Technicians (EPT), Helm Safety Officer (HSO), Aft Steering, and Helm / Lee Helmsman.

STANDING ORDERS EXAMPLE
USS XXXXXXX Instruction ####.#

Subj: COMMANDING OFFICER'S STANDING ORDERS

Ref: (a) List applicable references

1. Purpose. This instruction promulgates Standing Orders for USS XXXXX. This instruction amplifies references (a) through (xx), which contain other information basic to the Officer of the Deck's (OOD) responsibilities.

2. Content. These standing orders include my directives encompassing the following topics and situations:
   a. Standing Order #1: Responsibilities
   b. Standing Order #2: The Watch
   c. Standing Order #3: Conning and Maneuvering
   d. Standing Order #4: Required Reports to the Commanding Officer
   e. Standing Order #5: Commanding Officer Approval Items
   f. Standing Order #6: Navigation
   g. Standing Order #7: Restricted Visibility
   h. Standing Order #8: Man Overboard
   i. Standing Order #9: Anchoring
   j. Standing Order #10: Restricted Maneuvering Doctrine
   k. Standing Order #11: Engineering/Maximum Plant Reliability
   l. Standing Order #12: Steering Control
   m. Standing Order #13: Small Boat Operations
   n. Standing Order #14: Flight Operations
   o. Standing Order #15: Well Deck / Mission Bay Operations
   p. Standing Order #16: Towed Gear Operations
3. Responsibility. As your Captain, I AM ON DUTY 24 HOURS PER DAY, and responsible for the safety of this ship at all times. I depend upon you and trust you to assist me in keeping our Sailors and our ship safe from harm.
4. Action.
   a. If there is ever any conflict between the Fleet Standing Orders, my supplemental Standing Orders or the Night Orders, bring the conflict to my attention immediately and take positive action to operate safely while we resolve the conflict.
   b. The Navigator will maintain the Night Order book and keep a copy of these Standing Orders in front along with a monthly "Record of Acknowledgment" sheet, which will be maintained onboard for one year. Each Sailor standing watch in a control station will read and acknowledge they understand these orders monthly by signing the "Record of Acknowledgment." Supplemental Night

Orders will be prepared nightly or as appropriate and reviewed by cognizant authorities prior to my signature.

   c. Recommendations for changes or additions to this instruction may be made at any time through the Navigator. The Senior Watch Officer and the Navigator are responsible for the annual review of this instruction.

   d. All Bridge and Engineering watchstanders will review this instruction monthly. The content of this instruction will be prerequisite knowledge for all qualifying controlling stations, including, but not limited to: TAO, CICWO, OOD, SUWC, EOOW/RCO, CONN, JOOD, QMOW, Helm Safety Officer (HSO), and Helm/Lee Helmsman.

Commanding Officer

STANDING ORDER NUMBER 1

Responsibilities

1. Command Responsibility

   a. As the Commanding Officer, I am ultimately responsible for every action and inaction that occurs aboard this ship. Along with my trust and confidence in you as a watchstander in a controlling station, comes my expectation that you execute your duties to the utmost of your ability.

   b. NEVER HESITATE TO CALL ME. When reports are required, make certain I understand your report. In an emergency, concentrate on the safety of the ship and pass the word, "CAPTAIN TO THE (station)" on the 1MC. If a situation is not an emergency, and you are unable to locate me, do not hesitate to pass, "COMMANDING OFFICER, PLEASE CONTACT (station) FOR A ROUTINE REPORT."

   c. DO NOT ABDICATE YOUR RESPONSIBILITY OR AUTHORITY. As OOD, TAO, EOOW/RCO, and CSOOW, you are in a position of special trust and confidence. You must act always for the safety of the ship and CALL ME IF DOUBT EXISTS.

2. Watch Relationships

    a. The OOD is my direct representative and is ALWAYS responsible for the navigational safety of this ship. The OOD Underway is granted weapons release authority for crew-served weapons in self-defense. The Conning Officer (CONN) is responsible for issuing necessary orders to the helm and main engine control to avoid danger, to take or keep an assigned station, and to change course and speed following orders of proper authority. Normally a specified watchstander will be assigned as CONN; however whenever the CONN shifts to another watchstander, to the OOD, or if I assume the CONN, it will be announced to all personnel in the pilothouse. Only one officer will have the CONN at any time and nothing absolves the OOD of their responsibility for safe navigation, regardless of who has the CONN.

    b. The Tactical Action Officer (TAO) will be assigned during most underway operations, and is granted weapons release authority for weapons in defense of this ship. My Battle Orders outline the responsibilities of the TAO, but the assignment of a TAO does NOT relieve the OOD of his/her responsibility for the ship's safe navigation and operation. The TAO, or Combat Information Center Watch Officer (when the TAO is not present), is responsible to the OOD for navigational support as required in the NAVDORM. The Surface Warfare Coordinator (SUWC), in addition to their tactical responsibilities, is the primary surface contact management and contact avoidance watchstander and will make reports to the CICWO for contact management support.

    c. The Engineering Officer of the Watch (EOOW) / Readiness Control Officer (RCO) will be assigned during all underway operations and in-port operations when the engineering schedule dictates. The EOOW is responsible for the safe operation of our engineering plant and will provide resources for power, propulsion and steering as directed by the OOD or TAO (in combat situations).

    d. The Combat Systems Officer of the Watch (CSOOW) or equivalent will be assigned during all underway operations and in-port operations when the combat systems schedule dictates. The CSOOW is responsible for the safe operation of our Combat and Weapons Systems, and will provide resources for navigation, self-defense and offensive operations as directed.

    e. If, at any time, these supervisory stations disagree in the safe operation of this ship, I am to be called IMMEDIATELY.

3. Command Relationships

    a. Executive Officer. The Executive Officer runs the ship and is second in command. I trust the XO's experience and judgment implicitly, and the XO may relieve any watchstander in any situation when such action is necessary for the safety of personnel or equipment. The OOD is responsible to the Executive Officer for the execution of events contained within the Plan of the Day and will keep the Executive Officer advised of any changes that are required.

    b. Senior Watch Officer. The Senior Watch Officer is charged with the supervision of the shipboard watch organization. Immediately notify the Senior Watch Officer if you or any of your assigned watchstanders are incapable of standing their watch or completing their duties.

    c. Department Heads. The Department Heads are responsible for supplying the resources enabling successful execution of the ship's schedule. Keep the Department Heads informed of any changes you feel will affect our ability to accomplish our mission.

    d. Navigator. The Navigator reports directly to the Commanding Officer with respect to the ship's safe navigation. The Navigator shall advise the OOD of safe courses and speeds to steer; however the OOD must evaluate each maneuvering recommendation with regards to the actual situation.

4. Responsibilities

    a. The fact that the Captain or Executive Officer is in a controlling station does not relieve the watchstander of the responsibility to maintain full situational awareness, and to forcefully and positively state his/her opinion and recommendations for the safe operation of the ship.

STANDING ORDER NUMBER 2
The Watch

1. Conduct of the watch:

   a. Ensure the watch is executed per the sound shipboard operating principles. These principles are:

      i. Formality—Formality and the use of standard phraseology are important for clear understanding of your orders. Use it, and require all members of your watch section to do likewise. Additionally, address watchstanders by their watch station, billet, or rank/last name. Do not use first names or nicknames while on watch.

      ii. Procedural Compliance—Established procedures are defined and approved written instructions from higher authority. It is your responsibility to know the procedure, understand the procedure, and execute as directed.

      iii. Level of Knowledge—You must possess an in-depth knowledge of the systems you are operating so you can act with confidence and are able to recognize and correct abnormal conditions.

      iv. Questioning Attitude—Apply critical thinking and be proactive. Expect to find conditions that require action.

      v. Forceful Backup—Foster an environment of inclusiveness that values the input from subordinate watch stations. Have the courage to "speak out" and provide critical forceful backup when something is unclear or when improper actions are being taken. Communication up and down the chain of command is important, regardless of rank.

      vi. Integrity—Be honest and truthful. Disclose mistakes, errors, and limitations. Confront others and adverse situations when firm adherence to the standard of integrity is absent or compromised.

1. Ensure you are maintaining a proper lookout and use all available means such as surface-search radars and visual lookouts. When in visual

range, take precise bearings using alidades or bearing circles to observe trends and validate bearing drift.

2.   Prior to relieving the watch as a Controlling Station Supervisor, you shall:

a.   Ensure you and your watch team are rested and ready to perform your duties. To the greatest extent possible, we will use a watch rotation based on circadian rhythm and honor protected rest periods.

b.   Have a thorough knowledge and clear understanding of the shipboard material and operational status and any changes expected during your watch. You will visit all controlling stations, obtain a briefing by the station supervisor, and ascertain the tactical and technical understanding of scheduled evolutions and responsibilities. Seek amplification from myself, the Executive Officer, or the cognizant Department Head if you have any doubts.

c.   Ensure a complete exchange of information with the previous supervisor, to include:

i.   Tactical formation and organization, including our station and any unexecuted or expected tactical signals.

ii.   Awareness of the surface contact picture and intended course of action.

iii. Ship-wide material condition, Condition of Readiness, Weapon Postures, EMCON status, and Engineering Plant Alignment.

iv.   Any special evolution scheduled during your watch and the status of preparations.

v.   Officers of the Deck will relieve on the hour specified on the watchbill, the JOOD will relieve 15 minutes prior to the OOD, the CONN will relieve 30 minutes prior to the OOD. TAO will relieve 15 minutes past the hour specified on the watch bill.

d.   The OOD will, specifically prior to turnover:

i.   Understand the ship's position, navigational plan, and overall equipment status and ensure it supports the tactical situation. If the situation cannot be resolved, call myself, the cognizant Department Head, and the Navigator.

    ii. Review the surface contact situation to ensure compliance with the Rules of the Road, safety with respect to the prevailing conditions, and adherence to these standing orders. A proper number of qualified lookouts will be stationed as appropriate.

    iii. If gear is streamed, to include NIXIE, review the scope of depth of the gear, comparing it with water depth along the intended track before relieving. Ensure the planned track allows for significant depth beneath the gear if the ship becomes adrift.

  e. The actual change of the watch shall be made with care and formality, as the relieving supervisor is completely responsible for the watch once he/she has relieved. The relief of all supervisors will be made formally in each space and also on whichever Net or channel is monitored by the greatest number of stations and personnel, e.g., the CO's Battle Net. If I am in the space, request permission to relieve the watch and report turnover to me.

3. Watch reliefs may be delayed due to the operational environment at any given time if introducing turnover would create an unsafe situation or endanger us. You may decline to relieve the watch if:

  a. The ship is out of station or off PIM without explanation or proper reports having been made, or if position cannot be adequately determined.

  b. The tactical situation is unclear.

  c. The previous watch team has not adequately prepared for the turnover.

  d. The status of equipment found on your prewatch tour does not reflect the briefed status, and if the issue cannot be resolved.

  e. You are ill or otherwise physically incapable of standing the watch.

4. Should you decline to relieve, immediately inform me and the Senior Watch Officer. If the navigation picture is unsafe, inform me and the Navigator immediately.

5. We will incorporate the Plan, Brief, Execute, Debrief (PBED) process into not only planned special evolutions, but also day-to-day watchstanding. Conduct a formalized watch turnover brief led by the oncoming TAO and attended by the oncoming OOD, JOOD, SUWC, AAWC

(or other specified watchstanders as required by the TAO), prior to the start of staggered watch turnovers. The focus of the brief should be lessons learned from previous watch, status of current and upcoming events, systems status such as weapons, comms, link, and any other controlling station priorities.

STANDING ORDER NUMBER 3
Conning and Maneuvering

1. I may relieve the Deck and/or assume the CONN at any time. Normally, I will specifically inform the OOD of the duties of which he/she is being relieved; however, should I give a direct order to the helm or lee helm at any time, it will be understood that I have assumed the CONN and be so logged by the QMOW. If the OOD is in doubt as to the exact status in this regard, it is the OOD's responsibility to immediately clarify who has the CONN.

2. *Maneuvering.* When operationally feasible, take actions per USCG Navigation Rules and Regulations and notify me when this cannot be accomplished. Know where safe water lies and be prepared to maneuver toward it at every moment.

   a. Do not allow yourself to be distracted by lesser tasks during maneuvering situations, periods of high traffic density, or low visibility.

   b. Always look before you turn and verify the ship's response to your orders after you give them.

   c. Always maneuver per USCG Navigation Rules and Regulations Handbook and notify me whenever a situation arises where you believe compliance with the Rules of the Road is not feasible.

   d. Standard commands shall be issued by the conning officer in a clear voice with appropriate volume for the situation. (Provide examples.)

3. Contact Management

   a. All contacts with a CPA of 2.5 NM or less will be closely monitored until they are past CPA and at a range greater than 10 NM. If there is a disagreement between the Bridge and CIC as to an impending situation, notify me immediately. Take frequent visual bearings on all contacts to ensure adequate bearing drift exists. If you are unable to meet these requirements due to high traffic density, the OOD shall notify me immediately.

b. When in formation, maintain an accurate, up-to-date formation diagram of all ships in company on maneuvering board. Maneuver independently to avoid contacts and give a wide berth to navigational hazards.

c. Maneuvering board solutions will be calculated by both the Bridge and CIC for all contacts with an initial CPA of less than 2.5 NM.

d. Unless specifically ordered, maintain a minimum range of 2.5 NM from a surfaced submarine or one at periscope depth. Observe a minimum distance of 3 NM ahead, 2 NM abeam, and 1 NM astern of an aircraft carrier or large deck amphibious ship.

e. Transits are planned to avoid hazards, optimize safety, and meet mission requirements. Altering course to facilitate safe passage with other vessels is acceptable, but do not leave track just to avoid making contact reports. If conditions warrant a potential change to the track, contact the Navigator to report those conditions and make a recommendation, i.e., contact density, traffic flow, unplanned hazards, etc., make the current track dangerous or impractical and a suitable alternative may exist. The Navigator will implement changes to the track per the Navigation Bill with my approval.

f. High traffic density situations should prompt the OOD to station additional watchstander(s) in the pilothouse or request additional lookouts from the Senior Watch Officer to assist with contact management. The Bridge will inform me when this additional measure is taken. I may specify additional "on call" watchstanders on the normal underway steaming watch bill, but the OOD can call on any crew member to assist in maintaining the safety of the ship. Examples include:

i. Shipping Officers

ii. Additional OOD underway qualified Officers

iii. Department Heads

iv. Any capable MOBOARD, Comms, or RADAR operator(s)

4. Formation Steaming

    a. If doubt exists, maneuver out of station, sector, or screen and into open sea room.

    b. Signals received by radio or via the signal bridge will be simultaneously and independently broken by the Bridge and CIC. The Bridge will advise me if concurrence is not reached promptly.

    c. If emergency action is necessary, regardless of reason, keep other ships in formation informed using radio circuits and visual signals.

    d. While assigned a point station, maintain station within 2 degrees of bearing and 10% of range. For sector stations, remain within the designated sector. The Bridge will call me if we do not maintain station.

    e. Upon receipt of an IMMEDIATE EXECUTE signal, take the required action (put over rudder, increase speed, etc.) as the Bridge informs me of the signal.

STANDING ORDER NUMBER 4
Required Reports

1. I am always on duty. Call me if in doubt.

2. Contact Reports

    a. Notify me of any surface contact with a CPA within 2.5 NM. This report should be made before the contact reaches 6 NM. Contact reports shall be made in the following manner: "Captain, this is the (OOD/JOOD) with a contact report. The time is ___. We are on course ___° T at speed ___ kts. We have a (type of contact/AIS name) by (visual/radar/AIS), bearing ___ relative, off the (port/ stbd, bow/qtr/beam) at ___ yards, on course ___ ° T, speed ___ kts. Target angle is ___ with (significant/good/slight) (left/right) bearing drift [or: "Is CBDR"]. By (radar/moboard) the CPA is ___ yards off the (port/stbd) (bow/beam/quarter) in ___ minutes. This is (overtaking/head-on/crossing) situation and we are the (give-way/stand-on) vessel. My intentions are to: _____. This is/is not per the Rules of the Road. Combat (concurs/does not concur)."

b. In a fast-moving situation that requires quick action, the cognizant controlling station will report to me what you know immediately and supplement it when more information becomes available.

c. If a junior naval vessel requests permission to proceed on duties assigned, immediately grant permission and then the Bridge will inform me.

d. The TAO will notify me when other military vessels or military aircraft are operating in the vicinity, regardless of nationality.

3. General Reports

a. All occurrences you believe deserve my attention.

b. When you decline to relieve the watch.

c. Conflicting guidance from higher authority contrary to these orders.

d. Conflicting interpretation of tactical signals, maneuvers, or situations between any Controlling Watch Station.

e. All significant material casualties and corrective action.

f. All injuries to personnel. This will also be reported to the XO.

g. Any abnormal condition or alarm that cannot be immediately cleared.

h. When calling away the SNOOPIE team. If necessary, do not hesitate to set it first and inform me after.

i. When setting the Low Visibility Detail. If necessary, do not hesitate to set it first and inform me after.

j. Prior to alteration of the major engineering plant equipment or combat systems alignment not included in the night orders.

k. Anytime you intend to discharge waste not per Maritime Pollution Abatement Regulations.

l. Prior to granting initial "GREEN DECK" for helicopter operations.

m. Prior to loading, lowering, and launching small boats.

n. While underway, prior to authorizing work aloft or over the side.

o. Anytime a major evolution cannot be conducted on time.

p. When a Flag Officer or Squadron Commander is embarked, make similar reports to him/her or his Staff Watch Officer per appropriate staff orders.

4. Weather
    a. Marked changes in the weather
        i. Sustained true wind of 25 kts or greater.
        ii. Wind speed changes of 10 kts or more in one hour.
        iii. Increase in seas of 2 feet in a two-hour period.
        iv. Barometric pressure at or below 29.5 inches or a change of 0.04 inches in one hour or 0.10 inches in a four-hour period.
        v. If visibility changes significantly or reduces to less than 4 miles.
        vi. When temperature and dew point temperature are within 4 degrees of each other.
    b. If any unusual weather phenomena occurs.
5. Navigation
    a. When the ship's track will pass within 10 nautical miles of shoal water.
    b. Any time the ship's position is in doubt.
    c. When fixes plot outside the drag circle while anchored or there is indication of dragging.
    d. Whenever fathometer soundings differ by 10 percent from charted depth, or when the ship is in less than 100 ft of water.
    e. When encountering any unexpected buoys, navigation aids, or hazards to navigation.
    f. When unable to maintain the Plan of Intended Movement or Speed of Advance.
    g. Any time navigation equipment or steering gear fails a special evolution preventive maintenance check.
6. Communication
    a. Significant tactical signals.
    b. Loss of communications on any maneuvering or warfare commander circuit for a period of 10 minutes.
7. Maneuvering
    a. Unresolved contact tracking conflicts between the CIC and the bridge, especially when the bridge and CIC do not concur on course, speed, and CPA.

    b. If the ship deviates more than authorized in the Night Orders from the intended track to facilitate safe passage with another vessel.

    c. Report change of formation or station assignments or formation course changes immediately. Do not wait until the signals are executed to call me. Likewise, execute immediate execute signals and inform me as soon thereafter as practical.

    d. When in formation, report when we are off station more than 10% of range and/or 2 degrees in bearing; outside patrol limits; if unable to maintain station; if you do not understand the movement of the Guide or any other ships in the formation; or if any other unit is significantly off station and may present a problem.

    e. Breakdown of ships in company.

    f. When required to take immediate action to avoid risk of collision.

STANDING ORDER NUMBER 5
Commanding Officer Approval Items

1. Prior to conducting an evolution that could potentially place our ship and crew into a potentially high-risk evolution, we will discuss the evolution in a formal brief (for planned evolutions) and conduct the necessary ORM to ensure its safety.

2. Unless otherwise given, obtain my permission prior to:

    a. General

        i. Deviating from Standing Orders, Night Orders, or orders from Commanders exercising OPCON/TACON of the or any approved procedure such as those contained in EOSS, CSOSS, PMS, or other Fleet Guidance.

        ii. Discharging waste over the side.

        iii. Conducting casualty control drills.

        iv. Setting and securing the Restricted Maneuvering Doctrine (RMD).

        v. Turnover of OOD, TAO, and CONN when the CO is present.

        vi. Securing from General Quarters.

        vii. Changing approved watch bills.

b. Engineering

  i. When setting single valve protection to the sea, or any high energy or immediately dangerous to life or health (IDLH) system.

  ii. Main engine/prime mover startup (specify exceptions; for example, permission not required when inherent in another order such as setting maximum engineering reliability).

  iii. Tagging out specified equipment.

  iv. Rolling or stopping shafts.

  v. Opening reduction gears.

  vi. Aligning installed drainage.

  vii. Transferring flammable liquids.

  viii. Changing the electrical configuration of the ship.

  ix. Disabling installed Damage Control systems.

c. Weapons/Combat Systems

  i. Handling/transferring ammunition.

  ii. Testing magazine sprinklers.

  iii. Firing any weapon (Reference exceptions granted for self-defense).

d. Safety

  i. Entry into IDLH spaces such as tanks, voids, and spaces contaminated by toxic gas.

  ii. Working on energized equipment.

  iii. Bypassing equipment interlocks or safety devices.

  iv. Personnel going topside after dark when underway.

  v. Personnel going aloft or over the side while underway.

  vi. Exceeding heat stress risk stay times as listed in OpNavInst 5100.19 Series.

e. Navigation

  i. Securing navigation equipment (i.e., fathometer, VMS, GPS, INS, navigation RADAR, fluxgate compass).

  ii. Prior to closing within 10 NM of land/shoal or prior to crossing the 50-fathom curve.

      iii. Prior to entering another nation's territorial waters.

      iv. Deviating from planned track more than 2 NM laterally or greater than 2 hours ahead or behind PIM.

  f. Special Evolutions

      i. Launching/recovering small boats as discussed in Standing Order 13.

      ii. Commencing the UNREP approach, tensioning/de-tensioning CONREP rigs, and prior to receiving fuel or pumping to a receiving ship.

      iii. Removing stoppers and letting go during anchoring.

      iv. Launching/recovering aircraft as discussed in Standing Order 14.

      v. Prior to streaming or recovering towed bodies as discussed in Standing Order 16.

STANDING ORDER NUMBER 6
Navigation

1. The safe navigation of the ship is the most important responsibility as a Controlling Station Supervisor. If there is any doubt in your mind regarding the accurate position of the ship or the ability to remain in safe waters, slow or stop as necessary until the issue is resolved, and the OOD shall call myself and the Navigator immediately.

2. The Navigator will perform duties as outlined in OpNavInst 3120.32D (SORM) and CNSP/CNAP/CNSL/CNALINST 3530.4E (NAVDORM) as well as this Standing Order. Specifically, notify the Navigator when:

  a. You are in doubt about any element of navigation or the performance of any navigation watchstander.

  b. An expected aid to navigation is sighted 30 minutes or more ahead of schedule or not sighted within 15 minutes of expected time.

  c. Any unexpected aid to navigation is sighted.

  d. When fix intervals cannot be complied with the NAVDORM table below.

  e. There is a malfunction of navigation equipment.

AREA	DISTANCE FROM LAND OR SHOAL WATER	GPS FOM	MAXIMUM FIX
Restricted Waters	Less than 2 nautical miles	FOM ≤ 2	3 minutes
Piloting Waters	2–10 nautical miles	FOM ≤ 4	3–15 minutes conditions warrant
Coastal Waters	10–30 nautical miles	FOM ≤ 6	15–30 minutes conditions warrant
Open Ocean (Enroute Navigation)	Over 30 nautical miles	FOM ≤ 7	30 minutes or conditions warrant

3. Whether using charts or VMS, take fixes per our ship's Navigation Bill. Although VMS continuously plots the ship's position the requirement still exists to obtain a fix by an alternate source at least every third fix interval in restricted waters. Therefore, manual bearings and/or ranges will be provided by the Bearing Takers and CIC RADAR Operator and entered by the ECDIS-N Display Operator at least every nine minutes in restricted waters. The fix interval can be reduced when prudent based on prevailing conditions and operational commitments.

4. Station the Navigation or Modified Navigation Detail when required, and ensure the details are set in a timely manner. The navigation detail will be set prior to entering restricted waters. The modified navigation detail will be set per the Navigation Bill.

5. Transmit AIS per Fleet Commander guidance while transiting any traffic separation scheme (TSS) and/or any high-density traffic area unless otherwise directed by the TAO.

Restricted Visibility

1. Reduced visibility requires increased vigilance on the part of the supervisory and controlling stations.
   a. During reduced visibility, operational commitments will never override the safety of the ship. The speed of the ship will be determined as prescribed in the Navigation Rules.

b. Carry out, at a minimum, the procedures in the ship's Low Visibility Bill when surface visibility drops to 3 NM. Execute these actions sooner if you consider it appropriate to ensure the ship is fully prepared to enter low visibility.

2. In reduced visibility situations, particularly in dense traffic areas, the safety of the ship may be enhanced by transmitting our position via AIS. Consult with the TAO, and call me if in your judgment, AIS is necessary.

Man Overboard

1. During a Man Overboard under way, conduct the following actions concurrently:

   a. Throw a life ring and maneuver to recover.

      i. Man in sight: Prepare to conduct the recovery by the most efficient method for the prevailing circumstances. Ensure someone maintains visual on the man at all times until the recovery is complete.

      ii. Man not in sight: Prepare to conduct the recovery by the most efficient method for the prevailing circumstances. Employ all available means to locate the man, i.e., extra lookouts, electro-optical sights, night vision devices, additional units as necessary. The CICWO will give "expanding square" course recommendations if man remains unlocated.

      iii. Towed body deployed: Conduct a Racetrack turn and use the most efficient method of recovery available. Pass the word via the 1MC twice, "Man Overboard. Man the [insert towed body] detail." Operators will immediately cease any underwater transmissions.

   b. Ensure a smoke float is dropped as close to the man as possible unless there is a fire risk such as fuel on the water, e.g., in the vicinity of a crash site.

   c. Instruct all topside personnel to point to the man.

   d. Sound six short blasts.

e. Notify ships in company and the OTC, and via VHF Channel 16 issue a "PAN PAN" if necessary.

f. Pass "MAN OVERBOARD (port/stbd) SIDE. This will be a (small boat/shipboard/aircraft) recovery. All divisions submit muster reports to [insert station]" over the 1MC. Boat deck and foc'sle will automatically be manned.

g. QMOW and/or CICWS shall mark the man on VMS and DDRT/DRT/CADRT.

h. Break the OSCAR flag or energize pulsating red over red lights.

i. The CIC ensures any combat systems transmissions into the water and the fathometer are secured (for an actual event only), mark the man, and report bearing and ranges to the Bridge.

STANDING ORDER NUMBER 9
Anchoring

1. While at anchor, the following precautions will be taken:

   a. All watches set forth in the NAVDORM will be manned and will:

      i. Ensure that a fix is taken on the Bridge and CIC every 30 minutes (every 5 minutes if winds are greater than 25 kts) and compared for accuracy. If a fix falls outside of the drag circle, the VMS alarm activates, or you believe the ship is dragging anchor, immediately take another fix. If that falls outside the drag circle, immediately call the CDO and Navigator.

      ii. Guard all required circuits.

      iii. Ensure that the fathometer is continuously energized.

      iv. If necessary, prepare to get the ship underway to reposition and anchor.

   b. A qualified CIC Watch supervisor will be in the CIC and will:

      i. Guard all required circuits, including chat.

      ii. Maintain a radar watch to monitor nearby traffic and make a determination of risk of collision.

   c. An Anchor Watch will be stationed in vicinity of the anchor and will report status of the anchor to the Bridge/CIC every 15 minutes. The report should state the direction the chain is tending, the strain, and the amount of chain on deck (i.e., "the anchor is at twelve o'clock, moderate strain with 4 shots on deck").

d. At anchor, each duty section will have a minimum of one Engineering Officer of the Watch. One main engine will be available for immediate start (< 15 minutes) and steering units will remain aligned for starting from the Bridge.

2. Required reports while at anchor include:

a. All occurrences you feel deserve attention or whenever in doubt.

b. When a change in Readiness for Sea status is directed by the Immediate Superior in Command.

c. When an increase in Force Protection condition occurs, or a Force Protection notification is received by the ship.

d. When severe inclement weather is forecasted or approaching.

e. When boating operations or liberty launches must be suspended.

f. When dragging anchor.

g. Upon parting of a line while moored.

h. Prior to aligning PWT (gray water) or sewage (black water) over the side.

i. Prior to transferring ammunition.

j. Prior to externally transferring fuel or oily waste.

k. Prior to starting engines or generators.

l. Prior to rolling shafts.

m. Prior to high-powered radiation of any element of the combat system.

n. When experiencing challenges with the Defense Attaché, Husbanding Agent, local or base police, etc.

o. Any liberty incident involving host nation police.

p. Notification that a Sailor has been hospitalized, reported to the emergency room, or has an urgent medical need.

q. Upon receipt of an AMCROSS message.

3. Reference the ship's anchoring nomograph for determining the minimum length of chain and the horizontal distance from the ship to the anchor for flat and sloped bottoms.

STANDING ORDER NUMBER 10
Restricted Maneuvering Doctrine

1. As noted above, Commanding Officers must tailor this Standing order to meet their ship-specific needs.

STANDING ORDER NUMBER 11
Engineering/Maximum Plant Reliability

1. Due to unique configurations of engineering plants throughout the Surface Force, Commanding Officers must tailor this Standing order to meet their ship-specific needs.

STANDING ORDER NUMBER 12
Steering Control

1. Due to unique configurations of Steering Control throughout the Surface Force, Commanding Officers must tailor this Standing order to meet their ship-specific needs.

STANDING ORDER NUMBER 13
Small Boat Operations

1. The Boat Deck Safety Observer and the Boat Officer are the OOD's primary agents for safety during small boat operations.
    a. Minimum manning includes a Bow Hook, a Boat Engineer, and a Coxswain. The Bow Hook will often be manned by a SAR Swimmer, and a Boat Officer is usually used. If two boats are to be used, and not in a lifesaving capacity, the second Boat Officer and SAR swimmer may be waived at the OOD's discretion. The Boat Officer will receive a brief from the Bridge Team prior to launch covering ensuing operations.
    b. The small boat operations checklist will be completed prior to requesting my permission to launch or recover boats.
    c. The OOD shall maneuver to create a lee for small boat operations. Inform the boat deck and the coxswain if maneuvering is required to flatten the sea state such as when launching the small boat while the ship makes a slow turn.

STANDING ORDER NUMBER 14
Flight Operations

1. The Helicopter Control Officer (HCO) is the OOD's agent on the flight deck to ensure that all preparations are made correctly and that all aspects of the evolution are carried out safely.

   a. Set Flight Quarters in advance to permit thorough preparations, taking into account any alert or ready deck requirements.

   b. Complete the check-off list prior to helicopter operations.

   c. Deck status will be controlled by the OOD, with recommendations from the HCO. The OOD will inform me prior to authorizing Green Deck, and only when NWP 3-04.1 and NAVAIR 00-80T-122 environmental requirements have been satisfied for the applicable airframe.

   d. Maneuver the ship only during "Red Deck" conditions, paying special attention to Polar Plots and the status of the flight deck nets, especially during high-speed evolutions. Lowering and raising of nets will be at a safe speed for personnel.

   e. *AIRCRAFT IN-FLIGHT EMERGENCY.* Immediately pass the word "EMERGENCY FLIGHT QUARTERS" over the 1MC and the nature of the emergency, if known. Proceed at best speed toward the known or last known location; if the helo is in our vicinity, immediately come to Foxtrot Corpen.

STANDING ORDER NUMBER 15
Well Deck/Mission Bay Operations

1. Due to unique configurations and missions required for Well Deck or Mission Bay Operations, Commanding Officers must tailor this Standing order to meet their ship-specific needs.

STANDING ORDER 16
Towed Gear Operations

1. Whenever towed gear is deployed, the ship's effective dimensions increase in both length and navigational draft in proportion to cable scope.

Manage the contact situation and track appropriately.

a. While deploying, retrieving, or maneuvering with towed gear, follow guidance contained in the applicable technical manual.

b. Use sternway only in an emergency.

c. Navigational charts will be carefully monitored to ensure available water depth supports operations on the intended track.

d. The TAO shall notify the OOD whenever cable must be paid out or retrieved. Towed body depth will be recalculated for the new tow length by both the CIC and Navigation teams using nomograms in the applicable reference.

e. OODs will advise the TAO of intentions to change speed so that cable scope may be adjusted to maintain desired towed body depth.

Appendix B

MATERIAL CONDITIONS OF READINESS

The three standard conditions of material readiness that apply to U.S. Navy surface ships are the following:

X-ray Set when the ship is in almost no danger of attack or natural hazard, in a well-protected harbor or secured at home base, in fair weather during normal working hours. All fittings marked X-ray (X) are closed at all times except when in use.

Yoke Set and maintained at sea, when entering or leaving port during peacetime, in port during peacetime (other than normal working hours), and in port during wartime. All fittings marked X-ray (X) and Yoke (Y) are closed at all times except when in use. When open, the fittings should be so logged in the D.C. closure log.

Zebra Set during general quarters or any peacetime emergency evolutions and wartime battle situations. All fittings marked X-ray (X), Yoke (Y), and Zebra (Z) are closed and may be opened only on receipt of permission from D.C. Central.

The following classifications of fittings are found on board U.S. Navy surface ships:

X-ray Closed at all times when not in use.
X

Yoke Y	Fittings for which alternate Zebra accesses exist. Normally closed when not in use, the only exception being when condition X-ray is set.
Zebra Z	Normally open for operation of the ship, habitability, and access. Closed during battle or emergency evolutions and conditions.
William W	Ventilation and plumbing fittings normally open during all conditions of readiness.
Circle X-ray (X)	Fittings that may be opened without special authority to allow the transfer of ammunition and the operation of vital systems.
Circle Yoke (Y)	May be opened without special permission by personnel proceeding to battle stations but must be closed after use.
Circle Zebra (Z)	May be opened during condition Zebra on authority of the CO to allow the distribution of food, access to sanitary facilities, or the ventilation of battle stations and other vital areas. When open, must be guarded for immediate closure if necessary.
Black D Zebra D̲Z̲	Closed for darkening ship at night.
Circle William (W)	Nonvital ventilation and plumbing fittings normally open during condition Zebra but may be closed in the event of an NBC attack.

Appendix C

TYPICAL SCHEDULE FOR GETTING UNDER WAY

Date: _____

EVENT	RESPONSIBILITY	

72 HOURS PRIOR

1. Prepare charts for restricted waters transit.   NAV/CIC   _____
2. Senior QM and senior OS review charts.   NAV/CIC   _____
3. Prepare and submit OTSR request (if applicable).   NAV   _____
4. Prepare communications plan IAW OPTASK COMMS.   COMMO   _____
5. Submit port services request to Port OPS.   OPS   _____

48 HOURS PRIOR

1. XO reviews / CO approves charts and navigation brief.   NAV   _____
2. Post getting underway checklist on the quarterdeck.   NAV   _____
3. Pass the word: "The check-off list for getting under way is available for review on the quarterdeck."   OOD   _____
4. Make the following entry in the deck log: "Start getting underway checklist."   OOD   _____
5. Post S & A watch bill signed by CO.   SWO   _____

24 HOURS PRIOR

1. Prepare and submit MOVREP.   NAV   _____
2. Confirm gyros are on line and alarms tested.   CSOOW   _____
3. Commence pre-underway checks for   CSOOW   _____
   combat systems equipment.
4. Verify tugs/pilot/line handlers.   OPS   _____
5. Verify shore service disconnection schedule. OPS   _____
6. Conduct PMS check on anchor windlass.   AUXO   _____
7. Post approved COMMS plan in the   COMMO   _____
   pilothouse and in CIC.
8. Ascertain number of guests, ETA,   CMAA   _____
   and prepare berthing arrangements.
9. Power up and test the SCC. Test EOT   EDO   _____
   only after confirming all engines are secured.
10. Test steering IAW EOSS EOP.   EDO   _____
    Log in the deck log: "pre-underway
    steering checks complete IAW EOSS."
11. Engineering underway checks complete.   EDO   _____
12. Conduct test of alarms and   NAV   _____
    navigation lights.
13. Conduct navigation brief.   NAV   _____
14. All departments secure for sea.   CDO   _____
15. Inventory/update all pilothouse   NAV   _____
    publications.

12 HOURS PRIOR

1. CDO review status of getting under-   CDO   _____
   way checklist.
2. Compute gyro error. Compare repeaters   NAV   _____
   against master gyro. Log error in deck log.

6 HOURS PRIOR

1. Energize and check all CIC equipment.   OPS   _____
2. Conduct radio checks.   COMMO   _____

2 HOURS PRIOR

1.	Bring in command parking signs.	1ST LT	_____
2.	Begin faking lines out on deck. Remove frapping and rat guards.	1ST LT	_____
3.	Ascertain from the XO the uniform and time for setting the Sea and Anchor Detail. Pass the word: "All hands shift into the uniform for getting under way. The uniform for getting under way is _____. The ship will station the Sea and Anchor Detail at time XXXX."	OOD	_____
4.	Obtain outgoing mail instructions.	SUPPO	_____
5.	After obtaining permission from the XO, hoist in all boats as required. Rig in unnecessary rigs and ladders and secure the decks for sea.	1ST LT	_____
6.	Adjust and tune the pilothouse radar repeaters as necessary.	CE	_____
7.	Reboot navigation systems as required.	CSOOW	_____
8.	Test BTB radio.	NAV	_____
9.	Verify NVGs, wood chips, and chem lights are on station.	NAV	_____
10.	Test communications circuits in the pilothouse.	CSOOW	_____
11.	CDO and underway OOD walk main decks and note condition of shore services and securing for sea efforts.	CSO/OOD	_____

1 HOUR PRIOR

1.	Send mail ashore.	SUPPO	_____
2.	Pass the word: "All visitors are requested to leave the ship."	OOD	_____

3. Pass the word: "Check the setting of   OOD   _____
material condition modified ZEBRA.
Make modified ZEBRA reports to CCS."

30 MINUTES PRIOR

1. Pass the word: "Station the Sea and   OOD   _____
Anchor Detail. Station the Sea and
Anchor Detail. The ship expects to
get Underway for Sea at XXXX."
2. Shift the watch from the quarterdeck   OOD   _____
to the pilothouse.
3. Submit Draft Report to the pilothouse.   OOD   _____
Log in deck log: "Received the getting
underway draft report. Draft FWD _____
Draft AFT _____ Mean Draft _____
Displacement _____ "
4. Test anchor windlass.   1ST LT   _____
5. Make the anchor ready for letting go.   1ST LT   _____
6. Pass the word: "All departments make   OOD   _____
readiness reports for getting under way to
the Officer of the deck in the pilothouse."
Executive   _____
Combat Systems   _____
Operations   _____
Weapons   _____
Engineering   _____
Supply   _____
7. Receive manned and ready reports: OOD   _____
Ship Control (NAV, Pilothouse AFT Steering)   _____
Command and Control (CIC/CSMC)   _____
Communications Control   _____
Deck Stations (Forecastle, Fantail, Amidships,   _____
Anchor Windlass, Boat Deck) CCS

8. Start main engines (with CO's permission).   OOD   _____
9. Contact degaussing range.   ELO/EMC_____
10. Test BTB radio.   OOD   _____
11. Clear unnecessary personnel from   BMOW   _____
the pilothouse.
12. Ensure all force protection equipment   GUNNO   _____
is returned.
13. Test the ship's whistle.   OOD   _____
(CO's permission required.)
14. Disconnect pier services and check   OOD   _____
that sides are clear.
15. Take in spare breast lines.   1ST LT   _____
16. Disconnect telephone lines.   OOD   _____
(XO's permission required.)
17. Ensure all visitors have departed the ship.   CMAA   _____
18. Ensure that CODE HOTEL is closed   OOD   _____
up when pilot embarks.
19. Conduct time check from the pilothouse.   QMOW   _____
20. Test emergency alarms from the pilothouse.   BMOW   _____
21. Test fathometer.   NAV   _____

15 MINUTES PRIOR

1. Shift throttle control to the   OOD   _____
bridge IAW EOSS.
2. Remove/Rig in brow.   OOD   _____
(XO's permission required.)
3. Ensure pilothouse has positive   OOD   _____
steering control.
4. Report to the XO: "Sir (or Ma'am), the   OOD   _____
ship is manned and ready to get under way."
XO will report the same to the CO to
obtain permission to get under way.
5. Secure ventilation to pilothouse   EOOW   _____
(noise reduction).

10 MINUTES PRIOR

1. Make up tugs.   OOD   _____
2. Single up all lines.   OOD   _____
   (CO's permission required.)
3. Place Restricted Maneuvering Doctrine   OOD   _____
   in effect. (CO's permission required.)
   Ensure EOOW is notified. Every fifteen
   minutes, pass the word: "The Restricted
   Maneuvering Doctrine is in effect. Make
   no changes to equipment configuration."

UNDER WAY

1. When last eye is lifted off a pier fitting,   OOD   _____
   pass the word: "Under way." If after 0800
   and prior to sunset, pass the word:
   "Under way, shift colors."
2. Close up international call sign.   OOD   _____

SITUATIONAL

1. Secure anchor for sea.   OOD   _____
   (CO's permission required.)
2. Secure from the Restricted Maneuvering   OOD   _____
   Doctrine. (CO's permission required.)
3. Inform CCS when 3 NM from land.   OOD   _____
4. Secure Special Sea and Anchor Detail.   OOD   _____
   (XO's permission required.)
5. Strike the jackstaff and remove ship's   OOD   _____
   awards from the bridge wings (as applicable).
6. Conduct Sea and Anchor Debrief.
   The following personnel are required to attend:
   CO
   XO
   CONN

OOD/JOOD
NAV
CCS
OPS
CIC
Helm Safety Officer
Master Helmsman
Lee Helmsman
Amidships Safety
Forecastle Safety
Fantail Safety

Upon completion of this checklist, return to the QMOW for archive. Make deck log entry: "Getting under way checklist complete. No discrepancies." (If discrepancies found, note them.) Retain a copy on board for six months.

Appendix D

TYPICAL SCHEDULE FOR ENTERING PORT

Date: _____

EVENT	RESPONSIBILITY	

72 HOURS PRIOR

1. Prepare charts for restricted waters transit. NAV/CIC _____
2. Senior QM and senior OS review charts. NAV/CIC _____

48 HOURS PRIOR

1. XO reviews/CO approves charts and navigation brief. NAV _____
2. Post getting underway checklist in pilothouse. NAV _____
3. Pass the word: "The entering port/ restricted waters checklist is available for review in the pilothouse." OOD _____
4. Make the following entry in the deck log: "Commenced entering port/restricted waters checklist." OOD _____
5. Post approved S & A watch bill. SWO _____
6. Conduct port/liberty brief for foreign port. CMC _____

24 HOURS PRIOR

1.	Prepare and submit MOVREP.	NAV	_____
2.	Confirm gyros are on line and alarms tested.	CSOOW	_____
3.	Commence pre-underway checks for combat systems equipment.	CSOOW	_____
4.	Compute gyro error. Compare repeaters against master gyro. Log error in deck log.	NAV	_____
5.	Conduct navigation brief.	NAV	_____
6.	Contact port operations. Confirm pilot and time of UW. Find out anticipated harbor movements.	OPS	_____

12 HOURS PRIOR

1.	OOD review status of getting underway checklist.	OOD	_____
2.	Compute gyro error. Compare repeaters against master gyro. Log error in deck log.	NAV	_____
3.	Pump bilges prior to 50 NM limit.	EOOW	_____

2 HOURS PRIOR

1.	Begin faking lines out on deck.	1ST LT	_____
2.	Ascertain from the XO the uniform and time for setting the Sea and Anchor Detail. Pass the word: "All hands shift into the uniform for entering port. The uniform for entering port is ____. The ship will set the Sea and Anchor Detail at time XXXX."	OOD	_____
3.	Walk topside spaces ensuring the ship has a smart appearance.	1ST LT	_____
4.	Test BTB radio.	OOD	_____
5.	Test communications circuits in the pilothouse.	CSOOW	_____
6.	Confirm pilot pickup time for sea and anchor over BTB with harbor control/port ops.	OPS	_____

1 HOUR PRIOR

1. Pass the word: "Check the setting of   OOD   _____
   material modified ZEBRA. Make modified
   ZEBRA reports to CCS."

2. If necessary, rig accommodation ladder.   1ST LT   _____

30 MINUTES PRIOR

1. Pass the word: "Go to your stations all   OOD   _____
   the Special Sea and Anchor Detail. Go to
   your stations all the Special Sea and Anchor
   Detail." (Time will depend on situation.)

2. Place Restricted Maneuvering Doctrine   OOD   _____
   in effect. (CO's permission required.)
   Notify EOOW. Every fifteen minutes,
   pass the word: "The Restricted Maneuvering
   Doctrine is in effect. Make no changes to
   equipment configuration. Conduct no
   maintenance without the permission of
   the Officer of the Deck."

3. Submit Draft Report to the pilothouse.   OOD   _____
   Log in the deck log: "Received entering
   restricted waters draft report. Draft FWD_____,
   Draft AFT_____, Mean Draft_____,
   Displacement_____."

4. Test anchor windlass.   1ST LT   _____

5. Make the anchor ready for letting go.   1ST LT   _____
   (With CO's permission.)

6. Pass the word: "All departments make   OOD   _____
   readiness reports for entering port to the
   Officer of the Deck in the pilothouse."
   Executive   _____
   Combat Systems   _____
   Operations   _____

Weapons		_____
Engineering		_____
Supply		_____

7. Receive manned and ready reports: OOD _____
   Ship Control (NAV, Pilothouse AFT Steering)
   Command and Control (CIC/CSMC)
   Communications Control
   Deck Stations (Forecastle, Fantail,
   Amidships, Anchor Windlass, Boat Deck) CCS

8. Test BTB radio. OOD _____

9. Verify NVGs and wood chips OOD _____
   are on station.

10. Clear unnecessary personnel from BMOW _____
    the pilothouse.

11. Test emergency alarms from pilothouse. BMOW _____

12. Conduct a time check from the pilothouse. QMOW _____

13. Test fathometer. NAV _____

14. Ensure all force protection equipment GUNNO _____
    is ready.

15. Test the ship's whistle. OOD _____
    (CO's permission required.)

16. Report to the XO: "Sir (or Ma'am), OOD _____
    the ship is manned and ready to enter port."
    XO will report the same to the CO.

17. Ensure that CODE HOTEL is closed QMOW _____
    up when pilot embarks.

18. Close up international call sign. OOD _____

19. Make up tugs. OOD _____

MOORED

1. When first eye is lifted on to a pier OOD _____
   fitting pass the word: "Moored." If after
   0800 and prior to sunset pass the word:
   "Moored, shift colors."

2. Secure the Restricted Maneuvering   OOD   _____
   Doctrine. (CO's permission required.)

3. Secure anchor for sea/underfoot.   OOD   _____
   (CO's permission required.)

4. Secure main engines.   OOD   _____
   (With CO's permission.)

5. Secure Special Sea and Anchor Detail.   OOD   _____
   (XO's permission.)

6. Place ship's awards on the bridge wings.   OOD   _____

7. Conduct Sea and Anchor Debrief.
   The following personnel are required to attend:
   CO
   XO
   CONN
   OOD/JOOD
   NAV
   CCS
   OPS
   CIC
   Helm Safety Officer
   Master Helmsman
   Lee Helmsman
   Amidships Safety
   Forecastle Safety
   Fantail Safety   OOD   _____

Upon completion of this checklist, return to the QMOW for archive. Make deck log entry: "Entering port checklist complete. No discrepancies." (If discrepancies found, note them.) Retain a copy on board for six months.

Appendix E

SAMPLE LOW-VISIBILITY PROCEDURES

When it first becomes apparent that there will be a low visibility situation, the following steps shall be taken:

_____ Notify the Commanding Officer, TAO, and CICWO that the possibility of entering a low-visibility area exists.

_____ Establish radar contact plot on the bridge.

_____ Open bridge wing doors and station the Junior Officer of the Deck, or other bridge watchstander, on the bridge wing closest to the nearest known contact.

_____ If at trail shaft, shift to split plant.

_____ Ensure throttle control and steering control is at the Ship Control Console. Consider assigning a separate helmsman and lee helmsman.

_____ Notify EOOW of low visibility situation.

_____ Test the ship's whistle and check navigation lights.

_____ Announce "Station the Low Visibility Detail" on the 1MC.

_____ If between taps and reveille send messenger to verify personnel assigned to Low Visibility Detail are awake and en route.

_____ QMOW makes appropriate deck log entries.

_____ Augment the regular watch:

_____ Qualified lookouts posted:
FORECASTLE FOG LOOKOUT _____
FORECASTLE PHONE TALKER _____

FANTAIL LOOKOUT _____

FANTAIL PHONE TALKER _____

PORT AND STBD LOOKOUTS _____

_____ CIC manned and ready.

_____ Commence fog signals.

_____ Secure topside speakers.

_____ With the Commanding Officer's permission, set material condition ZEBRA on the main deck and below and make deck log entry when set.

LOW-VISIBILITY CHECKLIST AT ANCHOR

When it first becomes apparent that there will be a low visibility situation the following steps shall be taken:

_____ Notify CDO that the possibility of a low visibility situation exists.

_____ Have bridge watch report estimated visibility based on radar and charted position. Report all radar contacts and visibility at least every fifteen minutes.

_____ Test ship's whistle (CDO must authorize).

_____ Notify the CDO.

_____ POOW will make appropriate deck log entries.

_____ Augment the regular watch.

Qualified fog lookouts posted:

FORECASTLE LOOKOUT (CAN BE ANCHORWATCH) _____

FORECASTLE PHONE TALKER _____

FANTAIL LOOKOUT _____

FANTAIL PHONE TALKER _____

QUARTERDECK PHONE TALKER _____

_____ Bell manned.

_____ Gong manned.

_____ Commence bell and gong signals.

_____ Set material condition ZEBRA on the main deck and below and make deck log entry when set.

_____ If necessary, notify bridge watch to stand by ship's whistle, to warn approaching vessels.

Appendix F

SAMPLE TOW OR BE TOWED PROCEDURES

EVENT	RESPONSIBILITY	
24 TO 6 HOURS PRIOR		
1. Verify steering checks complete and logged in the deck log.	ENG	_____
2. Conduct a safety brief for ALCON. Discuss type of approach, safety precautions, and sounds signals.	1ST LT	_____
3. Determine from OPS:	OOD	
a. Rendezvous position		_____
b. Rendezvous time		_____
c. Condition of tow		_____
4. Lay out necessary equipment.	1ST LT	_____
5. Break anchor chain at least four hours prior to event if being towed. Log in the deck log.	1ST LT	_____
6 TO 2 HOURS PRIOR		
1. Ensure all sound-powered phones/circuits tested and status reported to OOD.	OOD	_____
2. Prepare all tactical signals for towing operations.	OOD/TAO	_____

3. Determine gyro error, log results in the deck log and magnetic compass log.   QMOW _____

4. Check gyro repeaters and master gyro for error.   QMOW _____
   AFT Steering _____
   PORT Bridge Wing _____
   STBD Bridge Wing _____
   SCC _____

5. Post gyro error on ALL gyro repeaters.   QMOW _____

1 HOUR PRIOR

1. Review all sound signals for towing with Helm Safety Officer.   OOD _____

2. Assume tactical command, if towing (with CO's permission).   TAO _____

3. Verify propulsion and electrical plant line up as per CO's Standing Orders.   ENG _____

4. Test the ship's whistle (with CO's permission).   OOD _____

5. Test all navigation and towing lights (if towing at night).   QMOW _____

6. Pass time check.   QMOW _____

7. Place bullhorn convenient to CONN and check battery.   QMOW _____

8. Ensure two laser range finders are on the bridge.   QMOW _____

9. Test emergency alarms from the pilothouse.   BMOW _____

45 MINUTES PRIOR

1. Pass the word via the 1MC: OOD _____
   "Go to your stations all the Towing Detail."

30 MINUTES PRIOR

1. Conduct radio checks on the required circuits.   CICWS _____

2. Check BTB radio.   OOD   _____

3. Towing stations manned and ready.   OOD   _____

   a. Ship Control

     (1) BMOW   _____

     (2) JOOD   _____

     (3) Helmsman   _____

     (4) Lee Helmsman   _____

     (5) Phone Talker   _____

     (6) Messenger   _____

     (7) QMOW   _____

     (8) Course/Speed Recorder   _____

     (9) Helm Safety Officer   _____

     (10) Lookouts   _____

     (11) AFT Steering   _____

   b. CCS (Inform EOOW of course and speed.)   _____

   c. CIC   _____

   d. FWD IC   _____

   e. Radio   _____

   f. Ready lifeboat   _____

   g. Deck Detail   _____

4. Set Restricted Maneuvering Doctrine   OOD   _____
   (with CO's permission). Log in the deck log.

5. If being towed, take all way off the ship   OOD   _____
   and pass the word: "Standby for shot lines
   forward from USS _____."

6. Once tow is made up, ensure a towing   OOD   _____
   watch is posted to observe the towline at all times.
   SAFETY NOTE: Ensure fantail is clear
   of all personnel when towing.

INFO NEEDED FOR EMERGENCY TOWING OPERATIONS

It is the OOD's responsibility to provide (if being towed) or receive (if towing)
the following information prior to undertaking the towing evolution:

1. Engineering plant status, including whether shafts are locked or unlocked, and if power is available to the anchor windlass.
2. Hull condition, including any weakened bulkheads or holes in the skin of the ship.
3. Condition of the steering gear (operable or inoperable).
4. Condition of deck machinery, including capstans, windlasses, and winches (operable or inoperable).
5. Available towing equipment on other vessel.
6. Tow ship readiness regarding rigging for a tow and breaking out the necessary equipment.
7. Will the crew remain aboard the towed vessel?
8. Establish a means of communications between ships when making up the tow and during the tow.
9. General trim of the tow.
10. Record drafts after the towed ship is in proper trim. (FWD _____ AFT _____)
11. Are all sea valves closed and wired shut?
12. Are all bilges free of oil and water?
13. Is the hull damage and/or flooding under control?
14. The rudder(s) should be centered and locked.
15. Are amber colored flooding alarm lights installed on the towed ship? (This is desirable if the towed ship is unmanned and flooding is a possibility.)
16. Are navigation lights installed and working on the towed ship?
17. If towing pads exist, bitts and cleats can be used but should be checked for handling the strain of towing.

NOTE: Return this checklist to the QMOW and log in the deck log completion of checklist.

Appendix G

SAMPLE DDG FLIGHT OPERATIONS PROCEDURES

1. Obtain the time of flight quarters   OOD   _____
    from CIC. Pass the word and ensure the crew
    is informed of changes to the published
    flight quarters schedule.

2. Determine helo mission (VERTREP,   OOD   _____
    HIFR, DLQ, PAX, MEDEVAC).
    Ensure the CO, XO, and CIC are
    aware of mission.

3. Determine best course for flight quarters.   OOD   _____
    Take into account winds and seas and review
    polar plot risk areas for intended course and speed.
    a. True wind: _____Deg T at_____Kts
    b. Relative wind: _____Deg T at_____Kts
    c. Barometer: _____
    d. Foxtrot Corpen: _____Deg T at_____Kts
    e. Pitch: _____
    f. Roll: _____
    d. PAX (number, names, etc.): _____

4. Pass the word: "Flight quarters, flight   OOD   _____
    quarters. All hands man your flight quarters
    stations. The smoking lamp is out on all
    weather decks. Covers shall not be worn
    topside. The dumping of trash is secured.

All personnel not involved stand clear.
Reason for flight quarters _____."
Repeat the word. Log in deck log.

5. Place HOTEL (FQ) or HOTEL ONE   OOD   _____
   (VERTREP) at the dip.

6. Notify LSE and HCO of all course and   QMOW   _____
   speed changes while at flight quarters.

7. Close up Ball-Diamond-Ball or   QMOW   _____
   energize Red-White-Red.

8. If at night energize blue stern light and QMOW   _____
   secure white stern light.

9. Confirm helo control circuit. Ensure the   OOD   _____
   circuit is monitored in the pilothouse
   and the bridge wings.

10. Establish comms and receive manned and ready reports from:

	COMMS	MANNED	READY
LSO	_____	_____	_____
TOWER	_____	_____	_____
CIC	_____	_____	_____
Crash & Smash Team	_____	_____	_____
CCS	_____	_____	_____
Boat Deck	_____	_____	_____

11. Test flight deck crash alarm.   OOD   _____
    Pass the word: "The following is a test of
    the flight deck crash alarm from the helo
    control tower and the pilothouse. Disregard."

12. Ensure flight deck nets are lowered.   HCO   _____

13. Ensure FOD walkdown is complete.   HCO   _____

14. Pass numbers to the HCO.   HCO   _____

15. Turn to F CORPEN for winds.   OOD   _____

16. As soon as manned and ready, and   OOD   _____
    checklist completed through step 15,
    request permission from CO to set Green
    Deck. Log in deck log.

17. Close up HOTEL or HOTEL ONE   OOD   _____
    for Green Deck.

18. While at flight quarters, pass the following OOD   _____
    word every fifteen minutes: "The smoking
    lamp is out on all weather decks. Covers shall
    not be worn topside. The dumping of trash
    is secured. All personnel stand clear."

19. HCO report aircraft ready recovery.   OOD   _____

20. Recover helo. Set Red Deck when helo   OOD   _____
    has landed and is secured on deck.
    Log in deck log.

21. Set Green Deck when helo is ready for   OOD   _____
    launch (CO's permission required).
    Log in deck log.

22. Receive "Ops normal" report from   OOD   _____
    aircraft via HCO. Set Red Deck. Secure
    Flight Quarters. Haul down HOTEL and
    day shapes. Adjust lighting appropriately
    for night steaming. Log in deck log.

NOTE: Upon completion of this checklist, return to QMOW.

Appendix H

SAMPLE UNDERWAY REPLENISHMENT PROCEDURES

EVENT	RESPONSIBILITY	
72 HOURS PRIOR		
1. Send replenishment request to UNREP ship.	1ST LT	_____
2. Post approved UNREP watch bill.	SWO	_____
24 TO 6 HOURS PRIOR		
1. Verify steering checks complete and logged in deck log.	ENG	_____
2. Determine from OPS:	OOD	
a. Rendezvous position		_____
b. Rendezvous time		_____
c. Replenishment course		_____
d. Order alongside		_____
3. Determine from 1ST LT:	OOD	
a. Station to be used		_____
b. Type of rig		_____
4. Determine from MPA amount of fuel requested.	MPA	_____
5. OPS/1ST LT conduct safety brief for ALCON.	1ST LT	_____
6. Verify time distance to rendezvous position.	OOD/CIC	_____

7. Determine from SUPPO if movies/   OOD   _____
   mail/other items to be transferred.

8. Determine from SUPPO/OPS the   OOD   _____
   number of pallets to be received.

6 TO 2 HOURS PRIOR

1. Fueling stations checked.   ENG   _____
2. Lay out necessary equipment.   1ST LT   _____
3. Determine gyro error, log results in   QMOW   _____
   deck log and magnetic compass log.
4. Check gyro repeaters and master   QMOW
   gyro for error.
   AFT Steering   _____
   PORT Bridge Wing   _____
   STBD Bridge Wing   _____
   SCC   _____
5. Post gyro error on ALL gyro repeaters.   QMOW   _____
6. Set up stadimeter IAW UNREP GUIDE   QMOW   _____
   and test laser range finder for JOOD.

1 HOUR PRIOR

1. Ensure all sound-powered phones/   OOD   _____
   circuits tested and status reported to OOD.
2. Review emergency breakaway procedures.   OOD   _____
3. Post call sign.   TAO   _____
4. Prepare all tactical signals for   OOD   _____
   replenishment operations.
5. Assume tactical command if OCE   OOD   _____
   (with CO's permission).
6. If OCE, assign ships to designated   OOD   _____
   stations. If not, take station as assigned.
7. Verify propulsion and electrical plant
   line up per CO's Standing Orders.   ENG   _____

8. Test the ship's whistle   OOD   _____
   (with CO's permission).

9. Test running, task, and wake lights   QMOW   _____
   if night UNREP.

10. Conduct time check.   QMOW   _____

11. Place bullhorn convenient to CONN   QMOW   _____
    and check battery.

30 MINUTES PRIOR

1. Pass the word via the 1MC: "Station the   OOD   _____
   Underway Replenishment Detail, Station
   the Underway Replenishment Detail,
   Station _____ (and ___)."

2. Pass the word via the 1MC: "The smoking   OOD   _____
   lamp is out throughout the ship."

3. Pass the word, via the 1MC: OOD   _____
   "The fantail is secured. Hold all
   trash and garbage on station."

4. Conduct radio checks on the   OOD/CICWS _____
   required circuits.

5. Check BTB Radio, if EMCON   OOD   _____
   conditions permit.

6. UNREP stations manned and ready.   OOD

   a. AFT Steering—inform AFT Steering   _____
      helmsman and Safety Officer of course. In the
      event of a casualty, steer nothing right/left of _____.

   b. Pilothouse
      (1) BMOW   _____
      (2) JOOD   _____
      (3) Helmsman   _____
      (4) Lee Helmsman   _____
      (5) Phone Talker   _____
      (6) Messenger   _____

(7) QMOW   _____

(8) Course/Speed Recorder   _____

(9) Helm Safety Officer   _____

(10) Lookouts   _____

(11) QMOW [ROMEO ready to break at the   _____
dip/BRAVO ready (closed up)/day shapes]

c. CCS (Inform EOOW of course and speed.)   _____

d. CIC   _____

e. Radio   _____

f. Ready Lifeboat   _____

g. UNREP Stations   _____
Station___Station___Station___

h. All station personnel in ranks.   _____

7. Receive draft report. Log in deck log.   OOD   _____

8. Mail/movies/other at designated station.   SUPPO   _____

9. Set Restricted Maneuvering Doctrine   OOD   _____
(with CO's permission).

10. All department heads make readiness   OOD   _____
reports for alongside replenishment.

a. COMBAT SYSTEMS   _____

b. OPERATIONS   _____

c. SUPPLY   _____

d. ENGINEERING   _____

e. WEAPONS   _____

11. If conducting simultaneous air operations
at night, use blue stern light vice white.   OOD   _____

READY TO COMMENCE APPROACH

1. Break ROMEO at the dip when   OOD   _____
manned and ready and ready to
commence approach.

2. Close up ROMEO and special day   OOD   _____
shapes/task lights on commencement
of approach (three hundred yards).

3. When CONN takes speed off, pass the   OOD   _____
word via the 1MC: "Standby for shot
lines fore and aft from USS/USNS _____."

FIRST LINE OVER

1. Haul down ROMEO   OOD   _____
when first messenger across.
2. Break BRAVO if receiving   OOD   _____
fuel or ammunition.

BREAKAWAY

1. Place PREP at the dip fifteen minutes   OOD   _____
prior to breakaway.
2. Obtain recommended course and   OOD   _____
speed from NAV with CIC concurrence.
Check surface picture.
3. Inform UNREP ship of   OOD   _____
breakaway intentions.
4. Haul down BRAVO when pumping   OOD   _____
ceases or ammunition is struck below.
5. Close up PREP when breaking last rig.   OOD   _____
6. Ensure all stations' personnel   OOD   _____
in ranks for breakaway.
7. Haul down PREP when all lines clear.   OOD   _____
8. Secure Restricted Maneuvering Doctrine.   OOD   _____

NOTE: Return this checklist to the QMOW and log in the deck log
completion of checklist.

Appendix I

GUARD MOUNT AND CLEARING BARREL PROCEDURES

Prior to assuming any armed watch and upon returning a weapon to the armory, watchstanders conduct a standardized procedure to ensure effective and safe transfer of weapons and clear understanding of the watchstanding environment and rules/conditions in place. This procedure is known as the guard mount procedure and should also be posted at the weapons issuance point to review.

1. Issue firearms and ammunition.
2. Conduct supervised clearing barrel procedures (Detailed process explained below).
3. Formation.
4. Conduct muster.
5. Inspect personnel for neatness, clean uniforms, proper equipment, and fitness for duty.
6. Brief personnel on applicable status of forces agreement (SOFA).
7. Brief personnel on prevailing rules of engagement (ROE).
8. Brief personnel on use of force.
9. Brief personnel on prevailing force protection condition (FPCON).
10. Brief personnel on current intelligence.
11. Brief personnel on previous watch events.
12. Brief personnel on special orders, events, and expected VIP visits.
13. Resolve personnel issues and concerns.
14. Post personnel to watch stations for turnover.

CLEARING BARREL PROCEDURES

The sole purpose of a clearing barrel is to provide a safe direction in which to point a weapon when performing any or all of the following functions:

1. Load and make ready.
2. Unload.
3. Unload and show clear.

At every duty station, written clearing barrel procedures shall be posted near the clearing barrel. The clearing barrel supervisor shall read each command slowly and clearly, while closely monitoring the process. The following procedures should always be followed prior to using a clearing barrel:

1. Inspect general condition of clearing barrel.
2. Inspect behind and adjacent to clearing barrel.
3. Clear unnecessary personnel away from clearing barrel.

Personnel should line up at the clearing barrel and, one at a time, follow the directions described below.

LOAD AND MAKE READY

On the supervisor's command "load and make ready," personnel will place their trigger finger straight along the receiver, keep the pistol pointed in the clearing barrel, and perform the following steps to take the pistol from Condition 4 (no magazine inserted, no round chambered) to Condition 1 (magazine inserted, round chambered, safety on):

1. Ensure the pistol is in Condition 4, with the slide locked to the rear.
2. Visually and physically verify that the firearm is clear and safe.
3. With the firing hand firmly gripping the pistol and the pistol pointed in the clearing barrel, rotate the pistol so the magazine well is inboard and clearly visible, while drawing the firing elbow in to facilitate control of the pistol.

4. With the nonfiring hand, remove a filled magazine from the ammunition pouch. Slide the index finger along the forward edge of the magazine until the finger is touching the tip of the round to ensure the magazine is filled.

5. Insert the filled magazine into the magazine well, verifying orientation of magazine with the index finger. With fingers extended, push the magazine with the heel of the hand until it is fully seated. Do not relinquish control of the magazine until it is fully seated.

   a. Due to the weight of a fully filled magazine, releasing control of the magazine early can cause it to fall out of the magazine well.

   b. Slapping the bottom of the magazine can dislodge rounds, which in turn may cause a stoppage.

6. Visually and physically ensure that the firearm is on safe.

7. With the trigger finger extended straight along the receiver, release the slide to chamber a round. Visually and physically verify the slide is fully forward. Ensure a round is chambered by physically checking the loaded chamber indicator. (Note: When there is a round in the chamber, the upper surface of the extractor protrudes from the right side of the slide. The protrusion can be felt by sliding a finger or thumb of the nonfiring hand over the top of the slide and across the extractor. This check is effective during both daylight and darkness.)

8. Ensure the safety is on and the hammer is forward. Assume a transport.

UNLOAD

On the supervisor's command "unload," personnel will place their trigger finger straight along the receiver, keep the pistol pointed in the clearing barrel, and perform the following steps to take the pistol from Condition 1 (magazine inserted, round chambered, safety on) or 3 (magazine inserted, no round chambered) to Condition 4 (no magazine inserted, no round chambered):

1. Visually and physically ensure the pistol is on safe.

2. With the nonfiring thumb, depress the magazine catch, remove the magazine, and hand it to the clearing barrel supervisor.

3. With the muzzle pointed into the clearing barrel, hold the firearm at a 45-degree angle. With the nonfiring hand grabbing the slide and cupped over the ejection port, lock the slide to the rear, ejecting the chambered round into the cupped hand. Hand the round to the clearing barrel supervisor. (A safe-eject device may be used for this step, if present.)

4. Visually and physically check the firearm to ensure it is clear and safe, making sure the magazine well and chamber are empty.

5. Bring firearm to administrative transport position. Turn the firearm over to relief personnel or return it to the armory. (Note: Whenever an M9 service pistol is transferred or returned to the armory it should be in Condition 4, with the slide locked to the rear.)

UNLOAD AND SHOW CLEAR

On the supervisor's command "unload, show clear," personnel will place their trigger finger straight along the receiver, keep the pistol pointed in the clearing barrel, and perform the following steps to take the pistol from Condition 1 or 3 to Condition 4:

1. Visually and physically ensure the pistol is on safe.

2. With the nonfiring thumb, depress the magazine catch and remove the magazine. Hand it to the clearing barrel supervisor.

3. With the muzzle pointed into the clearing barrel, hold the firearm at a 45-degree angle. With the nonfiring hand grabbing the slide and cupped over the ejection port, lock the slide to the rear, ejecting the chambered round into the cupped hand. Hand the round to the clearing barrel supervisor. (A safe-eject device may be used for this step, if present.)

4. Visually and physically check the firearm to ensure it is clear and safe, making sure the magazine well and chamber are empty.

5. Allow for a secondary inspection by the supervisor.

6. Bring firearm to administrative transport position. Turn the firearm over to relief personnel or return it to the armory. (Note: Whenever an M9 service pistol is transferred or returned to the armory it should be in Condition 4, with the slide locked to the rear.)

Appendix J

SUMMARY OF NAVY POLLUTION CONTROL DISCHARGE RESTRICTIONS

APP J-1			
AREA	SEWAGE ("BLACK WATER")	GRAY WATER	OILY WASTE
(0–3 NM)	No discharge.	If no pierside collection capability exists, direct discharge permitted.	No sheen. If equipped with OCM, discharge <15 ppm oil.[1]
(3–12 NM)	Direct discharge permitted.	Direct discharge permitted.	No sheen. If equipped with OCM, discharge <15 ppm oil.[1]
12–25 NM	Direct discharge permitted.	Direct discharge permitted.	If equipped with OCM, discharge <15 ppm oil. Ships with OWS or BWPT but inoperable OCM must process all machinery space bilge water through OWS or BWPT.[2,3]
>25 NM	Direct discharge permitted.	Direct discharge permitted.	Same as 12–25 NM.[2,3]
>50 NM	Direct discharge permitted.	Direct discharge permitted.	Same as 12–25 NM.[2,3]

AREA	SEWAGE ("BLACK WATER")	GRAY WATER	OILY WASTE
MARPOL "Special Areas" in effect	Direct discharge permitted.	Direct discharge permitted.	Refrain from discharging any oil or oily waste to the extent practicable without endangering ship or impairing operations. When necessary, same as 12–25 NM.[2,3]
Foreign Countries	Within foreign territorial seas (12 NM), see Visit Clearance or SOFA (as delineated in the Port Guide or LOGREQ reply). If sufficient guidance not available, no discharges within 3 NM when sewage reception facilities available. If not feasible, follow standards observed by host nation warships.	Within foreign territorial seas (12 NM), see Visit Clearance or SOFA (as delineated in the Port Guide or LOGREQ reply). If sufficient guidance not available, follow guidance above. If not feasible, follow standards observed by host warships.	Within foreign territorial seas (12 NM), see Visit Clearance or SOFA (as delineated in the Port Guide or LOGREQ reply). If sufficient guidance not available, follow guidance above. If not feasible, follow standards observed by host warships.[3]
Comments	Direct discharge allowed 3 NM under emergency conditions.	The collection of gray water inside 3 NM from shore and prior to pierside may significantly reduce tank capacity and might result in unnecessary overboard discharge of sewage before reaching pier facilities or unrestricted waters.	State/local rules may vary; check SOPA regulations. Submarines without BWPTs: After allowing adequate separation time, pump non-oily water phase, outside 50 NM, or as far from shore as practicable if the operations or operational capabilities of the submarine would be impaired by this requirement.

1 If operating properly, OWS or BWPT discharge will routinely be less than 15 ppm.
2 Surface ships without operable OWS must retain oily waste for shore disposal. If operating conditions require at-sea disposal minimal discharge is permitted beyond 50 NM from nearest land.
3 If equipped with OWS and OCM and operating conditions prevent achieving less than 15 ppm, limit discharges to less than 100 ppm.

AREA	GARBAGE (NON-PLASTICS)[1]	GARBAGE (PLASTICS)
(0–3 NM)	No discharge	No discharge
(3–12 NM)	Pulped or contaminated food and pulped paper and cardboard waste may be discharged >3 NM.	No discharge
12–25 NM	Bagged shredded glass and metal waste may be discharged >12 NM.[2]	No discharge
>25 NM	Direct discharge permitted.[3]	No discharge
>50 NM	Direct discharge permitted.[3]	No discharge
MARPOL "Special Areas" in effect	Discharge pulped or contaminated food and pulped paper and cardboard waste >3 NM. Discharge bagged shredded glass and metal waste >12 NM. (Note 6) Report all non-food, non-pulped, non-shredded garbage discharges to CNO (N 45) upon completion of operations.	No discharge
Foreign Countries	Discharge pulped or contaminated food and pulped paper and cardboard waste >3 NM from foreign coasts. Discharge bagged shredded glass and metal waste >12 NM.	No discharge
Comments	Garbage discharge should be processed to eliminate floating marine debris. Retain surplus material for shore disposal.	Record-keeping requirements exist for at-sea discharge. Minimal discharge authorized if plastic waste processor inoperable and necessary for safety of ship/health of crew. Report discharge commencement to appropriate operational commander.

AREA	GARBAGE (NON-PLASTICS)[1]	GARBAGE (PLASTICS)
Submarines are required to discharge only the minimum amount practicable.		
Submarines may discharge compacted, sinkable garbage between 12 NM and 25 NM provided that the depth of water is greater than one thousand fathoms		
If equipped, use pulpers and shredders for all discharges of food products, paper, cardboard, glass, and metal wastes. Shredded metal and glass must be bagged prior to disposal.		

1 Submarines are required to discharge only the minimum amount practicable.
2 Submarines may discharge compacted, sinkable garbage between 12 NM and 25 NM provided that the depth of water is greater than one thousand fathoms.
3 If equipped, use pulpers and shredders for all discharges of food products, paper, cardboard, glass, and metal wastes. Shredded metal and glass must be bagged prior to disposal.

APP J-3

AREA	HAZARDOUS MATERIALS	MEDICAL WASTES (INFECTIOUS AND SHARPS)
(0–3 NM)	No discharge	Steam sterilize, store and transfer ashore. No discharges.
(3–12 NM)	No discharge	Steam sterilize, store and transfer ashore. No discharges.
12–25 NM	No discharge	Steam sterilize, store and transfer ashore. No discharges.
>25 NM	No discharge	Steam sterilize, store and transfer ashore. No discharges.
>50 NM	No discharge	If health and safety are threatened, steam sterilize waste, package and weight for negative buoyancy, log, and discharge. No discharge of sharps permitted.
MARPOL "Special Areas" in effect	No discharge	Steam sterilize, store and transfer ashore. No discharges. If >50 NM and health and safety are threatened, steam sterilize waste, package and weight for negative buoyancy, log, and discharge. No discharge of sharps permitted.
Foreign Countries	No discharge	The packaging, handling, storage, transport, treatment, and disposal of infectious waste shall be as prescribed by applicable visit clearance, SOPA regulations, and port guides.
Comments		Dispose of all sharps ashore. Do not incinerate plastic, wet materials. Steam sterilization requirement not applicable to submarines. Other noninfectious waste may be disposed of as garbage and does not require steam sterilization.

Suggested Readings and References

This is not an all-inclusive list, but these are some of the major publications you will encounter in the standing of watches both on the bridge and in the CIC.

JOINT DOCTRINE PUBLICATIONS
DoD Dictionary of Military and Associated Terms
Joint Publication 1-0, "Doctrine of the Armed Forces of the United States"
Joint Publication 2-01, "Joint and National Intelligence Support to Military Operations"
Joint Publication 3-0, "Joint Operations"
Joint Publication 3-32, "Command and Control of Joint Maritime Operations"
Joint Publication 5-0, "Joint Planning"
Joint Publication 6-01, "Joint Electromagnetic Spectrum Management Operations"

NAVAL DOCTRINE PUBLICATIONS
Naval Doctrine Publication 1, "Naval Warfare"

ALLIED EXERCISE PUBLICATIONS
Allied Exercise Publication 1, "Allied Submarine and Antisubmarine Exercise Manual," AXP 1(E)
Allied Exercise Publication 2, "Allied Maritime Above Water Warfare Exercise Manual," AXP 2(C)

Allied Tactical Publication 1, Volume 1, "Allied Maritime Tactical Instructions and Procedures," ATP 1(G), volume 1

Allied Tactical Publication 1, Volume 2, "Allied Maritime Tactical Signal and Maneuvering Book," ATP 1(G), volume 2

Allied Tactical Publication 3 and 3(B), "Antisubmarine Evasive Steering," ATP 3(B)

Allied Tactical Publication 4, "Allied Naval Gunfire Support," ATP 4(F)

Allied Tactical Publication 8, "Tactics, Techniques, and Procedures for Amphibious Operations," ATP 8(C)

Allied Tactical Publication 28, "Allied Antisubmarine Warfare Manual," ATP 28(C)

Allied Tactical Publication 31, "NATO Above Water Warfare Manual," ATP 31(D)

Allied Tactical Publication 43, "Ship-to-Ship Towing," ATP 43(D)-MTP 43(D)

Also, the Exercise Tactic series and the Inter-American Navy series of publications provide information for operations with Pacific Rim and South American navies.

NAVAL WARFARE/TACTICAL PUBLICATIONS

NAVAIR 00-80T-122, "Helicopter Operating Procedures for Air-Capable Ships NATOPS Manual"

Navy Tactical Reference Publication 1-01, "The Navy Warfare Library"

Navy Tactical Reference Publication 1-02, "Navy Supplement to the DOD Dictionary of Military and Associated Terms"

Naval Warfare Publication 1-03.1, "Operational Reports"

Naval Warfare Publication 1-03.41, "Maritime Reporting System"

Naval Warfare Publication 1-10.11, "Tactical Action Officer (TAO) Handbook Quick Reference Guide"

Naval Warfare Publication 1-14M, "Commander's Handbook on the Law of Naval Operations"

Naval Warfare Publication 3-01, "Fleet Air and Missile Defense"

Naval Warfare Publication 3-02.1.4M, "Defense of the Amphibious Task Force"

Naval Warfare Publication 3-07.2, "Navy Doctrine for Antiterrorism / Force Protection"

Naval Warfare Publication 3-12, "Cyberspace Operations"

Naval Warfare Publication 3-13, "Navy Information Operations"

Naval Warfare Publication 3-20, "Navy Surface Warfare Manual"

Naval Warfare/Tactical Reference Publication 3-20.6 Series, "Class Tactical Manuals"

Naval Warfare Publication 3-21, "Fleet Antisubmarine Warfare"

Naval Warfare Publication 3-32, "Maritime Operations at the Operational Level of War"

Naval Warfare Publication 3-58, "Military Deception at the Operational Level of War"

Naval Warfare Publication 4-0M, "Naval Logistics"

Naval Warfare Publication 4-01.4, "Underway Replenishment"

Naval Warfare Publication 5-01, "Navy Planning"

Naval Warfare / Tactical Reference Publication 3-22 Series, "Aircraft Tactical Manuals"

Navy Tactical Reference Publication 1-03.5, "Defense Readiness Reporting System-Navy Reporting Manual"

Navy Tactical Techniques and Procedures 1-10.1, "Force Tactical Action Officer (FTAO)"

Navy Tactical Techniques and Procedures 3-01.5, "AEGIS Air Defense Core Tactics"

Navy Tactical Techniques and Procedures 3-01.11, "Maritime Air and Missile Defense Planning"

Navy Tactical Techniques and Procedures 3-02.1M, "Ship-to-Shore Movement"

Navy Tactical Techniques and Procedures 3-03.1, Volume 1, "Tomahawk Land Attack Missile Employment Manual"

Navy Tactical Reference Publication 3-07.2.2, "Weapons Handling Standard Procedures and Guidelines"

Navy Tactical Techniques and Procedures 3-13.14, "Surface Electronic Warfare Guide"

Navy Tactical Techniques and Procedures 3-14.2, "Navigation Warfare"

Navy Tactical Techniques and Procedures 3-20.1, "Surface Warfare Commander's Manual"

Navy Tactical Techniques and Procedures 3-20.3, "Surface Ship SUW Tactics"

Navy Tactical Techniques and Procedures 3-21.1, "Strike Group Antisubmarine Warfare Commander's Manual"

Navy Tactical Techniques and Procedures 3-21.21, "Submarine Approach and Attack Manual"

ALLIED AND NAVY COMMUNICATIONS PUBLICATIONS

Allied Communications Publication 113(AJ), "Call Sign Book for Ships"

Allied Communications Publication 117, "Allied Routing Indicator"

Allied Communications Publication 121(I), "Communications Instructions General"

Allied Communications Publication 123(B), "Common Messaging Strategy and Procedures"

Allied Communications Publication 125(G), "Communications Instructions Radio Telephone Procedures"

Allied Communications Publication 165, "Brevity Codewords"

Navy Technical Publication 4, "Fleet Communications"

Navy Technical Publication 13(B), "Flags, Pennants and Customs"

DEPARTMENT OF THE NAVY

Manual of the Judge Advocate General (JAGMAN)

Standard Organization and Regulation of the U.S. Navy (OpNavInst 3120.32D Change 1)

Uniform Code of Military Justice

U.S. Navy Regulations

U.S. DEPARTMENT OF HOMELAND SECURITY, U.S. COAST GUARD PUBLICATION

Navigation Rules and Regulations Handbook, 17 February 2018

WEBSITES

Joint Doctrine, http://www.jcs.mil

Navy Doctrine Library, https://portal.nwdc.navy.mil/ndls (CAC Enabled)

Defense Technical Information Center, http://www.dtic.mil/

Navy Warfare Development Command, http://www.nwdc.navy.mil/

BOOKS

Allen, Craig H. *Farwell's Rules of the Nautical Road.* 8th ed. Annapolis, Md.: Naval Institute Press, 2005.

Barber, J. A. *Naval Shiphandler's Guide.* Annapolis, Md.: Naval Institute Press, 2005.

Belenky, Gregory, Nancy J. Wesensten, David R. Thorne, Maria L. Thomas, Helen C. Sing, Daniel P. Redmond, Michael B. Russo, and Thomas J. Balkin. "Patterns of Performance Degradation and Restoration During Sleep Restriction and Subsequent Recovery: A Sleep Dose Response Study." *Journal of Sleep Research* 12, no. 1 (March 2003): 1–12. https://doi.org/10.1046/j.1365-2869.2003.00337.x.

Blank, David A., and Arthur E. Bock. *Introduction to Naval Engineering.* 2nd ed. Annapolis, Md.: Naval Institute Press, 2005.

Brittin, Burdick H. *International Law for Seagoing Officers.* 6th ed. Annapolis, Md.: Naval Institute Press, 2014.

Bruhn, Lt. Cdr. David D., USN, with Capt. Steven C. Saulnier, USN (Ret.), and Lt. Cdr. James L. Whittington, USN. *Ready to Answer All Bells: A Blueprint for Successful Naval Engineering.* Annapolis, Md.: Naval Institute Press, 1997.

Cutler, Thomas J. *Dutton's Nautical Navigation.* 15th ed. Annapolis, Md.: Naval Institute Press, 2004.

Felger, Daniel G. *Engineering for the Officer of the Deck.* Annapolis, Md.: Naval Institute Press, 1979.

Gagliano, Joseph A. *Shiphandling Fundamentals for Littoral Combat Ships and the New Frigates.* Annapolis, Md.: Naval Institute Press, 2015.

Knight, Austin M. *Knight's Modern Seamanship,* edited by John V. Noel. New York: Van Nostrand Reinhold, 1989.

Kotsch, Rear Adm. William J., USN (Ret.). *Weather for the Mariner.* 3rd ed. Annapolis, Md.: Naval Institute Press, 1983.

Kotsch, Rear Adm. William J., USN (Ret.), and Richard Henderson. *Heavy Weather Guide*. 2nd ed. Annapolis, Md.: Naval Institute Press, 1984.

Miller, Nita Lewis, and Michael Firehammer. "Avoiding a Second Hollow Force: The Case for Including Crew Endurance Factors in the Afloat Staffing Policies of the US Navy." *Naval Engineers Journal* 119, no. 1 (October 2007): 83–96. https://doi.org/10.1111/j.0028-1425.2007.00007.x.

Index

Note: *f* or *t* with page reference indicates figures or table respectively.

About the Authors

ADM James Stavridis, USN (Ret.), was sixteenth Supreme Allied Commander at NATO; has commanded a destroyer, destroyer squadron, and carrier strike group; and is dean emeritus at The Fletcher School of Law and Diplomacy at Tufts University. He is currently an Operating Executive with the Carlyle Group; and Chair, Board of Counselors for McLarty Associates.

RADM Robert P. Girrier, USN (Ret.), served as Deputy Commander Pacific Fleet and has commanded a mine countermeasures ship, destroyer, destroyer squadron, and two carrier strike groups. He is founder and managing member of Strategic Navigation LLC, a consulting company; and president of Pacific Forum, a private nonprofit foreign policy research institute focused on building security and stability in the Indo-Pacific.

CAPT Tom Ogden, USN, is Deputy Commodore of Destroyer Squadron Seven, forward deployed to Singapore. A naval strategist, he has served at numerous joint and naval commands, including command of a destroyer.

CAPT Jeff Heames, USN, is Commodore of Destroyer Squadron Twenty Three. He has held numerous positions ashore and afloat, including command of a destroyer.

The **Naval Institute Press** is the book-publishing arm of the U.S. Naval Institute, a private, nonprofit, membership society for sea service professionals and others who share an interest in naval and maritime affairs. Established in 1873 at the U.S. Naval Academy in Annapolis, Maryland, where its offices remain today, the Naval Institute has members worldwide.

Members of the Naval Institute support the education programs of the society and receive the influential monthly magazine *Proceedings* or the colorful bimonthly magazine *Naval History* and discounts on fine nautical prints and on ship and aircraft photos. They also have access to the transcripts of the Institute's Oral History Program and get discounted admission to any of the Institute-sponsored seminars offered around the country.

The Naval Institute's book-publishing program, begun in 1898 with basic guides to naval practices, has broadened its scope to include books of more general interest. Now the Naval Institute Press publishes about seventy titles each year, ranging from how-to books on boating and navigation to battle histories, biographies, ship and aircraft guides, and novels. Institute members receive significant discounts on the Press's more than eight hundred books in print.

Full-time students are eligible for special half-price membership rates. Life memberships are also available.

For a free catalog describing Naval Institute Press books currently available, and for further information about joining the U.S. Naval Institute, please write to:

Member Services
U.S. NAVAL INSTITUTE
291 Wood Road
Annapolis, MD 21402-5034
Telephone: (800) 233-8764
Fax: (410) 571-1703
Web address: www.usni.org